G000124247

It sure did beat working…

The autobiography of

Sam St Pierre

"Flying is one hell of a way to make a living – but it sure beats working." (Anon)

Published by

Latimer Publishing

Sheffield

Yorkshire

Copyright © Sam St Pierre 2012

All rights reserved. No part of this publication may be reproduced, stored in a
retrieval system, or transmitted in any form, or by any means, without the prior
permission of the publisher, except by a reviewer who wishes to quote brief passages in
connection with a review.

Every effort has been made to trace the owners of copyright material. All
photographs are the property of Sam St Pierre unless otherwise indicated. The events
described have been cross checked whenever possible and the author apologises for any
errors or omissions that may have arisen.

Printed by York Publishing Services Ltd

Dedicated to Jennie

Editor's Note

I first met Sam during the UK Mountain Soaring Competition (UKMSC) at Aboyne in 2003. My first entry to this competition was a steep learning curve. At the start of the week I watched in wonder as my fellow competitors charged through the most desperate parts of the Cairngorms with seemingly no regard for the lack of safe landing places. I can still vividly remember looking down to see Sam, in his DG200, dancing back along the ridges from Pitlochry when I never dared leave the safety of the fields near Braemar. Back at base I was despondent that I was truly out-classed and should perhaps go home. However, Sam and other competitors were soon imparting pearls of wisdom as to where there were safe fields and escape routes. With their encouragement, by the end of the week I was there with the rest of them and managed to safely transit Glenshee below the mountain tops; and so began my love of the UKMSC.

In subsequent years Sam shared some of his tales, not in any boastful manner but in one of pure delight at what can or might be done and the joy in such adventures. They all provided useful gems as to what is possible. His pioneering wave flying from Yorkshire is truly an example of how we stand on the shoulders of our predecessors, an inspiration to all modern wave pilots.

When we moved to join the Yorkshire Gliding Club (YGC) in 2006 I started to get to know Sam a little better. Sam continued to be a force to reckon with late into his flying career. In 2007 he still managed to give us a run for our money in the Northern Regionals at Sutton Bank where he finished 4th and I will leave it to you to work out his age. He also continued to win annual trophies at YGC taking those for the fastest 100km triangle in 2009, 2010 and 2011.

As to this book I have to say I never imagined I would become involved in editing a book, let alone publishing one. I had some free time and my wife, Simona, told me she had a draft of Sam's autobiography and perhaps I should read it. I settled onto the train from Sheffield to London one morning and thought why not have a quick browse? The next thing I knew was that my fellow travellers were up in the aisle because we had pulled into St. Pancras. I finished the book on my return journey that evening and decided this just had to be done. In getting this book to print I do have some co-conspirators who deserve mention for their support. They are:

Simona Latimer   Anne Silver
John Ellis   Peter Crawley
Graham Evison

Enough from me, here is the book and I hope you enjoy it.

Dave Latimer
December 2012

Foreword

I first met Sam in 1962 when I was stationed at Royal Air Force Geilenkirchen in the north of Germany, flying Canberras with 3(F) Squadron. Sam had already had an unusual flying career, starting as a National Service trainee pilot, progressing to a short service commission flying Sabres and then leaving the RAF to join Tasman Empire Airlines Limited (TEAL) as co-pilot of their Solent Mk 4 flying boat in the South Pacific. He had re-joined the RAF after that and was now with 5 Squadron, flying Gloster Javelin interceptors.

A Royal Air Force Germany Gliding Association Club (Nimbus) operated from Geilenkirchen, and this set the scene for our mutual involvement in gliding. Several other long term friends were made during this time, notably Dan Delap, Brian Connolly, Don Morris, John and Heather Hunter, and Jennie Hutty. I was responsible for Jennie eventually becoming Sam's wife, this resulting from a foursome evening out during a competition at Butzweilerhof.

We spent many hours working on gliders and ground equipment and also in discussion about the best way to go fast across country in gliders. Much Amstel was consumed during the latter.

In 1963 Sam and I acquired a Minimoa from the RAF Laarbruch gliding club. Shortage of paint (and funds) resulted in it being painted a somewhat inappropriate shade of pink. Unfortunately we never had the chance to fly it cross-country because we had no trailer and never quite finished the one we started to construct. Perhaps this was just as well; one can imagine the derision had we landed it at a German club site.

We had numerous expeditions to other gliding sites in Europe, mostly with a club glider towed behind the car. During these often impromptu tours we achieved our Diamond Goal flights in Switzerland in an Olympia 463, and gained mountain flying experience in Italy and Austria. Eventually the time came when we both had to move on and so the Minimoa was sold to an American club member, Don Wilson.

We both worked for Bristow Helicopters during the 1980s, myself flying helicopters from Aberdeen and Sam a variety of fixed wing aircraft in Nigeria. During those years, and since, we have met again at irregular intervals as competitors in gliding competitions and sometimes with Sam being crew for me and whatever glider I happened to have at the time. On these occasions I have gained some insight into the unusual, exciting and sometimes dangerous twists and turns of Sam's career both before and since our days at Geilenkirchen.

Enjoy Sam's stories from his amazing past.

Lemmy Tanner
December 2012

Contents

Chapter 1

The country years

"I hope I don't get airsick because I do get carsick and if I got airsick I couldn't be a pilot and then I'd have to go to work. (Extract from a schoolboy's essay on "What I want to be when I grow up")."

In 1938, when I was five years old, my father saw a flying circus poster and decided to take mother and myself for a joy ride. It was a long walk for a small child from our home at Goodmayes in Essex to a grass field a mile northeast of where the Second World War airfield of Fairlop was later constructed. I can just remember my excitement when we saw the brightly coloured little biplanes and my disappointment when Father said we weren't going flying after all. The only aircraft in which we could go together had a closed passenger cabin and he wanted to be out in the open. If the flying circus had operated an aeroplane with an open cockpit large enough for my parents and me and we had flown, almost certainly I'd have been airsick. No doubt I'd have been put off from flying for the rest of my life. Thirteen years later, when I was committed to flying training, sheer stubbornness kept me going until I got over the sickness problem.

In one way and another, water has also played a large part in my life and if I had been put off from aviation, I might have requested the Royal Navy for my National Service. An earlier, probably my earliest memory is of water. I have always had an image at the back of my mind of a boating lake, with bright red tulips flowering on the bank and my father rowing me towards a brick wall. Sixty years later this childhood memory was confirmed when one of my brothers sent me a photograph that I had never seen before. Air and water eventually came together when for two glorious years I became a flying boat co-pilot.

I have few other memories of my first seven years, although even at such a young age I can remember being terrified by Herr Hitler's rantings that I heard on the radio. I thought he would be after me personally and lived in dread of the day when the storm troopers might arrive. Eventually

Photo 1 - Sam with his father

war did break out. For a short time mother and I were evacuated to Aldeburgh on the Suffolk coast, but nothing seemed to be happening during the phoney war, so we returned to Goodmayes.

When things livened up in 1940 I was evacuated to the village of Bromham in Wiltshire. After life on the edge of London, the countryside was, to me, a small boy's idea of paradise. My foster parents were smallholders, with a few acres and a large number of chickens. Today, their approach to the care of children would no doubt have brought the wrath of Social Services down on their heads. Like the father in Arthur Ransome's "Swallows and Amazons", they had the view that "Better drowned than duffers – if not duffers, won't drown". So although there was plenty of discipline in the home, my friend from the Goodmayes School and myself were given a great deal of freedom after we had completed our chores. There were woods to explore, trees to climb, streams, ponds and a canal to fish in (and quite often fall into) and not far away the Roundway Downs to roam. "Tarzan" films were frequently shown in the cinema at nearby Devizes and Johnny Weismuller became our role model. Sometimes this led us into unintended scrapes. On one occasion we were happily sitting outside our stick, leaves and moss shelter in a large wood, roasting the only rabbit we'd ever managed to shoot with our bows and arrows. Suddenly the local policeman, perspiring heavily, crashed out of the undergrowth. We expected to be in deep trouble – he'd seen the smoke from our fire and thought there had been a plane crash. But beyond extracting our promise that we wouldn't light fires in the woods again, he let us off without reporting our misdeed to our foster parents.

At first I was sent to the Church School in the village, but I found myself being re-taught stuff I had learnt long before and kicked up a fuss until I was removed to the County School. There I flourished as a student, but frequently got into very hot water on the behavioural side. On one occasion, the day was so beautiful during the walk to school - about a mile and a half across the fields - that I got somewhat carried away with the bird song, the flora and fauna and my companion's profound views on the nature of life. It was fast approaching midday before we got within half a mile of our destination. I thought that if I picked a big bunch of wild flowers for the Head Teacher, I might get away without punishment. It didn't work.

I got into another scrape around this time. One day our class teacher handed us some geography books and said, "Turn to page xxx and read that chapter." That done, she said "Now children, close your book and write about what you have read." She didn't say "in your own words" or anything similar. Not having a very original mind, I produced a practically word for word copy of the original text and was promptly accused of cheating by copying from the textbook. I was in disgrace until a few days later when we were given Tennyson's "The Brook" to learn. After reading the poem a couple of times I was able to recite it without fault. Alas, I've lost that photographic memory in the years that have passed. I do though remember the subject of that geography lesson - it was about life on a South Sea coral atoll – and I'm sure it was in my subconscious memory when years later I went to see New Zealand but on arrival there took a job in Fiji!

In those wartime days, cars were a rarity and of course petrol was rationed. I can remember only one car ride in the three years I spent in the country. We walked everywhere until we were old enough for bicycles. It was four miles to the swimming baths, the library and the cinema at Devizes and a mile and a half to Bromham's Methodist Chapel on Sundays. Once we had learnt bicycling, we travelled much further, usually on our own. We joined the local Cub pack and I began to learn some of the arts of survival, which in later years proved invaluable.

Although we were away from the main aerial fighting regions, there was a fair amount of flying activity in the area. Keevil and Hullavington were not far away and we sometimes cycled over to watch the aeroplanes taking off and landing. I can remember seeing only one German aircraft flying, which I think was a Messerschmitt 109. This came across the school playground, very low and was gone in seconds. I don't remember seeing any German aircraft wrecks, but there were a few of our own. In fact, we saw and heard very little warfare. The most dramatic events involved no more than the occasional bomb during the night, probably jettisoned since there were no real targets in the area. We were quite pleased with these; they brought the underlying heavy blue clay to the surface. This was ideal for making marbles – proper "glass alleys" had long since become a memory.

I can't say that I had any special interest in flying or aeroplanes during my evacuee years. We did fly folded paper aeroplanes in the field behind the house and fooled with parachutes made from handkerchiefs and stones. I also wasted a lot of time one summer trying to make a pair of wings, spending many hours fastening chicken feathers onto opened out hessian sacks. The project never got off the ground. Plenty of feathers were available, but at some stage I decided that there were better things to do. No doubt, had I completed the project and failed to get airborne, I'd have concluded that I should have used rooks' or crows' feathers, since our chickens couldn't fly.

Undoubtedly I was destined to drown, but somehow I managed to avoid that fate. The first attempt was in the Devizes swimming pool, when I slipped out of my depth and was rescued by a bystander who realised that I'd been under water rather longer than was desirable. Then I fell into the local pond while fishing for newts. A fortunately placed strand of barbed wire came to hand, which, although painfully, enabled me to haul myself out. The closest call came when I was riding my bicycle along the Kennet and Avon canal towpath near Seend, with my five-year-old brother trotting behind me. Somehow my foot slipped on the pedal, I lost control and wobbled into the canal. The bicycle fell on top of me in such a way that I could not move, but lay on my back, sinking slowly into the ooze. I strained to keep my mouth and nose above water and, remembering one of Tarzan's exploits, with the hand that was free, plucked a hollow reed stem. If I sank further, I thought, I could breathe through this. David, bless him, remained calm and unaware of what my real predicament was. He didn't want to leave me, but I managed to persuade him to go on along the towpath to the road bridge to stop a vehicle and to fetch some help. Eventually he returned with an adult in tow and I was hauled out.

My interest in fishing began in that same Kennet and Avon canal, starting with the proverbial cane, cotton and bent pin. I never caught anything sizeable and although I insisted on eating the first few perch and roach that I did land, I soon decided that cotton wool stuffed with needles would taste just as good. There were some very large pike in the canal, but I was a little frightened of them, they looked rather like crocodiles to my young eyes and I would go somewhere else if one of them appeared in my fishing hole.

That happy country life came to an end in 1944.

Chapter 2

Grammar School, sailing and a lifeboat rescues a lifeboat

At Bromham primary I had passed the examination for grammar school and without my knowledge it was decided that I should return to my real home and attend the Ilford County High School at Barkingside, Essex. This was a bitter blow. My father was still serving in the Royal Air Force in Burma and I found it very difficult to accept my real mother. I hated suburbia and although we lived close to the edge of town, the nearby part of Essex seemed very dreary, flat and derelict, with much sad looking rough pasture just waiting to be built over. The school terms seemed endless; I couldn't wait for the school holidays and the chance to get away to the country, camping or Youth Hostelling. But school itself was enjoyable; I found the new subjects we were taught thoroughly interesting, especially maths and science. Outside school model aircraft became a major interest. I never had enough money to buy a diesel or glow plug engine, but built a series of gliders and rubber-powered machines and when Fairlop airfield was abandoned very soon after the war ended, flew them from there. I once saw a real sailplane fly over the airfield. The pilot could well have been Geoffrey Stephenson or Philip Wills on one of their pioneering cross-country flights of the immediate post-war era. Interest in gliding was further roused during a Youth Hostelling bicycle holiday when I paused at the top of Dunstable Downs and watched a Slingsby Falcon 3 two-seater soaring the ridge. It was a beautiful sight, with its transparent fabric showing all the detail of the interior wing construction of ribs and bracing wires. I didn't think I'd ever be able to afford to fly gliders myself.

I was an avid reader and buried my nose in many books while travelling to and from school by trolley bus. I soon discovered the Arthur Ransome stories in our local Carnegie Library and after reading "Swallows and Amazons" really fancied the idea of sailing. One of my school friends, John Barker, had a very small lugsail dinghy which he kept near Burnham on the river Crouch. He often took me there, sometimes leaving me on my own to learn how to sail it. Over a period of several months he introduced other classmates to this activity and eventually we had a gang of five keen sailors. John upgraded to a Yachting World Cadet and we progressed to dinghy racing at the Royal Corinthian Yacht Club, cycling the 35 miles to Burnham at weekends. Longer sailing holidays with hired dinghies followed; we camped once at Horsey Mere on the Norfolk Broads with a 14 footer. Then one of the local councils opened a sailing lake in one of the parks, with Firefly and GP14 dinghies. The pond was too small for racing, but we enjoyed chasing the ducks.

After several years of this inland sailing we became more ambitious and really wanted to go to sea. The opportunity arose when a number of RAF airborne lifeboats came on the market. I can't remember which of the group got lucky, whoever it was managed to persuade his parents to buy one. He had the boat moored at Erith, on the south bank of the Thames, a considerable distance downstream of Tower Bridge which was then the last bridge before the sea, but the free Woolwich ferry gave us a short-cut route.

The airborne lifeboat was carried by specially fitted aircraft such as the Lancaster bomber and could be dropped by parachute to downed aircrew. It was designed by Uffa Fox and like the 14 foot International racing dinghy of the day, was skinned with two diagonal layers of plywood with oilcloth between. It had enclosed buoyancy tanks fore and aft and in its original state, an outboard motor that lowered through an inboard well. We didn't have the motor; instead our boat had a gunter mainsail and a jib. We found it to be very fast and easy to handle in the winds we encountered on the Thames.

The summer holidays arrived and our plans made during the spring term came to fruition. The intention was to sail down the Thames, through the Havengore swing bridge into the river Roach, thence into the Crouch, downstream to the sea and along the coast to Yarmouth. We would sail from estuary to estuary – Blackwater, Orwell, Deben, Alde, Blyth - and camp ashore. We would visit places that were just magical names, like Pin Mill and stay a few days or move on as the mood took us.

We reached Canvey Island the first night and the river Crouch below Burnham via the Havengore and the Roach on the second. The next day began well enough. We left the Crouch and with a moderate beam wind from the shore, sailed across the Blackwater entrance and northeast along the coast. The miles slipped past and it seemed that we would reach the Orwell estuary early in the afternoon. Then, as we passed Frinton, a huge storm cloud formed over the coast. The sun vanished and the wind began to increase. We knew from all the sailing books that with no harbour nearby the safest place to be in a blow was well out to sea, in case the wind changed round to on-shore, so we headed south east with the wind behind us. The wind increased still more and before we had time to gain much of an offing, suddenly swung round to the northeast. We were on the starboard tack (wind from the right side) and, in what had become a gale; found that the boat would go no closer to the wind than ninety degrees. This put us heading into shore. We needed to go about on to the other tack and head southeast, to get further out to sea. But try as we might, the boat would not go about. Each time, as soon as the sails began to flap, she stopped turning and hung short of the wind's eye. We tried everything – lowering the jib and tacking with mainsail only, using the oars to help her round (back-watering one side and pulling the other), lowering the sails completely and rowing, all these with centreboard down or up – nothing would get her round. With such a strong wind, we were reluctant to try gybing round (turning down-wind, during which manoeuvre the sail blows violently across the boat) but in desperation, tried to turn round that way – and found she would go no further than to point with the wind on the quarter. By now we were in the angle between the shore and the pier at Walton-on-the-Naze. The situation didn't look too happy, embayed on a lee shore, wind howling, waves breaking heavily over the promenade wall a few hundred yards away. But we were on a lifeboat, after all! If we lowered the sails and dropped anchor, surely we could ride out the storm?

At first, with all the anchor rope out, we were dragging towards the shore, but well before we were among the breakers, the anchor held. We were cold, wet from the by now heavy rain trickling into all the gaps in our oilskins and fairly miserable, but fortunately none of us were feeling seasick. We huddled together with the sail pulled over our shoulders, getting as low as possible in the open boat and began to sing our repertoire of sea shanties. It was some time before one of us noticed that there were a lot of people on the pier and along the waterfront. What on earth were they doing standing there in that weather? Then we saw a red maroon flare explode above the town and then another. That's the lifeboat call out, we realised. Someone must be in difficulties. We scanned all round, but could see no other vessels. Oh dear, it must be us – if the coastguard thinks we are in trouble perhaps our situation is more serious than we believe. Better hoist an oilskin up the mast as a distress signal.

Half an hour later a proper RNLI lifeboat hove in sight to the north of us. Soon the crew had fastened a towrope to our bows and taken us on board. They seemed quite pleased to have had something to do, or perhaps it was, as they explained, that after a successful rescue they could broach the ship's rum supplies. There was enough for a couple of tots each for us as well!

Some of those readers who were and maybe still are fans of Arthur Ransome will have discovered that "Secret Water" does in fact exist, being the area of mud, marsh, islands and creeks behind the coast north of Walton on the Naze. The lifeboat towed us into this backwater and along "Amazon Creek" to the town. Here we were handed over to the ladies of the Shipwrecked Mariners Society. They took us to one of the town's rather smart hotels. Evidently shipwrecked mariners were a not unusual phenomenon, the hotel residents seemed totally unsurprised by the sight of five small boys dripping muddy water all over the carpets. We were given rooms for the night and told to go down for dinner when we were ready.

Our first thoughts were to keep our mouths shut and not tell our parents of this escapade, but the arrival of the local press changed our minds. We agreed it might be better that our parents heard a toned down version of events from us before they read a dramatic account in the papers. So we trooped off to the nearest public telephone with pockets full of change and took turns to spin them a yarn. I can't remember how my parents reacted, but it seems that all five of us must have been sufficiently convincing in our arguments, none of us were ordered to return home immediately. However, we ourselves decided to tempt fate no further, so, abandoning the idea of sailing to the Norfolk Broads, we stayed in the Backwaters.

We made our camp on the inland side of Ransome's "Flint Island". Although we didn't realise it we were exactly at the spot where he placed the "Camp of the Savages". For the next two weeks we explored the Backwaters, by boat at high water and in bathing trunks when the tide was out. We didn't know about "splatchers" (like snowshoes, but designed for walking on soft mud), but managed to get around the ooze by lying down and rowing with our hands. The mud soon washed off when we swam across the creeks and at the end of the day we had only to cross to the seaward side of "Flint Island" to find a sandy beach at all states of the tide. It must have been a warm summer, because I remember one night when the water was full of phosphorescent plankton, which glowed where the wavelets were breaking on the beach, or where we stirred the water with our hands.

I missed the best bit. For some reason, probably because I'd run out of money, I left before the others and hitchhiked back home. They eventually sailed the few miles from the Backwaters to the Orwell, where they got to know the skipper of one of the few remaining working Thames barges. He was bound for the port of London and taking them on board, towed the airborne all the way back to Erith.

My father had returned from the war in 1946 and after a spell working for his pre-war employer in the building trade, set up in business on his own as a painter, decorator and plumber. As the eldest son, by now of four, I was required to spend some of my out of school time helping him. I learnt a little about central heating installations, roofing methods and such, but I was not a very adept apprentice. The General School Examination School Certificate time came along when I was sixteen; I did quite well with six 'Very Goods' and three 'Credits' but was not too certain which way to go, with top grade 'Very Goods' and the lesser 'Credits' in both Science and Arts subjects. In any case, I was at a rebellious age and wanted out of school and home, so I went off to the Royal Air Force recruiting office. I almost got away, but the Head Master and my father leant on me and I was hauled back into two years of sixth form.

I sat for the General School Examination Advanced Level in the summer of 1951 and with four A levels won a County Major scholarship, which would have paid my way through University. But there was National Service to take into account. The option to defer this until after University was available, but I was more inclined to get it over with first. I did make a half-hearted attempt at gaining acceptance at Queen Mary College, London, but was not over disappointed to be turned down. While awaiting call-up, I found work with a small engineering company in Barkingside. One of their biggest selling lines was the manufacture of iron stair banisters and I progressed through cutting vertical rods to length, drilling holes in the ends, tapping threads in the holes to take bolts and eventually assisting in assembly of the finished item. I also had my first experience of Trade Union ideology. One day when I was operating the drilling machine, the swarf began to pile up around the drill bit. I swept it off onto the floor with my hand to get it out of the way and was promptly taken to task by the shop steward – "That's Fred's job, if you need your bench cleared, go and find him to do it". Something which would have delayed production for no more than a couple of seconds then took anything up to a quarter of an hour, depending on how far away Fred was and what he was doing when found.

A few weeks later my call-up papers arrived and with some relief I gave in my notice.

Chapter 3
"Square bashing", aircrew selection and ground training

At the local National Service reporting office I found that I had a choice as to which Service I could join and that I could request a particular Trade. With little expectation of any notice being taken of my wishes, I asked for the Royal Air Force and flying. Eventually my joining orders and travel warrant arrived. I was to report to the RAF reception centre for National Servicemen, Padgate, a few miles south of Blackpool, on 28 August 1951. When I arrived, I was even more surprised to discover that the whole of my intake would be going, after "square bashing", for aircrew selection.

For all that we were to see of Blackpool, we could have been on another continent – we were not allowed off the camp. For some of us, those who had led a sheltered home life, the sudden transition to communal living and harsh discipline was traumatic. I had no real difficulty with this; the barrack room was much like a Youth Hostel dormitory, although the 'bull' was to a higher standard and the supervision very much tougher. Some of the more sensitive souls were however reduced to tears.

I actually missed much of the early drill and other assorted unpleasantness. We all had a medical check soon after arrival and I was told that due to some unspecified ear problem, not only was I unfit for aircrew, but I would probably be discharged as unfit for service. So instead of marching around in the cold and rain I was given light duties. These consisted mostly of washing up oven trays and cooking pots in the "Tin Room" and peeling a never decreasing pile of potatoes. At least it was warm. As a change, I was once handed a Flight Lieutenant's "best blue" uniform and told to clean the buttons. I still remember the awe with which I touched the first pair of RAF "Wings" I'd ever come close to. It seemed that I would never wear them myself. But a few days later, without a further medical, I was taken off the light duties and sent back to the parade square with the rest of the squaddies. I never discovered what had been wrong and still suspect that somehow my records had been mixed up with someone else's.

We had a few days respite from our month of "square bashing" when we travelled to Hornchurch for Aircrew Selection. I remembered seeing a Tiger Moth flying from there before World War 2 practising spins and recoveries, but the Tigers had gone by 1951. We did get to see some aeroplanes, Spitfires of the Meteorological Flight. Hornchurch was just a few miles from home; we were allowed a 48-hour pass off camp one weekend. I took one of my new chums to visit my parents and to the Methodist Youth Club to show off our uniforms with the white disc behind the cap badge indicating our aircrew cadet status.

Nowadays computers are used for some of the aircrew aptitude assessments, but Heath Robinson might have designed several of the tests we undertook.

Two I particularly remember. The first used a large horizontally pivoted revolving drum dotted with a random pattern of flush brass studs. The candidate moved a pointer horizontally by means of a very loosely connected steering wheel, the aim being to guide the pointer over as many studs as possible. Presumably there was some sort of counter to keep the score. It was not easy to anticipate the degree of 'slop' to be allowed for and there were rapid decisions to be made as to which part of the drum looked like giving the best chance of picking up points.

The other test involved a board with one hundred square holes, in which there were one hundred square pegs. The top of each peg was painted half green and half red. Initially all the pegs were aligned with the green part away from the candidate. On the word go, the pegs were to be lifted out of the holes, turned through one hundred and eighty degrees and re-inserted with the red part away. I thought I had done quite well when 'stop' was called, I had about 60 of the pegs turned round, but when I looked at my neighbour I was horrified to see all but three of his turned. "That's one test I've failed for sure," I thought. I asked him later on how he had managed to be so quick. After some prodding, he confessed – all he had done was turn the first three pegs and then turn the whole board round! But if lateral thinking was one of the desired abilities, I guess he was a clear winner.

Evidently I hadn't failed that test after all, because I was one of those selected to continue to the next stage, aircrew grading. This was designed to separate out those who were not suited to flying at all and to sort the rest according to their progress into prospective pilots, navigators or air gunners. It entailed approximately 12 hours basic flying training in De Havilland Tiger Moth biplane two seat trainers at RAF Digby, a few miles south of Lincoln.

Digby was a long established Royal Air Force airfield, with permanent brick and steel hangars, but no hard surfaced runways, just grass. During World War Two it had been home to (among others) Spitfire Squadrons, but now the only resident aircraft were the Tiger Moths. On a good flying day the field gave the impression of a wasps' nest, with what seemed to be hundreds of yellow painted aircraft buzzing around in all directions. From what I remember there was no Air Traffic Control; the Tiger Moths had no radio. With the rest of the flying related subjects in Ground School we were taught the rules of the air which included who gave way to whom when landing and taking off. This seemed to work; there were no collisions during the month we spent there.

We were issued with the cumbersome kit needed for open cockpit aircraft – a heavy canvas Sidcot flying suit, leather fur-lined calf length boots, leather fur-lined gloves and silk inners, a canvas helmet and a pair of goggles. Dressed in these, we would not have seemed out of place on a Royal Flying Corps Squadron of the First World War. The Tiger Moth itself, with a few small modifications, could have passed as a Sopwith Camel or a Bristol Bulldog.

There were very few RAF personnel on the unit. The instructors were civilians, ex-WW2 RAF pilots. The atmosphere, in the air and on the ground, was very relaxed after the trauma of Padgate. On one occasion my instructor took control as we taxied out towards the take-off point, stopped the aircraft and producing a shotgun from beside his seat, loosed off with both barrels at a hare. He missed; otherwise I'm sure I'd have been dispatched from the cockpit to retrieve it.

My first flight took place on October 23 1951. The logbook entry reads:

Aircraft Type/No.	1st Pilot	Pilot, or 2nd Pilot, Pupil or Passenger	Duty	Single Engine Aircraft Day Dual
DH82a 112/51	Mr. Massey	Self	1, 2, 3, 4	.55

In fact this was copied into my first logbook from the single logbook page we were each given at Digby. Since there was no certainty that we would make the grade as aircrew, the powers that be weren't going to waste money by giving us each a complete logbook! DH82a was the official designation for the RAF version of the Tiger Moth. 1,2,3,4 under the "Duty" heading referred to the first few exercises - Aircraft Familiarisation, Preparation for Flight, Air Experience and Effect of Controls.

That first flight was a delight, although I soon discovered that I wasn't a 'natural'. We climbed past some fleecy cumulus clouds into a smooth clear sky and I was given the controls. The aeroplane would have done better on its own – after all, even non-radio controlled, free flight model aircraft manage quite well without a pilot. I was convinced that the slightest change of attitude needed immediate and positive action and over-controlled badly. My instructor laughed and told me to relax, I was only there to stop the aircraft going to Edinburgh when I wanted to go to London and the less I interfered the better it would fly.

From then on things went quite well, until a few flights later on when we started the stalling and spinning exercises. I soon found out that motion sickness was no fun. But somehow I managed to conceal my problem and continued through the other exercises until I had reached the 12-hour limit. Unfortunately, although my instructor considered I was ready for solo, the weather turned against me. It was not until 1964, 13 years later, that I flew a Tiger Moth on my own.

At the end of the grading course, I was told that I had been selected to continue training as a pilot. I couldn't really believe this was possible – from childhood I had thought that pilots were some sort of God. If they'd said I could be a navigator I'd have been more than satisfied, but a pilot? Wow! There must have been a mistake somewhere.

From Digby, we moved a few miles north to Kirton-in-Lindsey, No. 2 Initial Training School. Like Digby, Kirton was a pre-war grass airfield, with the standard brick and steel permanent hangars, brick built barrack blocks, Station Headquarters building, Parachute Section, Fire Section and so on of which the pattern was to become so familiar. In fact, if one had been set down in the middle of any of these "permanent" RAF bases, it would have been almost impossible to know **which** one it was. There was no flying involved at this unit. We were there to learn aviation theory and to receive instruction on the requirements of becoming a commissioned officer in His Majesty's Air Force. About half the time was spent in ground school, but we were also kept on the move from dawn to late in the evening with drill, rifle training, PT and outdoor exercises. In between, there was always something to be cleaned, washed or polished. As the old sweats used to say, "If it moves, salute it. If it doesn't move, polish it".

The small consolation was that we were allowed to leave the camp at weekends. Nowadays, between the fears of assault or theft and the equally alarming fear of being sued in the event of an accident, few drivers will stop for hitchhikers. In the 1950s, especially for members of the armed services, it was a very easy way of travelling. I thumbed my way home and back several times, but also, with one of my fellow cadets, explored all around Lincolnshire. On a nearer expedition we walked a few miles to the deserted World War Two airfield at Hibaldstow. We didn't stay long; there was an eerie, haunted atmosphere about the rusting Nissen huts and crumbling tarmac.

After ten weeks we had our final drill sessions, rehearsing the passing-out parade. Of approximately one hundred cadets on the course, all National Servicemen, initially seven only had failed selection for flying training. Of these, five were passed after interview with the Suspension Board and the remaining two were re-coursed. It seems that we were very much needed at that time, the Korean War was in full swing. I see from my diaries that the course behind ours had a 60% failure rate.

We now moved up the hierarchy scale, from Aircraftsmen 2 aircrew cadets to Acting Pilot Officers. Our pay also rose considerably from the four shillings per day (less stoppages) of an ordinary National Service 'erk'. In addition to a higher basic rate we received flying pay. I was at last able to buy some better wheels than those of the sit up and beg Raleigh which had served me so well during my high school days, but nothing too grand – just a lightweight drop handlebar bicycle with derailleur gears.

After a short leave, we reported to our assigned Basic Flying Training Schools – Anstey, Sywell and Desford or for my group, Booker, near High Wycombe.

Chapter 4
Basic and advanced training

In 1952 Booker airfield was out in the country. I remember a bright moonlit early spring night, when I bicycled across the fields down the hill to Marlow and heard dozens of nightingales singing in the woods. Booker is now known as Wycombe Air Park and is surrounded by housing estates, the M40 motorway and other busy main roads. It is also beneath the London Terminal Area and the airspace that we freely cavorted in is now restricted, reserved for aircraft under radio control bound for Heathrow and the other London airports.

The training aircraft were, as at Digby, De Havillands, but these were DHC1 Chipmunks, far advanced from the fabric covered, strut and wire, Tiger Moth biplane. Designed by De Havilland Canada, the Chipmunk was a low wing cantilever monoplane, with an all metal fuselage and a sliding cockpit canopy. Although we had a new aircraft to become familiar with, it was powered by the same Gypsy Major 4-cylinder piston engine, with the small modification of a six-shot cartridge starter.

My first Chipmunk flight was on February 20th, in WG401. Thereafter things didn't go too well for me, partly due to a 12-day break after my first three days flying while my instructor was away sick. A month later all my course mates had soloed but I was still grinding round the circuit after 9 ½ hours dual. When it finally happened, my first solo, on 21st March in Chipmunk WB293 was nearly my last. Not for any life-threatening reason, but because I came very close to damaging the aeroplane. Although many RAF pilots broke aeroplanes but were allowed to continue, they were usually rather further into their training, or already fully qualified. I recall reading about a Battle of Britain pilot, of whom it was said "He has destroyed at least ten aircraft, of which a few were enemy". I didn't have any credit side to my balance sheet.

I had just flown a few not too erratic circuits with my instructor. At the take-off position, he climbed out and told me to do one circuit on my own. Fortunately there was a hump in the middle of Booker airfield, so he didn't see what a mess I made of the landing. I touched down much too far into the field and barely managed to stop before running into the boundary hedge. I was so close – the propeller was only twenty feet from the bushes - that I didn't have room to turn round. I had to switch the engine off, climb out, push the aircraft backwards away from the hedge, lift the tail round, then climb in and start up again. I was most grateful for the cartridge starter – if it had been a Tiger Moth it would have meant hand swinging the propeller and I wouldn't have dared try that for fear of sending the aircraft off on its own!

There was no drama on my third solo, an hour of circuits and landings in WD285. I saw this particular aircraft 40 years later, at California City airport in the U.S.A. but unfortunately the owner was out of town so I didn't get the chance to beg a flight in it again for old time's sake.

There's an old wartime song, "An Instructor's Lament", which goes something on the lines of:

"What did you do in the war, Daddy?
How did you help us to win?
With circuits and bumps and stalls, laddie,
And how to get out of a spin."

It must have been a soul-destroying life for our instructors. Even after we made it to first solo, it took another 12 hours of circuits and bumps and stalls and how to get out of a spin before we moved away from the immediate area of the airfield and started doing practise forced landings, aerobatics, cross-countries and instrument flying. Aerobatics nearly ended my flying days; I suffered badly from airsickness. Fortunately my instructor was sympathetic and would let me stop throwing the aircraft around before I reached the vomiting stage. When solo, I would push things a bit further. There were two ways to deal with the inevitable result. RAF issue cape leather flying gloves made quite good sick-bags (but too expensive to throw away, we had to pay for any lost equipment). The alternative was to open the canopy and lean out. The first time I tried this I got it wrong, I was flying straight and most of it came back inside. I soon learnt to sideslip away from the side I was leaning out of!

Practice forced landings kept us alert. The easier one was the forced landing with power, something one might have to do if caught out by bad weather and unable to reach an airfield, or with the sort of emergency that made an immediate landing advisable. A suitable-looking field could be checked over from a low-level fly-past and if it proved no good another could be inspected. Forced landings without power were more difficult. Any time the instructor wanted to pile on a bit more pressure, he would pull back the throttle and announce that the engine had failed. After settling the aircraft into a glide descent, a scan all around would with any luck reveal a suitably large, level and smooth field where it should be possible to land safely. If not, the most suitable area for a controlled crash would have to do. We would glide down to fifty feet or so, by which height it was clear that we had or hadn't made a pig's ear of it and then open the throttle and climb away.

We learnt to fly on instruments, with our part of the canopy obscured by whitewash and were taught cross-country flying by map and compass. This culminated in a solo flight to another airfield, landing there, re-fuelling and returning. I flew to Sywell, in Northamptonshire, then an RAF training airfield, which I was to visit several times many years later. Near the end of the course we were introduced to night flying and had our first experience of the RAF Night Flying Supper. For some obscure reason, at RAF Flying Training Schools, after night flying, instead of returning to the Officers' Mess we went to the Airmen's Mess, where we were treated to eggs, bacon and tomatoes, known to the Royal Navy I'm told as "train smash"

At the end of the course on 6th May 1952, we had flown 60 hours on the Chipmunk. For the next stage we separated again and went to various Advanced Flying Training Schools, to fly either twin engined Oxfords or the single engined Harvard. At our new schools, we met up again with others from the original Kirton in Lindsey crowd. I was posted to RAF Wellesbourne Mountford in Warwickshire, to train on the Oxford.

This aircraft, designed and built by the Airspeed Company, was a military version of the pre-war Envoy. It was a low wing monoplane of wooden construction, fabric covered, powered by two Cheetah 10 radial piston engines. Being a 'tail-dragger', with a tail wheel rather than the more modern nose wheel undercarriage, it had a strong tendency to 'ground-loop', that is to keep moving in a straight line while spinning round – performing something like a handbrake turn in a car. I returned from a walk one day and was rather puzzled to see an Oxford sitting on the airfield boundary fence with its tail across the road. It looked as if it had landed on the hedge and stopped dead, but there was no real sign of damage. In fact, it had ground-looped and slid backwards.

The Oxford was somewhat old-tech even then. For instance it had no electric starter and the engines had to be started by a ground staff man squatting on the wing and cranking an inertia starter. If the pilot was not quick enough to throttle back when the engine started, the mechanic could be blown off by the propeller wash.

Flying the Oxford introduced us to the asymmetric power problem. In the air, with one engine out of action, thrust from the one still running applies a turning force. This turning force is countered by using the rudder to apply an equal but opposite turning force. Unfortunately the force available from the rudder is dependent on speed, a higher speed giving greater force. In cruising flight the speed available for twin engined aircraft from one engine is high enough for the rudder to provide enough force to keep the aircraft flying straight. But when speed is low and power on the good engine high, for instance when one engine fails while taking off, the rudder may not give enough force. It will then be necessary to reduce power on the good engine until engine turning force again equals rudder force. But then there may be too little power to accelerate or climb.

What it comes down to is that depending on the particular aircraft, its weight and various other factors like altitude, temperature, whether the undercarriage is up or down and flap setting, there is an airspeed below which if one engine fails it is not possible to keep the aircraft straight and climb away. For most modern aircraft, this speed will be achieved before the aircraft reaches take-off speed, but for some of the older types, an engine failure just after becoming airborne made an immediate landing (or crash) straight ahead inevitable. Above this airspeed the aircraft could be accelerated further to the correct airspeed for a climb. Even so, the rate of climb could be rather low. Inaccurate flying with the speed higher or lower than ideal could stop the aircraft climbing. The Oxford was in the 'older aircraft' category, but in the training role, was well below its designed maximum weight, so engine failures were not too serious a problem.

For some reason we did no formation flying until after the final handling test. Formation flying was a fairly staid exercise in the non-aerobatic Oxford. We would drone around in groups of four, one each side of the leader forming a level 'V' and one 'in the box' behind and below. From time to time the followers would change positions so each pilot would have practice at flying left, right and behind. After a few flights with instructors in all four aircraft we moved on to having an instructor in the lead aircraft only. On my last flight there was a shortage of instructors and I was asked if I felt I could lead three of my fellow students around. It sounded easy; I found out the hard way it was not. Thinking ahead is essential when flying, leading a formation requires thinking ahead squared.

At the end of this Advanced Flying Training course those of us who had satisfied the ground and flying examiners of our fitness to do so received the coveted 'wings'. These were presented at a passing out parade, attended by parents, aunts, uncles and girlfriends. The next step was the Advanced Flying course where we were to learn to fly jet engined Meteor or Vampire aircraft. Again we were split into smaller groups and I went to Weston Zoyland, situated a few miles east of Bridgewater in the flat, low-lying area of the Somerset Levels, to fly the Meteor, arriving there on the 4th November 1952.

I took the bicycle with me and explored the local area at weekends. There was some good coarse fishing available, notably in the King's Sedgemoor drain, one of the major land reclamation watercourses, but the countryside was not very exciting, except to bird watchers. There were some historic sites nearby. Marks on the walls of the church at Chedzoy were said to have been made by combatants sharpening their swords before the 1685 Battle of Sedgemoor. Glastonbury was not far to the east.

We had good relations with the permanent staff and instructors and got on well together in our small group of nine students. There were some pleasant old pubs around. We course members spent many evenings in the skittle alleys which were a feature of most of them, often in the company of our instructors and of course consumed as much 'scrumpy' cider as we could manage.

Flying started on 21st November after two weeks of ground school. My instructor was Sergeant Jack Sherburn. I was to bump into him again around 40 years later when he visited the Yorkshire Gliding Club for a glider flight, having retired from Shorts, the by then Belfast based aircraft builders for whom he had been a test pilot. The 'duty' for my first two flights was recorded as 'familiarisation', but it would have been described more accurately as 'a chance for Jack to show off both the aircraft and his own flying skill'. I was most impressed by the way the Meteor could perform the full repertoire of aerobatics with one engine shut down but still gain height – in the Chipmunk, aerobatic sequences always involved a loss of height. Another very noticeable difference was the lack of vibration. But there was a price to pay for the power, speed and smoothness – maximum fuel endurance (at high level) was about 1 hour 30 minutes. At high speed low down the fuel would run out in around 30 minutes. Also, engine failures on take-off were somewhat more serious than on the Oxford. Given plenty of speed, it was easy enough to keep the aircraft flying straight with one engine out of action, only a small rudder deflection was needed. At low speed however, the foot load for the full rudder deflection that was needed was very heavy. It was essential to adjust the rudder pedal position before flying so that the appropriate knee could be locked just 'over centre' with that leg extended and the rudder bar fully deflected. If the rudder pedals were not far enough away the strain of holding full rudder with a bent leg became unsupportable after a very short time. Too far away and full rudder could not be applied.

I flew my first jet solo, in Meteor Mk 7 WL344, on 1st December and continued with two flights in the single seat Mark 4. With my 20th birthday only five weeks away, I could just make the 'teenage jet pilot' claim. Many years later when the Royal Air Force began flying training from the outset on the Jet Provost this would have become the norm except that around the same time a policy requiring aircrew candidates to have graduated from University was introduced.

Until jet conversion my colleagues and I had led charmed lives. All had survived Basic Flying Training on the Chipmunk and Advanced Flying Training on Harvards or Oxfords. Things began to go wrong during the Advanced Flying stage. Of around 100 on my course at Kirton Lindsey, twenty or so were to die in the next three years, two at Weston Zoyland while I was there.

Undoubtedly this was caused by the step up to much faster and more technically complicated aircraft, allied to the fact that we were now pushing the boundaries of aviation. We were doing things that, with the knowledge that came later, should not have been done. For example, we were flying at very high altitude, in unpressurised aircraft, with simple oxygen systems. It was not realised that at very low outside air pressure even breathing pure oxygen still left the body short of the vital element. In later years a pressure jerkin, pressure mask and G-suit enabled

Photo 2 - Meteor F4   ©RuthAS

oxygen to be forced into the lungs, but in our day a few unexplained fatal accidents were probably contributed to by pilots suffering a degree of oxygen deficiency.

Even safety equipment, designed to save life, could cause fatalities. We sat on a pack containing a folded rubber dinghy, attached to our parachute harness. If we bailed out and landed in the sea, the dinghy could be inflated by activating a carbon dioxide bottle. One of my friends died when his dinghy inflated accidentally, forcing the control column fully forward, causing the aircraft to dive into the ground. So we were all instructed to provide ourselves with dinghy stabbers. A sharpened potato peeler, tied to one's overalls was popular. Inevitably one day someone's stabber came adrift during aerobatics and stabbed the pilot. A new improved stabber was devised, but something else went wrong. By 1972, when I left the Royal Air Force for the second time, the sixpenny potato peeler had mutated into a very expensive Martin-Baker knife. This was held in a sheath sewn to the overalls and could be released only by operating two separate catches.

There was also an aerodynamic problem with the Meteor itself, which led to several inexplicable fatalities. An aircraft would join the circuit and all would appear normal until, in the final turn, it would dive into the ground apparently out of control. Eventually it was discovered that although with the wheels up the airbrakes could be operated without problems in any conditions of bank, 'g', or yaw, if the wheels were down and a turn was unbalanced (i.e. with slip or skid) extending the airbrakes could lead to loss of control.

Some of the instructional techniques of the1950s were another factor. Nowadays single-engine training in multi-engined aircraft is carried out very circumspectly. Engines are never actually shut down for practice except at a very safe height, 3,000 feet being the minimum for a propeller driven machine and jets even higher. Engine failure after take-off is simulated by retarding a throttle and the shutdown drill is completed by touching the appropriate switches and levers without actually moving them. If anything goes wrong, the pilot merely has to open the throttle again. Our Meteor engine failure after take-off training was conducted by the instructor simply closing the fuel cock on one of the engines. This wasn't a simulated failure – it was a real one! Eventually the RAF came to the conclusion that more people were dying as a result of 'practice' engine failures than were dying following real failures.

My personal first near miss with the grim reaper came about halfway through the course. It was a fine day when I took off, clear blue sky and unlimited visibility. I climbed out to the northeast and reached 30,000 feet somewhere in the Cheddar Gorge area. After a couple of 360-degree turns, looking down to make sure that there were no other aircraft below and that I was over open country, I started to throw the aircraft around. Loops, stall turns, slow rolls, barrel rolls – and a lot of other peculiar and not too well co-ordinated manoeuvres. At first, there was no problem staying in the same bit of sky, the reservoirs below were an easy location point. But then a sheet of cloud started to drift across them. It was time to head back south-west towards the airfield. A hole in the cloud sheet gave me a visual position fix; I was going in roughly the right direction, but the cloud was becoming more continuous.

In itself, this was no real problem. We didn't have today's sophisticated navigation equipment, but there was a system known as VHF D/F, Very High Frequency Direction Finding. This entailed a ground operator listening to a pilot's radio transmission and by swinging a receiving loop aerial, finding from which direction the strongest signal was coming. He could then tell the pilot in which direction to steer towards the airfield. Once overhead, if there were no gaps in the cloud to descend through, the procedure was to fly away from the runway at an angle of 10 degrees from the outbound centre line, while descending to half the starting altitude. A turn of 190 degrees would then put the aircraft heading approximately towards the runway, approximately on the centreline of the approach. The descent continued and further bearings gave corrections towards the centre line. This was not a very accurate procedure. There was a time lag while the pilot spoke, the bearing was obtained and the controller gave the pilot a course correction. A jet fighter's high approach speed meant that it had to be pretty well lined up and on the centre line with, at the latest, about half a mile to go to touchdown. Achieving this by radio bearings alone was exceedingly unlikely. The pilot needed to be below cloud and with reasonable visibility far enough out to see the runway and then make the turns necessary to line up.

A better system was available, but not at Weston Zoyland. This was Ground Controlled Approach (GCA). The controller gave directions to the pilot from observation of a radar screen. This gave more accurate approaches. The controller was able to see the aircraft's radar echo relative to the ideal glide slope and would tell the pilot to increase or reduce his rate of descent accordingly. In azimuth, deviations showed up immediately and again the controller could give corrections without delay. Later on GCA was replaced by the Instrument Landing System (ILS), when an instrument in the cockpit showed, directly to the pilot, deviation in both glide-path and azimuth from a radio beam originating at the runway threshold.

On that day in 1953 when I arrived overhead base, I could see no gaps in the cloud below. Low cloud had quickly and unexpectedly rolled in from the Bristol Channel. The few other airfields within range were also reporting low cloud and poor visibility and none of them had GCA. ILS was just a dream of the future. I had no choice but to try a VHF D/F approach.

The outbound leg, procedure turn and first part of the inbound leg were in bright sunshine, but at 600 feet I slipped into the top of the cloud. One thing was going for me. The countryside all round Weston Zoyland was very flat and the only obstruction of any height (the church spire) was to the west of the airfield, on the opposite side from me. Anywhere to the east of the threshold I could descend to a very low altitude before hitting anything. I passed 500 feet, 400, 300 still in the fog. At 250 feet, I caught a brief glimpse of the ground.

Ahead and to my right, I spotted a road bridge over a canal and recognised it as the place where I had gone fishing the previous weekend. A couple of aircraft had landed while I was fishing, but they had passed on the other side of the bridge. I was too far to the left. As I made an S-turn to the right, I entered the cloud again. Straightening up on the last bearing I carried on gently down. At 200 feet I was still in the thick of it. I passed 150 feet – and hallelujah, vaguely visible through the murk, dead ahead, was the runway.

I was shaking when I climbed out of the aircraft.

Chapter 5
Ground duties and gliding

At the end of the Meteor course on 15 March 1953 and after an unexpectedly good final handling check flight with the course Commanding Officer, my Flight Commander and Jack Sherburn both tried to persuade me to 'sign on' for a short service commission or to apply for a permanent commission. Had I agreed, it would have saved me six depressing months. Every National Service course before ours had gone on for their last six months to Operational Conversion Units and Squadrons. We were just too late. The Korean War Armistice talks were progressing well and we were not expected to be needed. The luckiest amongst us were sent off to fly Spitfires on the Meteorological Flight at Hornchurch, some others went to Communications Flights where they acted as taxi drivers for the 'brass', flying Oxfords, Ansons and such. The rest, myself included, were found silly ground jobs. I was posted to Wildenrath in Germany, a 2nd Tactical Air Force base. This was one of the newly constructed 'clutch' airfields, carved out among the conifer plantations along the Dutch/German border, between Aachen and Arnhem. I was to be the Station Intelligence and Security Officer.

I never really found out what the Intelligence part of the post involved. There were certainly no spies reporting to me and no secret information came down from Headquarters. The Security aspect gave me nightmares. At Wildenrath there were two Squadrons of F86 Sabre fighters, the most up-to-date aircraft on our side of the Cold War and one of less modern Vampires. Those aircraft that were not in the hangars on maintenance were parked, unguarded, on hard-standing dispersal areas scattered among the pine trees. The base perimeter was about 15 kilometres in length. There was a barrier and a guardroom at the main entrance, but elsewhere nothing more than a single strand of barbed wire and at 100 metre or so intervals, "Eintritt Verboten" (No Entry) signs. Every day several hundred German workers – cooks, cleaners, clerks, labourers and so on - would come onto the base, solemnly presenting their passes at the guardroom, but thereafter freely moving around. I could only hope that someone occasionally checked them once inside. There were no British personnel specifically allocated to Security, although I could call on the services of around a dozen airmen of the RAF Regiment – if they weren't on other duties. And the Station Riding Club promised to keep their eyes open!

Until this posting to Germany I had never been out of England – not even into Wales or Scotland. Unfortunately I had opted for French as my foreign language for the GCE. As a twenty-year-old, with no experience of the world other than school and the relatively protected life of a trainee pilot, with not more than two words of German, I was rather out of my depth. The Intelligence and Security Office was in its own semi-underground bunker and there I went to earth. I was intending to try Civil Aviation after my National Service finished. Nobody at Wildenrath seemed to want me to do anything in particular, so I spent my time studying the Civil Aviation Act and Regulations in preparation for the Commercial Pilot's Licence examinations, hoping that I would never have to do anything serious!

This hope was dashed when one day two rather overzealous members of the RAF Regiment squad brought me a prisoner. They had found him near one of the dispersed Sabres. He didn't speak English or at least didn't admit to and the Regiment airmen didn't speak German, so things were at a bit of an impasse. All we could be sure of, from his identity papers, was that he was resident in East Germany. One of the German clerks from Station Headquarters was called in as translator. Our captive's story was that he was born in the nearby village, but went to the east before the war and had lived there since the war ended. He had managed to get permission to visit his family home and went for a walk through the woods he remembered from his childhood. To his surprise he came across an aeroplane and then these soldiers jumped out of the bushes and grabbed hold of him. A telephone call to higher authority at 2 TAF HQ elicited the advice that I should check the likelihood of this story with the local Mayor and if it appeared true, just let him go. Which I did.

Outside of work, I had a reasonably enjoyable time. I went on a few weekend trips with colleagues to Cologne and nearby places on the Rhine. Germany, eight years after the war, was a country of extreme contrast. In Cologne vast areas of bomb damage rubble remained, with many people still living in makeshift shelters. Not far away the riverside resort of Konigswinter was a place of smart cafes and hotels. I remember vividly the fantastic cream-laden cakes in one of the cafes. Back in England we still had food rationing!

By the middle of May, I had had more than enough of a desk job. I also had doubts about my prospects of a flying career in civil aviation. I needed more flying hours to qualify for a Commercial Pilot Licence; very few airlines were taking people without one. A four-year Short Service Commission (extending National Service by two years) was available and would get me back into flying, so I put in an application. Had I known it would take until November to get back into the air, I'd have gritted my teeth and stuck to the desk, my National Service was due to end in August.

My replacement as Intelligence and Security Officer didn't arrive until the 11th August. He was a keen dinghy sailor, in no time at all he had arranged for us both to go for two days racing on the weekend of 22nd August at the Steinhudemeer, a large freshwater lake near Buckeburg. A sailing match had been arranged between the RAF U.K. and 2nd Tactical Air Force teams. We could enter one of the open races on Saturday and if we showed any promise, might get to sail or crew in the 2 TAF team. When the day arrived, although we came last, we both ended up crewing in the remaining match races.

On September 22nd I finally had notice of my return to flying duties. I would be going back to Weston Zoyland for a Meteor refresher course on 27th October. I had a large amount of leave owing, so applied to clear from

Wildenrath at the beginning of October and spend three weeks at home. As usual, there was some administration problem with this apparently sensible notion, I could have the U.K. leave but would have to return to Germany to clear and then go directly to Weston Zoyland. So I opted instead to take the leave in Germany and arranged to go to the Steinhudemeer again, for fishing as well as sailing.

It was quite a trek getting there by train and in fact I didn't make it. The connections were such that I had to spend Saturday and Sunday night at Buckeburg. With Sunday to spare I went for a walk and at the airfield saw a group of servicemen flying an SG-38 open primary glider. This consisted of little more than an open seat mounted on a keel (on which the rudder pedals were hinged) hung below a wood and fabric wing by a bird's nest of struts and wires. Seeing my interest and after enquiry into my flying experience, they offered me a go. After 3 medium hops - launches to 200 feet and landings straight ahead - without disaster, I found myself flying full winch launches to around 1,000 feet with none of the aids – or encumbrances – that previous flying had accustomed me to. I decided that gliding beat both sailing and power flying.

The Buckeburg club flew only at weekends, but the members said that at Scharfoldendorf, not far away, there was gliding all week. So I cancelled the sailing arrangements and went by train to Hamelin and on by 'Kleinbahn'. This started as a tram in the town centre, but once out of the suburbs it took off down a main railway. The Scharfoldendorf stop was distinguished from the generally deserted countryside by no more than a signboard. No platform, no shelter, no sign of life and no telephone. But I saw a glider flying along the ridge behind the sign. There seemed to be no road leading that way, so I scrambled up what felt like a minor alp, only to find when I reached the top that the hangar doors were just being closed.

Scharfoldendorf had been a gliding centre since before the war and the RAF Germany Gliding Association had 'inherited' not only many gliders, the winches, workshops and a hangar, but also some very palatial accommodation. I was one of only two guests at the officer's hotel. My room was more commodious than any I had lived in while in the RAF. The evening meal was exceptional.

Next morning I met the CFI and told him my story. Bad news. "All the two seaters are unserviceable". Then the good news. "I'm just going to do an air test on the Grunau, if it's serviceable you can fly that. Watch what I do and I'll give you a briefing when I land."

So I watched, he flew round the circuit and landed. The briefing was very thorough, speeds to fly, heights to aim for at the landmarks round the circuit, only use the airbrakes when you are wings level on the approach, they act like the throttle on a powered aircraft and so on. "The gully between launch point and winch is smooth but steep, so if you get a cable break early in the launch you either stop before the drop or keep lots of speed and land uphill on the other side." The final words were "if you get more than 600 feet on the launch, do a few turns over the winch to lose height – there's no-one else flying."

I strapped in and watched the tractor bringing the cable leave the winch. It then disappeared for an eternity, before re-appearing a few hundred yards ahead. After the cable was attached to the glider there was a long wait between "take up slack" and "all out" while it tightened across the 200 deep gully. But the launch went well, and I released at around 800 feet.

Now one of the things one learnt in RAF training was to follow the briefing – exactly. If you were told to go off solo, climb to 20,000 feet and do half a dozen spins, you climbed to 20,000 feet and did half a dozen spins. Those instructors had eyes and spies, everywhere. So when I did my first turn to lose height, I was a bit disconcerted to find I **hadn't** lost any height. There was a funny little green ball bobbing up and down in an instrument which from schoolboy reading I recognised as a cosim variometer (an instrument showing rate of climb or descent). "I must be in one of those thermal things (a rising bubble of warm air)," I thought, "what to do?" So I widened the turn. "That's better, but the green ball is still showing some of the time. Widen the turn some more. Good, it's red all round now." Of course, I hadn't been briefed to use the airbrakes – except on the approach. So I descended to 600 feet and flew the rest of the circuit as briefed.

While we were closing the hangar doors at the end of the day, the winch driver came to speak to me. He was an ex-Luftwaffe Messerschmitt 262 jet pilot. The Germans were still banned from flying at that time but when no-one official was around he was allowed the occasional flight. "Ach, you English pilots are all the same. I launch you into a good thermal and you don't get the wing down, so you don't turn tight enough and you lose it." What could I say?

Unfortunately the weather for the rest of my stay was not suitable for soaring. I made another seventeen flights in the Grunau, but they were just circuits. The wind blew from every direction except towards the ridge and the air was too stable for thermals. I did not have the chance to put his advice into practice until the following summer in England.

Chapter 6
Return to flying

Back at Wildenrath on Tuesday 20th October, I found that my posting had been changed to Oakington, near Cambridge. The rest of the week was spent going round the station obtaining signatures on my 'clearance chit', a piece of paper designed to make sure that I had handed back any equipment I had drawn from such sections as sports, safety equipment and publications, that I had handed over the Intelligence and Security inventory, paid any money I owed for losses or damage and in general could be allowed to go out of immediate reach.

I travelled by troop train and ferry to Harwich. Ahead of me in line for the U.K. Customs were first a Group Captain and then a Leading Aircraftsman. I observed the Groupie declaring a number of small items including a camera he was carrying and being allowed through without having to pay any duty. The LAC was next; he declared the camera **he** was carrying and was asked to pay a moderate sum. He made a fuss, complained that the Groupie hadn't been charged, one law for the rich and so on, but the Customs Officer was adamant. In the end the LAC forked out the cash and, still muttering, went through to the railway platform. I saw him out there a little later and commiserated. "Ah, don't worry, Sir" he said, "I've got annuver ten ov'em in me kit bag!"

Oakington became a disaster for me – and Air Ministry probably thought they had picked a real loser. I arrived on 27th October and started flying again on the 30th, with two dual sorties in the Meteor 7. On the 3rd November I had another dual flight, followed by a solo in a Meteor 4. Just after I took off, another aircraft crashed on the runway, so I went to Graveley for my circuit practice, before diverting to Waterbeach, just a few miles away. With the return my total solo time for the day was 50 minutes. Two more dual flights on the 4th and 5th gave me a dual total of 3 hours. On Friday 6th I was not on the flying roster. On Monday 9th the weather was bad, so a group of us went to the PT hangar. There I got into a game of volleyball, slipped, fell on my left hand and broke my wrist. I did not know it, but it was to be 13 weeks (11th February) before my arm came out of plaster and 2nd April before I flew solo again.

Those four and a half months passed slowly, although from my diary life seems to have been full of activity. On the station I was given a variety of administrative jobs and I managed to scrounge occasional dual trips in the Communications Flight Oxfords and Provosts. I wasn't allowed to fly solo, at first the plastered arm made this impracticable and even when the plaster finally came off the Station Medical Officer wouldn't give me medical clearance. I took leave twice, once before and once after Christmas, on both occasions spending the time on Youth Hostel cycle tours of Devon and Cornwall. Weekends and public holidays seem to have passed in a whirl of sailing at Burnham on Crouch, coarse fishing in the fens, short cycle tours in

Cambridgeshire, Suffolk and Norfolk and visits home. Some of my schoolmates introduced me to the world of jazz; we spent evenings listening and jiving to Humphrey Lyttleton or Chris Barber and Lonnie Donegan at venues in London. I can still remember every word of Lonnie's skiffle group song "The Rock Island Line", which we sang along to even before it became a number one on the hit parade.

Finally I was passed fit for flying again and was posted to Worksop on 29th March 1954 for another Meteor course. I remember very little about the station, although I have a vague impression that it was a WW2 temporary airfield with Nissen huts and wooden buildings. I do know that our crew room was on the far side of the airfield from the Officers' Mess. It was a bit far to walk, so I signed out one of the 802 Raleigh sit up and beg bicycles that were on the station inventory. The trick was to wait for a Meteor taxying round the perimeter track and then fall in behind in the warm jet efflux. Maybe breathing exhaust fumes was not good for one's health, but at least one stayed warm.

Worksop's single seat Meteors were the Mark 8 version, the first RAF aircraft to be fitted with ejection seats. I was very apprehensive the first time I strapped in; I had visions of being shot into the sky if I so much as sneezed. But as with most things, familiarity, though it did not bring contempt, brought a degree of nonchalance. Soon the ritual of checking that the safety pins were in, sitting down, fastening the seat harness, asking for the pins to be removed and being shown them before they were stowed became just one of the ordinary things one did before flying.

Refresher flying covered much the same exercises as the Weston Zoyland jet conversion course, with the addition of spinning, which had been forbidden previously on the Meteor. This proved to be a good thing; on the very next flight after my dual spin training I managed the first (and last) unintentional spin of my whole flying career when I got a little over enthusiastic during a solo aerobatic session. That I was fooling about at night with one engine throttled right back may go some way towards explaining this departure from conventional operation.

When the course ended on May 19th I went on to Stradishall, near Haverhill in Suffolk for Operational Conversion. Stradishall was another of the permanent, brick and steel construction RAF stations. My first flight there was a dual check in a Meteor 7. The instructor was a somewhat fiery-tempered ex Battle of Britain Sergeant pilot. I was a little unsettled by the briefing before the flight, which went on the lines of "You can forget all the **** they taught you in flying training, now I've got the job of showing ******'s like you how to use the ******* aeroplane, you know nothing and you never will ..." It was like being back at Padgate. My unease was not mitigated when as we walked out to the Meteor 7 I glimpsed an aircraft a mile or two away diving vertically downwards, heard a loud explosion and saw a mushroom of thick black smoke rising from behind the distant trees. We took off; during the 55-minute sortie the comments from the rear seat were scathing and by the time we landed I fully expected to be sent packing. The instructor proved to a bad guy/good guy rolled into one, during the debrief he was quite complimentary and affable.

All the previous courses had involved roughly equal amounts of dual and solo flying. On the Operational Conversion course it was assumed that we knew how to fly an aircraft; we were being shown how to use it in combat so we did very little dual. The techniques of aerial combat were imparted mostly by briefings, followed by formation flights led by an instructor. The early part of the course concentrated on flying in the 'finger four' battle formation, invented by the Luftwaffe in WW2. This was before the days of air to air missiles; by flying almost in line abreast, spread out with about a thousand yards between the two outermost aircraft, those two pilots could keep a watch across the rear of the formation and see any attackers coming from behind before they were within gun firing range. The inner two pilots could then concentrate on the sky ahead, looking for targets. The problems came when the whole formation needed to turn through large angles; simply all turning at the same rate would have put the four aircraft in line astern after ninety degrees. So we learnt how to do cross-over turns, where the aircraft on the outside of the turn started by turning more rapidly, crossed behind the leader and then eased his turn so as to end up in line abreast again but on the opposite side. On the second half of the course we learnt air gunnery. We began with cine photography 'attacks' on another aircraft, then cine on a towed banner and finally two live firing sorties on the banner.

We had plenty of fine, warm weather during the course and spent many hours sunbathing on the grass in front of the hangar, idly discussing a great variety of subjects, not all related to flying. One of the pilots spent much time scribbling in notebooks; in later years I read and enjoyed all Gavin Lyall's novels. Another of the course pilots, Brian Thornton, had a motorcycle and let me try riding it. This encouraged me to upgrade from my pushbike. I had been cycling 50 miles to Burnham on Crouch at weekends to go dinghy sailing; although the exercise had no doubt been good for me the journey was somewhat time-consuming. On Brian's advice I bought a Francis Barnett 200cc two-stroke.

That brought another minor problem. The new ease of travel led me to see what else the surrounding area offered in the way of entertainment and I discovered the Cambridge University Gliding Club at Marshall's Airport just outside the city. From then on several weekends were wasted, while I dithered between going gliding and going sailing. On the occasions I did make my mind up, it seemed that whenever I chose sailing, the weekend weather would turn to flat calm and puffy cumulus cloud, no good for sailing but ideal for gliding. If I went to Marshall's, it changed to a howling wind and no thermals.

Perhaps because the CUGC gliders had been purchased with members' hard earned, begged or borrowed cash rather than looted like the RAF Germany Gliding Association's, the instructors were not so blasé about letting a power pilot loose without any dual instruction. I had to fly under supervision in the

T21 two-seater for a while. But after I was allowed to fly solo again, in a single seat, strutted Prefect, I eventually managed to find one of those thermal things, get the wing down, stay in it and by exceeding 15 minutes above the low point of the flight, gain the 'C' certificate badge.

At the end of the Operational Conversion course, for reasons best known to the Air Ministry and at the time apparently in spite of all logic, two of us, Brian Thornton and myself, were posted not onto a Squadron equipped with the two engined Meteor, but to 66 Squadron which flew single-engined F86E Sabres at Linton-on-Ouse, 10 miles north of York. With hindsight, I realise that possibly this did make sense – maybe Air Ministry knew that the Meteor would soon be replaced by a series of single engined day fighters. In fact, even when the next twin engined fighters came along, the engines were so close together (either vertically as in the Lightning or horizontally in the Javelin) that the old problems of asymmetric power when flying with one engine failed no longer existed. When we arrived at Linton on 13th September 1954 our new Squadron Commander welcomed us with the news that he wasn't going to have the bother of converting us to the new aircraft on the Squadron and he would get us sent back into the Meteor world. However, Air Ministry insisted that we were to join 66 Squadron. So it was arranged that we should go on the next available Sabre conversion course, starting on 4 October at Chivenor in Devon.

With nothing useful to do for two weeks, I was able to take leave and made my way to Sutton Bank, home since 1934 of the Yorkshire Gliding Club. There I met Bob Swinn, the Resident Instructor and his deputy, Henryk Dokter. The club fleet was fairly limited; a T21 and a T31 for dual training and Cadet and Tutor single seaters. These were all wood and fabric, strutted, low performance machines. I don't remember seeing much in the way of privately owned, higher performance gliders, but I expect there must have been a few.

When compared with today's YGC, the 1954 club facilities were rather primitive. The gliders were housed in an earth-floored, corrugated iron roofed blister hangar. The clubhouse was a wooden shack, with a coke stove. A horsehair stuffed sofa occupied much of the space in the main room; it would have had many a tale to tell had it been able to talk! Bob and his wife Sue lived on site in a caravan. Winter life up there, 1000 feet above sea level, must have been bleak. The area around the site was a heather covered plateau with little to break the wind; the trees in the mature fir plantation of today were then no more than six feet high. Even in September the wind blowing up the west-facing ridge that enabled me to stay airborne without power was fairly chilly. The seven flights I made added four hours fifteen minutes gliding time to the five hours achieved in the previous 66 launches, which shows the advantage of a ridge site over a flat one.

The 'busman's holiday' over, I made yet another train trek, to Chivenor, via London, to take my kit packed in its ammunition box. This was before the Beeching axe. If waiting for connections could be endured it was possible to travel directly cross-country by rail to almost any destination but it was usually quicker to travel via the hub. Next weekend I went back to Linton for the motorbike.

Chivenor was not one of the permanent RAF Stations, but was a rather motley collection of wooden huts erected during WW2. Situated on the estuary of the river Taw, it was in the area immortalised in Henry Williamson's "Tarka the Otter", "Salar the Salmon" and "Tales of a Devon Village". There were only ten of us on the course; Brian Thornton and I were the oddballs, all the rest having gone through the Harvard/Vampire single engine training sequence. So we two were singled out for special treatment and did Vampire conversion training before flying the Sabre. There was a marked contrast between the Vampire and Sabre conversions. The Sabre course involved two weeks of ground school, going deeply into the aircraft's electrical and hydraulic systems, the engine's fuel, oil and starting systems and the emergency drills for engine fire and so on. We even spent time in the hangar with the aircraft on jacks, practising the various emergencies that raising and lowering the undercarriage could entail. For the Vampire, I was given two short flights in the Mark 11 two-seat trainer, then an hour to read the Pilot's Notes for the single seat Mark 5. That done, one of the instructors came to the aircraft with me, assisted me to strap in, started the engine for me and then stood on the wing while I taxied to the end of the runway. Only then was I left to my own devices.

After the somewhat hulking Meteor, the Vampire 5 felt like a toy. We two ex-Meteor pilots, in conversation with the other course members, found some amusement by referring to it as the "Wheelbarrow" (apt enough with its twin boom layout) or the "Kiddycar". But in fact it was, as was to be expected from any De Havilland classic, a responsive and forgiving fighter.

With Sabre ground school over, first solos on type began. The system was for a staff pilot, in another Sabre, to formate on the trainee and be ready to give advice. We all assembled to watch the first victim. Immediately after the pair were off the ground, it became obvious that this aircraft was of a different breed to the Meteors and Vampires we were used to. The student's aircraft twitched from side to side and up and down like a demented dragonfly. When our own turns came, we found out why. The controls were so sensitive that it seemed one had only to think "go left" or "go up" and the machine responded. More than the slightest pressure on the stick and the pitch or roll attitude would change rapidly. In fact, at higher speeds full aileron would give a rate of roll, if sustained, greater than the pilot could take. Seated above the axis of roll, he could be subjected to enough negative "g" to suffer from "redout" (where blood is forced into the head). This is much more dangerous than excessive positive "g", since it could rupture blood vessels in the brain.

Once we had learnt the feel of this new style machine, we found it to be streets ahead of the Meteor and the Vampire. It was the first production aircraft designed to 'break the sound barrier', but in truth there was no barrier – the thin swept wing design overcame all the control reversal, buffeting and other problems that earlier aircraft had. Later fighters could reach supersonic speeds in level flight, but the Sabre did not have enough power for this. The best way to achieve supersonic speed was to climb to around 40,000 feet, fly level at full power until the airspeed reached a maximum, then roll upside down and gently pull through into a vertical dive. The rate of descent was around 60,000 feet per minute! This gave a maximum of about 15 seconds to hold the vertical, while the Machmeter needle wound slowly to just past 1.0. Other than the Mach indication, there was no way of telling that the magic speed had been reached. Then it was throttle right back, airbrakes out and pull out of the dive in short order. For some reason this exercise was not included in the Chivenor course, we had to wait until we joined our Squadrons. We couldn't sneak off and do it anyway during the course; we were being watched by radar all the time.

Half the flying exercises were individual handling sorties, practising circuits, aerobatics, stalls and instrument let-downs. The others included low and high-level battle formation, close formation and the always enjoyable tail chase. The instructor leading the sortie would perform a series of aerobatics and the students, in line astern, tried to follow his every move. The one at the back had the most difficult task, or if he felt idle the simplest. There was an inevitable lag in the response of the first follower to the leader, the second follower to the first and so on. Sometimes tail end Charlie would find that the one ahead of him would be starting a manoeuvre such as a roll when the leader was finishing his. The simple answer was to omit the manoeuvre entirely.

Although there was no air-to-air firing for us on our conversion course, there was a nearby gunnery range. Some Tempest (single piston engine) fighters, used for target towing, were based at Chivenor. The pilots were nearly all Polish and had an unusual way of flying a landing circuit. They would dive towards the banner drop area just left of the runway, release the banner and then pull up into a loop. At the top, inverted, they put the wheels down (up?), throttled right back, continued the loop while lowering landing flap and plopped onto the runway. Very spectacular! But something I was never tempted to emulate. I don't think it would have worked in the Sabre.

By the end of the seven week course, I had accumulated 13 hours flying in the Sabre and an assessment of "Above the Average" as a fighter pilot. Just how this was assessed beats me, with no two-seater Sabre in existence. The assessment could not have been on the basis of an instructor flying with me, or on gunnery, since we did none. I suspect the assessments were allocated on a lottery basis to keep the course statistics on line!

Chapter 7
66 Squadron

When Brian and I arrived back at Linton-on Ouse we found that a new C.O., Squadron Leader 'Sammy' Osbourne, had taken over the Squadron. We were put onto 'B' Flight, led by Flight Lieutenant 'Bush' Barry. As his nickname would imply, Bush was from Australia. I learned some time later that he had worked his passage to England on one of the last four masted clippers. I really envied him that experience; the closest I had been to true blue water sailing was on a school visit to 'Pamir' when she was docked in the Port of London a few years previously.

Photo 3 - Who gets there first can fly it.
L to R   Brian Thornton, Norman Glass, "Kiwi" Connell, Chas Spinks, Jonny Ditmas, Ray Williams, "Ben" Gunn, Pete Riley and Pete Foard
© Crown Copyright/MOD 1955

Even in 1954 there were constraints on how much flying a peacetime RAF pilot was allowed, although I did manage four sorties in one day on several occasions.

Bush had a system for rationing out the available hours. He kept a board in his office with his pilots' names alongside a chinagraphed bar chart and monthly total. At the end of each month our logbooks had to be submitted for verification. Bush was always baffled by the way three of his flight, Brian, 'Kiwi' Connel and I always seemed to have done more flying than anyone else. What he apparently never cottoned on to was that we three would sneak into his office when he was flying, carefully rub out the end of our bar charts and alter the totals downwards to match.

Car ownership in the 1950s was not widespread. On 66 Squadron only the C.O., the two Flight Commanders, two of the married junior pilots and three of the other 19 owned four wheeled vehicles. A few of the rest of us had motorcycles. For a reason I never quite fathomed, although our rival 92 Squadron's pub was only two miles away at Newton-on-Ouse, "our" pub was the Punchbowl in York's Stonegate, ten miles away. When a spontaneous move for an evening's 'thrash' erupted among the mostly unmarried junior members, some would pile into whichever of the three cars were currently more or less driveable and the rest onto the motorbikes. After a few beers at the Punchbowl in Stonegate we might move to the De Gray Rooms, or the Assembly Rooms to take in the dances held there. Day-time visits to York could involve a lunch beer and leer session at Betty's, where downstairs one of the rooms had a wall covered with signatures of the WW2 aircrew who used to frequent the place, or, if we had female company, tea and toasted teacakes at the Willow Tree café. I had a slightly unusual day out once, when I was invited to York races by two sisters. We made a fair amount that afternoon, not by winning on the horses, but by the two old pence a bottle that we got from the beer tent for the empties we collected!

We on B flight had a slight advantage on the social side. Two of the three unmarried car owners were on our flight. One of them was Don Christmas; we had more Christmas parties than the normal one per year. But when it came to a sortie off camp, there was a tendency for a stampede towards the other two cars; Don's had one wheel smaller than the other three, which made cornering quite interesting.

Promotion examinations for those aspiring to the rank of Flight Lieutenant were held in February 1955. Early in the New Year our Station Commander, Group Captain Denis Spotswood decreed that all those eligible to sit them **would** sit them. Being absolutely certain that I would be leaving the RAF in less than a year and would not have achieved sufficient time as a Flying Officer to obtain promotion before leaving, I submitted a "Sir, I have the honour to…" letter suggesting that I might be excused. No way. "You **will** sit the examinations" thundered the reply. Lectures were laid on, attendance was compulsory, but I wasn't very enthusiastic about taking notes or memorising any of the information. Some of the keener candidates organised evening revision sessions amongst themselves, but the squash court and the bar kept me away, until the day before the exams I had a rush of blood to the head and spent the afternoon with one of those groups. I was punished for my indolence when we came to the three-hour Air Operations paper. After one hour, I'd put down all I could think of on two sides of A4 paper. To pass the examination required full marks for at least five of the questions; I had answered only four. My Squadron Commander was invigilating, I asked him if I could leave, but he persuaded me to review my work. I looked round at all the others furiously filling page after page, managed to add a couple of sentences and then asked again for and obtained, permission to quit.

A month or two later the Station Commander gathered us all together and read out the results. " Flying Officer Smith ... Pass. Flying Officer Jones ... Pass. Flying Officer Black ... Fail. Flying Officer St. Pierre (Growl and glare) –... Pass." Possibly, the person who had marked my papers was so relieved not to have to wade through yet another ten pages of verbiage that he added marks for brevity and handwriting sufficient to bring me up to the pass standard. More probably, something went wrong in the system for allocating results to candidates. To ensure anonymity, our names did not appear on the papers, instead we each had a number. If that **was** what happened I can only say "Sorry and thanks!" to the poor soul who got **my** results.

Due to various misdemeanours, I was not one of Group Captain Spotswood's favourite officers! He went on to become Marshal of the Royal Air Force Sir Denis Spotswood GCB, Chief of the Air Staff. Maybe I should have hitched my wagon to his star. But thanks to his refusal to let me duck the promotion exams, I did reach the dizzy rank of Flight Lieutenant after I re-joined the RAF some years later.

Photo 4 – Author and ground-crew during exercise "Beware"

© Crown Copyright/MOD 1955

On the 19th March 1955 the Squadron went to Acklington, north of Morpeth, for a month's concentrated air-to-air firing practice. The Sabre had six .5 inch machine guns, three each side of the nose air intake. We fired at a banner about 6 by 30 feet, towed by another aircraft. Usually there were four fighters per tow. The ammunition was painted with a sticky, coloured substance, each pilot having a different colour allocated. Occasionally an unlucky shot would sever the towline and the banner would be lost, but usually it would be dropped back at base. Then we would count how many of the holes in it were marked by our own colour and watch the cine-camera film of our attacks. There seemed to be little correlation between what the camera showed as a good firing sortie and what the actual score achieved turned out to be. The guns were supposed to be "harmonised" so that all six streams of bullets converged at a distance of 200 yards, but maintaining the harmonisation was always a problem. My scores usually ranged from zero to around 30 percent, but on one occasion I had an unbelievable 96%. Probably the armourers had inadvertently loaded all of the other pilots' aircraft with 'my' coloured ammunition!

Social life at Acklington alternated between "Sweaty Betty's", a nearby village hall where dances were held, the movie palace at Morpeth and the RAF Mess. A visit to "Sweaty Betty's" started with a trek along the 1001 steps – the railway line from just north of the camp to the road bridge at Broomhill. Railway sleepers are placed at a most inconsiderate distance apart for a normal sized walker; by the time we had reached the road bridge and climbed up the embankment we were ready for a reviver or three in the pub conveniently situated just there. Often enough that would be as far as we got and we wouldn't reach the dance hall. I always thought that was why we called the pub "The Trap"; I was astonished many years later when I drove past to find that really was its name.

I had two unpleasant experiences during this detachment. On the 29th March a very heavy rainstorm hit the airfield just before I arrived back from an air firing sortie as number two to Jed Gray. We didn't have enough fuel left to go anywhere else; Ouston, the nearest airfield, was also closed due to bad weather. The visibility was down to about 500 yards when we arrived overhead Acklington. We made a few orbits waiting for the storm to clear, but it got worse. When we had no more than ten minutes fuel left, we had to try to land. Jed led the way round a circuit and I had difficulty keeping him in sight from no more than 300 yards behind. At 200 feet above the ground, on the final approach, I had made up my mind that I didn't have enough fuel for an overshoot and another circuit, so if I didn't see the runway in the next few seconds it would be a case of full throttle, climb until the engine stopped a minute or two later and eject. I saw Jed overshoot but as I started to open the throttle to follow him caught a glimpse of the threshold lights away to my right. A rapid jink got me lined up and I threw the Sabre at the runway, touching down much too fast, but there was a strong wind against me and I managed to come to a stop before running off the end. I didn't think Jed would have enough fuel left to get round another circuit, but he made it – just.

A few days later I had my first and only accident in a powered aircraft. With the runway wet and no wind, I had to use the full length of tarmac. I tried to touch down just after the threshold, but misjudged my height and caught the main wheels on the four-inch lip where the hard surface began. The result was visually quite spectacular; the aircraft leapt about 50 feet into the air before I could catch it with the elevator and ease back down onto the runway. From the loud clang, I knew I had bent something. After shutting down, I had a look and saw that the wing surface around the right undercarriage leg was somewhat wrinkled. Fortunately the damage was not too severe; the aircraft was repaired and flying again within a week. The C.O. was very kind, said he was sure I'd never do that again and reported the damage as due to accumulated heavy landings. I went to look at the grass undershoot area when flying had finished; there wasn't a trace of wheel marks in the soft soil before the runway. I could only have been 3 inches too low at most – but when it comes to undershoot accidents, a little bit too low is similar to a woman being a little bit pregnant.

Later on, back at Linton, air-to-air firing gave me another of those moments which are described in the old saying that flying consists of many hours of boredom interspersed by occasional seconds of sheer terror. Our local firing range was situated off the East Coast, between Whitby and Flamborough Head. Before a firing sortie, one pilot was sent out to 'clear the range'. This involved a low-level pass out to sea. When a surface vessel was sighted in or near the range area, its relative position, distance and direction of movement was reported to the range controller, who was following the search aircraft on radar. Unfortunately, to see small fishing boats meant flying below radio and radar coverage, so the procedure was to pull up sharply until in radio and radar contact.

I was doing the search one day in not the best of weather – although the visibility below cloud was very good, there was solid stratus from 2000 feet all the way up to 20,000. I had seen a couple of vessels, climbed into cloud, made my report and dived back below cloud again. Another fishing boat appeared. I pulled up again and made the mistake of looking back over my shoulder at the boat just before entering cloud. When I looked at the instruments, they made no sense to me. The artificial horizon was rolling one way, the turn and slip needle was on the stops, apparently showing a turn in the opposite direction and the compass was spinning. Dis-orientation had got me and I couldn't work out what to do. The only instrument that gave me hope was the altimeter, which was winding upwards, although more and more slowly. This was it, I thought. If I couldn't sort out what was happening and finished up diving out of cloud, there wouldn't be height enough to recover before hitting the sea. If that altimeter stopped showing a climb, I was getting out. My first take-off without a landing loomed.

The airspeed was rapidly decreasing, the altimeter only just showing a climb and joy! I burst through the cloud tops into a bright blue sky and above my head a flat white sheet of cloud gave me an instant visual horizon. One wing was down (or was it up?) and the nose was above the horizon. I was in an inverted, climbing, banked attitude. We always said, when practising instrument flying "one peek (sneaking a look outside) is worth a thousand scans (of the instruments)" and in this situation the truth of the adage was not in question. I lowered the nose to just above the horizon, simultaneously rolling the wings level (the right way up), took more than a few deep breaths and decided my fuel state gave me good reason to fly sedately back to Linton.

I had another near miss some months later. The Royal Observer Corps (ROC) established during World War Two was still in existence, although not in operation. In wartime, their particular concern was low flying enemy aircraft, which of course would not be picked up by our radar. The ROC observer would report by landline any sightings, giving the type, number and direction of flight of such to the nearest Fighter Control Centre. There a Fighter Controller would make a radio call, giving the observed position, time of observation and direction of flight of the targets to a designated fighter interception formation (usually just a pair). The defending fighters would also be too low to show on radar, so the Controller could not direct them onto the target. Instead the leader of the defending formation would plot the target's position, allowing for a minutes' delay between ROC observation and Controller's message, on his map. With his own position established from ground features he would then work out an interception course to the target.

We would occasionally practice this sort of interception exercise, known as 'Rat and Terrier'. With no active ROC the leader of one pair of Sabres acting as target (the rats) would simulate the ROC/Fighter Control system by transmitting the position he **was** in and the direction he **was** going one minute ago every two or three minutes. On this occasion I was the leader of the terrier pair. We were flying at 600 knots, about 300 feet apart in line abreast. I had plotted the rats heading east from the York area over the Yorkshire Wolds south of Malton and I was heading south across the Vale of Pickering on what seemed to be a perfect ninety-degree intercept. To see the rats, we were as low as we dared be; a camouflaged target aircraft shows up much better from below against the sky than from above against a backdrop of fields and woods. We swept up the scarp slope of the Wolds from below. Just as we reached the crest so did the rats, head-on to us up the dip slope and also staying as low as they dared to avoid being seen. There was no time at all to take avoiding action, we 'threaded the needle' with their leader passing between myself and my number two. He had made a ninety-degree turn after transmitting his last position, just as an enemy aircraft might have done after being observed by the ROC.

When the ground was not visible and without ground radar observations, only a very rough idea of one's position could be maintained, unless the aircraft had radio aids to navigation fitted and the appropriate ground radio beacons were within range. There were not many of either in the early 1950s. We had two navigation receivers in the Sabre. One was the Distance Measuring Equipment. This displayed the distance from a selected DME ground beacon and was very accurate. Unfortunately there were not many DME ground beacons either. We drew distance circles on our maps round such beacons as there were. When out of sight of the ground, or uncertain of position from ground features, obtaining a range from one beacon, then tuning another, gave us two possible positions (where the two circles intersected). Sometimes one of the two could be ruled out as impossible, but if not, distance from a third beacon resolved the ambiguity. Of course, the aircraft would have moved during the time it took to obtain the distances, so when flying in formation the leader would ask his wingmen to tune different beacons. When he needed a 'fix', he would use a pre-arranged code word on the radio and the wingmen would reply with their ranges from their assigned beacons.

Less accurate was the Radio Compass. This could be tuned to a variety of ground transmitters, from ground Non-Directional Beacons specifically provided for navigational purposes through to ordinary radio broadcast stations. A needle on the instrument panel dial then pointed towards the transmission site. It was not very accurate, thunderstorms or another station on roughly the same frequency could deflect the needle and if the station was a long way off, radio waves would have been deflected when they bounced off the ionised upper layers of the stratosphere. When a commentary was being broadcast from a cricket match at Headingley a favourite trick was to fly past, low and fast at full throttle, with the Radio Compass tuned to the BBC, just to hear one's own aircraft and the commentator muttering about the noise.

During the 1950s a big effort was being made to eradicate tuberculosis. Mobile units were travelling around the U.K. and X-raying the chest of as many of the population as they could entrap. One of these units came to Linton and whereas civilians could decline to be X-rayed, we were ordered to submit. There was a degree of panic amongst the "brass" when around fifty percent of the pilots' X-rays seemed to show they had the disease to varying extents. It was thought there had been something wrong with either the film or the procedure but, as a precaution, they were stopped from flying. A day or two later, repeat X-rays of those pilots showed no abnormalities, but some of a different group of aircrew again showed all the X-ray signs of TB. It didn't take too long to establish that this phenomenon was directly related to recent flying. The medics put their minds to the problem. Eventually they concluded that when breathing air, only the oxygen (1/5 of the air) would be absorbed immediately from the tiny air sacs (alveoli) in the pilots' lungs. The remaining nitrogen would keep the alveoli inflated while carbon dioxide from the blood was returned. But when 100% pure oxygen under high 'g' was being supplied, in some of the alveoli all the oxygen could be absorbed and they would completely collapse. It would take a considerable time for them to re-inflate.

Only when this had been established did we pilots compare notes and all confess to frequent chest pains, which lasted for several hours. None of us had dared report sick for fear of being permanently grounded.

One of the pilots on 'B' Flight, John Connel, was from Auckland, New Zealand. His tales of wilderness back country full of deer and wild pigs where one could spend weeks without seeing another human, stories of rivers and lakes teeming with monster trout where it was unusual to encounter another angler and descriptions of mountains, glaciers, lakes and beaches were enough to set me thinking seriously about leaving England for New Zealand. I think what crystallised my determination to go there was a Lake District experience in the summer of 1955. I thought it might be interesting to see the sunrise from the top of Scafell, England's highest peak, on Midsummer's Day. So I rode across on the Francis Barnett the afternoon before and parked it in a disused quarry. With an alarm clock, sleeping bag and groundsheet I set off up the mountain to find a sheltered spot near the summit before dark. Early next morning the alarm sounded. I crawled out of my sleeping bag to see a brilliantly clear starlit sky and full of hope for a spectacular sunrise, made my way the last couple of hundred yards to the summit. As I drew near, I heard voices. Then more voices, then a veritable cocktail party of chatter. In the dim light, I saw a crowd, a host - not of golden daffodils, but of people – no solitude for me! In fact, there wasn't even standing room up there. That settled it; England was no place for me. I wanted someplace where I could get away from people.

A week or two later British Overseas Airways Corporation nearly changed my ideas and the whole course of my life. Air Ministry had circulated a questionnaire many months earlier asking for names of those pilots who were interested in the prospect of airline flying when they left the RAF and I had indicated my interest. I had forgotten all about this when out of the blue, four months before I was due to leave the RAF, a signal arrived from Air Ministry saying that a dozen or so of us from Linton-on-Ouse were ordered to report to BOAC Headquarters at London Heathrow Airport at 09.00 hours on Wednesday 13th July.

The other 66 Squadron pilot on the list was John Rumbelow and he was one of the very few car owners amongst us. As this was an official movement, not only would we get an allowance (known as a rate one) to cover food and lodging, but if we went in his car, he could claim mileage allowance. Regardless of the reason for the trip, this seemed like a bit of money for old rope.

On arrival at Heathrow we found ourselves with another hundred or so RAF pilots being briefed about BOAC and its training procedure for prospective flight crew employees. We were then interviewed individually. My own interview was a most weird experience. There were three senior BOAC people and an RAF Group Captain in the room. I was asked a number of questions about general flying matters, to most of which I didn't know the answers. Then one of them asked me if I knew when BOAC was formed – I couldn't answer except to say that I thought it had started before the war as Imperial Airways. So did I know when the RAF had come into being? I tried to avoid the Groupie's eye when I confessed that I didn't know that either! The next question was "Why did I want to join BOAC?" My reply rather took them aback – I did intend to find employment as a civil pilot when I left the RAF but I had no particular wish to join BOAC, I'd just gone along because I'd been ordered to by Air Ministry, I intended to go to New Zealand when I left the RAF, but in a few years' time I might be interested! Not surprisingly I was dismissed with the comment that there didn't seem to be much point in continuing the interview.

I landed from a Sabre flight at lunchtime the following Tuesday to be told that "Rumbles" and myself were to report to Air Ministry at 09.00 next day, 20th July. So once again we took the road in John's car with another Linton pilot and I spent the night at home in Goodmayes. At the Air Ministry next morning we met up with nine more pilots, all from Fighter Command. We learned that BOAC wanted us and they, Air Ministry, had agreed that we could have early release to start training with the airline on Monday 25th! After some discussion, we all agreed that we needed a little more than two days to settle our affairs with the Service and trooped out to Heathrow, where we persuaded BOAC that Monday 2nd August would be more realistic.

I can't imagine how, remembering how different travel was in those days – the A1 was just a two way road – but somehow we got back to Linton-on–Ouse that evening and I managed to get back to Heathrow for a BOAC medical (by train) on Friday. Then I made what was either a mistake, or perhaps in view of the way my life went later, a lucky move. I went on a pub-crawl with some of my old school friends that evening. After a good few beers I came to the conclusion that BOAC had no right to shanghai me, that I didn't want their job and I **was** going to New Zealand. This resolution survived next morning's hangover and I sent a telegram declining their offer. Who knows what might have happened if I'd accepted? John Rumbelow did; many years later he retired from BOAC's successor, British Airways, as a senior Boeing 747 captain.

The rest of that autumn passed in the usual round of flying, fishing and gliding, beer sessions and parties and a few days walking in the Lake District. I managed to keep one of the Tutor gliders airborne for five hours in ridge lift at Sutton Bank, gaining the duration leg of the Silver "C" badge.

Two of my Sabre flights and one that didn't happen, were especially memorable. The first was on a night reinforcement exercise to Geilenkirchen in Germany with six aircraft, when I made one hour of the three-and-a-half hours total night flying of my Sabre career. The Geilenkirchen Squadrons made us most welcome; I was handed my first beer of the evening before I'd even got out of the aircraft. Their hospitality continued next morning, when we were taken across the border into Holland for shopping and lunch. A hotel in Heerlen where I ate Chicken Jambalaya would be first stop on my dream gastronomic tour of the world if I could go back in time as well as place!

The second flight was a Battle of Britain anniversary fly-past with 15 aircraft. We flew at low level below cloud over Catterick, Thornaby, Acklington and Turnhouse (Edinburgh) airfields, in a "vic" (V formation) of three "vics" of five aircraft. This was a pretty, but somewhat unwieldy arrangement. I was in the worst possible position, on the outside of one of the two rear "vics" which put me on the inside of turns towards me and outside of everyone else on turns away from me. On the inside it was very hard to slow down enough not to end up leading the whole formation and on the outside full throttle was barely enough to keep up with the pack. That was difficult, but when the whole formation turned round to go back to Linton, we discovered that the cloud had lowered and was covering the hills to the south. We had to climb through 12,000 feet of it; the proximity of 14 other aircraft when I could barely see the wingtip of the one next to me made concentration on the one I could see a major priority

The flight that didn't happen? It was the day I nearly broke my personal record of four sorties in a day. I strapped in for the fifth and went through the start-up procedure. Something went wrong; even with my almost soundproof crash helmet on, I heard a bang. I thought the "Houchin" (the ground power unit) had backfired, but then saw that the engine rpm gauge was showing zero. Within seconds a fire engine, an ambulance and the Station Commander's and Wing Commander Flying's staff cars were clustered round me. It transpired that just about everyone on the station had heard the bang and thought that someone (me) had inadvertently fired themselves out on their ejection seat! The problem had been that the engine had not turned over; when first fuel and then a spark had been added there had been an explosion within the combustion chambers.

My service was due to end on the 14th November 1955, but I had four weeks terminal leave to take before then. The Squadron Commander and Flight Commander were both kind to me; I continued flying right up to the last possible day, October 14th, the Friday before my leave started (the Squadron was stood down for the weekend). One of my last Sabre flights remains vividly in my memory. It was a cold, clear day, with no natural cloud, but the deep blue sky was criss-crossed with white condensation trails; it seemed the whole Royal Air Force fleet was in the air. The scene was reminiscent of wartime Battle of Britain photographs and movies. I was given an air test to do after a minor problem had been rectified, which took a few minutes to complete. After that I was free to enjoy myself. I prowled around and "attacked" anything I saw, mostly Meteors and a couple of Canberras. Tangling with our Meteor-equipped rival fighter squadron from Rufforth was really not very fair; the Sabre was a much faster and more manoeuvrable machine.

To my everlasting regret, I never had the opportunity to fly Spitfires, but this was compensated for by the Sabre, which I felt was the jet equivalent. In later years military flying became more technology focussed, with missile and radar systems. The Sabre was a point-it-and-squeeze-the-trigger fighter. It had no vices, pulling too hard in a turn simply led to a juddering stall, any tendency to spin was easily stopped by relaxing the back pressure on the control column. With the throttle closed, the aircraft could be held in a full stall with the nose high and steered around with rudder. One particularly enjoyable manoeuvre was started from a run at maximum airspeed to the runway threshold. A pull up to a vertical climb put the aircraft over the centre of the airfield; with full power still applied an input of aileron started it rolling. Seven or eight complete rolls later and 20,000 feet or so higher the aircraft would run out of airspeed. Stop the roll, chop the power, a stall turn and the aircraft would be pointing straight down. Airbrakes out, aileron to start rolling again, seven or eight complete turns on the way down and then it was time to pull out of the dive. Completing the show with a practice forced landing without touching the throttle again would be a bonus.

Photo 5 - F86E Sabre during exercise "Beware", mission accomplished.
Author centre.　　　　　　　　　　　　　　© Crown Copyright/MOD 1955

At that time my next few years' future had been clear in my mind. I would leave the RAF, take the examinations for my Commercial Pilot Licence, then go out to New Zealand and find a flying job there for a couple of years. After that, I'd see what came along. However, I had still not quite completed the 50 hours gliding at Sutton Bank which was needed for me to be able to claim the subsidy from the RAFGSA, so during my last week of active service I arranged to stay on in the Mess at Linton for some of my accrued leave in hope of doing so. This decision was, unexpectedly, to lead me to a lot of anguish.

Chapter 8
New Zealand or not?

On Saturday 29th October I went to the wedding in Harrogate of one of the squadron pilots. There I got into conversation with two girls, Gloria and Olga, who seemed to be old friends. Until then, I'd never been sufficiently interested in any female to consider changing my plans, but Gloria was different. I had arranged my final departure from Linton with a lift to London on the 2nd November, but on the day after the wedding I was conned by Brian Thornton and Don Christmas with a story that Gloria and Olga had said they would like to come to the informal dance being held in the Mess on Friday the 4th and were hoping someone would invite them. So I stayed on at Linton a bit longer. I knew Olga's surname and place of work, but of Gloria only that she worked at the Wetherby Employment Exchange. I telephoned Olga, invited her and asked her to ask Gloria to come as well. "Oh, the first time I met her was Saturday, I don't know how I could contact her, can I bring one of my friends instead?" was the reply. I could hardly say "No" or "Oh sorry, it was Gloria I wanted to come, cancel the invitation!"

With two guests already, I thought I might as well be hung for a sheep as for a lamb. So I gave telephoning the Employment Exchange a try and asked to speak to "a girl called Gloria who I think works there" It was Gloria herself on the other end of the line. I learnt that she hadn't said anything about wanting to go to the dance, this was the first she'd heard about it, but she would like to attend. I now had three guests.

I spent the next couple of days working hard on Brian and Don and eventually managed to persuade them that since they had got me into this tangle, they should look after Olga and her friend and leave me free to escort Gloria. She telephoned me on the Thursday evening before the dance to ask about transport; when I said I'd go to her home on the motorbike but I'd get taxis to Linton and back, she said "Don't bother with taxis, I'll go on the bike." This definitely sounded like my sort of girl! Even when we left the dance at 2.30 a.m. and found thick fog outside, she still wouldn't let me call a taxi. It took an hour and fifteen minutes to drive the eleven miles to Harrogate.

At the dance, Brian escorted Olga. Some months later I heard through the grapevine that they were going steady. Many years later I bumped into Don in Malaya and discovered that he, not Brian, had married her.

I went home by train on the evening after the dance, having arranged with my father to go back to Linton in his van on the 10th. Ostensibly this was to collect my kit and the motorbike, but seeing Gloria again was the real motive. That was the start of three month's dithering. One day I would be chasing a possible passage to New Zealand, the next looking for a flying job in England so I could stay near Gloria. Between November and March I went back to Yorkshire another three times by motorbike or train. Nowadays, when I am usually ready for bed by 9.00 in the evening, I find it hard to believe how much stamina I had as a young man. My diary shows for one of these trips:

Saturday 17 December 1955

06.00	departed home (Goodmayes) on motor bike.
13.00	arrived Linton (230 miles, no motorways then and it was only a 200cc two-stroke)
13.00-17.15	Lunch, arranging lift, bathe and change
17.15-19.50	Motorcycle lift to Boroughbridge, bus to Harrogate, walk from bus station to Gloria's home at Bilton Grove Avenue.
19.50-21.55	Party at Gloria's.
21.55-23.10	Bus to Harrogate centre, taxi to Linton.
23.10-04.00	Squadron party in crew room at hangar.
04.00-04.40	Taxi to York, drop off two girls (other pilots' guests) and on to Ned Kelly's (another 66 Squadron pilot), where I had arranged that Gloria could stay the night
05.10	Walk from Ned's to railway station to catch 06.15 bus to Linton
06.00	Arrive railway station – there is no 06.15 bus – because it's Sunday!
06.05 – 08.35	Walk the ten miles to Linton (not enough cash on me for a taxi!)
08.35 – 12.30	Breakfast, one hour in bed, talk to friends, motorbike to Ned's.
12.30 – ??	Brunch at Ned's, then visit York Minster with Gloria, walk around city, tea and movies, see her onto bus home, motor bike back to Linton, then a session in the Mess bar with Brian Thornton and Kiwi Connel until well after midnight.

That's about 2 hours sleep in 36 hours

And then next morning I left Linton at 09.30 and rode the motorbike 230 miles back to Goodmayes!

Between these Yorkshire visits, I fitted in studying for, sitting and passing the ground examinations for the Commercial Pilot Licence; taking and passing the flying test, in a Chipmunk at Hamble, near Southampton; getting the licence issued; a visit to Cambridge for a job interview; a week's gliding at Lasham; a visit to Headley Court, the RAF hospital near Alton where two of the 66 Squadron pilots were being repaired after accidents (non-flying); numerous pub-crawls with old school friends; several classical music evenings at the Festival Hall; the musical "South Pacific"; the movie "Mr. Roberts" and chasing up various possibilities of a passage to New Zealand.

The job interview was on the 18th February 1956, with Marshalls, an aviation company based at Cambridge. They had contracts to overhaul and test-fly a variety of RAF aircraft, ran a flying club and did some charter work using

Dragon Rapides. The job involved participation in all these activities, with the prospect of taking over from their Chief Pilot when he retired; all their existing pilots were close to retirement. The variety of flying appealed, although I was not over-enthused by the prospect of test-flying the Brigand, one of the RAF machines. I had heard of the apocryphal report by the prototype's test pilot. "Access to the cockpit of this aircraft is difficult. It should be made impossible."

Marshalls did not offer me employment on the spot, but said they would write to let me know. Before their letter arrived a travel agent called me to say a cancelled passage on the 'Orontes' to Australia on the 20th March would almost certainly be available, he would let me know for sure on the 5th March. Marshalls' letter arrived on the 3rd offering me employment. I more or less made up my mind that if the Orontes travel fell through I'd take the job. But when I went to the travel agents on the 5th March to see if the cancellation was definite, it was, so I paid the £125 fare, arranged to collect the ticket two days later and wrote to Marshalls declining their offer.

When I think back, I am quite amazed at the self-confidence I evidently had. I knew no one in New Zealand; all I had was John Connel's parents' address near Auckland. I had to hope that I could get a passage from Sydney onwards to New Zealand soon after arriving in Australia and that after a month's shipboard and Sydney spending I'd still have enough cash to pay for it. I certainly wouldn't have the funds for a return ticket. But I just had to go.

The next two weeks passed in a round of farewells to relatives and old school friends, including a final trip by motor bike to Linton-on-Ouse on the 9th March. I said my goodbyes to the Yorkshire Gliding Club and the Squadron and on the Sunday had a last day out with Gloria. We went to Fountain's Abbey by motorbike; it was a gloriously sunny day but bitterly cold; the snowdrops, large double ones, were in full bloom around the old grey stone buildings. Gloria and imminent springtime combined almost made me change my mind and stay, the following few days after I said goodbye to her were not the happiest of my life.

Chapter 9

Slow boat to Sydney

The 20th of March 1956 started as a warm sunny early spring day, so pleasant that it made leaving England seem even more of an utterly stupid thing to do. My parents took me to Tilbury, where the SS "Orontes" lay alongside the wharf. We arrived at midday and I took my rucksack and one suitcase to the 'not wanted on the voyage' baggage loaders. Then we went on board to leave my three 'wanted on the voyage' suitcases in my cabin on 'G' deck, as far down in the bowels of the liner as it was possible to get. Finding the cabin was difficult enough; the ship was a labyrinth of passageways and stairways. Finding the way back to the gangway took even longer.

The ship's tannoy "all ashore that's going ashore" call came. We said our goodbyes and mother and father went to stand on the wharf, looking up to where I was leaning over the boat deck rail. Paper streamers were thrown from wharf to ship and from ship to wharf. Today's easy, cheap and rapid travel was unimaginable in those

Photo 6 - S.S. Orontes

days. Many of the passengers were emigrants travelling on £5 assisted passages; they probably expected never to see their relatives again. Those streamers were possibly the last contact they would ever have and the emotion was tangible.

At 3.30 p.m. the ship's stern started to move away from the wharf, pulled by a tugboat and the streamers broke one by one. It took an hour or so for the tugs to manoeuvre the liner through the lock gates at the exit from the dock and then we were under way down the Thames. By now the day had turned overcast and cold in keeping with the "What **have** I done?" thoughts that haunted me. I wanted to watch the lights of the seaboard towns as we rounded the North Foreland and steamed off down the Channel, but the wind chill factor caused by the ship's motion kept me inside most of the evening. I went to my bunk bed in a mood of deep depression.

Next morning the mood had changed and I started to enjoy the new experience. Perhaps one day, when oil runs out, the cost of alternative aircraft fuels may become prohibitive and passenger liners, coal (or even wind) powered will make a come-back. There was a special magic about a long sea voyage. There was nothing one could do to make the ship go any faster. The only way to approach the 36-day passage to Australia was to lie back, forget the outside world and enjoy the luxury of having all one's material needs taken care of. There was all the time in the world to "stop and stare". I spent many hours leaning on the rail at the stern of the ship, idly watching the wake, sea birds or other ships and day-dreaming about any of the many possible futures in life. Sometimes wandering albatrosses followed the liner, riding the invisible air currents created by the wind and the ship's motion. Now and again a school of dolphins would appear and take up station in the bow wave. I remember a glass-calm day in the Red Sea, when shoal after shoal of flying fish burst from the water, maintaining the impetus of their flight by sculling with the extended lower lobe of their tail fins and leaving a small zigzag wake. I watched until the show was completely over, with no feeling that I should be busy 'doing something'.

The first port of call had been Gibraltar, but we arrived at night and were anchored offshore for only an hour or so. At Naples we had just the morning to explore the city, then at Navarino Bay in Greece again we had no more than a couple of hours anchored off-shore while a number of Greek emigrants were brought out to the ship. From then on we had the chance to go ashore for eight hours or more at Port Said, Aden, Colombo, Fremantle and Port Adelaide, but I was too broke to take any of the available tours. At Melbourne, where the ship stayed for three days, I did manage to get out into the Dandenong hills by train and bus. All I remember seeing of Australian wild life was a fox!

The Orontes was a one-class, effectively economy-class ship, but the food on board was first class. The duty-free bar was always an attraction. There was plenty of entertainment laid on; special dinners for such occasions as crossing the equator, two fancy dress parties, dance evenings, table horse racing, movies on deck (once we reached warmer climes), a cribbage competition and so on. The game of deck quoits was popular among the more energetic passengers. There was a completely new

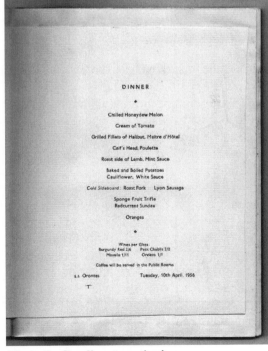

Photo 7 - Goodbye to rationing

dimension to table tennis on board. Playing uphill when the ship rolled towards you was easy whether defending or attacking, but when the table tilted downhill it became very difficult. Swimming in the small pool on the upper deck was also an interesting experience when the sea was rough. Dancing could be tricky; on one occasion as we sailed along the south coast of Australia the boat took a very severe roll; chairs, tables, the pianist and the dancers slid gracefully across the floor and finished up in a heap. Great fun.

The ship's library was well stocked; towards the end of the voyage I found "Doctor at Sea" by Richard Gordon on the shelves and was highly amused at how closely events on our voyage corresponded with those in the novel. Even the shipboard romances. One couple on our voyage met on board, got engaged at Colombo, married in Melbourne and honeymooned in Sydney. I might have gone the same way; I was introduced to a charming girl as we cruised across the Mediterranean. She was on her way to Australia to marry a doctor she had met in England and had become engaged to by letter, but she hadn't seen him for over twelve months. We spent a lot of time together for the rest of the voyage but as a penniless vagrant I went no further with her than spending hours leaning on the rail looking for whales, sharks, porpoises and icebergs, talking, dancing, playing deck quoits and going for long walks at some of the ports of call. It didn't help my honourable intentions when the ship's entertainment systems incessantly played a current hit parade number…

"I'd like to get you,
On a slow boat to China,
All to myself, alone"

I did feel that the voyage could have gone on forever.

Orontes docked in Sydney before breakfast on the 26th April. It was 12.30 before I had gathered all my belongings and cleared customs. Two of the passengers had told me they were sailing for Auckland at 15.30 on the "Wanganella", so I telephoned the shipping agents to see if there was a last minute passage available. They said, "Call again later". I took a taxi to the railway station where I could rid myself of the encumbrance of rucksack and four suitcases at the left luggage office and somehow found time to visit two aircraft operating companies before calling the Wanganella agents again. There **might** be a first class cabin they said. I abandoned that idea (too expensive even if 'might' became 'there is'), telephoned a hotel to book a room and went to Thomas Cook's to see what the alternatives were. There were two (apart from finding work in Australia). I could fly across the Tasman Sea any day, or wait ten days and travel on the TSS "Monowai" to Wellington. Air travel was extremely expensive in those days. I calculated that the nightly hotel rate of six shillings and six (old) pence – $32^1/_2$ p in new money - plus ten day's living plus the liner fare would work out cheaper. I should arrive in New Zealand with around £25 left, whereas flying would leave me about half that. The "Monowai" it had to be.

The hotel, in Kings Cross, wasn't exactly the Ritz. I shared a bed with a car worker, not simultaneously though. He worked on the night shift in a car factory.

There was plenty to do in Sydney even on limited money. Travel by tram or ferry was cheap and there were lots of interesting walks around the harbour and along the shore south of the Heads. I went to the movies a couple of times, to the earliest – and cheapest – of the sessions at 11 a.m. Prices rose progressively at 2, 5 and 8 p.m. Visits to art galleries, museums, the botanical gardens and some of the mid-day classical music broadcasts in Hyde Park filled more hours. I also lost some of the weight I'd amassed on the Orontes. There was a café near the harbour bridge where a breakfast of steak, egg, tomato, chips, bread and butter and a large pot of tea varied in price from two and six (12 ½ p) to three and six (17 ½ p) depending on the day of the week. Most days I made that my main meal and ate bananas or tinned sardines or peanut butter rolls for lunch and dinner. At the end of ten days I was about £8 poorer and rather more than ten pounds lighter than at the start. My RAF pay had been £2.50 a day with all found - clearly the cost of living in Australia was rather less than that in England.

I just happened to be walking across the Harbour Bridge on the 3rd May when the Orontes passed underneath on her way back to England. I stood and watched as she disappeared round a promontory further down the harbour, feeling that now I really had burnt my boats. At 3.30 on the 5th I was sailing beneath the bridge myself on board the Monowai.

Chapter 10
New Zealand and the flying boat

I have no pleasant memories of the five-day voyage from Sydney to Wellington. The Monowai was a two-class ship, I was in the cheap end of the boat and in fact couldn't have been nearer the end, in the last cabin on the lowest deck at the stern. Monowai was much smaller than Orontes and although I had survived the England to Australia voyage without seasickness, I succumbed minutes after we left the harbour and entered the Tasman Sea. It made little difference to me that we Cabin Class passengers were confined to the after end of the ship, I never felt well enough to want to go far from the washroom or my bunk. After arrival in New Zealand, I discovered from the Wellington local paper that this had been the roughest 'Monowai' passage on record.

We berthed at Wellington on Wednesday 9th May 1956. I was lucky; my kit was almost the first off the boat. I left it with the Railway staff at the wharf to be taken to the station, intending to take the overnight train to Auckland, near where, I had been told, many of the country's top dressing operations were based. After a meal in town I managed to fit in visits to the Royal New Zealand Air Force recruiting office, the New Zealand National Airways Corporation office, a top dressing operator at the airfield and the Civil Aviation Administration's office. There I filled in some forms to get my U.K. licence validated and was told I could complete the validation in Auckland. Everyone I spoke to was very friendly and helpful, even though the RNZAF, NZNAC and the top dresser were not recruiting at that moment.

The train was scheduled to leave at 7.15 p.m., but was delayed for half an hour by problems with the overhead wires for the first, electric, stage. Not much further on the wires ended and the rest of the journey was steam hauled. It was a shame that I could not travel during the day, I missed seeing one of the railway world's more spectacular engineering feats – the Rairimu spiral. Here the narrow gauge railway climbs a major escarpment. The line follows one side of a narrow spur, then turns into a tunnel, emerges on the other side of the spur, but keeps turning into another tunnel, to come out again directly above the first part of the spiral. Thus, if travelling in one of the rear carriages, one can see the locomotive higher up going in the same direction as oneself. Unfortunately, by the time the sun rose, we had passed all the best scenery. I also missed, but by choice, the rugby scrum for tea and sandwiches at each station – no catering was available on the train.

We arrived in Auckland at 9.30 a.m. on Thursday 10th and somewhat bleary-eyed, I left the train. All my kit went into the left luggage store, where I discovered it could be left free of charge for a month – very useful. I bought a newspaper and discovered right away that the employment situation in New Zealand was rather different to that in the U.K. The newspaper was about the size of the "Daily Telegraph" – and there were about eight pages of small, three line advertisements of situations vacant. Since I had no more than £10 sterling left and no return ticket, I found this somewhat heartening. There was also a nearly full page of accommodation vacant ads, so very soon I had sorted out somewhere to stay.

There wasn't much time to waste – that £10 wouldn't last very long, even at £2 per week for bed and breakfast! So I had a wash and a shave and set out to look for gainful employment. First stop was the Civil Aviation Office at Mechanic's Bay on the shore of Waitemata Harbour. There I was given a briefing on New Zealand Air Traffic Control Regulations, in preparation for validation of my U.K Commercial Pilot's Licence. I walked back to town, by then it was too late to think about going out to the airport to find the top dressing operators. Seeing the Tasman Empire Air Lines passenger office, I went in to make a not too serious enquiry about their recruitment situation. They directed me to their Personnel Department – back at Mechanic's Bay of course. Luckily they had a vehicle going out there so I got a lift.

From then on events followed with somewhat breath-taking rapidity. I went to the receptionist, said I had a pilot's licence and was looking for a job. She made an internal phone call, said "Go up the stairs, turn right, second office on the left and you'll find Captain Brownjohn, the Operations Manager." The door was open, he indicated that I should enter and sit opposite him at the desk and before even saying "Good morning" (or, it was more likely, "How're yer going mate?") he produced a tin of rolling tobacco and a packet of papers and passed them across the desk to me. This was something of a facer, I thought perhaps the ability to "roll-your-own" might be part of the selection requirements. I had tried DIY cigarettes occasionally back at Linton-on-Ouse, but I was a bit out of practice. I managed to fumble a ragged cigarette together and answered some questions about my past history. These appeared to satisfy and I listened with a sense of disbelief to a description of a possible offer of employment, starting immediately.

TEAL were looking for a co-pilot for their sole remaining Short Solent Mark IV flying boat ZK-AMO, based at Suva, the capital of Fiji. The boat operated a scheduled service on what was known as "The Coral Route". This went from Suva through Satapuala at the western end of Upolu, the second largest island in Western Samoa, then to Aitutaki atoll in the Cook Islands and on to Papeete, the capital of Tahiti. In the busy season this was a weekly trip, with an outward night stop in Samoa, two nights in Tahiti, another Samoa night stop on the way back and then three nights in Fiji. In the low season the flight operated fortnightly, with the Tahiti stopover extended to three nights. There was also a once monthly service to Nuku'alofa, the capital of Tonga and every three months a flight to Auckland for overhaul. If I was interested, would I come back tomorrow (Friday) at 11.30 for further interview with himself and one of their Senior Training Captains? A series of images flashed through my mind. That long, long ago geography lesson in primary school, the musical

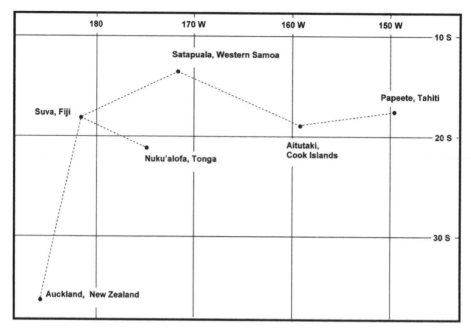

Figure 1 - The Coral Route

"South Pacific", the film "Mr. Roberts" I had seen in London with John Barker and saw again on Orontes. As today's vernacular has it, is the Pope a Catholic? I certainly was interested!

Next morning at 11.30 I went back to the Mechanic's Bay office. After a very short discussion I was asked to return at 14.30 for a formal letter setting out the offer of employment. When I went back, I had no hesitation in signing my acceptance. Subject to passing a medical on Monday morning, I would be paid £NZ 650 per annum while training and after three months, when qualified as co-pilot, would go on line at a salary of £NZ 1050. The salary didn't really enter my head – if I'd had any money left I'd have paid **them** for the privilege of being a flying boat pilot in the South Pacific!

On Monday I passed the medical and was ready for ground school, which I thought would be organised on lines similar to my RAF experiences. No such thing. I was shown into a large room, with a picture window looking out over the harbour towards Rangitoto Island, given a pile of technical manuals on the Solent and its Bristol Hercules engines, copies of the New Zealand Air Navigation Regulations, the TEAL Operations Manual, a book on Air Navigation and various other bits of reading and told to get on with it. If I had any technical questions to which the books didn't give the answers, I should go into the hangar and ask the engineers. There seemed to be no urgency despite the rapidity of my recruitment – it would be the end of June before I could take the various examinations. This was fortunate. Wandering around to find people who could answer my queries frequently became necessary, but usually involved a fair amount of general chat before getting to the point. Activity outside in the harbour was a constant distraction, with cargo boats, liners, ferries, motor boats and yachts going every which way and small Widgeon amphibian aircraft occasionally alighting or taking off. Then there were a few sessions in the link trainer and some tutorials from the experts on instruments, engines, navigation and so on.

As a break from study, I was given a jump seat ride on one of the Auckland – Sydney – Christchurch – Sydney – Auckland DC6 flights. I went to Mechanic's Bay to meet the crew and reported to the Captain, Phil Lecouteur. As I was a spare hand, he asked me to fetch the crew car from the Company garage while he dealt with the weather forecast, crew briefing and other paper work. My protest that, although I had flown supersonic fighters, I had never driven a car was dismissed with "Now's the time to learn then – go and fetch it anyway." To my continuing dismay, he then made me drive the 20 miles or so out to the airport, which in those days was at Whenuapui, north of the city. Fortunately the roads in 1956 were much less busy than they are today. The main problem I had was when stopped at traffic lights on an uphill slope. On the motor bike, a foot on the road had been enough to hold position while de-clutching, selecting first gear, re-engaging the clutch and opening the throttle to pull away when the lights changed. The concept of hand brake replacing leg on road didn't occur to me, so there was a backward lurch before each getaway. But what caused the rest of the crew finally to rebel and get me thrown out of the driver's seat was an excursion onto the pavement while trying simultaneously to change gear and negotiate a sharp corner.

Back in Auckland, with an income of £12 a week, room rent of £2 a week and around £2 a week for food, I soon saved up the £10 needed for a second hand bicycle. At weekends, I started to explore the city and the surrounding countryside as far out as Titirangi to the north-west and Ardmore airfield to the south. There was a gliding club at Ardmore, but every time I went they seemed to be having one problem or another and I never saw any flying. By the end of June I had saved enough to move up to a motorbike. I bought a second-hand 200cc Triumph Tiger Cub for £70. Riding this was a little tricky on the mostly unsealed gravel roads. There was no way I would emulate the Kiwi motorcyclists, most of whom rode around in bare feet; the mere thought made me cringe!

On the 6th of June the Solent 4 ZK-AMO arrived from Suva for maintenance. During the next two weeks I had plenty of time to talk to the crew about the Coral Route operation. They told me that our flying boat afforded the only airline connection from the outside world to Tonga, Samoa, the Cook Islands and Tahiti. The first flight on the route had been in December 1951, using a Solent Mk. 3. There was a World War Two airstrip near Satapuala in Western Samoa, another at Rarotonga in the Cook Islands and one at Bora Bora 200-odd miles to the north west of Tahiti, but there were no regular air services to them. Tahiti had no land airstrip at all.

Photo 8 - I thought it was supposed to be a flying boat!
Solent ZK-AMO hauled up the slipway for maintenance

Courtesy of Mark Mabey

The only other aircraft that ever flew to Tahiti from outside of the Society Islands were Royal New Zealand Air Force Sunderlands from Fiji and a Sandringham flying boat operated by Sir P.G.Taylor from Australia; these went there no more than once or twice a year. The two Catalina flying boats based at Tahiti operated purely local services apart from very occasional visits to Auckland for maintenance. Tahiti was also hard to reach by other means. Two or three cruise liners passed through each year and Messageries Maritimes ran infrequent liner services with the Tahitien and the Caledonien. A few tramp steamers delivered cargo and took a small number of visitors. The only other way to get there was as crew on an ocean-going yacht; many a skipper found himself re-enacting the Bounty Mutiny when one or more of his crew deserted and vanished into the districts with a Tahitienne vahine.

The two weeks also gave me the opportunity to look around the aircraft. I did not travel on a civilian airline as a passenger until the 1970s, so I don't know how different the passenger arrangements on our Solent were from those on the landplanes of the 1950s. I suspect that we were a long way behind them, almost back in the wicker chair, pilot in an open cockpit, pre-war Imperial Airways style. None of the knees against the seat in front, elbows in, praying mantis posture while eating the plastic wrapped, pre-prepared microwaved meal that one suffers today. There was no first, business or economy class distinction, the aircraft was spaciously laid out as a one-class entity. All but the four seats in the lower deck aft cabin were arranged facing across large tables as in today's Intercity trains, with plenty of leg room. There was a real galley, where meals were cooked to order using fresh ingredients. Meat, fish and similar perishables were kept in a dry ice refrigerator. Meals were served directly to the tables, set with tablecloths, quality china, glass, silver-plated cutlery and linen napkins.

Photo 9 - Those were the days....

Courtesy Colin Hunter

The passenger entrance, at the rear on the port side, opened onto a set of wide steps down to a lounge style cabin with four seats arranged as a settee along the starboard side of the aircraft. Aft, a door opened into the rear luggage/freight hold. Forward, a central waist-high door through a watertight bulkhead led to the first of five compartments, each separated by similar bulkheads. The first and second were 6-passenger compartments, with the spiral staircase to the upper deck on the starboard side of the second. Forward again, to left and right were the washrooms and a ladder leading upwards onto the flight deck. Then came two more 6-passenger compartments. Another door through a full bulkhead gave entry to the front hold, which also had a door to the outside on the left used as the crew entrance. Forward again, the mooring compartment was reached through another full bulkhead. A boat hook, the anchor and some cable were stowed here and an upward opening hatch gave access to the mooring bollard on the nose.

The flight deck above was rather larger than one would find today – but there were five flight crew. Behind the two pilots, on the left-hand side, the radio operator and the navigator sat facing the side wall, each with a large table. On the right side there were two crew rest seats and centrally placed, the

Photo 10 - Author re-visits the Solent flight deck in 2006

astrodome – a Perspex bubble - from which the navigator took sextant readings. The view of the night sky from here was spectacular. Little of the dimmed flight deck lighting leaked past one's body and in the middle of the South Pacific there was no external light pollution.

Next rearwards came the Flight Engineer's station. Situated between the four engines and close to the main spar, this was the noisiest place in the whole very noisy aircraft. The Bristol Hercules radial sleeve valve piston engines had two banks of seven cylinders each, which with two per cylinder meant a total of 112 spark plugs. Probably the most up-to-date piece of equipment on the aircraft, a cathode ray tube ignition analyser, now and again enabled the Flight Engineer to announce "We'll need to change the number two plug on number eight cylinder of number three engine when we get to…"

Aft of the Flight Engineer's station was the galley and after that the upper deck cabin. This, being well above the waterline, did not need watertight bulkheads. Here the 16 passenger seats were arranged in forward facing rows. At the front of this cabin a ladder gave access to an emergency escape hatch in the ceiling

There was of course no in-flight entertainment but the crew told me that around school holiday periods, children travelling from or back to their homes could sometimes fill the lounge cabin at the rear of the lower deck and entertain the few other passengers able to hear over the engine noise with their ukulele and guitar music.

Although the Solent had 44 passenger seats, on our operation three of these were needed for the extra crew we had to carry. Being the only aircraft operating regularly in the area between Fiji and Tahiti, we had no shore-based engineering facilities, so we carried two ground engineers on every flight. Then there was the Flight Clerk, who looked after the paper work, took bookings, sold tickets and carried out other administrative duties. With five flight crew and three cabin crew (two stewards and a stewardess or one steward and two stewardesses) that gave a ratio of one crew member for each four passengers!

It is interesting to compare the Solent with a more recent four-engined aircraft of about the same weight, such as the British Aerospace 146-100, the first version of the 146 to go into service.

	Solent Mk.4	BAe 146-100
Wing Span	113 feet	86 feet
Maximum All Up Weight	79,000 lbs	84,000 lbs
Cruising Speed	200 mph	450 mph
Range	2000 miles	2000 miles
Flight Deck crew	5	2
Cabin crew	3	3
Passenger seats	44	57[1]
Maximum fuel capacity	22,860 lbs	20,640lbs
Cruise fuel consumption	300 gallons/hr	580 gallons/hr
	2250 lbs/hr	4650 lbs/hr[2]
Passenger air miles per lb. of fuel	3.91	5.52
Passenger miles per gallon	29	44

As with most things in modern life, technology brought better function (in this case speed) at a lower cost. In addition to better fuel economy, there were improvements in radio communications, navigation equipment and aircraft systems, which removed the need for Radio Operators, Flight Navigators and Flight Engineers. Of course, this latter saving might well be counterbalanced by higher costs of maintenance of the more sophisticated systems.

---

[1] The Solent could carry a full load of 44 passengers plus their baggage with full fuel. For any aircraft the maximum allowable take-off weight is fixed, so the weight of passengers plus baggage plus cargo plus fuel is fixed. Modern aircraft are generally more flexible than the Solent. They have fuel capacity such that with the tanks full, to stay within the weight limit the number of passengers has to be limited to less than the number of seats that can be fitted. Fewer passengers can be carried further or more can be carried a shorter distance. Full fuel in the BAe 146-100 gave approximately 2000 miles range, but the passenger plus baggage number had to be reduced to around 57. Later versions of the 146 would be more efficient still.

[2] Jet fuel is heavier than piston engine fuel, hence the different conversion factors from gallons to lbs.

When the maintenance was completed on 19th June the aircraft returned to Suva. I was given another break from study and went on the flight as supernumerary crew. We hit some fairly rough weather half way through the seven-hour flight and I had my first encounter with the inter-tropical convergence zone, which was to become only too familiar in later years in Africa. At one stage all four engines were throttled right back, but we were still climbing at more than a thousand feet per minute. The weather had cleared up to small puffy trade wind cumulus in a clear blue sky for our arrival at Laucala Bay, the flying boat base just south of Suva on the main island, Viti Levu. As we descended I had my first view of a tropical coral reef and lagoon from the air, one of the most beautiful sights on the planet.

I didn't have time to explore Suva on that first visit, with a 5.30 a.m. wake-up time for a pre-dawn taxi ride to the small airport at Nausori in prospect. The cross-island air service to Nadi[3] was operated by another De Havilland aircraft, the low-wing monoplane three-engined Drover. The flight at low level across the island's rugged interior was a geography lesson in itself, with the rain shadow effect of the mountains very apparent. The southeast half, where the prevailing trade winds dropped their moisture, was verdant rain forest. In the northwest dry sugar cane plantations covered the low-lying plain.

From Nadi I sat on the jump seat of a TEAL DC-6 back to Auckland.

---

[3] Languages in the South Pacific have few consonant sounds. When the missionaries put the Fijian language into writing, they were able to use some of the 'spare' consonant letters of the alphabet to represent diphthongs. Since a hard 'c' as in 'cat' sounded the same as the 'k' in kite and a soft 'c' as in 'cease' sounded the same as the 's' in 'sea' the letter 'c' was going spare, so they used it to represent the diphthong 'th'. There was no hard 'd' so they used 'd' to represent the diphthong 'nd'. Thus 'Nadi' is pronounced 'Nandi' and 'Laucala' is 'Lauthala'.

Chapter 11
Sailing experience useful

My flying boat air training began in Auckland on 23rd July, in the standby Mark 3 Solent, ZK-AMQ. I went as supernumerary crew on an air test flight and admired the view as we flew to the Coromandel Peninsula and back. On the return I was let into the co-pilot's seat and flew the circuit and landing. During this and subsequent training flights, I began to learn about the peculiarities of flying boat handling.

The first thing to understand was that there were no brakes! Reverse pitch propellers, which, by twisting the blades enabled forward or reverse thrust, were in existence in the 1950s, but for some reason were not fitted to the Solent. With them life would have been a lot easier. Once the Solent's engines were running, the aircraft inexorably moved forward. Even with the engines at idle the Radio Officer (who normally attended to slipping and mooring up to the buoy) would not have the strength to release the mooring loop from the bollard in the bow against the pull of all four propellers. So the slipping procedure was for the two outer engines to be started, the mooring cast off and then the inners to be started while on the move. There was no water rudder; steering was achieved by a mixture of the normal rudder and differential throttle on the engines.

Photo 11 - It was indeed a flying boat.
ZK-AMO Aranui on her moorings at Mechanic's Bay, Auckland
Courtesy Peter Lewis

Engine run-up checks were the next hurdle. These required taking the engines up to fairly high power (30 inches of boost), checking the magnetos one by one and exercising the propellers from fully fine (take-off) pitch through to fully coarse (cruise) and back. We were relatively fortunate, the thrust at the specified power from two engines was not quite enough to drive the aircraft out of displacement hull mode to planing hull mode, so we could check the inners together and then the outers, without the speed increasing too much. The Catalina which I later saw in Tahiti, being two-engined, had to check one engine at a time and would spin round in demented circles first one way, then the other.

In normal circumstances there is no great need to keep a landplane's wings level by control inputs during take-off and landing ground runs, the undercarriage takes care of that. The seaplane was different. The wing floats were relatively fragile and it was important to keep the wings level so that the floats did not touch the water at anything other than low speed. I found this part of the proceedings came fairly naturally, having been accustomed to take-offs and landings in gliders, which had only one wheel and had to be 'flown' to keep the wings level as long as possible after landing. Keeping the flying boat straight was another matter. On take-off, the torque of all four propellers caused the aircraft to veer off to the right and the right wing to go down. Until sufficient speed had been obtained even full left rudder was not enough to stop the swing. So take-off commenced with full left rudder and full left aileron. All four engines would be opened up to about three-quarters power, then the left outer throttle was left behind while the other three throttles were taken up to the stops. The left outer was then used to steer the aircraft until the rudder became effective. Finally the last engine could be eased up to full power and with good luck and a fair wind it might just be possible to get the rudder centralised before the aircraft left the water.

Alighting was simpler, with the engines at idle there was not much torque effect and rudder was usually sufficient to keep straight. Of course it was important to keep the wings level and the floats out of the water, until "off the step" and down to a low speed.

Mooring was achieved in much the same way as in a sail boat, by turning into wind down-wind of the buoy and

Photo 12 - Vital but draggy

cutting all the engines at just the right moment so that the aircraft would coast into wind, slowing down all the way and ideally come to a momentary stop just as the bow reached the mooring. This gave the Radio Operator time to grapple the mooring rope eye with a boathook and slip it over the nose bollard, before the boat drifted back with the wind and the mooring rope became tight.

Alas, it didn't quite go according to plan on the one and only time I was given the chance to operate the boathook a year or so later. When we arrived at

Mechanic's Bay that day the wind of about 10 knots was blowing directly into the angle between the harbour sea wall and the two hundred metre long breakwater. I was standing in the open mooring hatch, boathook at the ready, white topped flat hat on my head, with all the headquarters staff watching from the shore as Captain Joe Shephard positioned the aircraft, turned into wind and cut the engines.

We coasted up to the buoy. The mooring rope eye was held in a forked stick with the rest of the rope coiled round it - looking rather like a cobra poised ready to strike. I got hold of the eye with the boat hook and then couldn't seem to get it detached from the stick. The boat came to a halt and started to drift back. I managed eventually to get the eye loose and rapidly hand over handed the boat hook to get hold of the loop. I had got it to within half an inch of slipping over the nose bollard when the rope became taught.

Well, yachtsmen will know how relatively easy it is to push a boat weighing many tons away from a jetty – and how trying to stop the same boat when it is drifting into the jetty is an exercise in futility. I thought all I had to do was hang on, I could stop the drift, haul back towards the buoy and slip the loop over the bollard. The boat hook slowly slid through my grip. I hung on. Now the light line securing the boathook to the aircraft slid slowly through my grip. I hung on. Eventually the securing line became tight. A loud "twang" – and two feet of the stringer to which it was tied and a square foot or so of hull skin flew past my head. Fortunately the resulting hole was well above the water line!

Joe re-started the two outer engines and we held off while a launch re-coiled the mooring rope on the buoy, retrieved the boat hook and brought it to the rear door. Then we went round for another attempt, this time with the Radio Operator occupying the mooring hatch. I was never asked to try mooring up again.

There were some emergency procedures unique to flying boats. A perforated or broken off wing float could mean loss of the machine if it tipped over to that side when on the water. Thin lifelines were stowed in ceiling boxes each side of an escape hatch opening onto the top of the fuselage. The procedure then was to turn the aircraft so that the wind was blowing from the side of the damaged or missing float. The lifeline had dog clips attached at intervals. The Flight Engineer would take the end of the rope, with its dog clip, out onto the down-wind wing. The Navigator took hold of the next clip and followed him out. Finally the Radio Operator took the last clip. Near the wing tip, the Flight Engineer attached his dog clip to a ring bolt and corresponding ring bolts were located where the other two crew members would by then be positioned. All three would then cluster at the wing tip hanging on to the life-line. Their combined weight was enough to stop the float-less wing going down and the aircraft capsizing in any reasonable wind force from the opposite side. This procedure was not without hazard. I was told that some years previously a float was lost in Wellington Harbour one dark and stormy night. The Flight Engineer fell off the wing and was very fortunate to be rescued.

Damage caused by debris striking the main hull was always a possibility. I think that up to three of the seven watertight compartments could be perforated without the boat sinking. If the hull were damaged, the waist-high watertight doors in the lower cabin would be secured closed by heavy-duty dog-clamps. In the case of severe damage during take-off, the aircraft would be flown to some place where it could be run ashore onto a beach before it filled up and sank.

Although alighting on the open sea in an emergency was possible, there was a high probability of damage to floats and propellers if the waves were more than a couple of feet in height. Later on I did once encounter very rough water for take-off inside the lagoon at Tonga. The battering was such that my windscreen split from top to bottom. I had to press against it for the rest of the flight to stop it blowing in!

The slipway at Mechanic's Bay led up to a large concrete apron and to the hangar where major maintenance was carried out. When this was necessary, beaching gear, consisting of undercarriage legs encased in balsa wood, was floated out to the boat and attached to the fuselage. The boat would be towed to the slipway and hauled out by a crawler tractor. I heard about the time when this went slightly wrong. It was midsummer and low tide. Unfortunately it had just rained and the slipway was well covered with algae. The tractor driver got to the point where the flying boat was almost completely out of the water when the tracks lost grip. Slowly the whole combination slipped backwards, with the driver frantically operating throttles, brakes, clutches and gears, all to no avail. Game to the last, he went down with his ship. The onlookers saw a last despairing puff of smoke from the tractor's exhaust and his hat floating on the surface, before he reluctantly let go of the controls and rose out of the depths.

Widgeon amphibians of Tourist Air Travel also used the TEAL slipway. TAT was managed by Captain Freddie Ladd and was a small, mostly charter, operation with a few scheduled runs. At that time the harbour bridge was still a dream. TAT's scheduled services included what was probably the shortest in the world, from one side of the harbour to the other; about five minutes from water take-off to water landing. Freddie also ran a schedule to the Great Barrier Island. When there was spare capacity on the return flight from there to Auckland he would buy as many crayfish as he could carry and sell them from the aircraft on arrival – there were always some hopeful people waiting. Someone told me that this eventually led to a prosecution for selling fish without a fishmonger's licence. The story was that Freddie defended himself, quoted the example of a noble lady who used to promenade the streets of Paris with a lobster on a lead and said "So, yer' onour, my crayfish are all alive and I'm selling them as pets. Don't need a licence to sell pets." Case dismissed![4]

---

[4] Freddie's own account in his autobiography "A shower of spray and we're away" is a little different but why spoil a good yarn?

Photo 13 - Sold out of crayfish, Freddie Ladd's Widgeon

Eventually I had passed all the ground examinations, the Type Rating flying test and the New Zealand Instrument Rating flying test. ZK-AMQ had gone to Suva to operate the Coral Route while the Mk.4 ZK-AMO was engaged in a few Suva-Auckland-Suva shuttles so my line training began with a flight to Suva in her. We night stopped at the Grand Pacific Hotel. This was definitely a bastion of Empire. Despite the heat and humidity, with air conditioning just a dream of the future, the hotel information included the statement that "Gentlemen are required to wear suits in the public rooms." Left to myself, I'd have gone somewhere else to eat my dinner in shirt-sleeved comfort, but it did not seem diplomatic for me go off on my own when the whole crew were assembled together.

We flew back to Auckland next day in seven and a quarter hours and I spent a few days organising storage for the motorbike, selling the push-bike and packing. On the 20th August I moved to the Suva base permanently.

Chapter 12
Fiji and the Coral Route

TEAL had arranged accommodation for me at a guesthouse not far from the centre of Suva. This was a wooden, corrugated iron roofed bungalow set in a medium sized garden, with randomly placed canna lilies, paw-paw trees and cassava all around. The toilet was in a concrete shed in a corner of the back garden; another concrete shed held two showers and washbasins, all with cold water only. The veranda at the back had been partitioned off to form rooms. Air conditioning was managed by leaving shutters open for the wind to blow through – there were no glass windows. Some of the other residents could have stepped straight out of a Somerset Maugham novel. These included Mike, an alcoholic Irishman, who held long conversations with himself while asleep; Madame Claire, the local hairdresser and two old Suva hands, mystery men who kept very much to themselves. Meals were prepared by a middle-aged Indian woman. I found out what the 'Bounty' of mutiny fame was all about when breadfruit featured at almost every meal. But although the slaves apparently wouldn't eat it when it was finally introduced to the West Indies, I found it was quite palatable when baked.

ZK-AMO went back to Auckland on the 21st, for a major overhaul. The plan was for my base training to begin two days later, when the Mark 3, ZK-AMQ was due back from Tahiti. It was unfortunately – well, for me unfortunately, but the crew probably felt otherwise – delayed in Tahiti for three days with a fuel leak. So my first flight round the "Coral Route", on the 27th August 1956, with Captain Ed Allison, was as a supernumerary crewmember.

We departed from Laucala Bay at the very civilised hour of 9.00 a.m. The first leg, to Satapuala in Western Samoa passed over or close to many small islands and reefs. With no pressurisation we stayed low (on most flights at about 6,000 feet) from which height the beauty of the coral seascape was quite breath taking. The deep ocean waters were of an almost gentian blue, while within the fringing reefs the shallow lagoons were rainbow coloured with a mix of greens and yellows, dappled with the purples and reds of coral heads. Some of the islands were hilly and heavily wooded; others were barely above water and covered by coconut palms. One almost perfectly circular island intrigued me. It was quite clearly of volcanic origin, but what made it rather special was that its perfectly circular crater was full of water, in the middle of which was another circular island with a round lake in the middle. In the centre of that, a very tiny group of rocks just broke the surface. An island in a lake in an island in a lake in an island.

Although the flight took only four hours, we were flying eastwards, so it was late afternoon on the 26th August by the time we arrived at Satapuala. The 26th is not a mistake; we did indeed take off on the 27th and land on the 26th. We had crossed the Date Line on the way. The passengers and I received TEAL

Date Line crossing certificates to prove it. From that day onwards, I have always kept my watch on Greenwich Mean Time, now known as UTC. When moving frequently from one time zone to another, it is very easy to forget whether one has reset one's watch or not. It is easier to remember the time difference and apply it to what the watch shows. And of course, when flying, all Air Traffic Control times are given in UTC.

Photo 14 - Moored in the Satapuala lagoon

The flying boat alighting area at Satapuala was a single "runway", which had been created by dynamiting out coral heads within the fringing lagoon. There was a turning circle at each end and a mooring paddock half way down. The edges of the strip were marked by sawn off 45 gallon oil drums mounted on scaffold poles; for night operations floating kerosene flares were lit.

We were ferried from our mooring to the Satapuala jetty by a motor launch. From there we were taken about twenty miles to Apia, the capital, on one of the most consistently beautiful drives I have ever encountered. The road stayed mostly close to the shore, between seawards-leaning coconut palms and red, pink or white frangipani trees. A few hundred yards across the pearlescent lagoon brilliant white spray rose from the swell crashing onto the reef. Every village had its breadfruit trees, patches of banana and taro, clumps of hibiscus bushes and at least one whitewashed church. The houses (fales) were set well apart on stone platforms two or three feet high in a closely mown communal lawn. They were oval in shape, with palm or pandanus thatch roofs supported on 30 or so vertical coconut trunk posts. They had no permanent walls; plaited pandanus or coconut frond blinds could be lowered to keep out the rare driving rain or cold wind. Outside each fale, stands made from the fleshy trunks of banana trees were decorated with hibiscus and frangipani flowers threaded onto stripped coconut palm frond ribs. By each village small thatched huts (fale itis) stood on stilts in the lagoon, connected to the shore by a walkway of coconut logs or planks. Although they were very picturesque, they had a somewhat utilitarian function, being the communal privies. Showers were not only communal, but also uninhibitedly public, being simply standpipes in the grass areas between the fales.

Photo 15 - On the road from Satapuala to Apia

In Apia, we stayed at Aggie Grey's Hotel, a two story wooden building on the landside of the waterfront road with a fine view across the 'harbour' to the wide passage through the reef. The gap was in fact so wide that there was no real protection from the fortunately rare storms. The wreck of 'Adler', a German warship caught by a storm more than fifty years previously, was still visible on the coral. Aggie was reputed to be the inspiration for "Bloody Mary" in James Michener's book "Tales of the South Pacific" which was made into the "South Pacific" hit musical I had seen in London.

Most of the crew and the passengers had individual rooms in the main building, but the Flight Clerk and myself, as the two most junior crewmembers, shared a bungalow in the grounds. This was of unusual construction, the lower part of the walls were made of empty beer bottles set in concrete. A practical solution to a waste disposal problem and providing good insulation against the tropical heat. Usually, all the crew gathered there soon after arrival for sandwiches and soft drinks and then dispersed for a few hours sleep before leaving the hotel at around two a.m.

Photo 16 - The bottle house at Aggie Grey's hotel

Before we arrived back at Satapuala, the launch went out to the strip to set up the flarepath then returned to ferry us to the aircraft. After the outboard engines had been started the Radio Operator released the mooring rope and we moved out from the mooring paddock while the Captain and Flight Engineer started the inners. It was my job to lean out of the side window holding the aldis lamp (carried to enable us to make visual signals to the ground or water) and to sweep the light beam from side to side ahead of us to illuminate any floating debris. Meanwhile the Captain and Flight Engineer carried out the engine run-up checks. There was just enough time to finish these and the pre-take-off checks, before reaching the turning circle. Then we swung round into wind and opened up to full power. After an agonisingly long time ploughing through the water, the boat lifted onto the step and pattered across the wavelets slowly gaining flying speed. Once airborne it seemed to jump forward, free from the drag of the sea.

This leg of the flight took just over five hours. During the night part of the cruise, the steward came onto the flight deck to take our breakfast orders. We ate first, so that the cabin crew would have time to cook and serve the passenger meals between dawn and our landing. The menu, listing fresh temperate and tropical fruit, fruit juices, cereals, eggs, bacon, sausage, tomato, bread rolls, toast, jam or marmalade, tea and coffee would not have shamed a four star hotel.

Flying against the sun, the dawn truly came up like thunder, with very few minutes from the first paling of the eastern sky to full daylight. On this my first flight, when dawn came, there was nothing to be seen below except the deep blue Pacific. Occasionally on later flights, depending on just how far down track we had reached by dawn and how close to track we were, we might see Palmerston Atoll. This was the only speck of land in the 700 miles between Tutuila, the last island in the Samoan group and the first of the Cook Islands.

Our destination on this leg was Akaiami on the reef of Aitutaki atoll. The atoll was roughly triangular, about 12 km. on each side. The main, inhabited island, about 6 km. long, lay in the northern corner of the lagoon and there were 15 small motus (islets) mostly strung along the eastern reef. Akaiami was one of these. The motu, crescent shaped, was only half a kilometre in length and 200 metres across from the coral sand beach on the inner side to the rough broken coral seaward coast. 200 metres further out across the shallow platform reef, the ocean swells broke in flashing spray. For an international airport Akaiami had rather few facilities – three 'runways' like those at Satapuala and a population (when we were not there) of precisely zero. Apart from a partly cleared area round the terminal buildings - three palm thatched huts near the coral jetty - the whole motu was thickly covered with coconut palms and bush undergrowth. There was a well; even though the motu was nowhere more than a metre above high tide level this provided sufficient fresh water for toilet and washing facilities via a storage tank. On flying boat days a launch came from the main island (population a few hundred) with half a dozen island girls and a mechanic. The girls served fruit juice, tea, coffee and sandwiches to the passengers while the mechanic helped the Flight Engineer to refuel the aircraft. The fuel was pumped by hand from 45-gallon drums, ferried to the aircraft by launch from a fuel dump well away from the passenger terminal. Refuelling took over an hour and a half; there was plenty of time for the passengers and the rest of the crew to swim or sunbathe and socialise. By the time we re-boarded the aircraft a family party atmosphere was well developed.

There was a dream-like quality to the Aitutaki experience. With the gentle chattering of coconut palm fronds in the soft Trade Wind breeze as a musical background, the white-hulled flying boat moored on the opalescent lagoon just looked so right. I was told the Samoans had named the Solent "Vailili", - "Water bird"- it had the air of a seagull floating calmly with its tail cocked up, turning gently from side to side to keep facing into wind. It took little imagination for it to grow the masts and rigging of Captain Cook's "Endeavour", for our passengers to become bare-footed pig-tailed seamen and for the flight crew to metamorphose into cocked-hatted braided naval officers of the 18th Century bartering with the Polynesian inhabitants.

The onwards flight to Tahiti took another four hours, with little but ocean to see until the dramatic island of Moorea, a few miles short of our destination. We were in the descent as we passed by to the north, just below the level of the highest peaks, the remains of an ancient volcano. The views into the two bays were incredibly beautiful, turquoise blue tongues of water extending into the island, fringed by coconut palms hanging over white sand beaches, between

Photo 17 - The essence of the coral route

Photo Courtesy of Captain Maurice McGreal

cardboard cut-out ridges covered, even on the vertical razor-edges, by brilliant green vegetation.

  As we rounded the north-eastern point of Moorea, the island of Tahiti came into view. Surrounded by a fringing reef, with a narrow band of flat land on the coast, the island's interior was a jumble of high, densely wooded mountains, with deep valleys stretching inland. Orohena, the highest peak at 2241 metres and the triple peaks of the Diademe were crowned with orographic cumulus cloud, but otherwise the island was bathed in sunshine. There was little sign of habitation along the shore; the omnipresent coconut palms hid all but occasional glimpses of houses and the narrow round the island road. Here and there passages through the reef gave access to the lagoon.

From Papeete, the capital, westwards to the point of Faaa in the northwest of the island there was a deep channel between a platform reef attached to the shore and the seaward reef. The channel width varied between little more than two hundred metres and half a kilometre or so. This was our alighting area.[5]

We made our approach over the town, with a row of ocean going yachts moored stern on to the waterfront road to our left and splashed down opposite a small island on the right. We turned back and moored up to one of the big ship buoys just off the Papeete waterfront and disembarked onto the wharf at the centre of the town. I learnt that occasionally a cruise ship would be berthed alongside the wharf; Papeete harbour was blessed with very deep water right up to the shore. On this, my first visit, we had the wharf to ourselves. Half the island's population seemed to be waiting for us outside the customs shed. We and our passengers, were soon festooned with 'heis' (flower necklaces). Our baggage went into a fumigation room for a couple of hours as a precaution against introduction of the coconut beetle, a pest in some of the Pacific islands. While we waited for its return we went to our agent's office to collect our daily allowance money, in French Pacific Francs. This was a most impractical form of currency, there were no coins of sufficient value to be of any use so virtually all transactions had to be made with notes. Even small denomination notes were on the large side; buying a round of drinks required the use of a piece of paper, crumpled and filthy from much handling, the size of a handkerchief.

With funds for our stopover we adjourned to the first floor balcony of the Bar Maurice, overlooking the main street. I tasted the first of many 'Hinanos', the local beer, while watching the fascinating activity in the street below. There

Photo 18 - Watering hole for the crew

---

[5] Partly vanished under the airport built in the 1960s.

were few private cars. Most of the four-wheeled vehicles were either taxis or covered trucks. Inside, the trucks were crammed with passengers; outside the roofs were festooned with bunches of bananas, chickens and pigs in cages, baskets of fish and fruit, mysterious cloth-wrapped bundles and other odds and ends. Polynesian faces predominated among the passers-by, with quite a large number of Chinese and a sprinkling of Caucasians. There were some pedal cycles and many 'mobylettes' (bicycles with a small motor on the front frame which lowered onto the front wheel). The riders were mostly Tahitiennes wearing brightly coloured 'pareu' cloth dresses, many of them with waist length dark hair. When travelling as pillion passengers, they rode side-saddle. Almost everyone, male and female, had a hibiscus, frangipani or tiare tahiti flower tucked behind his or her ear.

Eventually our luggage was released and we moved along to the hotel. 'Les Tropiques' was situated about three miles to the west of town, between the round the island road and the lagoon. The reception desk, bar and partly roofed dining patio were together in one area at the water's edge, with a wooden jetty from the patio stretching out across the inshore platform reef to the edge of the deep water channel. Guests were accommodated in bungalows scattered among the coconut palms. All the buildings were constructed, except for the concrete floors, of local materials. The frames of the 'fares'[6], built of coconut palm trunks and timber from purau trees, supported roofs thatched with coconut palm fronds or the longer-lasting pandanus leaves. Much of the construction was tied together with cord made from coconut fibre, rather than being nailed. Internally there were no ceilings; one could see the underside of the roof and the unintentional decorative patterns formed by the lacing of the thatch to the roof poles. Nor was there any glass; window openings could be closed by shutters made of woven bamboo strips in wooden frames.

There was time for a shower and an hour's rest before dinner. When we assembled at the bar Moorea was silhouetted against a flaming sunset, its jagged peaks like the crest of a crouching stegosaurus. As darkness fell flaming bundles of palm fronds wielded by Tahitian fishermen appeared on the inshore platform reef. The men were carrying 45-gallon oil drums, sawn-off at top and bottom, which they plunged into the shallow water and then beat with sticks. It seemed that any fish trapped in the drum would be stunned and would float to the surface. They were then scooped out and placed in the floating bamboo fish 'traps' towed by the fishermen.

A waitress brought us menus. It was clear that I was another step away from austerity Britain. The Orontes menu had been lavish; the Les Tropiques menu was a cornucopia of Tahitian, French and Chinese specialities. I was so overwhelmed by the choice and my lack of knowledge as to what most things were that I panicked and asked for roast pheasant, one of the few things that I

---

[6] There were many different dialects in the Polynesian language. In Samoa, the houses were 'fales'. In Tahitian 'l' was replaced by 'r'.

did recognise although I had never eaten it before! Later in my Tahiti days I was to discover a wealth of culinary delight. There was first and foremost 'poisson cru', i'a ota in Tahitian, which was raw fish soaked in lime juice and garnished with coconut cream. I still make this 40 years later in England, with tinned coconut cream from the supermarket and halibut replacing the mahi mahi fish of the South Pacific. At a small Chinese restaurant in town I usually asked for foo yung har, basically prawn and egg with various other ingredients. At the Royal Tahitian Hotel freshwater prawns in batter were a favourite. Not so easily come by was the varo, or mud lobster. It looked like an eight inches long wood louse, but it was sweeter and more tender than any lobster from Maine. At parties, anything from an umu (earth oven) was not to be missed. This method of cooking was found throughout the Polynesian triangle. A fire was lit in a pit and rocks were heated on the coals. When the flames died down a variety of seafood, meat, fe'i (cooking bananas) and vegetables, wrapped in leaves, was placed on the rocks and then the umu was covered over with sand and left for half a day or more. Sucking pig from the umu was so tender it could be cut with a fork. Something I could never bring myself to try was fafaru. This also took a long time to prepare. Chunks of fish were placed in an earthenware pot filled with seawater. The pot was left in the sun for three or four days and topped up with more seawater when necessary. Naturally the fish went rotten. It could be eaten at this stage, but was not considered to be quite what it should be. The best fafaru was that which had been made by pouring the liquid residue from the first batch into the next lot to be made and then again... and again. After the fourth recycling it was beginning to come right! If fafaru featured at an outdoor occasion, I found it best to stay upwind.

All this was in the future. That first night I was not much bothered what I was eating. There were too many other things to be savoured. The hupe, a gentle night wind that flowed down from the mountains was just strong enough to set the overhanging coconut fronds rustling and just cool enough to make a cardigan optional. It added the scent of rich damp earth with hints of vanilla and copra to that of the sweet-smelling heis of tiare tahiti and frangipani which we and the other guests were wearing. Across the lagoon the endless procession of ocean swells broke on the reef, the spray phosphorescent in the starlight. The muted rumble of the breakers formed an unceasing background accompaniment to the music of a small band. And the music! A steel guitar, some ukuleles and drums playing not the languorous hulas of Hawaii but the foot-tapping, finger-snapping fast rhythms of popular songs of the day in the Tahitian language (one of which was nothing more than an advertisement for 'biere hinano' – the local beer). The pace increased even further when a vahine, dressed in the full traditional regalia of 'grass' skirt, couronne, plaited bracelets, anklets and waist band decorated with sea shells put on a solo display of the ori tahiti dance.

The crew had decided to make sure that I was properly introduced to Tahiti on my first visit, so after dinner we bundled into several taxis and took off for town. They gave Quinn's Tahitian Hut a miss on this occasion and took me to Zizou's, one of half a dozen small 'boites' in the town itself. We pushed in through the narrow doorway…

I think this was one of the defining moments of my life. The one small oblong room, with a bar across the narrow end, was seething with a densely packed crowd, dancing to another local band. Most of the dancers were Tahitians and the dance was, to put it mildly, somewhat uninhibited. In no time at all our male crew members were led onto the floor by vahines and the stewardesses by tanes. I had until then been somewhat straight-laced, reserved, almost puritanical, but it was quite impossible not to fall into the spirit of the evening and join wholeheartedly into the revels. Sometime later we moved further afield, to the Lido, another nightspot in one of the districts. I must have been really letting go; although the Lido is recorded in my diary I've no remembrance of where it was or what it was like! All the diary shows is that we returned to the hotel in the small hours, that I spent most of the next day recovering and that I went to bed early that evening in preparation for the next morning's flight.

The return to Fiji seemed almost an anti-climax; I'd seen it all on the way out! We left Les Tropiques in the dark and took off just after dawn. Once again we swam at Aitutaki while the aircraft was refuelled, then flew on to Samoa for a longer night stop with a daylight departure for the last sector. Three days off in Suva gave me a chance to investigate the Yacht Club and to accept an invitation for a trip into the interior, to a picturesque pool at the foot of a small waterfall surrounded by rain forest.

Chapter 13
Night flying the Solent

On the 4th September the aircraft was ready for my delayed training. The fringing reef at Laucala Bay was a long way from the shore, so the lagoon was very wide. It also had a sandy bottom and there were no coral heads inside the reef, so we had no set 'runway' areas, but could take off directly into any wind. Before we took off, our control launch would do a sweep of the expected take-off run to look for any debris. If the water was flat calm, the sweep also rippled the surface. This made a big difference to the flying boat's take-off distance. In a flat calm, there was nothing to break the suction under the hull. A ripple enabled air bubbles to be swept behind the 'step' and quickly set up the cavitation needed for the aircraft to rise from displacement mode to planing mode. With no large river entering the bay there was rarely any problem with debris, but on one occasion we were delayed for ten minutes while the launch chased some whales away.

As part of my training I was required to carry out some night flying take-offs and landings, but a flight to Tonga and technical problems prevented this before the next scheduled Coral Route flight on the 7th, so once again I went as supernumerary crew. Joe Shephard, the Senior Captain at Suva, commanded the flight. Joe was probably the most experienced still active flying boat pilot in the world at that time. He had flown boats all through WW2 and continued on boats with TEAL when the war ended. I don't think he had flown a landplane since his early flying training days.

Things took an unexpected turn on the second leg 45 minutes after our night take-off from Satapuala when the port outer engine began to vibrate and lose power and we returned for a night landing. Investigation revealed metal in the oil filter, so an engine change was required. This was TEAL's first engine change in Samoa; it took four days. There was no slipway so it had to be done on the water. We had to borrow a large pontoon, which took a day to arrive and then rig up a crane to lift the unserviceable engine out and the new one in. Disconnecting and re-connecting electrical cables, fuel and oil lines with the aircraft bobbing up and down on the lagoon wavelets was not too difficult, but taking out the engine mounting bolts, removing the engine, lifting the new engine into place and inserting the mounting bolts had to wait for flat calm conditions. We had a Samoan diver on hand the whole time to retrieve any tools or bits and pieces that dropped into the sea.

When we were ready to go on the 13th ZK-AMO was still in the throes of its major maintenance and was not available to help us get back on schedule. By sheer chance Sir P. G. Taylor's Sandringham (converted Sunderland) flying boat happened to be in Tahiti on one of his flying boat safaris, so TEAL chartered his aircraft to bring our passengers from Tahiti to Aitutaki, meet us there and take our Tahiti-bound passengers back with him. We would not be back in Suva in time for our next scheduled service but Ansett of Australia still had an operational Sandringham; they were chartered to operate it for us. We passed them on our way back to Suva, one of the very few times when there was another aircraft in the sky within a thousand miles of us!

The technical aftermath of this episode kept the aircraft unavailable for my night flying training, so, on the 20th I made yet another Coral Route flight as supernumerary. This time we had three nights in Tahiti. The first evening was relatively quiet. I spent it at Les Tropiques with the other crewmembers, gathering all the information I could about the island until two in the morning. I was rather attracted by a French-Tahitienne girl at another table and danced a few times with her until she left with her friends.

Next morning, from the end of the hotel jetty and with the aid of a face mask and snorkel tube I had my first look at the underwater world. The shallow inshore reef fell away there almost vertically; the face of the reef vanished into a blue haze and the bottom was not visible. Later, in other parts of Tahiti and in Fiji I found much better coral and a vastly greater variety of fish, but there was so much to see even in this relatively poor habitat that I was overwhelmed by the experience. The variety of shapes and colours of fish was amazing. Another astonishing thing was the way they seemed to take no notice of me, swimming close by my facemask and only moving away if I reached a hand out to within a few inches of them. When one walks past a pool of fish they dart away into cover, but they seem to treat a human in the water as nothing more than a big harmless animal. I was fascinated by an octopus that lurked in a shallow cave about ten feet down, it slithered out from time to time and as it passed over different colours of coral, changed its own colour to match.

With another 36 hours before our next flight we went on the town in a big way on the second night. I was introduced to more of the nightspots, Quinn's Tahitian Hut being the most famous, or perhaps that should be infamous, of them all. Located in what was then the centre of town, just behind the Customs building, it had a long frontage onto the Rue Pomare. Old Tahitian women ambushed the clientele as they approached the bat-wing doors, selling heis of Frangipani and the sweet-scented Tiare Tahiti, a species of white gardenia. Inside, a single large dimly lit room with a dance floor was surrounded by small alcoves, bamboo-walled, each containing a table and ten or so chairs. At the inner end there was a small platform about six feet above floor level; there the two star girl singers Mila and Phyllis rendered the hits of the day, mostly Tahitian although "Que sera, sera" was a very popular number. From time to time they would be displaced by a vahine performing the Ori Tahiti; usually this resulted in demands for her to descend to the dance floor, where she would be surrounded by half a dozen young men. The spectacle could perhaps be best described as rape without contact; the male part of the action being rather explicit.

In the following months we would occasionally pop into Quinn's for a daytime Biere Hinano and I was often there late in the evenings when we were not flying the next day. Alas, it is now long gone. Maybe it was demolished to make way for a more commercial building, but the sheer exuberance of the tightly packed clientele dancing to the thudding beat of the piano, guitar and drum band used to cause the whole rather flimsily constructed bamboo and palm thatch building to bounce and sway as if being shaken by an earthquake. Perhaps it simply fell down in the end.

Photo 19 - Quinn's Bar

Courtesy Harold Stevens

On the last day of this stopover the Flight Clerk, Don Patterson, guided me round the Papeete shops, mostly Chinese owned. There seemed to be no specialist stores, each one sold practically the whole range of goods from armchairs to zip fasteners, piled on the floor and shelves in no particular order. They all dealt in rolls of brightly coloured, boldly patterned cotton pareu cloth and shirts made from the same material. A simple six feet by three feet length of pareu cloth had many uses; it could be wrapped round the waist as a cool, comfortable garment at home; the ends could be brought between the legs and tucked into the waist wrap forming a swim suit; it would roll into a pillow and it was always useful as a Dick Whittington type carry bag.

In one of the stores we encountered the girl I had been dancing with on the first night. It seemed a good idea to invite her to show us her favourite restaurant and have lunch with us. She led us to a small alley near the Cathedral. We could have been in France. It was a small place; a two story whitewashed frontage with louvred window shutters, sandwiched between its neighbours. A dozen seats were set round tables on the pavement outside and about the same number inside. The tablecloths were chequered in red and white and a red and white striped awning provided shade. The owner and his wife were French, as was the menu.

We were the only customers and after a long discussion with the owner about his specialities of the day we spent a leisurely three hours over a bottle of wine and a meal. I set up a date for our next visit to Tahiti with the girl, Suzanne; she said she would be waiting on the quayside when we arrived.

Back in Suva, aircraft serviceability and availability came together and at last I was able to complete my night flying training. This proved to be rather different to land-based night operations. At Laucala Bay the first problem arose when the launch crew laid out the flarepath. The 'flares' consisted of waterproof battery operated lamps, each one with a flotation collar, an anchor rope and a grapnel. The coxswain would do his utmost to hold a dead straight run into wind, while his assistant, with the aid of a stopwatch, dropped each lamp overboard at regular intervals. This procedure should have resulted in a perfect, straight set of 'runway' lights. Unfortunately the lagoon depth varied, there was always some cross current and when the coxswain looked back at the end of his run some of the lamps would have drifted more than others. From water level the result was a purely random scatter of light sources bobbing up and down in the wavelets. There wasn't much that could be done to rectify this, so we just kept all the lights to one side. The lagoon was wide enough and deep enough all over so it really didn't matter where we splashed down.

With no reference objects each side of the 'runway' height judgement was another problem. The aircraft's landing lights did not help. The water was usually so clear that while the bottom of the lagoon was well lit, the surface was invisible. So no attempt was made to judge height. The technique was to set up an approach at a speed 10 knots above the stall, with the engine power adjusted to give a rate of descent of 200 feet a minute and just keep going until impacting the surface. Then the power was cut and the stick was held right back until the boat slowed down and "fell off the step", that is, sank into the water after planing over the surface. The same technique was necessary in daytime when the water was smooth. After a few bounces on my first, second and third landing, I began to get the hang of it. After the fourth, fifth and sixth, Captain Joe either decided he'd had enough or I was good enough, I'm not sure which! But he signed me up as having completed all my training.

Chapter 14
Coral Route routine and engine failures

On the 4th October I set off down the Coral Route this time at last earning my keep as a fully qualified co-pilot. We didn't get far. Shortly after take-off the Flight Engineer, Bob Shea, came on the intercom to say that the port outer engine, the one we had changed in Samoa, was acting up with the torque fluctuating. We turned back, were towed into the Braby pontoon, the engineers checked the oil filter and again there were specks of metal in it. Another engine change was required. My Tahiti date had gone for a ball of chalk, but more seriously we had earned a black mark from Aggie Grey. She didn't like flying and had been intending to go by ship to Apia, but had been persuaded by our sales people to fly with us. Now she had not only been frightened, but had literally missed the boat and there wouldn't be another one for months.

There was a slipway at Laucala Bay, so the engine change was done on land where it took three days instead of Samoa's water-bound four. We had no problems with the aircraft on the delayed flight, but were a bit concerned when we received a radio call on the way to Aitutaki asking us to look for the "Inspire", a trading schooner which had been stolen from Rarotonga in the Cook Islands. She was carrying 70 drums of our aviation fuel, which should have been delivered to Aitutaki. Our future operations were in jeopardy; urgent messages went to our Mechanics Bay Headquarters to get some more fuel organised.

Not surprisingly, Suzanne was not waiting to meet me on the wharf when we arrived three days late. While we were waiting at the Bar Maurice for our bags to be fumigated, Don Patterson hung over the balcony and chatted up three Tahitiennes in the street below. Soon he had arranged for them to meet him, our temporary Radio Operator and myself that evening at the Vaihiria café. I didn't realise how efficiently the coconut radio operated; Suzanne learnt of this plan and when we got there she was waiting with a few choice words. One of the other three girls discreetly dropped out and we all went along to Quinn's.

Later that evening, after the girls had gone home, we saw one of Tahiti's 'Le Trucks' waiting for a full load before it set off for the Lido and decided we should finish the evening there. Basically a flatbed truck, brightly decorated, with a wooden roof and bench seats along each side, the vehicle was one of the many which operated informal, un-timetabled 'bus services all around the island. It was a hilarious ride, with the mostly Tahitian passengers singing to the music of a guitar and several ukuleles. When we set off, the driver was sitting almost outside the cab operating the accelerator, brakes and clutch, while his girlfriend was steering. No one seemed to think this was out of the ordinary! We stopped wherever people wanted to get on or off, with the driver collecting fares as they disembarked.

After the return flight to Suva, we flew one more passenger service in AMQ on the 12th October, to Samoa and back the same day and made a training flight on the 16th. Another crew brought ZK-AMO from Auckland and took AMQ back there on her last flight. She was scrapped soon after, although I heard a rumour a few years later that the hull was turned into a restaurant somewhere in North Island. With the expectation of no problems with the younger Mk 4 we flew another Coral Route schedule starting on the 19th and were not impressed when on the last leg back into Suva on the 23rd the number two engine developed an oil leak and we had to shut it down. But that was the last of the major aircraft problems during my time – bar one. A year later, on the way from Samoa to Aitutaki, we had a major failure of the number two engine. I just happened to be looking across the cockpit at the engine when it blew. I heard the bang even through my headset and saw a sheet of flame burst out of the cowling. We rapidly turned off the fuel, feathered the propeller, operated the fire extinguisher and turned back to Samoa. At first we were unable to maintain height and gently descended to where the three remaining engines gave enough power to stay level at 2,500 feet. Then another engine started to fluctuate. The Captain, Maurice McGreal, got the two ground engineers to position themselves near the cargo holds, with carving knives from the galley, ready to cut the baggage loose and throw it out. The next two and a half hours were somewhat nail-biting, but the situation got no worse and we landed back at Satapuala for another on-the-water engine change.

Those first few trips set the pattern for the next two years, with the occasional variation of the monthly day returns to Nuku'alofa, the capital of Tonga and three-monthly visits to Auckland for maintenance. With the Mk. 3 ZK-AMQ withdrawn from service the two week turnaround at Auckland meant no air services at all to Tonga, Samoa, the Cook Islands or Tahiti for that period. It did give me a chance to see more of New Zealand. During one of these visits I went to Rotorua on the motorbike and toured the thermal areas. I was most impressed by the central heating system in the house where I stayed. It used water from an underground hot spring!

At Tonga the usual five-hour stopover didn't give time for much more than a leisurely lunch. On the way to the guesthouse in one of Tonga's very few motor vehicles we passed through the only cross roads on the island. A policeman stood on traffic duty on a small thatch-roofed platform at the centre of the crossing. With maybe as many as two trucks or cars per hour passing by his main responsibility was to ensure the safe passage of King Tui Malila, the Royal Tortoise, on his occasional rambles through the town. The tortoise had been presented to the King of Tonga around two hundred years earlier by Captain Cook and had survived both a traffic accident and a fire.

My most memorable Tonga stopover was on the occasion of a formal visit by two Civil Servants from the U.K. Colonial Office. Prince Tungi laid on a mid-day feast to which we also were invited. A palm thatch awning had been constructed in a grassy clearing. We sat cross-legged beneath this on each side of a long rectangle of banana leaves laid on the ground. A Tongan girl sat behind every guest, selecting especially tempting items for him and waving a raffia fan to keep him cool. The food, sucking pig, chicken, seafood, plantains and yams had been cooked in an umu, prepared by some of the convicts from the island's prison!

Another memory is of a choir singing Handel's "Messiah" in the Tongan language. Polynesians generally have very good singing voices, some of the ancient chants are voice only and a full-throated areare'a has the 'tingle factor' in full measure.

At the Suva home base, the guesthouse began to pall. Fiji was very Empire in its ways. One of the Suva institutions was the Defence Club, effectively for whites only, although Lieutenant-Colonel Ratu Sir Edward Cakembau, a Fijian, was an honorary member. The 'Defence' name was explained by Club Rule number 4 - "All members undertake by accepting membership to place their services at the disposal of the Government of the Colony of Fiji to assist in any emergency that may arise." The Club, a rambling single-storey wooden building with a corrugated iron roof, had a bar, a library, several billiards tables and a few bedrooms and I moved into one of these. A club servant brought me tea and toast each morning. For lunch and dinner on the days I was in Suva I ate out at one or other of the restaurants.

Ratu Edward was one of Fiji's paramount Chiefs. He was a most imposing figure, well over six feet tall and broad to match. He invited a couple of us to the royal box at the town's cinema one evening. On the walk from the Defence Club to the movie house, every Fijian we met went down on his knees until the Ratu had passed. His rank of Lieutenant Colonel was not honorary, but was earned in the British Army. When asked what his Regiment was, he would usually reply "the South Sea Highlanders" He also had a string of military and civilian honours behind his name, including the knighthood. On one occasion when an American woman wanted to know his full title he reeled it all off, "Lieutenant Colonel Ratu Sir Edward Cakembau … etc., etc., adding 'QFC' at the end. She fathomed out all the abbreviations except that one, which, when she persisted, he translated as "Queen's favourite cannibal!"

Suva town held a flower festival in September, with floats prepared by various organisations and businesses. One of our sales staff organised TEAL's entry. Naturally it was based on a real float, one of our spares. Led by Philip, a Fijian ground staffer, we visited a local village to obtain flowers. We were invited into one of the houses. It was very different to the lightweight airy fales of Tahiti, but surprisingly cool inside.

The walls, made of reeds, were a couple of feet thick. There was no gap between the walls and the roof and no windows, just one very small door in each of three of the sides. A most imposing bed stood at the end without a door. At the opposite end was a fireplace. The only other furniture was a chest of drawers. We sat down on a deep layer of mats and went through around an hour and a half of speech and ceremony before a selection of flowers was brought to us. On the way back to town we gathered a few more. Despite our efforts we didn't win.

A canal near the city centre with adjacent colonnaded two storied buildings mirrored in calm blue water was most picturesque and gave rise to the 'Venice of the South Seas' appellation favoured by the Suva tourist industry.

Photo 20 - Suva Canal

The Yacht Club was situated at the entrance to a narrow creek further along the harbour. At close quarters this creek was rather less salubrious; an oil-slicked surface hid a bottom of thick black ooze, which clung tenaciously to one's feet when launching the boats. I joined the Club and bought an 'Idle Along' racing dinghy, naming it "Meteor". Although it was only twelve feet long, a two-foot bowsprit and a main boom which extended three feet behind the stern enabled a most impressive spread of sail to be carried, requiring the agility of a panther to keep the craft balanced in anything but the lightest of winds. So much so that I only sailed it with the smaller sails designed for strong winds and rarely took part in races. Even so, I shudder to think now of the foolhardiness of my youth. There was no built-in or airbag buoyancy. I had no life jackets. The only emergency equipment was a bailer and a single paddle. The sails were well past their sell-by date; I spent almost as much time repairing them as I did sailing.

Mostly I would sail within the harbour or round the inshore passage to Laucala Bay with one or two other T.E.A.L. residents or visitors, but quite often we would sail out through one of the reef passes, along the outside edge of the reef and back in through the next pass. Perhaps the tropical sun had fried my brains; on one occasion I bought a couple of bottles of orange drinks and some bananas and sailed out of the harbour across thirty miles of ocean to a small motu on the reef around the neighbouring island of Mbbenga. There I spent the night in a shelter made using the mast, boom and sails.

Maybe the experience justified the risk. I will always remember waking up some time in the early morning and in the light of a full moon seeing thousands upon thousands of tiny transparent ghost crabs marching in the same direction along the beach. Shining my torch towards them stopped them all in their tracks; switching the torch off set them in motion again. The dawn was spectacular too, the moon was still high and the combination of its light and the sunlight spreading up from below the horizon gave the cloudless sky a dream-like quality of luminescence. The return to Suva, beating into a very fresh trade wind, was not so pleasant. A

Photo 21 - "Meteor" rigged and ready to go

failure of the sails or rigging would have left me drifting westwards into an empty ocean, with the New Hebrides archipelago some 400 miles away.

The Yacht Club had a roofed area for storing some of the dinghies but I did not stay in Fiji long enough to get off the waiting list for this; 'Meteor' had to stay outside. It never occurred to me to buy a boat cover. I had a simpler way of stopping her planks from shrinking in the sun and letting in the water. When not being sailed, she spent her time sunk three feet below a marker buoy.

Apart from the Yacht Club, I had few interests in Suva, which was a very staid and stuffy sort of place where one had to be very

Photo 22 - Author and "Meteor" in Suva Harbour

careful not to do the not done thing. I was much more taken up with the hedonistic, carefree, riotous life of Tahiti, although it did take me a few months to get rid of all my inhibitions. I was a bit disadvantaged to begin with because at Les Tropiques I was sharing a room with Don Patterson, the flight clerk. A six-room u-shaped bungalow enclosing a paved area open to the lagoon was reserved for the five flight-deck crew, one of the stewardesses and the flight clerk. Seven into six meant that Don and I, as the two most junior members of the crew had to share. My budding romance with Suzanne came to an end when one evening she gave me a lift back to Les Tropiques on her mobylette and I then didn't ask her to spend the night in my bed.

During my first few months of Tahiti stopovers, by day I explored the countryside and beaches and by night, the restaurants, bars and nightspots. There was a sealed, though often pot-holed road all round the main part of the island, which one could circumnavigate leisurely by mobylette in a day. I found one idyllic place on the eastern coast, where a stream from high in the interior ran between some large smooth rocks into the lagoon. There were many coral heads in the lagoon, with an incredible number of fish in an infinite variety of shapes and colours. After drifting around with a snorkel and face mask in the blood-heat lagoon one could paddle into the stream and wash off the salt in the icy cold fresh water and then climb out on the rocks without getting one's feet covered with sand.

Exploring the restaurants was helped by the way we could eat in any establishment on the island and sign the bill, which the owner would later present to our agent in Papeete for payment. This did enable a certain amount of fiddling; it was always possible to sign for a full meal that included the most expensive items on the menu and thus cover the cost of less expensive meals for oneself and a guest. It was rumoured that certain crew members went even further and signed for a complete stopover's meals in the most expensive restaurant in exchange for cash (minus a small "handling fee") as soon as we arrived and then by patronising the much cheaper places had enough left for beer and taxis. Some years later after I had left I heard that the Company had decided there was too much fiddling going on and decided to pay a daily meal allowance instead. This had to be set according to the prices at the hotel where the crew stayed. Les Tropiques' restaurant was not the highest-priced, but very close to it. After a few months the Company discovered the new arrangement was costing them more. They hadn't allowed for the fact that crew members were frequently hosted by the island's residents and also preferred to eat in a variety of places, most of which were considerably cheaper than the hotel. Naturally the crew firmly resisted any attempt to change back!

Christmas 1956 came and went. It didn't last long. We left Samoa at daybreak on 25th and crossed the International Date Line half an hour later, when it immediately became the 26th. I never had the luck to make up for it by crossing the line from west to east on Christmas Day.

Chapter 15
DIY surgery (almost)

On the first of February 1957 we flew from Suva to Samoa, overnighted and went on to Tahiti next morning. About seven that evening I began to feel sick with a stomach ache. Our steward gave me some Lomotil, but it didn't do much for me. There was a plan for a crew sortie down town, but I felt too ill. Our stewardess, Sheenagh Rennie, who had been a nurse, said she would check up on me when they returned. When she came back just after midnight the pain was so bad that she went to fetch our company doctor. He came fairly soon and gave me an injection and some pills, but these didn't help either. By six in the morning I was convinced I had appendicitis and got Sheenagh to go and find the doctor again. He saw me several times during the day, but thought it was just a case of food poisoning. We were supposed to leave for Aitutaki that afternoon, but Captain Joe could see I was in no way fit to fly so he delayed the flight.

After another bad night, at five in the morning I was in really dreadful pain, shivering continuously and literally screaming. Sheenagh came and piled blankets on me and sent Don off to find the doctor again. He arrived around seven o'clock, but still didn't think I was in serious trouble and went away saying he'd look in again at ten. A few minutes after he left, the pain completely stopped. I didn't realise that this was the effect of an appendix bursting and not having eaten for two days, I was hungry. So off I went to get some breakfast. Meanwhile Sheenagh had gone with the doctor, to convince him that I should be in the hospital. When he came back with the hospital surgeon, they were a bit horrified and said yes, they did think I had appendicitis, the pain had gone because the appendix had burst, I shouldn't have eaten anything and they were taking me to the hospital for an appendectomy.

I felt perfectly fine, but reckoned they knew best, so off we went. The surgeon took me into the operating theatre, which was just a wooden walled room with a table in the middle – no shiny tiles, stainless steel equipment or air conditioning. He pointed at the table, said "Get undressed and lie down on there" and went out of the room. So I complied and lay there quite calmly watching a lizard catching flies on the ceiling. My calm evaporated when a young lady came in brandishing a cut-throat razor! Yes, I was on a small island in the middle of the South Pacific, but I did think the medical facilities would have been slightly more sophisticated than this. Panic subsided when she made me understand that the razor was not to be used for the operation, but just to shave around where the incision was to be made.

That done, the surgeon came back, gloved and gowned. "I'm giving you a Pentathol injection, start counting backwards from one hundred" he instructed. I got quite a long way, far enough to comment "How long has this been in stock?" before lights out. I woke up in the Papeete hospital, on my back with a large pack of ice on my stomach, a drain tube from the incision and a drip tube in my arm.

That evening, the crew came to visit and I heard what was to be done to get the boat back to Fiji. By chance, our navigator Pat Halse was on leave. Another of our DC6 captains, Phil LeCouteur's brother Cliff, had taken Pat's place on the flight. More fortunately, Cliff was also an ex-Solent pilot. So Joe had got clearance from New Zealand's Civil Aviation Authority to fly with Cliff acting as both co-pilot and navigator. Just as well – otherwise, with no land runway on Tahiti and no other regular flying boat service in the South Pacific, the only way T.E.A.L. could have got a replacement co-pilot to Tahiti would have been either to persuade the Royal New Zealand Air Force to fly from Fiji to Tahiti, or to send the replacement by ship!

Whatever, it would have taken a minimum of three days. This sort of delay had occurred in the past, before my time. There was an occasion when an engine failed on the take-off run at Aitutaki. The take-off had to be abandoned. There was no way to get a spare engine there by ship. The only passage through the reef was narrow and shallow, everything went ashore in small surfboats. Even our full fuel drums were floated ashore. A Hercules engine was a bit too much for this to be attempted.

Although a spare engine could have been flown in to the land strip there was no slipway to haul the boat out of the water and no barge big enough to carry the engine out to the flying boat for an on-water change. So some WW2 disused buildings were resurrected to house the passengers. Everything that was not essential was removed from the aircraft – the seats, galley, toilets and so on. Considerably lighter than normal, the aircraft was then flown out on three engines, with just the two pilots on board. The passengers remained marooned for about ten days. It seems there were no serious complaints, they all enjoyed the unintended holiday.

Now I was a castaway in the Papeete hospital. There could have been a worse place. At the time I had spent a total of 33 nights on the island, 20 or so days. I had met a few people once or twice, but didn't know anyone well. Each day a stream of visitors arrived, most of them bearing flowers, fruit or books and some just coming to keep me company. The coconut radio had spread the word, whether the islanders knew me or not, the TEAL flying boat meant a lot to them and they weren't about to let one of their few outside world connections languish alone on their island.

For the first three days my only nourishment was glucose, via a drip. In fairly typical French fashion, when I was offered my first solid meal, the question was "Do you want wine or beer with it?" I was allowed to get out of bed that day and the day after that the Solent arrived back. The crew came and took me away – straight to the Bar Maurice and then to Les Tropiques. They left me behind when they flew back to Fiji, which was about as disappointing as breaking the bank at Monte Carlo would have been.

Photo 23 - Les Tropiques waitresses Gaby and Noreen with author "recuperating" after appendectomy

I spent the next five days gently pottering around the hotel, snorkelling off the jetty and sunbathing and the evenings down town in Quinn's, Zizou's, the Col Bleu or another of Papeete's watering holes listening to the live music and regretting that I was too sore to dance. In my innocence I thought this blissful existence would continue until I had recovered enough to resume flying, but I was brought down to earth next time the plane returned when I was carted off back to Fiji and then sent on to New Zealand.

Chapter 16
Introduction to family life

When I returned to Tahiti four weeks later, the crew accommodation arrangements had been altered and I now had a room to myself. It took very little time for me to discover the truth in one of the popular songs of the time:

Les femmes d'Amerique,
Elles sont tres jolie,
Mais pour les avoir,
Il faut des dollars,
Tandis qu'a Tahiti,
On les a pour rien,
Vive Tahiti,
Le pays des amours.

"On les a pour rien" wasn't entirely correct. L***** was a waitress in one of the hotels, a Junoesque, friendly, always happy girl from one of the outer islands. A senior citizen American tourist staying at the hotel had been propositioning her from the first day of his arrival. She was not interested, but finally out of the goodness of her heart gave in – on condition that she would receive a small present. Came the morning, L***** had to get up and go to work, but the American reneged on the deal and said he wouldn't give her anything. Looking round, she saw his false teeth in a glass of water, so she snatched them and left. When he arrived for breakfast, he demanded their return, but, said L*****, "No present, no teeth". So he called in the gendarme, who was sympathetic but refused to take any action. After a couple of days existing on pap, the tourist gave in, but by then L***** had decided the whole episode was too much of a joke to bring to an end. She put the teeth on a high shelf behind the bar and every time the American appeared she would take them down and gnash them at him. It wasn't long before the coconut radio had spread the story all round the island. When he eventually left with us on the flying boat, still sans teeth, our stewards were ready for him with the special lunch of the day – grilled steak.

After half a year on the route and some experience of unusual food items like the raw fish in lime juice I had lost my dietary inhibitions and was ready to try almost anything. Two things I was never ready for, the fafaru and the sea cucumber entrails which Samoan children would try to sell us as we went by on our way to town. In Samoa, I did try the palolo. This was a sort of worm that lived in the coral reefs; on two nights of the year it emerged to spawn in untold billions. When prepared for eating it turned a vivid green. I can't say I'd go out of my way to eat it again, it tasted of nothing much in particular. Samoan pigeons though were rather special; the short open season for shooting them coincided with the ripening of a particular berry on which they fed, imparting a delicious sweet flavour to their flesh.

At Papeete in June 1957 I met an Australian whose tales of outback life intrigued me. One evening he asked me out to dinner at the Royal Tahitian Hotel where he was staying. There he introduced me to his vahine, Frida and told me he was about to return to Australia. He explained that, although he wanted to take her back with him the 'White Australia' policy then in force made this impossible and he asked me to look after her. I muttered some sort of yes, O.K., but thought little more of it. Two weeks later she met the Solent and said that Charlie McPhee, an artist, had invited her and me to dinner at his place. I met Charlie at the Bar Maurice and he drove me out to his house in Arue where his wife, Elizabeth and Frida were waiting.

While Elizabeth prepared the meal, Charlie showed me some of his work. He had adopted the same technique for oil painting on black velvet as the one Edgar Leeteg had developed. This involved the use of very thinned down paint, so that each hair of the velvet remained separated, even where multiple layers of paint had been applied. Each painting took months to finish, each layer of paint had to dry thoroughly before another could be added, so a production line system was used with many paintings, sometimes multiple copies of the same subject, being worked on each day. The resulting works, particularly the portraits, were very striking, having an almost 3-D effect.

After dinner we returned to Papeete for a round of the town nightspots, then drove back past Arue to 'Lafayette'. I'm told it is long gone, but in the fifties it was 'the' place to finish up an evening. Quite why is hard to understand, it was really little more than an open-sided barn, with a waist high bamboo and thatch wall and posts holding up the thatched roof. Bamboo shutters between the top of the wall and the eaves would be lowered during the day when Lafayette was closed. The single room had a planked dance floor and a bar along one end. Perhaps it was the location, just across the road from the lagoon, or maybe the live Tahitian music that gave it a special charm.

That first evening we danced, drank Hinano and sang along with the band until the wee small hours. Eventually I realised that I hadn't seen either Charlie or Elizabeth for a while and peering outside saw that their car had gone. I mentioned this to Frida who said, "Oh, they went home an hour ago." "I'd better find a taxi to take you home and me to Les Tropiques" I suggested. "No need, my house is just half a kilometre away, we can walk there and you can stay with me" she replied.

At that time Arue was out in the country; there were small houses at intervals on both sides of the narrow road, but there was access to the black sand beach almost everywhere. Frida's house was set among coconut palms just a few metres from the lagoon edge. Across the lagoon there were gaps in the reef to the left and the right, but opposite the house the reef protected the beach from storms. Three separate 'fares', one the kitchen, one with the living room and bedroom and the third holding the shower and toilet were connected by covered concrete paths. The whole complex was thatched with pandanus. Here I discovered the significance of the 'house of singing bamboo' lyric in the musical "South Pacific". The outer walls of the fares were built of a single row of vertically placed whole bamboo poles, loosely held between double horizontal lengths of timber at top and bottom. The bamboos varied from little finger to thumb thickness. When the wind blew, these vibrated at different frequencies. As the wind fluctuated, it seemed that an orchestra of panpipes, piccolos, flutes and other woodwinds was playing from beneath the palm trees.

Photo 24 - Frida on the jetty at Les Tropiques

I dropped out from much of the TEAL crew's social round during Tahiti stopovers for the next ten months, spending my time with Frida and her three children. I did take in some of the 1957 Bastille Day (14th July) celebrations with the crew.

Photo 25 - Ready-made family

Chapter 17
Bastille Tahitienne and briefly New Zealand

It is hard to understand just why the Tahitians should have made such a big event out of the Bastille festival. As the colonised, one would expect them to have little enthusiasm for the celebrations of their colonisers. But they kept the party going for two weeks. To start with, they closed off the Boulevard Pomare along the waterfront. A timbered dance floor was then constructed across the road, with tiers of seating all round except for the VIP platform and the band area. This was the venue for the Governor's Ball. Although this might sound to be a very grand and exclusive occasion, it was in fact open to all who cared to turn up. The Governor would be in all his finery, epaulettes, ostrich plumed hat and medals. His lady would be in a Parisian gown. The dress of the other participants ranged through all the variations down from highly formal to a pair of shorts, no shirt and no shoes. It would not be unusual to see the Governor's wife dancing with a bare-footed taxi driver or the Governor with a waitress from one of the island's restaurants.

Next to the dance floor, along the landside of the road, temporary kiosks of bamboo and palm thatch were set up. Here one could try the coconut shies, hoopla, rolling coins onto a squared table and other minor gambling games. The prizes varied; one stall had a suckling pig as its big attraction. One of our crew, with his vahine for the evening on his arm, made the minor mistake of trying his luck on his way **to** the ball and won the first prize. He wasn't about to waste time returning to the hotel to keep it safe. So he made his way to a table near the dance floor and tied the piglet to the table leg. He was a bit worried about leaving it unattended while he went to dance. Although Tahitians were generally honest, a lost-looking suckling pig might have been too much of a temptation. But – aita peapea[7] – he simply tucked it under one arm while holding the vahine with the other when he went onto the floor. No one took any special notice of this; far less conventional behaviour was to be seen any day of the week.

Other events such as pirogue races, dance and music competitions, javelin throwing (where the aim was to hit a suspended coconut, not see who could hurl the javelin furthest) and of course many feasts and parties at places all round the island kept things going.

The Solent was due for maintenance in Auckland in August; we flew down on the 14th. Don Patterson borrowed his father's car and took me to the Chateau Tongariro via Waitomo. The glow-worm cave at Waitomo was memorable. After cautioning us to make no noise, the guides used overhead cables to pull

---

[7] A frequently heard Tahitian expression equivalent to "No problem", "It doesn't matter", "Why worry?" etc., according to context.

us along an underground river in a punt. Overhead in the velvety darkness the glow-worms shone like stars in the densest part of the Milky Way.

Knowing no better, when we arrived at the Chateau we hired boots, skis and poles and took the chair lift to the top of the then dormant volcano. Never having skied before, we had great difficulty getting down again. Traversing across and down the slope was O.K., but trying to turn while upright for a traverse in the other direction was too much for us. We became fairly expert at sitz turns. Stop, sit down, take off the skis, turn them round to face the other way, stand up, put them on and set off on the other tack! The descent to the crater lake was definitely beyond us. The more expert could ski down to the lake, strip to swimming gear and plunge in. It was desirable to stay near the edge; further out the up-welling hot water could cook the unwary.

We returned to Suva and the Fiji - Samoa - Aitutaki - Tahiti routine on the 27th August. On the 6th September we made an unscheduled flight to Tahiti, carrying a movie team on their way to location for a French film "Le Passager Inconnu". Halfway between Aitutaki and Papeete I had my closest contact with celebrity when Martine Carole was invited onto the flight deck. She wanted to try flying the machine, so Joe got her to sit on my lap. I guess he gave me the honour because he was rather too large around the middle himself!

The sometimes light-hearted behaviour of flying crews was less seriously criticised in the 50s than it would be today. One Tahiti arrival evening I went for dinner in the hotel and as I passed by the reception desk, one of our passengers intercepted me. "What was your stewardess up to this morning? Was there a search on for a missing boat or something?" he asked. "What do you mean?" I said. "Well, every few minutes in the last hour of the flight, she kept going to the back of the cabin. She kept looking out of the window one side and then shot across to look out the other." I couldn't think of any reason for this, we on the flight deck hadn't asked the cabin crew to look out for anything and there were no islands she might have wanted to see.

It was some time later before I got the story. Meeting our new stewardess in the mid-ships toilet area the Chief Steward had asked, "Have you read the Operations Manual? "Oh yes." she replied. "Well, you can't have read it properly – look at this!" Whereupon he opened the toilet door, a cloud of white vapour poured out and he quickly closed the door again. "When we get back to Fiji, read the Ops Manual again – properly. You'll see that it's your job to make sure the plugs are in the washbasins whenever we are going into cloud, if you don't, the whole cabin could fill up with it." Of course, he'd arranged the "cloud" by putting a handful of dry ice in the wash basin and turning on the tap.

1958 began with some interference from the weather, with a tropical cyclone heading towards Fiji at the same time as us in the first week. It won; we waited in Samoa for 24 hours. On the next schedule a week later we were warned of very rough water as we approached Samoa from Suva. It certainly was rough. As usual, whenever we touched down onto anything more than a slight ripple, the passengers asked Joe if he had let the co-pilot do the landing. When the water was glass calm they always congratulated **him** on the smooth arrival.

As we drove into Apia, we saw monster ocean swells crashing onto the reef, throwing up fountains of spray. Although there was no wind, the swell was heavy enough to cause large, damaging waves on the normally placid lagoon. Many of the 'fale itis' were in a sorry state, some floating, others leaning at crazy angles and still others with their connection to terra firma washed away. In town, opposite the gap in the reef, the swells were breaking onto the sea wall at the edge of the main road, which was littered with football sized chunks of coral and rock. There was very little tide in the central South Pacific, a foot or two at most, but during the afternoon as high tide approached the waves started washing right across the road, at times waist deep and the spume was flying over the top of the two storey buildings lining the inland side of the street.

Photo 26 - Heavy swells breaking over Apia waterfront January 1958

Our night departure from Samoa was quite interesting; although the tide was by then low the lagoon was still quite rough. The stewardess told us that one of the passengers had been seasick while we were taxi-ing to the take-off point. An unusual occurrence on an aircraft! Aitutaki reported heavy swells on the reef by the main island, but the lagoon was well protected and calm, as was the lagoon at Tahiti. We had dinner at Les Tropiques; there was no more than a light breeze but something peculiar was happening. The water level in the lagoon was much higher than normal, occasionally covering the jetty and periodically it would drop rapidly by a foot or two, causing the water to rush out, roaring around the jetty piles like a river in spate.

Next day I went to Arue. Frida was worried about the house; waves were breaking on the beach and almost reaching her walls. We went for a walk with the children; there was much flood damage. Smashed pirogues and fallen coconut trees were pounding up and down on the shore, one house had vanished and the road was washed away at one point. Yet there was still no wind. There was nothing that could be done to save the house if the situation did get worse so in typical "Aita peapea" Tahitian fashion Frida left the children at a friend's house and we went to the Grand Hotel for dinner, followed by a tour of the night spots until 3.30 a.m. We went to the more sheltered Les Tropiques for the rest of the night.

By the time we went for breakfast the swells had diminished and the lagoon was calm again. We went to town in the afternoon. There were (unusually) two cruise ships in port. The "Lurline" was moored against the quay, but the "Caledonian" was on a buoy out in the harbour. She had been moored astern of the "Lurline" but had rolled so heavily that she had pulled some of the bollards out.

Sputniks 1 and 2 were then the only artificial satellites orbiting Earth; there were no meteorological observations from space and there were very few meteorological reporting stations in the South Pacific. In the absence of wind, we thought that the huge swells must be the results of a seismic disturbance somewhere nearby, but when we went to the Met office before dawn next morning for our departure we learnt that a ship had reported another tropical cyclone to the northwest of Tahiti, apparently moving towards Aitutaki. Dawn was a very feeble affair, with a dark cloud ceiling low overhead, hiding all but the lowest part of Moorea. Joe Shephard decided a 24-hour delay was in order. By 7.30 we were back in our rooms at Les Tropiques. Soon after, it started to rain; the hotel could have been under the Niagara Falls such was the intensity of the downpour. I could see no way of staying dry on the walk over to the dining room for lunch, so I put my clothes in a waterproof bag and went across in my swimming trunks. When I got there rain was pouring through the ceiling, so there didn't seem any point in changing. No one took any notice of my unconventional dining attire.

During lunch the wind arrived and soon reached around sixty miles an hour. We heard that the meteorological office had pieced together what little information they had and believed the cyclone had turned through 180 degrees towards us and was now only 130 miles away. Ready for the worst, the crew settled down for a mammoth liar dice session.

"How I survived the hurricane" would have made a good story, but it didn't happen. Later that afternoon the rain stopped, the clouds evaporated and the wind died away. Next morning, there was some doubt whether we would be able to depart, the normally six foot wide stream flowing into the lagoon between the hotel and town had become a raging torrent the previous afternoon, carrying all sorts of debris with it. Joe sent me in the launch to check our take-off run. We pulled a couple of large logs out of the way but the other heavy flotsam was beyond the point where we would be airborne. We didn't get the hoped-for extra day in Tahiti.

When we arrived in Samoa there were still very heavy swells bursting on the waterfront road near to Aggie Grey's hotel, but apart from a littering of coral boulders no serious damage.

Photo 27 - A Fale iti before the storms

Chapter 18
What next?

The next few months slipped by. On one New Zealand maintenance stopover Roy Tomlin, the chief of TEAL's motor department took me to visit a friend for a fishing trip in the Bay of Islands. We arrived at Pahia after dark and rowed out to the motor launch on which we were to spend the night. The water was full of phosphorescence; the dinghy's bow wave glowed in a luminous V pattern and molten green fire dripped from the oars. The idea next day was to fish for Marlin, but it didn't work out. We needed Kahwai or other smaller fish as bait and the baitfish weren't biting.

On another New Zealand run we went north to the Waipoua Forest to see the country's largest tree, a Kauri named Tane Mahuta. Its circumference then was 43 feet; it is probably very little more today since it was believed to have taken more than twelve hundred years to get to that size. The beach nearby was noted for its toheroas, large mussel-like shellfish. They lived buried in the sand and could move underground remarkably quickly. They were semi-protected; there was a short open season, a size limit and a daily bag limit. Metal digging implements were forbidden; using them would damage the undersized toheroas. We dug with our hands and soon had the 50 over four inches minimum length that we were allowed. Our hosts cooked them for us as soup that evening and in fritters next morning; they were delicious.

With two captains and myself in Fiji and the captains also being qualified in navigation one of us or the navigator could be left off the roster for some of the flights. This gave me the chance to visit other parts of the island. One time Don the Flight Clerk, one of our stewards and his wife and I spent four days in a bungalow on the lagoon edge halfway between Suva and Nandi. The lagoon there was no more than twelve feet deep; a white sand beach shelved gently into the water. Further out isolated coral heads rose from the bottom, looking like Disney castles with spires, turrets and arches. Clouds of small fish in luminous colours swirled around the coral pillars and larger ones peered suspiciously out of the hollows. Further out again, the lagoon shallowed onto the fringing reef.

At low tide we could walk out to the very edge of the coral flat, the ocean swells would rear up thirty or forty yards out and rush towards us until we could look upwards at fish swimming in the glass-clear water a few feet away. Then the wave would topple and crash down in white foam, its energy spent in a harmless surge around our legs.

The Korolevu Beach Hotel was not far away. We went there once to an evening of Fiji dance and feasting. One of the war dances was quite scary, finishing with the Fijian men, their faces streaked with coloured paint, brandishing their clubs and spears and charging directly at the audience. It was not hard to imagine them forgetting the present and reverting to the not far distant days of conflict and cannibalism. Earlier on I had met a very old man who had eaten 'long pig' in his youth.

The feast was excellent. I tried octopus for the first time and really enjoyed it. I have eaten it all around the world since then, but it has always been rubbery and tasteless. The secret must be in the cooking method, I suspect that the Fijians used an earth oven, which cooks very slowly and retains moisture.

At Suva, as well as sailing and racing the Idle Along, I had a few weekends crewing on the 'Tamatea', a 36-foot Bermudan sloop. We always started out from Suva with the self-draining cockpit filled with cans of beer and ice cubes; the owner's judgement of our capacity was brilliant, we never ran out but there were never more than a very few cans left on our return. On the Saturday evening we would anchor off one of the mainland beaches or outlying islands and go ashore for a driftwood-fired barbecue. At least half the crew played guitars or ukuleles and we would sing into the night. Those who fell over first managed to find a berth below, the rest collapsed on deck or on the beach.

Our short stopovers in Samoa didn't allow time for much touring or socialising, but we did have a few evenings out when weather or aircraft problems delayed us. Samoa had been a German colony until the 1914-18 war and German/Samoan families were high in the social order. We were invited by the daughters of one of these families to a home movie evening and saw "Rock around the Clock", which was our first contact with Rock and Roll music.

By the middle of the year I had begun to feel unsettled. Perhaps I was going 'troppo', as the old hands called it, or maybe I started to fear that I was doing so. There was some uncertainty about TEAL's future, it was rumoured that the company might be taken over by QANTAS. The Solent operation had been expected to finish in August, with TEAL operating a DC-6 land plane direct from Suva to Bora Bora, linking with Resau Aerienne Interinsulaire's Catalinas for the120 miles from there to Tahiti, but the N.Z. Minister for Air had requested the Solent's extension for up to two years while the disused wartime strips in Samoa and Aitutaki were re-built. On the 'going troppo' side, staying in Tahiti had its attractions and possibilities. I had been putting out feelers about joining RAI. They had lost one of the Catalinas in a landing accident in February, but had a replacement on its way and were expected to expand. An American company was trying to set up a new airline using a Constellation from Honolulu to Bora Bora and a Solent Mark 3 from there to Tahiti. I wrote to them and had a reply saying that they were not yet ready to start recruiting but would keep me informed. Moves were afoot to build a new airport on Tahiti itself, which would inevitably lead to air services being started to many of the outlying islands. Another way-out notion was that I'd spend a few years working and saving while I built a cruising yacht on which I could retire and sail around the Pacific for the rest of my days.

On the other hand, getting away from the islands might save me from the fate of so many Europeans who slipped into a South Pacific beachcomber's existence. I met several of them around Suva and Papeete. One had left the

Royal Navy at the end of the war with enough money to buy a Motor Torpedo Boat, with the idea of carrying tourists around the Mediterranean. That didn't pay; he made a living by smuggling cigarettes until he was caught. He moved to Tahiti and bought a schooner; again it didn't pay. His next venture was a chicken farm on land owned by his Tahitian girlfriend. The hens didn't lay enough eggs; by the time I met him, he was living off the last few chickens, having eaten the rest.

New Zealand offered the chance of a job with Freddie Ladd's Tourist Air Travel. Roy Tomlin had told me that Freddie had asked if Roy thought I might be interested in flying the Widgeons. I had told Gloria when I joined TEAL that I was on a two-year contract; she had recently written saying she was looking forward to my expected return to England. I had a romantic notion that if I did go back to England I might pick up where I had left off with her and if I did get a job with TAT or another New Zealand operator, I might persuade her to emigrate to New Zealand with me.

One effect of my uncertainty was that I broke off my relationship with Frida, I think this was part of the not wanting to end up beach-combing aspect. There are few things in my life that I regret, but I am ashamed of the way I walked out on her. I never saw her again, but I did hear later from one of her friends that she had settled down with someone else and was 'tres contente' with 'un tres gentil homme'.

In July my immediate future was settled without my input. I received a letter saying that I was to be transferred back to Auckland for conversion onto the DC6. In itself this was not such a bad thing, moving to a more advanced aircraft was a good career step. My problem was that the Company wanted me to agree that I would stay with TEAL for at least another five years. Even the two year extra commitment I had taken on for my extended National Service had seemed a life sentence; five years appeared an eternity. I wrote to the Company saying that although there was nothing they could do if I gave the guarantee they asked for and subsequently broke my word, I was not prepared to give it.

I fully expected that there would be some further discussion and negotiation and I would be able to stay on the flying boat operation until its future was settled. Maybe I could have a couple of months unpaid leave and use my airline travel concession to visit home and Gloria before committing myself to the DC6 conversion. Instead another letter arrived terminating my employment after the next Fiji to Auckland flight in August. No one likes to think they are dispensable; my pride was hurt. I should have made my feelings known but my reaction was "if that's the way they want it, well, *** them, I'm off". So during the next three Tahiti round trips, I made my farewells to my Tahitian, Samoan and Cook Island friends and in Fiji sold the dinghy and packed my few belongings. I left Fiji on the morning of 14th August 1958 and co-piloted the aircraft on the seven-hour flight to Auckland, which brought my total time on the Solent to 1,788 hours. That was my last ever flight off or onto water.

ZK-AMO carried on operating the last International scheduled flying boat air service in the world for another two years, making her final Coral Route flight in September 1960. People often ask me why flying boats died out, when they could alight on any reasonably sized piece of water, without the enormous cost of an airport. Unfortunately flying boat operation isn't that simple. For a start, there are many populated areas of the world where there aren't any large bodies of water within a reasonable distance of major cities. On the ground at airports, the aircraft are directed along marked routes, with radio control and at the busier ones traffic lights, enabling taxying in close proximity. Runway and taxiway lighting would be extremely difficult to arrange on water. Water-borne vehicles can't be manoeuvred as precisely as land-borne ones. When a land aircraft stops, it stays in one place – there are no currents and it takes a very strong wind indeed to move an aircraft with its brakes on. Wind and currents make it practically impossible for a flying boat to remain in one spot. The area required for taxying, parking, servicing and loading/unloading more than a few flying boats at once would be enormous. And then there is the problem of bad weather approach aids, like the Instrument Landing System. These need to be fixed firmly in one place, not bobbing up and down in the waves. The logistics of ferrying fuel, freight and passengers to and from the aircraft at a major flying boat base, on the scale of, say, Heathrow, would be mind-boggling. There is also the problem of other users of most water areas. On our Coral Route operation, we had no exclusive right to the lagoons or harbours; we had to avoid other craft when landing or taking off. Auckland Harbour in the 1950s was relatively uncluttered, but finding a clear area on which to alight near the 'City of Sails' today would be quite a problem.

Chapter 19
House recycler, docker, farm hand and barman

My intention on arrival in New Zealand was to spend a short time playing the tourist and then look for a passage home. This plan was scuppered by New Zealand hospitality. Firstly Roy Tomlin and his wife Ruth invited me to stay with them and then kept suggesting I stayed a bit longer so they could show me more of North Island. This usually involved going off on a Friday to stay the weekend with friends and sometimes staying at home for the weekend while friends stayed with them.

To remain solvent I took on several temporary jobs. One was with an entrepreneurial character who made a living by carefully demolishing old houses and selling the salvaged materials for new buildings. Virtually all the houses in Auckland were built of Kauri, a long-lasting timber from trees that were almost extinct by the 1950s, having been logged out or cleared for farming. In Northland many of the grass paddocks were still littered with the skeletal stumps of these once magnificent trees, which rivalled the giant sequoias of the United States for size and longevity. Kauri timber was therefore a valuable commodity and with other items like lead piping, sanitary fittings, window glass and even carefully extracted and straightened nails, gave him a more than adequate income. Unfortunately he was later on 'done' by the Inland Revenue. For years he had declared a very low income and had paid no tax. It seemed that the IR Department had a couple of people whose sole job was to scan the 'For Sale' columns in the newspapers and compare the value of items offered with the claimed income of the offerers. He couldn't explain just how he'd come by the cash to buy the 'Bechstein Grand Piano, only five years old' he wanted to sell.

Another part time job was that of 'seagull', which was the full-time dockers' epithet for casual workers on the Auckland docks. I did this only on those weekends when visitors came to Roy's, because it paid time-and-a-half rates on Saturdays and double on Sundays. It was not exactly hard work. This was before the days of containers; we were unloading small items like cases of whisky, boxes of canned goods, sacks of rice and such by hand, using porters' barrows. Each ship had three teams allocated. While one team was in the ship's hold loading the barrows, one was on the dock unloading and the third was waiting for the first to emerge from the hold. The waiting team then entered the ship, the unloading team took a rest and the emergers unloaded. So Sunday working was paid at almost treble time rate for the time spent actually doing anything productive.

The plans for an early return to England ended while Cliff Lecouter was paying me for some garden landscaping. "You can't leave without seeing South Island. Get yourself a second hand car and have a look round" he said. I didn't take much persuading. He gave me a long list of people I had to visit and give his regards to; I bought a pre-war Austin Twelve, packed my worldly belongings into it and set off for Wellington and the inter-island ferry.

New Zealand in the 1950s was still very much a pioneering country, especially South Island. The Automobile Association map I purchased indicated "unexplored" for most of the West Coast of South Island. Few roads were tar-sealed. Even the main North Island highway from Auckland to Wellington was loose gravel for most of the way. The ferry I travelled on was a far cry from today's roll-on roll-off high-speed catamaran 'Lynx'; cars were hoisted on board by crane. It went to Lyttelton near Christchurch rather than Picton in the Marlborough Sounds, so it was an over-night voyage. Christchurch in those days looked so much like a small English town, but with better weather, that I spent a couple of days there trying to persuade myself that perhaps I didn't want to go back home.

The road from Christchurch to Timaru must be the most boring in New Zealand. Almost dead straight, it passes through flat country with small mixed farming fields often hidden by coniferous hedges planted as windbreaks. Until I returned there in 1997 my only abiding memory of the road was of the bridge across the Rakaia River. Opened in 1939 and New Zealand's longest at just over a mile, the bridge was exactly as I remembered it, a low concrete structure, one of the few things that hadn't changed in the intervening 40 years.

After a night in Timaru and another at Dunedin, my next stop was at a sheep farm near Berwick, in an idyllic situation to the east of the Lammerlaw Range. A side valley, heavily wooded on the slopes each side, ran down from north to south, opening out into a flat area of grass paddocks by the dirt road leading up the main Waipori valley. The farmhouse, with a clump of cypresses, was situated on a knoll at the head of the flats to the side of a trout stream. The track from the main road to the house crossed the stream by a cast iron bridge, which looked strong enough to have been built for a railway.

The owner, Bill Kofoed, had a very laid-back approach to life. He had cleared and grassed small areas on the valley sides but many of his sheep would be hidden away among the trees. When shearing time came round, his view was that there was little to be gained by charging all round the slopes mustering, the sheep would come down to the stream when they were thirsty enough, or into the pastures when the grass on the hill was eaten out. Where his neighbours would be out at all hours at lambing time, he reckoned that enough lambs would survive without his aid, losing a few didn't matter. He didn't bother to plant potatoes for the kitchen; at some time in the past one of the paddocks by the road had been used for arable crops and a patch of potatoes remained growing wild in an awkward corner. Easy enough to dig a few out when needed!

Deer of many species, possums, rabbits and hares, with no predators to keep their numbers down, had all become pests since their introduction into New Zealand. Deer were not common on this farm, instead there were bush sheep, descendants of the earliest introductions. Their competition for the available feed was not a problem, but their inter-breeding with the farmed animals was hindering efforts to improve the bloodlines with expensive imported merino rams. When the opportunity arose to gather a band of friends, relatives or visitors like myself, Bill organised a sheep shoot. Some of us would be stationed in strategic positions and the others drove the animals out from the bush. The farm lambs were de-tailed when young, so the instructions were very simple – "If it has a tail, shoot it!" Cliff LeCouter had loaned me a .22 rifle, which did not require a licence although a .303 did. So I was told to take out the bush lambs.

I also got entrapped into a hare shoot one night. Armed with a shotgun, I stood in a sawn-off 45-gallon oil drum lashed onto the back of a tractor, while Bill drove at full tilt round the paddocks swinging a spotlight from side to side until he located a hare. Deflection shooting had not been my forte in the Sabre; coping with the deflection from a moving tractor to a running hare, while trying not to be bounced out of the oil drum, was beyond my capabilities. The hares won hands down.

The Government paid bounties on the four pests mentioned, claimable at any Post Office. All one had to do was present the defined animal part. I think that for rabbits or hares it was ears; for possums it was the tail.

One of the local characters made a living out of these bounties; his particular speciality was the possum. He trapped these instead of shooting them. That way he could cut off their tails, then let them go to breed more possums and so maintain his source of income!

My next move took me across the Lammerlaw Range, an area reminiscent of the North Yorkshire Pennines, to Heriot. I stayed there a few days with another of Cliff LeCouteur's friends, who took me on a very successful trout fishing trip and an unsuccessful sea fishing expedition. The sea fishing target was Blue Cod, apparently the most sought-after of the country's saltwater species. We fished from a rocky platform at the foot of some high cliffs and caught nothing; when the tide came in we had a little more success spearing flounders from a nearby sandy beach.

From Heriot I crossed over into the Clutha valley and followed the river past Roxburgh and Alexandra. The country was now much more rugged, with mountains rising to 5,000 feet each side of the road. At Clyde, just north of Alexandra, the river emerged from the Cromwell Gorge, where the fast-flowing Clutha left very little room for a road and a railway. The two interwove, with un-gated and un-signalled narrow angled intersections. In places the railway ran for ten yards or more down the centre of the road. I had been cautioned about driving through the gorge at night; the single headlight approaching from the opposite direction would as likely as not be on a locomotive rather than on a motorcycle! Both the original road and the abandoned railway now lie beneath the waters of Lake Dunstan, formed by the Clyde Dam. The old town of Cromwell was also drowned, although some of the buildings were rescued and re-erected on the shore of the new lake.

At Cromwell the Karawau River comes in from the west to join the Clutha. The first few miles from Cromwell are now an arm of Lake Dunstan, but from Ripponvale through to Queenstown the Karawau Gorge is today little changed from the way I remembered it, except that there are few traces of the 1950s road still visible. In the 50s I drove across the wooden Karawau bridge, 15 miles from Queenstown, where the old road crossed from the south to the north bank. Built in 1880, the bridge has long been closed to traffic and is now used for bungy jumping.

Just north of the new concrete bridge over the Shotover River, 10 km. from Queenstown, another old wooden bridge can still be seen, although it is fenced off to road or foot traffic. A tarmacadam road along the riverbank leads past the bridge, this, south of the bridge is part of the old road. On the right just before the bridge a single story building, now a bed and breakfast house, was the 'Ferry Inn' in the 1950s. It was owned by Fred 'Popeye' Lucas, although his wife Lorie was the licensee. Cliff LeCouteur had suggested I called in to say 'hello' to Popeye. When I walked into the pub in December 1958 there was no problem recognising him, the likeness to the cartoon character was uncanny, even without the corncob pipe!

Once again I was invited to stay for a few days as a family rather than paying guest. After several days, when each time I indicated I should be moving on but was pressed to stay a bit longer – "you haven't seen … ", "been to…", "tried the…" I said I'd only stay if there was something I could do to help out with the pub. This was countered by a statement that if I did help, I would be paid. So we came to an agreement that I would take on the job of barman.

The legal closing time in those days was six p.m. and pubs were closed all day on Sundays. Lorie stuck to the Sunday observance laws but for the rest of the week we were, shall we say, flexible. Being well off the beaten track we got away with it until the local policeman walked in at 10.00 p.m. one evening. Like rabbits going to ground when a fox appears on the scene, the clientele departed through every doorway. The copper was quite mild. He said he'd had no choice but to stop, because he was driving back from the Arrowtown courtroom with two of the Magistrates. His main beef was that he'd had to walk two hundred yards from the nearest place on the road where he could park because of all the other cars outside. Matters were not helped by Lorie's small pyjama-clad son, who burst into the bar saying "Mummy, Mummy, a lot of men ran through my room and jumped out of the window". "You see. Mrs Lucas", he reproved "it even frightens the children" But he left it at that, merely suggesting that perhaps Popeye should convert the tennis court into a car park.

A month or so later the full majesty of the law descended, in the form of a flying squad from Dunedin. It was just after eleven p.m. and I had my back to the door, drawing a tot of whisky from an optic. When I turned round, the bar was full of blue uniform. This time there was no escape, there was more blue outside each window. We would still have got away with it; when asked, "When did you buy that drink?" everyone said "Oh, I didn't pay for it, Mrs. Lucas is giving a party." Except for one idiot, who admitted to buying his drink ten minutes earlier. I didn't go to court; Mrs. Lucas pleaded guilty on my behalf and paid the £5 fine.

We did not always keep the bar open far beyond the legal hours; when trade was slack we would close shop fairly well on time. I had many opportunities to fish the evening rise on nearby Lake Hayes. In those days it was primarily a rainbow trout water and the size of the fish I caught was remarkably constant; ninety percent were between four and five pounds. I visited the lake again in 2000; there were no rainbows then, just brown trout and perch.

Chapter 20
Scenic flight, Greenstone River and Milford Track

Popeye's main business was not the pub, but Southern Scenic Airservices, based at Queenstown. When he bought the pub, his great rival, Fred Ladd of Tourist Air Travel, sent a telegram on the lines of "Congratulations brilliant move. Get back paltry wages pilots earn when drown sorrows your pub near airfield" Southern Scenic flew a variety of small aircraft. They operated a few scheduled services, air-dropped supplies for the New Zealand Government and other organisations, seeded lakes and rivers with trout fry and tried out just about anything that could be done by or from aircraft, but their most lucrative activity was, as the name implied, scenic flights over the Southern Alps. On one of the rare occasions when one of these scenic flights was not full Popeye offered me the empty seat.

The aircraft was a De Havilland DH89 Dominie, the military version of the Dragon Rapide, a seven-seater biplane of pre-war vintage. With its struts, wires and Gypsy engines it was effectively a two-engined Tiger Moth, well suited to the all grass airfield of that time. We took off across Lake Wakatipu and climbed into the mountains. After showing us mountain peaks, snowfields, glaciers, waterfalls, herds of deer and other features of the Alps, Popeye descended into one of the deeper glacial valleys and flew close to the southern wall, passing almost within the spray of yet another cascade. He then turned ninety degrees and flew straight towards the opposite cliffs, which dropped a sheer two thousand feet to the river below. Casually draping his right arm over the back of his seat, he turned to face the passengers and began a long discourse on the geology of the region. I don't know about the others, but as the rock face ahead loomed closer and closer I had an almost overwhelming desire to shout at him to look where he was going. Just as I started to raise my hand to gesticulate frantically and alert him to the now imminent disaster, still looking back at us he turned sharply left down the valley. All part of the show, he told me later, he had practised the speech until he'd got the timing perfect and he liked watching the passenger's facial expressions.

Eventually it became time to move on, but before leaving Queenstown I wanted to see from the ground some of the backcountry that I had seen during the flight. So I left my car and belongings at the pub, threw a sleeping bag, some clothes and a large piece of polythene into my rucksack, carried my fishing rod in one hand and a bag of eatables in the other and went down to the jetty in town from where the coal-fired twin screw steamer "Earnslaw" sailed on her journeys round Lake Wakatipu. 51 metres in length, she had been pre-fabricated at Dunedin on the coast, taken by rail to Kingston at the southern end of the lake, assembled there and launched in 1912. In the 1950s there was no road access to the western side of the lake so the Earnslaw was a lifeline for the sheep station residents over there. Even today the dirt road from Kinloch at the north end of the lake finishes just 10 km. south at Elfin Bay. My destination was a farm jetty a mile or two further south, near the mouth of the Greenstone River.

I spent a week on the Greenstone, fishing my way up to Lake McKeller near the source and met only one other person. On the first day I had been looking for a musterers' hut some way up the valley, but by evening still hadn't found it, so I made a shelter with the piece of polythene and some poles cut from a shrub and spent the night in that. In the morning I woke to the scent of frying bacon and followed my nose a few yards through the bush. A walker from the other direction **had** found the hut and was cooking his breakfast. The rest of the week I saw no one.

There were many red deer in the valley; I almost collided with a small group of them when I rounded a bend in the trail through a patch of bushes. Another indication of the remoteness of the area was the small bird that flew down to perch on my knee when I sat with my back against a tree for a breather! When I re-walked part of the Greenstone track in 2001 I met dozens of other walkers and the sound of aircraft and helicopters on sight-seeing flights to and from Milford Sound was unceasing.

In 1959 the Milford Track was another of my must do's. It was only thirty miles across the mountains from Queenstown to Te Anau Downs where walkers joined the launch for the lake cruise to the start of the track, but a hundred miles drive. I took my fishing rod with me. At Glade House, the first hut on the track, I asked one of the staff how many anglers had fished the Clinton River since the season opened some three months earlier. "You're the first" was the reply. The first day's walk had been very short and there was time not only to investigate the fishing before the evening meal, but also time enough for the resulting catch of rainbow trout to be cooked and shared with some of the party.

Next day we continued upstream along the bank of the Clinton River to the Pampelona Hut. On day three we followed the river further upstream before climbing over the McKinnon Pass and descending to the Quintin hut. We were fortunate to have recent rain to keep the many waterfalls flowing and then dry weather for the walk. The river was glass-clear and I marked down a couple of good pools where large rainbow trout were lying. We reached the hut early enough for me to rush back over the 3,500 feet high pass and have a couple of hours fishing before dark. We stayed two nights at Quintin; three five-pound trout provided the next evening's meal for those who had missed out at Glade House.

Nowadays helicopters are available to carry things to otherwise inaccessible places, but in 1959 all the supplies for the Milford track were taken in by mule. Except the grand piano at the Quintin hut, which took pride of place in the lounge. That had been ferried across Milford Sound and then transported to the hut by leap-frogging it, strapped to a bogie cart, over two lengths of narrow gauge railway track.

From Quintin the trail led alongside the Arthur River and past Lake Ada to Milford Sound, where we boarded a launch for a short tour of the fjord. We were lucky again with the weather, although the saying is "It only rains twice a week on average at Milford – the first time for four days and the second for three." We had rain overnight to fill the waterfalls and the clouds broke during our boat trip so we could see them. The weather stayed fine for the spectacular coach ride back to Te Anau Downs via the Homer Tunnel and the Eglington valley.

Photo 28 - My pre-war Austin, still going well

Re-united with the Austin, the touring continued, criss-crossing South Island. I've lost track of the sequence, but I traversed the three major passes through the Southern Alps (Haast, Arthur's and Lewis) and saw Mt. Cook from the Hermitage and Mt. Aspiring from Glendhu Bay near Wanaka. In the autumn I was in the Roxburgh area in the Clutha River valley. Atlantic salmon had been introduced to the river many years earlier, but when the Roxburgh dam was built they could get no further upstream; the pool below the dam was, in the season, crammed with them. I wanted to try the fishing but needed to top up my funds, so I found a motor camp where I could stay very cheaply and worked for six weeks picking apples. Financially this stay was a success, but like the hares at Berwick, the salmon also won hands down. The closest I got to catching one was having a fair sized fish follow the spinner to within two feet of the bank, but then turn away.

Finally time ran out and a return to England beckoned more and more. I went back to Auckland via the Lyttleton ferry and Wellington and started organising a passage home. This took a while; I had hoped to spend some time in Tonga, Samoa and Tahiti on the way but there were not many ships travelling between these places and after investigating various possibilities I found there would be more time than I could afford at Tonga and Samoa between sailings. After a few weeks I had to settle for a passage on the Southern Cross to Tahiti, calling at Suva, Fiji for a few hours on the way. I would then have six weeks in Tahiti before departing on the Johan van Oldenbarnevelt via the Panama Canal, Fort Lauderdale (the port for Miami) and Bermuda, en route to Southampton.

While I was waiting for sailing day, John Connel, the colleague from 66 Squadron days, arrived in Auckland on leave. His three uncles were camping at Lake Tarawera, near Rotorua, on a trout fishing expedition and John invited me to join them with him. At the road's end we embarked on a small boat, which took us to the eastern end of the lake near the Tarawera River outlet. A hundred yards into the tea tree bush, we found our tent. I thought I knew what camping was; but this was camping de luxe. Full standing room in an army-style square tent, a carpet over the groundsheet, iron bedsteads with mattresses, sheets, pillows and blankets – and two armchairs! The fishing was superb, with the majority of the rainbows we caught in the 8 to 15 pound range. The uncles had set up a fish smoker in a natural chimney in an overhanging rock; with our contribution to the catch they had nearly half a ton of smoked trout to take home. They complained that it had been a poor season – no twenty-pounders that year.

That fishing expedition rounded off my gap year in New Zealand. Why I didn't stay there is a mystery to me now. I had the chance to re-join TEAL when one of the Operations management staff told me I could go back to them for the DC6 conversion without signing any five-year agreement. Perhaps the thought of living in or near Auckland didn't appeal, I much preferred South Island. New Zealand is an incredibly varied country; one doesn't have to go far to find just about any type of scenery or geological feature. Geysers, glaciers, fjords, alpine mountains, live and extinct volcanoes, mighty rivers, vast lakes, waterfalls, temperate rain forest, near desert, badlands, deserted beaches, extensive cave systems – New Zealand has it all, but most of it in South Island.

I sold the car in Auckland in mid-July and travelled to Wellington by coach to embark on the Southern Cross.

Chapter 21
Homeward bound with diversions

The Southern Cross was quite new, having entered service in 1955, but I thought not up to the standard of the Orontes. Post-war austerity was still evident in her design. In particular, the cabin partitions were very flimsy. As one of my cabin mates remarked one morning, "You can hear the fellow next door change his mind!"

A ticket to travel on a ship was rather less flexible than an airline ticket. If you missed the boat, well, tough. There wouldn't be another one along for a good few months. My Southern Cross ticket to Papeete carried the warning that if, due to weather conditions, the boat couldn't get into the harbour, I would have to pay the cost of onward carriage to the next port where the shipping company would disembark me with no further responsibility for my onward travel or for my return to the missed out stop. I was nearly stranded with insufficient funds at Suva, in Fiji, when I went ashore to see my old colleagues. After a fairly beery session, I set out back to the ship in what should have been good time, only to find the streets near the wharf solidly blocked with a throng of spectators and a police band. When at last I fought my way through to the edge of the wharf, the ship's bow lines had been cast off, the bow was swinging away and all the gangways had been pulled in. The only entrance still open was near the stern, with a four-foot, widening gap between the door and the wharf. Fortunately it was a downhill jump.

Arriving at Papeete I found little had changed from when I had left a year before, but somehow the ambience had gone out of the place for me. Perhaps it was simply that I wasn't in the company of the crew. Living there at my own expense rather than TEAL's might also have had something to do with it; it was not the cheapest part of the world for a tourist and my funds were limited. I took a room in a hotel for a few days and then was asked if I could "house sit" a bungalow near the centre of town while the owners, friends of Roy Tomlin, were away. A couple of weeks there put me far enough behind the spending line that I was able to fund a visit to Moorea, travelling on one of the inter-island schooners. Although they had engines, many of them still used sail propulsion whenever the winds were favourable. The journey was short enough that I didn't have to use the "fare iti". This was a privy suspended on poles over the stern; I heard that in a rough sea it could give a dizzying ride.

I had seen Pao Pao (Cook's) Bay many times from the air but the view from the deck of the schooner was even more breath taking. Framed by cardboard cut-out ridges, with riotous vegetation tumbling down to the shoreline coconut palms and the rainbow tinted shallows of the shelving reefs, deep blue water in the channel mirrored the trade-wind sky above. The only signs of human life along the bay were a few small palm-thatched fares, some built out over the water on coconut trunk piles. At the head of the bay more fares were clustered along the shore. The largest of these proved to be a small hotel, where I found a room. It transpired that I was the sole non-resident 'popa'a' on the island at the time and my arrival caused considerable interest. During the next few weeks I was shown around the village and the vanilla plantations, taken to the reef on snorkel and spear gun trips, invited to attend a wedding and in general treated as one of the family.

The wedding led on to a picnic. It was suggested that my contribution could be two cases of Hinano beer, some cans of butter and a couple of loaves. When the truck arrived next morning there didn't seem to be much, in truth there was nothing, in the way of eatables to be seen on board. We stopped at the village store for my purchases, which seemed somewhat inadequate for the number of people in the party, but my suggestion of a few tins of this and that was firmly rejected as unnecessary.

After bumping a few kilometres along the coast road we came to a bridge over a small stream. The truck stopped. I sat in amazement as the whole crowd of Tahitians leapt into the water and vanished up-stream. The sound of laughter and much splashing diminished then resounded as they returned, laden with newly plaited baskets brimming with fresh-water crayfish. Another stop and another foray resulted in a haul of 'fei' (like bananas, but needing cooking to be palatable) and limes. The food situation was looking up!

Further along the road, a pirogue was waiting for us on the beach. Several ferry trips took us to a small motu in the lagoon. Here I was introduced to the technique of throw-net fishing. Even my rather inept handling soon produced a haul of six-inch long sardine-like fish, plus a few larger parrotfish and rock cod. A fire was started and small rocks were put on

Photo 29 - Transport across the lagoon

the coals. While the fei, the larger fish and the crayfish were grilling on these, we dealt with the 'sardines'. We made bowls from large leaves pinned together with palm midrib splinters into which we squeezed the limes. Then the fish heads were cut off and the entrails drawn out. Holding the tails, we sloshed the fish a few times (according to taste) through the lime juice before eating them raw. The notion of raw fish may disgust many people, but this way they were delicious! So too were the grilled fei, fish and crayfish.

After the meal and a bottle or two of Hinano a doze in the shade of the tafano trees was indicated. Later we swam in the lagoon, sang a few Polynesian songs to the accompaniment of a guitar and ukuleles and finished off the beer before returning to the mainland and the village.

Moorea produced a small amount of vanilla, the seed pod of a climbing orchid plant. I went up into a hanging valley with the son of one of the vanilla 'plantation' owners and a girl whose task was to hand-pollinate the orchid flowers. It seemed that there were no moths on the island with long enough tongues to reach the nectar, so the flowers could not produce fruit pods without human aid. It was a three-hour round trip and the 'plantation' was no larger than an average garden. There were only twenty or so flowers on the plants when we got there. It did not seem a very economic crop to me, but I suppose time was no object in island life and the task of fertilising the vanilla was just a side product of a pleasant stroll.

Scuba diving was in its early days, I did not have the chance to try it, but spent much time drifting around in the blood-heat warmth of the lagoon snorkelling. On our way to the reef for one of the snorkel trips we put ashore halfway down the bay. My companions dug around one of the bushes and cut off some of the roots. They pounded these between two rocks, then wrapped the crushed material in leaves. At the reef, they placed the prepared packets in holes in the coral. A few minutes later a variety of fish floated to the surface. The Tahitian lads scooped some of the fish up and put them into fish traps made of split bamboo. Those they did not keep recovered and swam away unharmed a little later. Evidently the roots contained some sort of narcotic.

One day I hired a mobylette bicycle and went all round the island. The road was no more than a sand track on the narrow flat area between the mountains and the lagoon. There was very little habitation; just a few thatched huts grouped together at long intervals, among the ever-present coconut palms. On the southern shore I came across a half derelict jetty built out of coral blocks and walked out to the end. It was a strong trade wind day, the lagoon was full of white horses and there was a sort of steely look about the ocean beyond the reef. To this day I remember the feeling of utter desolation I experienced. I cannot explain why I was so affected. It may have been the impact of the emptiness before me, with nothing but ocean between the Antarctic and myself. Perhaps the Tupapaus (spirits) of the glory that once was Polynesia were hovering in the vicinity. Or maybe it was simply that I knew my time in the Islands was running out and I had the premonition then that I would never return. Whatever the cause, I fled back to Cook's Bay without stopping.

A few days later I went back to Tahiti and a few days later still the Johan van Oldenbarnevelt arrived en-route to Southampton. I went on board the ship late in the evening garlanded with heis from friends and after leaving my kit in the cabin, went back on deck for a last look at Papeete. Legend has it that as the ship departs one should throw a hei into the sea. If it drifts ashore, it means one will return, if it drifts out to sea, then it betokens a last farewell. Mine sank!

I think I was incredibly lucky to have seen Tahiti when I did, before the airport was built and the tourists started flooding in and before the nuclear testing began at Mururoa, which caused an influx of military personnel to Papeete. Tahiti in the 1950s was such a happy-go-lucky place. Tahitians didn't really need to work; there were plenty of fish in the lagoons and coconuts on the palm trees. Wild coffee grew on the hillsides; breadfruit, taro, bananas, plantains, sugar cane, oranges, limes, pamplemousse and many other fruits were to be found in the vallees. The streams were full of freshwater crayfish (small ones frequently came with the flush water in the Quinn's urinals!). There were wild pigs and wild fowl in the mountains. Some paid employment was available, but the staff turnover was very high. A Tahitian or Tahitienne would take a job, but as soon as enough had been earned to buy the bicycle or whatever it was they wanted they would quit.

One had to be careful not to be too complimentary when admiring any possession of a Tahitian. Don, the flight clerk and I were on our way to town one day when Don said to the driver "Fati, that's a very nice shirt you're wearing". "You like it?" Fati asked. "Yes" said Don. Whereupon Fati replied "It's yours" and started to take it off –while still driving! The few tourists that did reach Tahiti and stayed at "Les Tropiques" would find that on departure the staff would give **them** gifts rather than expecting tips. This "what's mine is yours" attitude extended beyond material possessions. A Tahitian friend would say "That's my mother over there". A day or two later, a different mother might be introduced and the following week yet another. Very confusing, until you learned that it was common practice for a mother to give a child to a sister, cousin or even a friend, sometimes receiving a different child in return. There was really no need of orphanages in Polynesia; no child could possibly be homeless.

Theft was unknown; there was no need to lock one's hotel room, house or car. Once, on the flight back to Suva, I realised that I'd left my TEAL shoulder bag behind. When we returned a week later, I retraced my steps round all the places I might have left it. Finally I came to the Vaihiria café on the waterfront, went to the counter and said "I lost my TEAL bag last week, I might have left it under the table where I was sitting", turned to point out, "over ...." and there it was, under the table. My camera and money were still inside when I retrieved it.

Prostitution also was virtually impossible; there were too many enthusiastic amateurs for the oldest profession to compete with. I once had an embarrassing experience at the Lafayette. I was on my own and when I went in I was invited to join a group of Tahitians. In the early hours I was getting on well dancing with a vahine who spoke very little French. I spoke only a few words of Tahitian, between dances another girl helped with translation. At closing time we hung back while everyone else left. When we went out hand in hand what seemed to be a serious argument (in Tahitian) was going on between one of the men and the rest of the group. I asked the French-speaking girl what was happening. "Oh, it's just that her husband doesn't want her to go to your hotel with you" she told me. I rapidly let go of the vahine. "No, there's no problem, he doesn't mind you sleeping with her, but it will have to be at their house" she continued. I politely declined this offer and took the French-speaking girl back to the hotel instead.

I have never returned to Tahiti and think it better that I do not. "Never go back" is usually good advice; one can go back in space but not in time. Many older Tahitians refer to the 1950s as "La belle époque" and indeed for me it was. I am sure that if I did go back I would be very disappointed, not only by the physical changes that have taken place with most of the old familiar buildings, shops, bars, restaurants, hotels and other visible features replaced but also by the changes in life style. On my way to New Zealand by Air New Zealand 747 in 1998 I asked the stewardesses how they liked Papeete and was horrified to be told that they didn't go out of the hotel, it was too dangerous. From all I have read and heard, it seems that tourism has fatally altered the way Tahitians used to live. Better that I remember Tahiti as it was.

Chapter 22
Completing the circumnavigation

The Johan van Oldenbarnevelt was a pre-war ship and retained a degree of faded elegance although by 1959 she had become a one-class vessel. As I was to discover later in their pubs, the Dutch favoured a heavy decorating style, even the tables were carpeted! The liner also laid claim to the longest name of any ship in the world, so she was generally referred to as the JvO. A few years later she was bought by a Greek shipping company, re-fitted and re-named Lakonia. Superstition has it that one should never re-name a ship. Within a few months of the name change Lakonia caught fire on a cruise to the Canary Islands with the loss of 128 lives. She sank west of Gibraltar while being towed towards port a week after the fire started.

There was no drama on my voyage home; we ploughed our way across an ocean that lived up to its Pacific name. I was feeling fairly miserable for the first few days, regretting my impulse to leave the Southern Hemisphere and as we passed through the Marquesas close to one of the larger islands I found the temptation to leap overboard and swim to the shore for a beachcomber's life almost irresistible.

A day or two into the voyage I learnt from a fellow passenger that there were some empty bunks in steerage, although when I bought my ticket I had been told the only berth available was in a two bed cabin. I went to the purser and was able to change to steerage, with the difference in fare to be refunded after arrival in England. This allowed me to spend my reserve of cash on board, with no need to retain anything for the U.K. Having enough to keep myself in beer and cigarettes for the rest of the journey and a bit to spare for a trip ashore at Bermuda, cheered me up considerably. Steerage accommodation was reminiscent of Youth Hostel dormitories or RAF barrack block rooms, with around fifty two-storey bunks, but because JvO was a one-class ship we were not confined to the steerage section and were allowed anywhere in the passenger areas.

After passing the Marquesas there was nothing but empty ocean to see until we arrived at Balboa. The Panama Canal was much more impressive than Suez had been, the immensity of the Pacific side Miraflores and Atlantic side Gatun locks was awe inspiring. The English canal system with its narrow boats was a dinky toy set in comparison. Recently in 2003 I see that a modern cruise ship paid a record toll of $217,500 dollars for a transit through the canal. The Johan van Oldenbarnevelt probably cost little more than that when she was built in the 1930s.

We must have passed through the chain of Caribbean Islands at night, I remember seeing nothing until we steamed into Fort Lauderdale in Florida. There was a group of Tahitians on board on their way to the U.S.A. to join the Mormon Church. They were being met at Fort Lauderdale, entertained for the day and then taken to Miami airport for onward travel. None of them spoke English and they asked me to accompany them as a translator. So I had a free day out with them and saw a little more of the U.S.A. than just the quayside at Fort Lauderdale. The only thing I remember from that first visit 'stateside' was that we went to the airport on an expressway, our host missed the turn into the airport and we had to drive about 10 miles further to a flyover junction to get back to the airport slip road. Of course, there had been no motorways in England when I left, so the situation was new to me.

Bermuda was the last stop on the voyage. Somehow the sight of scarlet pelargoniums set against whitewashed walls brings the island into mind even now. I recall little else other than a bare almost tree-less landscape with many white-washed single storied houses set in colourful gardens, a cloudless sky and a luminous sea dappled with white horses.

Chapter 23
Ice cream and re-treading

When the JvO arrived at Southampton in October my parents met me and I went back to stay with them in Goodmayes. The employment situation for pilots was dire; no airlines seemed to be recruiting. I had just ten American dollars left in ready cash. I had the refund from the JvO fare to claim and I hoped I might be able to regain a loan of £50 that I had made to a friend four years earlier. I soon found out that I needed at least ten hours flying recency before I could revalidate my U.K. pilot licence. I needed gainful employment to pay for this, but I had no qualifications for anything other than flying, so I found work with Walls Ice Cream Limited, selling from a van. They had modernised from the 'stop me and buy one' tricycles of pre-war times. The pay was low, but there was a commission on sales.

A working day began with calls at specific houses, farms and other locations, moving on afterwards to driving the streets of housing estates, mostly those in the then new town of Harlow. Walls' policy was to stick to a regular timetable for ad hoc sales, relying on customer loyalty to wait for Walls rather than buying from the first van that came by. Competition was fierce, Lyons, Tonibells and a variety of others toured the estates and often enough one of the opposition would have cleaned out a street just before I arrived.

On Wednesdays I had a fairly short morning round. This left me with two hours to spare before a 13.30 visit to a girls' boarding school. Rather than trying the bells around another housing estate, I used this time to hire an Auster from the Stapleford Tawney flying club. People would remark on the strange flying uniform (cream coloured, Walls issue) I was wearing. I did suggest to Walls' management that with a spotter plane, radios and a team of vans we could keep ahead of the opposition in a town until they gave up, then we could move on to another town and sort them out there, but this idea was rejected as unethical.

Eventually I built up enough recent flying to satisfy the original requirements, but by then the goalposts had been moved further ahead. I needed still more hours and also to renew my instrument rating. All my letters to airlines had either been ignored or answered with "don't call us, we'll call you."

I had good memories of the RAF and fighter flying, so early in 1960 I applied to re-join. In short order, a telegram arrived requesting my presence at Hornchurch for interview. There were just two officers on the interview board, a Wing Commander and a Squadron Leader. The latter had been a Flying Officer on 66 Squadron at the same time as myself, the interview became more of a "What happened to so-and-so?" session than anything formal. Towards the end I found it hard to keep a straight face when the Wing Commander asked the Squadron Leader if he had been annoyed by the noise of the ice cream van touring the married quarters during the TV news the previous evening. I didn't tell them that I was the culprit!

Soon after, I received notification that I had been accepted for a 12 year Short Service Commission, with the option of release at the 8 year point. I 'signed on' and duly reported for duty at RAF Hendon on the 16th March.

As I unpacked my few possessions in the Officers' Mess room allocated to me, I felt that I had come back home after years in the wilderness. Everything, the layout of the building, with its anteroom, bar and dining room, the furniture and the décor, seemed exactly the same as the Linton-on-Ouse Mess I had left four years earlier. When the civilian batman brought me my tea next morning, those four years could have been just a vivid dream. Before coming fully awake to the here and now I half thought I'd be flying a Sabre again that day if I could persuade 'Bush' to put me on the programme.

After ten days gentle re-introduction to Service life at Hendon I was sent to RAF Manby near Louth in Lincolnshire, where the Royal Air Force Flying College was based. Like Hendon, it was a 'permanent' RAF airfield with the familiar brick and steel hangars and brick and concrete office and accommodation blocks. There I was even more gently re-introduced to RAF flying. The atmosphere was most strange; it felt more like a Flying Club than a military establishment. There were only half a dozen of us on the refresher flying course, known by the staff instructors as "re-treads". We would toddle down to the hangar more or less when we felt like it and be asked, "When would you like to fly?" Sometimes, having expressed our wishes, the response would be on the lines of "Sorry, we don't have an aircraft available" or "there isn't an instructor free then" followed by " but we could fit you in this afternoon/tomorrow morning/whenever, if that would be convenient". And rather than having to follow a fixed syllabus, we would be asked, "What would you like to do today?"

The aircraft were 2-seat piston-engined Provosts, rather more powerful than the Chipmunk and fully aerobatic. Several of the other course members had previously, like myself, flown day fighters. Between us and unbeknown to the instructors, we would arrange to meet up somewhere over Lincolnshire for an illicit 'dogfight', instead of the instrument flying practice or other less interesting exercise we were supposed to be engaged in. The Provost handled nicely, but had one unpleasant failing; during aerobatics the cockpit would sometimes fill with fuel fumes. This tended to limit my aerobatic sessions; I would eventually feel airsick and have to fly straight and level with the canopy partly open until the nausea passed away. I had that as an excuse should I be caught 'dogfighting' – I was desensitising myself against motion sickness.

The course finished on 22nd April. Nothing much happened for a week, then I managed a few flights as safety pilot, keeping a look-out while the other pilot flew on instruments, until my next posting came through. This was to Strubby, a few miles away, for a jet refresher course. Strubby had been a WW2 temporary airbase and had wooden huts for offices, crew rooms and messes.

Although lacking some of the comforts of a permanent station Mess, the Officers' Mess at Strubby felt more homely and was certainly livelier, than that at Manby.

There had been little change in RAF jet training since 1952. The two-seat aircraft used for the refresher course were still Meteor Mk.7s, indeed one of them, WL344, was the very one in which I made my first solo jet flight back at Weston Zoyland. Meteor Mk 4 single seaters had been phased out, replaced by the Mk.8. The main difference in the flying exercises was that most sorties finished with a ground-controlled approach rather than a visual re-join. Practice double engine failure forced landings were a new feature, perhaps because many Squadrons were equipped with single engine Hunters.

At the end of the 34 flying hours course on the 23rd July I was given a 'high average' assessment and assured I would be sent on the Hunter day fighter Operational Conversion course I had asked for. The next course was already fully booked; I'd have to wait so in the meantime I was to go to Linton-on-Ouse as Adjutant of an Air Training Corps summer camp.

Linton village and the RAF station looked much the same as they had five years earlier, although the Sabres had gone. When I went into York on the first weekend it too was much as I remembered. Even today there has been little change to the city centre, except for the one-way systems and the amount of traffic. It is difficult to imagine how one used to be able to park a car almost anywhere, even right outside Betty's or the Assembly Rooms. Unthinkable now. Naturally I went into the old 66 Squadron favourite pub, the Punchbowl in Stonegate. The barmaid looked at me and without saying a word turned to the shelf behind the bar, took down a bottle of Newcastle Brown (my favourite tipple in 1955), carefully poured it into a glass and slid it across the counter. Only then did she ask "Are you back for long?"

The administrative side of the adjutant's job was not too onerous; there were plenty of opportunities to fly the Chipmunks and Piston Provosts provided for the cadets' air experience flights. I will never forget one youngster who seemed most apprehensive when we went out to fly. "You won't do any banking, will you Sir?" he asked. I tried to explain that if I didn't bank the aircraft it wouldn't turn round and we'd end up flying straight ahead till the fuel ran out. I promised that the weather was smooth and I'd fly very gently. Somewhat dubiously, he accepted this. We had been airborne for ten minutes, flying straight ahead and I was about to start a very gentle turn back towards the airfield when he piped up "Can we do a loop, Sir?" "Well, yes, but are you sure you want to?" I asked. "Yes please Sir" he answered. So we did. "Can we do another?" So we did. "What else can we do?" I showed him slow rolls, stall turns, rolls off the top of loops… and of course, banking. In the end, I was the one who wanted to quit. Perhaps he was just a wind-up expert.

The five weeks Linton detachment was followed by two weeks at Ternhill near Shrewsbury, again flying ATC cadets in Provosts and Chipmunks. Then came the bad news. Someone due to start on the next Javelin conversion course had fallen by the wayside and to keep the numbers correct I was to take his place. The Javelin was a night/all weather fighter. I couldn't see a lot of fun in flying around unable to see where I was going, nor, never having been much of a team player, in flying with a navrad (navigator/radar operator) telling me what to do! I really did want to fly the Hunter, as the British equivalent of the Sabre I was sure it would suit me. There was one small compensation. The Javelin Operational Conversion Unit was based at RAF Leeming, alongside the A1 road in North Yorkshire. I would be close to the Yorkshire Gliding Club of fond memory and there was also an RAF gliding club at Leeming itself.

Chapter 24
Conversion to the "Flatiron"

The Javelin course began on the 18th September. I got off to a bad start by having a good old whinge about how I'd been cheated out of my Hunter conversion and by telling all and sundry what I thought about night flying. Naturally that did me no good whatsoever. I compounded my 'attitude problem' (as it was called) one night after landing from a particularly unsuccessful practice interception sortie. What should have happened was that from the time my navrad picked up the target (another Javelin) on the aircraft's radar, we should have followed a curve of pursuit guided by his calling for turns with gentle (30 degrees), hard (45 degrees) or harder (60 degrees) of bank and for adjustments to speed, so that we ended up with a very small closing rate around 200 yards behind the target. I was then supposed to visually locate and identify the aircraft. We had tried half a dozen interceptions; none were successful. We either lost the target from our radar, rolled out much too far behind, or were closing so rapidly that I had to break off so as not to run into the back of the target.

I walked into the crew room feeling more than a little fed up with myself and the whole night fighter scene, to be greeted by the Course Commander, a Squadron Leader saying, "You look knackered". Without thinking I replied "Yes, I must be getting old". He then took me into his office and said that he thought I shouldn't be on the course, I was scared of flying. My reply that "As a psychologist, Sir, you make a bloody good plumber. Why do you think I spend my time every weekend flying gliders?" was not the most diplomatic. Eleven years later, when I left the RAF, I managed to sneak a look at my personal file. His comment on my end of course assessment was "This Officer looks and acts like a man ten years his senior." I don't think that was meant to be a compliment on my maturity! Actually I suspect that he didn't realise that I was a 're-tread' and **was** nearly ten years older than the rest of the course members.

In course of time I began to appreciate the Javelin, but after the Sabre I did find its aerobatic limitations a bit of a bind. The RAF flying "Bible" originally titled Air Publication 129 but later renumbered as AP 1234 had a section on the requirements for an aircraft to be acceptable for service. One of these was that it must be possible to recover normally from stalls and spins. Somehow the Javelin got past this. With its vast triangular wing and its relatively small tailplane high on the fin, as the aircraft stalled the tailplane and elevator would be blanketed by the now turbulent airflow from the wing and it would simply 'mush' with the nose up at a high rate of descent. Pushing the stick forward had no effect. The only way to recover from a stall was to boot on full rudder, pull the appropriate throttle back and convert the stall into a spin, from which the aircraft could be recovered with normal spin recovery action. This was not terribly practical – many thousands of feet would be lost. Rumour also had it that normal spin recovery didn't always work straightaway – a few pilots who had spun had not recovered until they had told the navrad to eject! As a result, manoeuvres in the vertical plane – loops, stall turns, vertical rolls and so on were prohibited.

My return to gliding wasn't all that exciting. Given the right wind and air mass conditions, air flowing over hills can behave like water flowing over a rock, causing waves downstream. Fly the glider on the up-going side of the wave and it will climb. Although Leeming was ideally placed just downwind of the Pennines for such mountain lee waves in westerly winds, the RAF club did not have an aircraft for aerotowing, so all launching was by winch. This didn't get us high enough to contact the wave on the few days it was there and it was too late in the year for thermals. All I managed was a large number of 5 minute circuits. Sutton Bank was not far away so I went there a couple of times to renew my acquaintance with Henryk Dokter and ridge flying.

The RAF Gliding and Soaring Association had by this time become well established and had set up a wave exploration project at Crosby-on Eden near Carlisle, by a strange coincidence (really?) close to an RAF Maintenance Unit commanded by Group Captain 'Paddy' Kearon, one of the founders of the RAFGSA. The semi-scientific aspect of investigating the meteorological phenomenon of atmospheric wave motion gave the RAFGSA an excuse to ask for service personnel (RAFGSA members naturally) to be sent there on detachment duty instead of them having to take leave. When the Javelin course finished in January 1961 I managed to get myself detached there for a week. Crosby is now a fully active civilian airport, but in those days it was a disused relic of WW2. The corrugated iron hangars and some of the huts were still there, but were not in too good a state of repair. We were accommodated at the Maintenance Unit, but each night one of us was detailed to sleep in one of the huts at Crosby as some sort of deterrent to unwanted visitors. It was an eerie experience, with odd creaking and banging noises coming from the hangars as the wind tugged at loose bits of corrugated iron. One felt that at any moment the ghost of one of the long-dead WW2 Hurricane pilots who flew from there might come knocking at the door.

There was no wave during my stay, but I made my first aerotows, on both ends of the rope. Driving the Chipmunk tug came first, with no more than a briefing on how to tow a glider – life was much less regimented in those days. I did have three dual tows in a two-seat Slingsby Eagle glider before flying the Olympia single-seat sailplane on a solo tow.

Chapter 25
Belle Epoque 2

On January 25th 1961, with the Operational Conversion course completed, I joined No. 41 Squadron, equipped with Javelin Mk.8's, at Wattisham in Suffolk. In memory, the next nine months were a second golden era in my life. I remember only the sunny days and the warm evenings, although there must have been **some** bad weather. There was an RAFGSA Gliding Club on the station, flying the Javelin on the Squadron was much more enjoyable than it had been under the pressure of the Operational Conversion Unit at Leeming and I bought myself four wheels in the shape of a Morris Minivan - there was no purchase tax on vans! There was even some unexpected sea trout fishing at Flatford Mill, where one could park right outside the Mill itself. It's now a half-mile walk from the nearest car parking area.

Mostly I remember the gliding during those months. There was no ridge nearby; staying airborne required the use of thermals. I achieved the Silver 'C' height badge, which needed a gain of height of 1,000 metres, in May and unintentionally made my first two landings away from base, the first at Ipswich Airport and the second at Debach, a disused war-time airfield. Two flights on the same day were particularly memorable.

Both of them involved flying in cloud, at which I was very inexperienced in gliders, although I had done plenty in powered aircraft. The glider was an Olympia, a post-war copy of the pre-war German Meise. The first of these two flights was relatively gentle. It was a day of small puffy cumulus clouds when I took off and flew from thermal to thermal below the clouds until one particularly strong one took me to cloud base at 4,000 feet. I decided to try a bit more cloud flying, expecting to gain just a couple of hundred feet of extra height in the small cloud above me, but as I went round and round the lift got stronger and the light diminished. The altimeter wound up past 5, 6, 7 and 8 thousand feet, with the rate of climb increasing all the time until at 9,000 feet I was climbing at over 1,000 feet per minute. Just below 10,000 feet the lift died away. I levelled the wings and after a few seconds popped out of the side of the cloud a few hundred feet below its top. The sky was a brilliant blue, the air was completely smooth and all around the tops of the other cumulus clouds were well below me. I drifted gently around, savouring the 'monarch of all I surveyed' feeling but, as always, Isaac Newton won and I sank back into the turbulent, shadowed world below.

On a second flight later that day I encountered a line squall. Thunderclouds sometimes form in lines across the direction from which the sun is shining. Rain falling from the back of the clouds drags cold air down with it. This cold air flows outwards from the line and on the sunny side, undercuts air warmed by the sun-lit ground. The rising warm air keeps the storms going on that edge and so the whole line advances, sometimes very rapidly bringing short-lived gale force surface winds. There are usually two distinct cloud base levels, with a vertical wall of cloud upwards from the lower level and a 'canopy' of higher cloud extending outwards from the wall. On this flight I found smooth, very strong lift in the angle between the wall and the canopy and soon was climbing into the higher canopy cloud. I tacked to and fro in the cloud, edging in towards the squall on each tack and found there was a very sharp distinction between the smooth lift and a turbulent area inside the main cloud. If I went too close to the turbulence it felt as if a giant hand reached out, grabbed the wing tip and shook it violently, but as soon as I edged away a few feet it all went smooth again. It was too good to last. At around 9,000 feet it started to rain and at 10,000 the rain began to freeze on the glider. Ice blocked the pitot tube, where air pressure is measured for the air speed indicator, so that fairly vital instrument for flying in cloud stopped working. It was time to leave. The Olympia had very powerful airbrakes, with them open it was impossible to exceed the maximum safe speed of the glider even in a vertical dive, so I opened the brakes, let go of the controls and waited until I fell into the clear air below cloud base. The only problem then was that I no longer had enough height to get back to Wattisham. The disused airfield of Debach was nearby; the runways still looked in reasonable condition, so I made my first proper away landing, one that was not at an active airfield or gliding site.

I don't remember any Javelin dramas, either personal or other colleagues' during this time. Apart from a three-week session of air-to-air gunnery in July, work settled into a routine of two weeks day flying alternating with a week of nights, until on August 11th the whole Squadron flew to Geilenkirchen on the Germany/Netherlands border north of Aachen. We operated from there until the 28th September, then flew back to Wattisham in formation.

On arrival back at home base, we learnt that 41 Squadron was to detach half a dozen aircrew to 5 Squadron at Laarbruch, also on the Germany/Netherlands border about 60 miles north of Geilenkirchen. I was to be one of them. I had one more Javelin flight at Wattisham, then took some leave before departing for Laarbruch on the 30th October, leaving the Minivan and most of my kit behind, expecting to be away for just a month. The days passed; our detachment was extended once, then a second time. Two and a half months later, by mid-January 1962, we were getting a bit cheesed-off and started agitating either to return to Wattisham or to have our detachments converted to postings. Among other things we were still officially on the strength at Wattisham and so were still paying Mess bills there!

We got our postings and I continued with what turned out to be a four and a half year stint in Germany.

Chapter 26
Skiing, surviving and (a lot of) gliding

I went back to Wattisham to collect the Minivan and my few possessions and settled in to the Second Tactical Air Force routine. It soon became non-routine. Standard advice in the Services was "Never volunteer for anything." Those in authority had ways to induce a disregard for this wise guidance. Attending the 2 ATAF Winter Survival course was not compulsory, but the eight days (six before the survival phase and two after) of free skiing offered to volunteers ensured a good take-up rate. I was one of the 'mugs' on the February 3-17 course.

Headquarters for this detachment was established in the Zur Post hotel at Bad Kohlgrub, near Oberammergau in Bavaria. The pre-survival week was fairly intensive, with lectures from 8.30 to 10.00 a.m., skiing until 16.00 and, fitted around tea and dinner, another two and a half hours of evening lectures finishing at 22.00. Our ski instructress, we discovered, was a champion skier, but far from fluent in English. Her instructional 'patter' was restricted to two commands – "Follow me" and "Lean more forward" and one piece of advice – "The more you bend your knees, the slower go your skis". The ski slope we used was relatively gentle, but suffered from a minor defect for the majority of us, who had little or no ski experience. There was no flat area before the gully at the bottom and the only way out was across a dogleg wooden bridge. Fortunately the V-shaped fence acting as a funnel and the sides of the bridge itself were smoothly planked, few of us managed to decant onto the flat area at the foot of the T-bar beyond the bridge without at least one ricochet off the wooden panels. We had all been equipped with black overalls, the predominately German civilian users of the slope soon learnt to scatter when we came anywhere near them and if we attempted to share a T-bar with them would turn a pale shade of white and politely decline the honour.

The fun ended when we were trucked out to the survival training area. We were split into teams of four. Each team was provided with a single one-man seven-day ration pack and an onion. This was the food supply for the next seven days. Our teams were dropped off at intervals just after sunset for night treks of around 15 km. straight line distance through a farming area with, we were told, several hundred ski-equipped German soldiers seeking to capture us. The heavy knee-deep snow covering made for tough going and the apparent need to move from cover to cover greatly increased the actual distance travelled. Our team didn't actually see any of the opposition, nor did the others we asked when we arrived at the destination. We came to the conclusion

Photo 30 - Winter holiday

that the several hundred ski-equipped German soldiers seeking to capture us were just a wind-up invention to make our hike longer and slower than it need have been.

The rendezvous, which we reached just after daylight, was a glade in a fir forest on the edge of a river. This was to be our home for the next six days. Our first task was to build a lean-to shelter and get a fire going. This would have been easier had we not been forbidden to use other than dead wood. Previous courses had already scavenged the surrounding area out to half-a-mile or so; finding firewood and attending to the other necessities of living in the wild between the morning and afternoon open-air lecture sessions became an endurance test. Cold weather survival depends on keeping warm; with no chance of more clothing this means either exercise or a fire, but exercise burns up food energy. Our three meals per day consisted, typically, of an Oxo cube sized piece of cheese, half a ship's biscuit and a sucrose sweet. It was debatable whether the warmth generated by the fire compensated for the energy burned gathering firewood from a distance. We certainly became very hungry!

The subject of the afternoon lecture on the fourth day was rabbit - how to catch, kill, skin and cook it. The unfortunate White Belgian used in the demonstration didn't have a chance. Even before it had been skinned, when the instructor said "You can eat the eyes raw – anyone want to try?" twenty hands shot into the air. We ended up with one fifth of a rabbit per team. Unbeknownst to the underlings of our four, our leader, being a bit of a psychologist, had calculated that our morale would be at its lowest on the fourth day and had been squirreling away part of each day's rations so that we could have a relative feast that evening. The remaining rations were taken out of the metal pack and put aside. The rabbit portion, the onion and the enhanced ration for our supper were soon simmering in the improvised saucepan, while we warmed ourselves by the fire, drooling over the entrancing odours arising from our stew.

As the radio programme catch phrase went, "Some mothers do 'ave 'em". For no good reason one of our team decided to stir up the fire. In so doing he managed to tip the ration tin over. Had we been in a real survival situation, I think he would have been in the pot himself within minutes.

There was an RAF Germany Gliding Association club at Laarbruch. Soon after returning from the survival course I began to fly with them. Later that year, on 24th April, I made my Silver 'C' glider distance flight (50 kilometre or greater), from Laarbruch, more or less by accident. It was very hazy with visibility of no more than two miles when I took off in a Meise. This was the German original from which the Eon Olympia was copied. It had been designed and built for the cancelled 1940 Olympics and was a single seat wood and fabric machine with a cantilever wing, of high performance for its day. Launched by winch, I found a weak thermal and started to climb, circling gently. The lift was stronger on the east side of the circle than on the west, so I shifted towards the stronger side. The lift strengthened, but again it was greater to the east. I moved further east still. This process continued until at around 3000 feet a wall of cloud appeared through the murk; I recognised an approaching line squall. I was by now over the launch point and looking down I could see the trees waving wildly in the gust front caused by the squall. I reckoned that I would have difficulty landing back safely at Laarbruch; the wind direction and speed would be changing unpredictably. If I was going to have to land away from the airfield I might as well explore the line squall first, so I straightened out and flew north-westwards along the wall of cloud, with a now visible shelf of higher cloud above. The lift increased further and soon, although I was flying at 80 knots (maximum rough air speed), I reached 6000 feet and had to partly open the airbrakes to avoid climbing into the cloud. It took only 20 minutes to cover the 50 kilometres required; I was near the Dutch National Gliding Centre at Terlet, which would be a good place to land. I could expect assistance to look after the glider, maybe even take another launch if it looked possible to fly back to Laarbruch after the squall had passed through. This cunning plan failed; on the descent I encountered severe turbulence and it became obvious that the squall was too close to Terlet for a safe landing there. The only solution was to climb as high as possible close to the squall, then glide directly away from it and land in calm conditions.

There were two farm hands working in the field next to the one in which I landed, 89 km from Laarbruch. They looked at me as if I was crazy when I asked for their help to move the glider into the shelter of a hedge and to tie it down because of the big wind that was coming. When it did, they were most impressed by my prescience! This flight completed the three requirements (height gain, duration and cross-country distance) of the Silver 'C' gliding certificate.

Gliding progress thereafter was rapid. The RAFGGA competition was to be held at Geilenkirchen in May. I was given a Grunau Baby 2 to fly. The Minivan was not powerful or heavy enough to tow a glider trailer, so I bought an old Opel Kapitan. We were allowed a ration of petrol coupons, which enabled us to buy petrol from the German filling stations at a greatly reduced price. With two cars I got two rations, which just about covered all the extra mileage that being involved in gliding entailed. The Grunau 2 was a rather low performance machine even then. It did have the advantage of a very low stalling speed and a skid rather than a wheel, which meant it could be landed in an extremely short distance. If there were no obstructions a piece of grass the size of a tennis court was ample. In those days the majority of tasks set in competitions were free distance, on this occasion they all were. I didn't do particularly well, but did make four more field landings in the five days when the weather was fit for cross-country. It would have been five, except that I couldn't find a thermal to get started on the first day, so didn't leave the airfield.

In June the Chief Flying Instructor, "Stu" Mead, gave me a morning's instruction on how to instruct, with three flights and then turned me loose as an instructor. Life was less formalised then; nowadays becoming a gliding instructor involves a vast amount of study and many flights with an examiner simulating a student. I was to make over 450 flights instructing, including sending my own navrad (and a good few other people) solo before the system changed and I went to the RAFGSA Centre at Bicester for a proper instructor's course.

By the end of the year I had another five field landings under my belt, a furthest distance of 120 kms and had flown solo in 19 glider types. The highest performance of these was the Ka6, but for looks the gull-winged Minimoa beat them all. In still air the Ka6 could fly about 33 miles from one mile high, the Minimoa, 28, both around half as far as today's highest performance sailplanes.

There was a British Forces Education Service school at Laarbruch. One of the female teachers was learning to glide. In the Club bar after flying she had a penchant for dancing on the table. I kept well clear – little did I know what was to be my future.

Meanwhile in what pilots who don't fly gliders would call the real flying world my Javelin hours accumulated. Mostly we practised high level interceptions, which, when you've done a few, become a little boring. We did have some breaks; a few air-to-air gunnery sorties and a couple of visits to other NATO air forces. On one of these, in June, we went to Skrydstrup in Denmark for three days, during which we made a formation fly-past over Copenhagen. But even at Skrydstrup I wasn't away from gliding; a Danish Air Force Gliding Club flew from there. One of their members, a military pilot, showed me a Meise sailplane in which he'd nearly come to a sticky end. He had been doing an aerobatics display and went a bit too fast. All the fabric and most of the structure behind the main spar inboard of the ailerons on both wings tore away. With only a little more than half the wing area remaining the stalling speed was very high, but he managed to land the glider by maintaining twice the normal approach speed until just above the ground.

At Laarbruch, apart from continually practising interceptions we had to keep two Javelins on Quick Reaction Alert, otherwise known as Battle Flight, at all times, in case a real interception was required. From time to time we would be 'scrambled' and would go haring off towards the border between East and West Germany. We didn't know whether there was a real target or if it was just the Fighter Controllers playing games with their opposite East German numbers. Just short of the border we would be told to turn ninety degrees left or ninety degrees right, then a few minutes later 180 degrees to the other direction and so on back and forth until we were down to the minimum fuel to get home. Occasionally, when the weather conditions were right, we would see one or a pair of condensation trails to the east, mirroring our every turn. We could never work out whether it was our man trying to fool them, or theirs trying to fool us!

One evening around this time several of us were in the Mess bar when a Mess steward came in and said "There's an outside call from Flight Lieutenant Pinker, he wants to speak to anyone from 5 Squadron". One of the group picked up the phone and we heard half the conversation. "You want to be picked up from where?" ...... "The pub in Weeze?" ..... "Stop messing about, I know you're at the QRA hangar on Battle Flight" As he was about to hang up, a look of doubt came on his face. This **was** an outside call. "O.K. Chas, what happened?" It transpired that they had been 'scrambled' and shortly after take-off one of their engines had caught fire. The emergency drill had not sorted the problem out. With the fire spreading, his pilot had ordered him to eject.

Chas entertained us later on with his story. As soon as he landed he had rolled up his parachute, rushed into a nearby wood and was halfway through digging a hole to bury it before he remembered that the war had been over for twenty years. He had flown on bombing raids over Germany during World War Two and had automatically started the escape and evasion actions learnt during those days. Jim Adams, the pilot, nearly left it too late to eject and landed almost on top of the burning wreckage of the Javelin.

Chapter 27
Geilenkirchen and a five star out-landing reception

Photo 31 - Javelin Mk9 XH903 which the author flew on 5 Squadron
Courtesy Adrian Pingstone

At the end of October No. 33 Squadron, based in the U.K. at Middleton St. George (now Teesside Airport) was disbanded. Their aircraft, Mark 9s and most of their aircrew were re-deployed to Geilenkirchen and some of us joined them there, forming a new 5 Squadron. I was soon in trouble. The Geilenkirchen Gliding Club's aircraft, vehicles and equipment shared the hangar that 5 Squadron was allocated. Naturally enough, our Squadron C.O. was not too pleased with this situation. Soon after arriving I was made Officer in Charge of Gliding. So began a battle that was to last until I left (and probably thereafter as well). He wanted the Gliding Club out, but there was no-where else for us to go. He tried various tactics, mostly to do with fire hazards. The Station Fire Officer would tackle me with "Your winch is in the hangar full of fuel, take it away." I'd reply "There are at least six Javelins in the hangar full of jet fuel, which is just as flammable as the diesel in our winch, will they be moved out as well?" Another time it was "All those bits of engine and stuff in your alcove are a fire hazard. If anyone drops things like that it could cause a spark." "Oh, really?" I asked, "So do our ground crew use plastic spanners when working on the Javelins inside the hangar?" To be fair, the C.O. didn't take it out on me in my squadron pilot role.

On the gliding side, 1963 was an interesting and varied year for me. In June a cumulo-nimbus cloud climb took me from a launch height of 1,000 feet to 13,000 feet. This was enough for the gain of height leg (3,000 metres) of the gold 'C' certificate. The climb was not in the least dramatic. Cumulo-nimbus clouds can be very rough on powered aircraft, which, flying straight through, pass instantly from strong up current to strong down current. In my glider I was circling within the confines of a rising air stream, climbing at more than 1,000 feet per minute in silk-smooth air. I didn't have oxygen on board so had to break off the climb. It was a little rough leaving the lift and flying out of the side of the cloud but the main problem was that by then the cloud was dumping heavy rain on the airfield and the visibility was too poor to land back. I slipped across the Dutch border to the abandoned WW2 airfield at Beek (Maastricht) where a Dutch gliding club operated. Unfortunately the weather didn't improve enough for me to take a launch and fly back, so a trailer had to be sent to retrieve the glider and me. Although this was long before European Union days, we never had the slightest problem crossing the Dutch, Belgian or French borders with an empty trailer going one way and a glider in it coming back. The only documentation we had was a letter we'd typed ourselves on RAF headed paper and our RAF identity cards.

In July, I flew in the 1963 RAF Germany competition, held at Venlo in Holland. This time I was allocated a Weihe. Although it was a pre-war design, it was still of relatively high performance compared with even the most recent machines, so I really had no reason to be proud of winning the first two days. I should have won the whole competition, but my crew managed to damage the glider during the retrieve from near Koblenz in Germany on the second day. I lost two out of the five competition days making repairs and finished third overall.

The fourth day's retrieve was memorable for other reasons. Up to then I had had generally friendly receptions from landowners I had dropped in on. This time the hospitality was lavish. The field was next to a road and close to a village. The glider had barely come to a halt before it was surrounded by a crowd of children and a few adults. I was busy fending off the small fingers poking at the fabric wing surfaces and the hands waggling the control surfaces, while trying to calm the excitement with my very few words of German, when a large Mercedes pulled up by the field entrance. A chauffeur opened the passenger door, an imposing-looking gentleman got out, barked a few words of command and the crowd fell back to a respectful distance. Turning to me, he said "You vill vait here a little time, zen you vill go viz me." I duly waited a little time and a photographer arrived. Pictures of the glider, me and the glider and myself were taken. Then, after one of the adults was ordered to watch over the glider, I was ushered into the car and we drove a few miles to a large house. A butler opened the door. My host said "You vill vant a telephone, ja? You know how to use it?" "Yes please and yes I do" I replied. He led me to the 'phone and left me. I got through to the Competition organisers at Venlo and told them where my retrieve crew would find me. I had been flying for four and a half hours, it had been hot and sweaty with the sun beating through the Perspex canopy, but I thought the way the butler approached me bearing a large snowy white bath towel was a little pointed. "Ze bathroom ist three doors on ze right," he told me, "you vill find clean trousers and shirt zere."

Photo 32 – The Weihe in the field near Hachenburg

Refreshed and wearing a change of outer garments, I returned to the front hall. My host intercepted me and asked me how long I thought it would be before my crew arrived. "Oh, about two hours, if all goes well," I answered. " Good, before I show you round my factory, would you like some strawberries and perhaps a beer?" he asked me. Strawberries and beer consumed, I was taken to the building next door, which proved to be a printing works. I had the full tour, with an explanation of the whole process. This was of course long before computers. I don't remember much about it now, but printing then involved a lot of lead and the typeface being set up in frames of some sort.

My crew arrived at about 7.30 p.m. and before we went to de-rig the glider they were refreshed with a stein of beer each. As we prepared to leave for the field with the trailer, I told my host that it was the normal practice for the pilot to treat the crew to a good meal on the way back to base. I asked if he could recommend a nearby hotel and invited him and his wife to join us there. "It's a bit hard to find," he said "so bring the trailer back here and we'll go in my car."

We had a magnificent meal and a fair quantity of beer. I called the Maitre d' over and asked for the bill. "Nein, Herr ***** has told me to put it on his account" he told me. No protest of mine could change this. It was getting a bit late and I said we should really be on our way. "No, you must wait just a little" our host insisted. We had another beer. Then a man came in selling the local evening newspaper and we were presented with a copy each. The Weihe and I, with photographs, were front-page news!

HACHENBURG. Gestern um 16.30 Uhr landete der englische Segelflieger Lt. A. St. Pierre unweit Hachenburg nach einem Flug von Venlo, wo er um 12 Uhr mit neun Kameraden gestartet war. Die Flugroute war vorgeschrieben.

Photo 33 - Front page news

A few days later I set off in my Kapitan for Aosta in Italy with Lemmy Tanner, a Canberra pilot and keen glider man. We towed another of the club's gliders, a Ka6, in its trailer. I had put the car in for a service before we left. Apart from a stop on the way to have weld repairs done on the trailer, all went well to Bex, below a 10,000-foot mountain just southeast of Lake Geneva. Lemmy knew a member of the gliding club there, so we called in, but his friend wasn't there. "Can we fly our glider here?" we asked. "Certainly, rig it and we will give you an aerotow" we were told. Neither of us knew anything about gliding in the mountains; we had expected to be given check flights by one of their instructors, but it seemed they didn't think it was necessary. "So what do we do?" we inquired. "Just fly close to the mountain where the sun shines on it, there you will find rising air and you will climb" was the advice. We rigged the glider, tossed a coin and I won.

I saw another glider below me; it seemed to be climbing towards me. My wing tip was about fifty feet from the rocks. "Perhaps I'm not close enough," I thought. I flew half as far out. The Ka6 wasn't sinking so fast, but it still wasn't going up. In desperation I moved closer still. Not until I had to lift the wing tip over the small bushes dotting the mountainside did I start to climb, but then it was like being in an express lift. I tacked all the way up to the peak, then pulled the airbrakes open and dived down to give Lemmy a go.

Next day we continued south and toiled our way up the Saint Bernard Pass road. After what seemed several hours of first gear crawling we thought we must be almost at the top. We were slightly disconcerted when we saw a road sign indicating "Keine Anhanger". Trailers forbidden or not we weren't going to turn round and go back. Not that we could anyway on the narrow twisting road. A few yards further on we were much more than slightly disconcerted when the car's gearbox seized! Outside we could feel the heat radiating from below the car and could smell hot oil.

We walked round the next bend and saw that the summit was just a hundred yards further on. After giving the gearbox an hour to cool down we investigated under the car. The explanation was not hard to find. The filler plug at the rear of the gearbox was missing. This had been no problem during the long drive on the flat country from Geilenkirchen to Switzerland, but during the climb up the pass the gearbox had been tilted backwards and most of the oil had run out.

Photo 34 - Kapitan en-route to Aosta - St. Bernard Pass

Once everything had cooled down we managed to drive the car and trailer to the top of the pass, but there a death rattle from below the car announced the final demise of the gearbox. We didn't dare leave the trailer unattended at the summit, not knowing how long it would be before we could get back to it. The subsequent free-wheel drive down the multi hair-pinned Italian side of the pass, with frequent stops to allow the brakes to cool off, was the stuff nightmares are made of. Luck held; just where the road levelled out in the Aosta valley we found a garage. The gearbox repair took most of the next day.

We flew a familiarisation flight around Aosta airfield on the 15th July and asked what time we could get a launch next morning. "Oh, sorry, we will not be flying tomorrow, we have to fetch the body from the mountain" said the Chief Flying Instructor. "What body?" we asked. "The glider pilot who crashed up there". "When was that?" "Oh, just before Christmas!" It seemed that snow had buried the wreck site and they'd had to wait for it to melt. Next evening we asked again what time we could fly the following morning. "Oh, sorry, we will not be flying tomorrow, we have to go to the funeral!" We did fly on the two days after that, but the weather was not really suitable and then we had to leave to get back for duty.

Photo 35 - Waiting for the brakes to cool

The rest of the month continued the away from home theme when the Squadron flew to the Royal Netherlands Air Force base at Leeuwarden for a week of air-to-air gunnery. My logbook shows nine flights in six days and a best score of 33%, but all I remember is the excellent satay buffet the Netherlanders put on for us. The Dutch seem to have the knack of taking indigenous cooking from other parts of the world and improving on it.

Chapter 28
Minimoa and first Diamond

In August 1963 our Geilenkirchen gliding club ran out of winch cable. For some reason we could not get any from the normal suppliers, so we telephoned the Laarbruch club who said they had some spare. I went with Lemmy to collect it. In the hangar we saw the Minimoa that I had flown the year before. It was de-rigged and leaning against a wall, covered with dust and cobwebs. When we asked why it looked as if it hadn't been flown for months, we were told that it needed new fabric, new control cables, the glue was suspect and the club had decided it was too was old to be worth spending money on. They were going to burn it on Guy Fawke's night. We made them an offer, on the basis that a few Deutschmarks towards their club funds was better than nothing. So for 250 Dm (equivalent to £25), slightly more than one week's pay, we had a glider of our own, complete with airspeed indicator, altimeter and variometer (rate of climb or descent indicator). We arranged that we would collect it on the following weekend.

Photo 36 - All our own

The Laarbruch club members expected that we would turn up with a trailer, but instead Lemmy and a tug pilot from the Geilenkirchen flying club arrived with a Tiger Moth and a towrope. I went in the Minivan, helped to rig the glider and held the wingtip for the launch. After releasing at Geilenkirchen, Lemmy soared locally for a couple of hours, then I took a winch launch and flew another half-hour. At club flying rates, those two flights went a long way towards recouping our outlay! However, we weren't completely mad, didn't press our luck any further and took the glider to a local maintenance facility for a thorough check, replacement of control cables and re-fabricing. That cost another 2,000 Dm or so. Then came re-painting. We had some white and some red paint, not enough of either to do the whole job and not sure we had enough of either to do wings with one and fuselage with the other. So we mixed the two and ended up with a shocking pink. This did not impress the Duke of Edinburgh when he visited the station a few months later.

When I was posted from Geilenkirchen, I left my share of the glider with Lemmy; when he was posted he sold it to an American for what we had spent on it. Thirty-odd years later Lemmy was contacted by a Dutchman seeking the glider's history; he had just bought it in the USA for $20,000!

In October we took the Javelins to Valley, on Anglesey, for Firestreak air-to-air missile firing practice. Theoretically we should have fired one missile per crew, but between target failure, missile failure, bad weather and range problems only a third of us actually succeeded. I didn't; the best I got was flying in formation with another aircraft and seeing his missile launched. Whether it actually hit the target is another matter. All I can say is that it was probably just as well that we never had to use the Firestreaks in anger.

1964 began with a lesson in the patience that gliding often requires. Lemmy and I took the club Ka6 to Issoire near Clermont Ferrand in Central France; a site famed for its high altitude glider flights in mountain lee wave conditions. We didn't get the right conditions for wave or anything else during the ten days of our visit and flew one circuit of about ten minutes each. But the food and wine were good, especially lunch at the 'Routiers' just outside the airfield.

A gliding instructor's course, at Bicester in early March, lasted five days and gave me an official, British Gliding Association, Full Category Instructor certificate. Also in March our Minimoa was returned to us with the work completed and we began to get used to it. By modern standards it was very heavy on the controls, but that made it very stable, once centred in a thermal it would go round and round almost on its own. Unfortunately the gull wing made it impossible to fit onto any of the club open trailers; closed trailers were an absolute no-no for it. We started building a trailer, but both of us were posted away before it was completed. Not being able to take the risk of a field landing meant we couldn't go far away from base, but on one especially good day I flew to Beek (Maastricht), landed, took a winch launch from the Dutch gliding club there and flew back to Geilenkirchen. All of 15 miles each way!

The 1964 RAF Germany Gliding Competition was held at Butzweilerhof near Cologne, starting on the 17th May. There I met my nemesis. One evening during the competition Lemmy had arranged to go out for a meal with his girlfriend. The table top dancer from Laarbruch was at the competition as a general helper. Seeing that she appeared to be on her own that day Lemmy suggested that I should invite her out also and we two should join him and his partner. This seemed a good idea at the time so I did just that. We had a pleasant evening out and from then on Jennie and I gradually became, as modern parlance has it, an item.

Lemmy and I flew alternate days in the Rheinland, a very neat little machine, until I caught the wingtip on a tree trunk after landing on the sixth day. With one foot of the wingtip taken clean off we couldn't fly it until it had been repaired, so we took it to our Minimoa fixer. With gliding out of the way, I spent the last couple of days of the competition sightseeing with Jennie. I learnt that she was seven years younger than I, had two older sisters and her father owned a paint factory. During the rest of the year I frequently drove up to Laarbruch at weekends, sometimes staying in the Mess there and sometimes taking Jennie to stay in the teachers' quarters at Geilenkirchen. She continued gliding until she left Germany but never went solo. One of the essential lessons in any flying training was recovering from stalls and spins, which she didn't want to do. I couldn't persuade her to, nor could anyone else.

A couple of weeks Javelin flying followed the competition. Then I had some leave available and so did Lemmy. We had heard good reports of another gliding site in Switzerland at Grenchen, situated at the foot of the Jura mountain range. We borrowed the club's new Olympia 463 and set off down the autobahn. On arrival we found a very thriving and active club, with aerotow launching. We introduced ourselves and were invited to fly our own machine without any requirement for a site check. Looking around we saw a few of the very newest sailplanes, the precursors of today's all fibreglass and carbon glass machines. They were built using balsa wood covered with fibreglass, which gave a much smoother and therefore more efficient surface, especially to the wings. We rigged our rather boxy, old-fashioned wood and fabric Olympia and began casually attempting to con flights in their gliders in exchange for them flying ours. They didn't exactly fall over themselves with enthusiasm.

The Juras, though not as high as the main Alps to the south, rise to a respectable 5,000 plus feet, in a long gentle curve facing south-southeast. With the scarp face that side, until late afternoon the sun shines on the steep dry rocky slope, heats it and the air on the slope is in turn heated by the surface. A narrow curtain of hot air then slides up the slope, almost independent of the general wind direction. We soon learnt how to exploit this anabatic wind. We moved close to the face and tacked our way up to the ridge crest. Once there, we flew a few feet above the ground, with one wing overlapping the crest and the other out over the valley. Ahead the top of the ridge itself could rise at what seemed an incredibly steep angle, but the glider would rise with it; one could feel buoyancy in the air. With no need to circle, a high speed could be maintained along the ridge.

On the sixth day of our stay the weather looked especially fine. It was my turn to fly. The local pilots were all talking about a task to a turning point 156 kms along the ridge to the west; this seemed a good one for me to try as an out and return for the goal diamond leg which requires at least 300 kms.

I started out in fine form; running along just above the ridge crest gave me a high speed in strong and consistent lift. Near the Col de la Faucille things got a little difficult, but knowing no better and bearing in mind the confidence with which those local pilots had said the task was a piece of cake I pressed on. I had a horrid twenty minutes stuck above a rather inhospitable forested area, before a thermal broke away from a car park and lifted me to safety. The turning point, Roche Franche, was, as the Swiss pilots had told me unmistakable – a cubic block of rock jutting above the general ridgeline. I took the photographs needed to prove I had been there and set off on the return leg. At first there was no great difficulty, but by then the sun was getting rather far round to the west and no longer heating the scarp face very well. An incautious attempt at climbing in a weak thermal drifted me over the northern, dip slope of the hills and I suddenly found myself too low to get back over the crest into the low country to the south. Although I could not see into it, I knew there was another deep valley to the north. I didn't know if there were any places to land there, but reckoned that if I got over it I could turn westwards and follow the river down into flatter country in France. The next few minutes were a bit fraught. I was only twenty feet above the rocky, unlandable ground and the dip slope was little steeper than my glide angle. Ahead of me there was a small lip just before the drop into the valley; I would not have cleared it had there not been a narrow break where a stream had cut its way through. Even so, I had to put one wing down and sideslip through the gap. Then instantly I had three thousand feet of air beneath me – and almost immediately I hit a very strong thermal which took me back up to cloud base high above the top of the hills. From then on I used thermals to stay high, running at ridge-top level would no longer have worked. A good height gain around 25 miles from home enabled a long cautious final glide and almost seven hours after take-off I was back at Grenchen with Gold 'C' distance and a Diamond Goal in the bag.

The Swiss pilots took us out for a celebratory meal and drinks that evening. They had all turned back before the turning point, because the conditions were, they thought, not good enough. Next day, Lemmy declared and flew the same task, with similar difficulties to mine. The Swiss pilots, now thoroughly impressed by the performance of our ordinary-looking Olympia, decided they would like to try it after all and offered us their machines to fly in return. Regretfully we had to decline the offers – our time was up and we had to leave for Geilenkirchen.

In July the Squadron went to Leeuwarden again for more air-to-air firing, this time for four weeks. Before we went I had found out that we would be doing our own banner towing, using Meteors. It seemed a good idea to get in on this, so I had a dual check in a Mark 7 that happened to be around at Geilenkirchen. Once I was up there pulling the banner I began to wonder if it was such a bright notion; when I watched the Javelins' gun flashes in my mirror it sometimes seemed that the Javelin concerned was pointing straight at me! But it did give me my best month's total flying on an operational

Squadron, even if more than half was on the Meteor. Joe Sim, who had been my navrad at Laarbruch, went along for the ride on one of the banner towing flights. Before becoming a navrad he had started pilot training at Cranwell, but for reasons unknown to me had failed the course. I let him fly the aircraft when we were towing. He seemed to be doing perfectly well, so I talked him round the circuit and landing back at Leeuwarden. At some time after I had left the Squadron, he got back into pilot training and eventually flew Harriers.

Chapter 29
Tiger Moth adventure

After the Squadron returned from Leeuwarden Jennie told me she was going to see her parents in England during the school summer holidays. I said I would meet her at Dusseldorf airport when she arrived back on the 5th September and would drive her to Laarbruch. A week before her return the Chief Flying Instructor of the RAF Geilenkirchen Flying Club asked me if I could fly their Tiger Moth G-ASPZ to Biggin Hill, near London on the following weekend, for its Certificate of Airworthiness check. When I told him that I had arranged to meet Jennie, he replied "Well, take her with you". I then said it was 12 years since I'd last flown a Tiger and then only dual, but if he would give me a dual check and I could fly a few circuits, I would make the flight. Within minutes I found myself checked out and flying a Tiger Moth solo for the first time.

During the next week I planned the flight. G-ASPZ, like most small private aircraft in those days, had no radio or radio navigation equipment. There were many small airfields where radio was not mandatory or often not even available. One would arrive overhead, look down at the signals square which displayed markers giving various bits of information including circuit direction and then fly a circuit to land accordingly. Flying from place to place could be almost as formality-free as driving a car. I decided to refuel twice en-route, at Ghent in Belgium and Lympne in Kent, both small grass airfields where radio was not mandatory.

Jennie arrived from Liverpool on a DC3 airliner next Saturday at 8.00 a.m. It would have taken around three hours to drive her to Laarbruch, then return to Geilenkirchen, but only 30 minutes to go to Geilenkirchen directly. The Tiger was not equipped for night flying; if I took her to Laarbruch I was unlikely to reach Biggin Hill before dark and if I night stopped en route I had no chance of returning to Geilenkirchen in time to be back on duty for Monday morning. There were only two options; take her to Geilenkirchen and persuade someone else to take her on to Laarbruch or do what the CFI had suggested and take her with me.

When she had cleared through the airport formalities, I asked somewhat diffidently "How would you like to go back to England with me today and come back tomorrow?" "How?" she asked. "Well, er… it's like this…" I explained about the Tiger Moth trip. She queried, "What's a Tiger Moth?" I told her it was an open cockpit, two-seat, propeller biplane. . "Will there be room for my luggage?" she asked. "Not all of it." I replied, "just take a change of clothes in that small bag and leave the rest in my car." "Won't we get wet if it rains?" was the final question. I convinced her that the rain would be deflected over our heads by the windscreens and we'd stay dry.

With that, with no more ado, she agreed to go with me.

Photo 37 - Jennie is fastened in

The Tiger Moth was all fuelled and ready when we arrived at Geilenkirchen, so after a short delay while someone found her some overalls, goggles and a flying helmet we set off for Ghent. I had no problem finding the way by map and compass, there was no low cloud and the visibility was good. From Ghent we flew at 1000 feet below cloud on a more or less straight track towards Lympne. As we approached the Belgian coast the weather deteriorated, with a heavy rain shower reducing the visibility to half a mile or so. Without intending to, I was able to prove to Jennie that indeed you don't get wet flying an open cockpit aircraft in rain! Once through the shower the visibility picked up. At the coast I followed the shoreline to the unmistakable departure point of Cap Griz Nez and then set out on the Channel crossing, aiming well to the left of track so that when we made landfall I would know that turning right would take me towards Hythe, from whence Lympne would be easy to find.

Three quarters of the way across we flew into another shower. The rain became heavy and the visibility decreased. Fortunately the sea was fairly choppy, with whitecaps showing through the murk, so I knew I could see far enough ahead to avoid hitting any obstructions on the English coast. When the beach finally appeared we had been forced down to a few hundred feet by the lowering cloud base and it became apparent that this was more than just a small shower. We had been in the air for almost two and a half hours. Fuel was getting low; we would soon have to land somewhere.

We were not in real danger, I could put down safely on one of the fields just inland, but that would have put paid to any chance of getting back to Geilenkirchen in time to avoid being absent without leave! I turned right and followed round the curve of St. Mary's Bay until Hythe came in view, made a tight turn onto northwest and held my breath. A couple of minutes later I spotted a windsock, then some white runway markers and landed straight ahead on the grass.

I left Jennie at the refuelling pump while I went to the airport office to pay the landing fee. There I was made to await the arrival of the airfield manager, who gave me a dressing-down for having landed in such bad weather. I was also told I would not be allowed to leave his office until he considered the weather had sufficiently improved.

It took nearly an hour to get back to Jennie who was still waiting at the refuelling point. She was a bit miffed, not because I'd been away so long, but because she had been interrogated at some length by a Customs officer. He had asked her many questions, to few of which she knew the answers. She knew where we had come from but not much else. The main questions revolved around "Where had we cleared customs outbound in Germany?" She didn't know the answer because in fact we hadn't cleared Customs anywhere. I had become so used to flying the Javelin and gliders across borders and landing in other countries with no formalities that the notion of clearing out of Germany hadn't even entered my mind. "Is he coming back?" I asked. "No, I just kept saying 'I don't know' to him and in the end he seemed to get fed up and went away" she replied. "Let's get out of here quick before he does come back" I suggested and the weather by then having cleared, we were soon on the last leg to Biggin Hill. From there, after handing over the aircraft to the maintenance company, we made our way by taxi to the railway station. A train to London, an overnight boat train across the Channel, a meandering set of train connections through France and Germany and finally another taxi took us back to Geilenkirchen. I still had to chauffeur Jennie to Laarbruch so she would be there for school on Monday morning and then drive back to Geilenkirchen so I would be in time for Met briefing.

A week later the Squadron had another exchange visit, this time to Bodo, north of the Arctic Circle in Norway. I went as a passenger in a Beverley, a lumbering, noisy, draughty four-engined monstrosity. I parachuted out of one a few years later. Deliberately, I hasten to add; it wasn't that unreliable!

We flew a few Javelin sorties intercepting and tangling with Norwegian Air Force fighters. I was 'bounced' by a Sabre on one occasion. I twisted and turned but couldn't shake him off. The only answer was to try the Javelin's 'last ditch' manoeuvre. I rolled upside down with full power, pulled into a vertical dive, then chopped the throttles and opened the airbrakes. The Javelin's airbrakes were enormous; it was like running into a brick wall. There was no way any other aircraft could slow down enough to stay behind it. As the Sabre shot in front of me I was able to pop the airbrakes in, open the throttles and get a second or two of cine-gun photography of him.

Back at Geilenkirchen there was a heavy snowfall one weekend in November while Jennie was visiting. We borrowed skis from the PT section and spent an afternoon falling down the only slope within 30 miles – the embankment behind the rifle range. It was Jennie's first time on skis; she seemed to enjoy it very much. So Lemmy and I hatched a plot. Innsbruck was another noted site for wave flying. He would invite his girlfriend and I would invite Jennie to go there for a week's skiing at Christmas. I didn't tell Jennie the other half of the plot, so it wasn't until we met up with Lemmy in Austria that she discovered he was towing a trailer with the Olympia 463 in it. Relations were a little strained until we had devoted the first two days entirely to skiing. By then she was glad to have a rest day.

We found the gliding club at the international airport – not many airliners flew into Innsbruck in those days. One of the members said the club would give us aerotows, but we had to go to the control tower to get permission. There we had a somewhat confusing discussion with the controller, who told us we could take off but must not land on the airport. This seemed a bit strange, we didn't fancy going off blindly to land into some unknown field and anyway we could see the local club gliders landing back on the airport. Light eventually dawned – we could take off from the **runway**, but must land on the grass. The next hurdle was a long form to fill in. Glider Registration number? Oh dear, as a RAF Germany Gliding Association glider it didn't need an official one and we hadn't got round to putting a Geilenkirchen identification on it. So we wrote down "GK11". Then "Insurance Policy Number?" The policy was in the other car at the other side of the airfield. We drove round to get it. Having observed the controller look through his binoculars at the gliders from time to time we thought we'd best put "GK11" on the side of ours while we were there. We made a passable job of it – with Jennie's bright red lipstick.

Alas, when we took the Insurance Policy back to the tower and started to copy the details, we found that we'd brought the expired Certificate from Germany instead of the recently renewed one, so we couldn't fly at all. As it turned out, we didn't miss much; there was no wave during our stay.

Life became a little complicated after that holiday. Jennie's British Families Education Service contract at Laarbruch was due to end with the 1965 school summer holidays. She had been offered and had accepted another BFES contract in Malaya to start after the holidays. I thought I would have until she left Germany to make up my mind about whether I wanted to make our relationship permanent, but out of the blue in February I received a notice of posting myself. The Indonesian Confrontation with Malaysia was in progress and a number of crews were needed to reinforce the two Javelin Squadrons at Tengah in Singapore. I would be travelling on an air trooping flight in mid-March to join 64 Squadron. Jennie managed to get her BFES Malaya job changed to BFES Singapore and I bought the engagement ring. I gave her the Kapitan and took the Minivan back to England, where I arranged to ship it out to Singapore.

Chapter 30
Singapore and Borneo

Although it was great to be back in the tropics after five-and-a-half years and away from the cold of a German winter, Singapore was a little disappointing. The sea was not the clear blue of the South Pacific, there were no coral reefs surrounding the island and it was very much more built up than Tahiti or Fiji had been.

Soon after arrival, I was sent on the Jungle Survival course. Compared with the rigours of the Winter Survival course, it was a piece of cake. We spent two days in the classroom at Changi, learning about the plants and animals that we could eat, how to find, pick or catch and cook them, the many uses of a parachute and its webbing, how to make shelters and so on. Then we went to the area of jungle that still remained in the middle of the island around the reservoirs. There we were shown some of the plants and animals that we had heard about. Finally, we spent four days deep in the jungle in Malaya.

It was fortunate that food was the least of our concerns in that tropical situation; most of the food we eat in colder climes is needed to keep us warm, keeping warm in the Malayan jungle was no problem at all. The only edible thing we saw that we had any hope of picking or catching was a poor old tortoise; we couldn't bring ourselves so low as to make a meal of him.

On the first three nights we slept in four-man shelters we had built, but on the last night we made individual roofed hammock shelters using parachute material and cord. Although we were only a few yards apart, the sense of isolation was overwhelming. The night noises were alarming; undoubtedly most of the whistles, screeches, growls and barks were made by completely harmless creatures, but every rustle from the undergrowth made one think of tigers or snakes.

In mid-May, after six weeks area familiarisation flying from Tengah, I went in an RAF Hastings to join the Squadron's detachment of half a dozen Javelins at Kuching in Sarawak, North Borneo. Our job was to patrol the Malaysian part of Borneo to lend support to our ground troops and to intercept any Indonesian aircraft. These were most likely to be low-flying troop carriers, such as the Hercules, so we flew at low level, 500 feet or so above the ground. We had none of the modern navigation equipment carried in today's military aircraft and navigated by map, compass and stopwatch. Flying low made this difficult; such landmarks as there were would be hidden behind trees and hills. Flying higher to make the navigation easier would have given greater exposure to any enemy ground weapons there might be. The low level requirement gave us an excuse to get **really** low, where the aim was to run across one of the calm bays at 500 or so knots and then pull up and look back to view the wake we had left!

At high altitude, a jet engine's normal fuel consumption is less than low down. Also, jet engines are most efficient when operating at maximum revolutions. High up, with both engines at maximum, the Javelin's speed would stabilise at about the best range speed, but down low the engines had to be throttled well back to maintain best range. Both engines would be running at a very inefficient, low revolutions per minute setting. Much better range or endurance could be obtained by shutting down one engine and running the other at maximum or near maximum continuous revolutions. So we carried out our low-level patrols over Borneo with one engine shut down.

South of Kuching there was no problem complying with our strict orders not to cross the border; it ran along the crest of a long escarpment. It was more difficult further to the southeast, where the terrain was flatter, with less distinctive hills. This was long before extensive logging. Virtually the whole of Borneo was covered by dense rain forest, which hid the few roads, the tracks and all but the largest rivers. Apart from half a dozen on the coast, there were no large settlements. My new navrad Tony Bradley and I got it wrong once. One leg of our patrol ran from a distinctive and for once visible river junction towards a small, unpaved airstrip close to the border. A minute before the expected time of arrival we saw an airstrip, but instead of being dead ahead it was out to the left. I was a bit suspicious, so I turned round and went back to the previous turn point.

We checked our heading and time calculations and tried again. Same result. "That must be it," we thought. So I turned left and flew towards the airstrip. Then we saw part of a Hercules wing sticking out below a thatched covering with a blackened area behind one of the engines. A few days earlier we had heard a report from the Army that they had shot at and hit an Indonesian Hercules, which had caught fire and disappeared back across the border. Our Intelligence Officer was very interested in our report and we heard no more about our transgression. I was full of admiration for the Indonesian pilot – it was a **very** short airstrip, even for a Hercules.

The Javelin had quite a good glide performance. With both engines at idle it could glide well over 100 nautical miles from 40,000 feet. This glide performance could be used to gain around 10% better range than that obtained by cruising normally at height, in a similar fashion to the climb and glide procedure familiar to pilots of sustainer or self-launcher gliders. The aircraft could be climbed to high altitude with both engines at full power, then one engine could be shut down and the other throttled right back. A long glide down to near the ground would follow and then the shutdown engine would be re-lit ready for another full power climb.

This technique got me out of trouble one day when the weather at base was very poor and I had to divert a long way to another airfield. Over reliance on it almost got me into real difficulty some time later. We were engaged in a combined RAF/Royal Navy exercise. The fleet was steaming north along the West Coast of Malaya. We were flying low-level patrols around the fleet ready to intercept any attack by 'enemy' aircraft. The 'enemy' were in fact also acting as fighter control, using their radar to direct our intercepts onto themselves. But they had been lurking out of range for the first three days, presumably waiting for a moment when our air cover broke down. We were pretty fed up with the lack of action.

My navigator/radar operator and I had been circling around the ships for half an hour or so with no 'trade' and had agreed that we had enough fuel remaining for another five minutes before returning to our temporary base, Kuala Lumpur. This was the only airfield within range and was about 25 minutes flying time away. We were jolted into action when the 'controller' said "We have a target for you 50 miles to the west, can you take it?" How could we possibly turn this offer down? So away we went and a few minutes later saw the first 'enemy' aircraft of the exercise. We simulated an attack with some cine photography and broke off to return to base.

As I opened up to full power to make the climb which would put us in gliding range of Kuala Lumpur, the fire warning light for the starboard engine illuminated. There was no choice but to shut the engine down. It might have been just a spurious warning but if it was for real the engine could explode within a few seconds. But now the climb and glide technique was not possible. All we could do was fly at best single enginted low-level range speed and hope for the best.

We made it back – just.

Some of our pilots found themselves flying on one engine or none for another reason. In unusual temperature conditions with heavy rain the engine casing could cool rapidly and contract onto the rotating turbine blades, whereupon the engine would seize or shed blades and possibly cause fire or other damage.

After the loss of several aircraft a fix for this 'centreline closure' was designed. A ring of abrasive material (Rockide) was attached to the inside of the casing around the relevant blades. If centreline closure occurred the tips of the blades would be ground off without seizure. It sounds daft; one might ask, "Why not give the blades more clearance in the first place?" However, that would have reduced the engine's performance. This way, if the problem occurred, the engine (and aircraft) would be saved and the blades could be replaced to restore the engine's designed thrust.

There was not a lot of entertainment at Kuching. We had to be fairly careful; there was always a possibility of incursions from Indonesia. We occasionally went into town with armed escorts to the golf course or in the evenings to the open-air eating-places in the market square. This had suffered a grenade attack a few months earlier, but Ah Tek's sweet and sour fish was worth the risk.

Two weeks at Kuching were followed by a couple of Javelin flights to Singapore and back and then a move to Labuan at the north-eastern corner of Borneo. The airfield there was at an easy walking distance from the beach.

With even fewer facilities than at Kuching swimming and fishing became the main off-duty activities. We flew more low-level patrols; sometimes Mount Kinabalu was a useful landmark from a long way away, but usually there was too much cloud to see it.

I had to divert to Jesselton (now called Kota Kinabalu) after one patrol when a large thunderstorm made Labuan unlandable. Jesselton was a civil airport; we had no RAF facilities there. I followed the marshaller's directions to a parking spot near the terminal building and shut down. Mistake. I expected to be refuelled from a mobile bowser, but discovered there wasn't one; re-fuelling was done from underground tanks at the other end of the apron. The problem was that the Javelin's engines were started by a cartridge system and there were only two cartridges per engine. One per engine had been used on start-up at Labuan. I could start one engine only to taxi to the refuelling point, but wouldn't be allowed to keep it running while refuelling. It might be possible to take-off on the other engine only and then do an air start, which needed no cartridge (the engine would be wind milling) but even if the runway had been long enough my superiors would take a very dim view of such action. 40,000 pounds of night fighter was a bit much for the two of us to push to the refuelling point but a few handfuls of Malaysian currency attracted enough onlookers to solve the problem.

The start of August saw me back in the fleshpots of Singapore for two weeks and then it was Borneo again for another eight, so I missed Jennie's arrival. That was my last Borneo detachment, confrontation was winding down. In all my time there, the only Indonesian aircraft I saw was that Hercules on the ground and I observed no other sign of the opposition troops. One of our Javelins did render aid to some of our Army colleagues who were under attack in a jungle clearing. The aircraft couldn't actually **do** anything. It was totally unfitted for ground attack, but when the engine afterburner system was switched on it sounded very like a bomb burst. The Indonesians thought they were under attack from the air and fled. Otherwise the closest I got (so far as I know) to combat was by proxy. For some reason my navrad Tony flew with another pilot one day. They were fired on by an anti-aircraft gun and came back with a shell hole in the wing.

Chapter 31
Snared by the table dancer

After the bamboo and thatch 'basha' accommodation at Kuching the somewhat austere Officers' Mess at Tengah felt like a 5-star hotel. I settled into my permanent room and the Squadron routine. In Germany almost all our flying had been at high level, 30,000 feet and upwards. In the Far East we spent much more time at low level. At night this was a bit nerve-racking, especially over the sea between Malaya and Java, where there was only an occasional surface light from a ship. We would fly in pairs on practice interception exercises, taking turns as target and interceptor. The target flew at 500 feet, the interceptor a bit lower so that the target would not be hidden among surface returns on the aircraft's radar. In the pitch black darkness sixty degrees of bank at 450 knots just a few hundred feet above the waves left little margin for error.

Tengah was on the northern side of the island and Jennie was living with some other BFES teachers in a guesthouse down town. The Minivan had arrived, so off duty I had wheels to visit her. We explored the city and the shops, preparing for our wedding. In those days Singapore hadn't been sanitised, it was full of anarchic character. There were places like Cook Street, with tables and chairs in the roadway and Chinese cooks producing all sorts of goodies on braziers or Primus stoves. Then Bugis Street, where many an innocent serviceman might pick up a very attractive girl only to find later that 'she' was something else. A floating shantytown filled one of the waterway inlets, with hundreds of families living on sampans.

Most anarchic of all was the traffic. There seemed to be no rules; overtaking either side was normal. The greatest hazard was the pick-up taxi. These would frequently overtake other vehicles and then, seeing a likely looking passenger waiting at the roadside, would brake hard right in front of the one they had just passed. I lost my temper with one of the taxi drivers one evening. The fifth time he did this to me I jumped out of the Mini, ran to his door, reached in through his open window, grabbed the ignition keys and hurled them into the roadside vegetation.

There was no gliding in Singapore in 1965. Instead I took Jennie to the RAF Tengah Yacht Club on the Johore Strait, a few miles west of the causeway which was then the only link between Singapore and Malaya. (Another has been built since). Sailing there was not easy; the tide ran very strongly. She had never been in a dinghy before that, but she enjoyed the sailing very much, so I bought a 16-foot Snipe racing dinghy. From then on we spent most weekends at the Club, usually with a morning and an afternoon race. When she was crewing for me we got along pretty well, but after I had crewed for her in the ladies' races a few times she refused to let me in the boat when she was at the helm, citing my incompetence with handling the jib sail. There are twice as many pewter cups on the sideboard here at home inscribed "J. P. St. Pierre" as there are with "A. H. G. St. Pierre" on them! Perhaps that tells me something about our relative abilities.

On the 8th November Tony Bradley was on leave and so missed a drama. I was teamed up with another navrad for a week. But for pure chance, we would probably have made a Martin-Baker (ejection seat) let-down that night. We went out to fly, but the aircraft's starter system didn't work, so we were allocated another Javelin. While we were airborne the first aircraft's starter was sorted out and another crew flew it. On their return they were unable to get the wheels down. Belly landing a Javelin was a positive no-no, so they followed the SOP (Standard Operating Procedure), pointed the aircraft out into the ocean and ejected into the water off Changi beach. The air-sea rescue boat was on its way almost before they hit the water and another Javelin was soon airborne looking for them with its "Violet Picture" – a radio device which indicated the direction to their emergency radio location beacon.

After the first search aircraft had been airborne for 50 minutes and would soon have to return I went with my crewman to take over. Overhead Changi we picked up an emergency beacon transmission, took a bearing, then went north to a point on the Malayan coast and took another bearing. Plotting these two gave us a location for the beacon. We reported this to the rescue co-ordination centre, but they said that it couldn't be correct, the downed crew had already been picked up by the launch and were well on their way back to shore. They had their beacons with them. We insisted that we were still getting bearings from well out to sea.

When no contact could be established with the first search aircraft it was realised that it too had gone missing and the transmission we were receiving was from its crew. Eventually the navrad was found floating in his dinghy and was rescued, but there was no trace of the pilot. It subsequently transpired that he had put his aircraft's wheels down and the landing lights on and had made a low pass over the first crew to indicate that they had been located, but he had then flown into the water.

The navrad could not remember hitting the sea, the first thing he knew was that he regained consciousness sitting in his dinghy and switched his emergency beacon on. Evidently the impact had somehow caused his ejection seat to fire and the automatics took over, saving his life. When the aircraft was finally located, it was virtually undamaged. The pilot appeared uninjured, but was still strapped into his seat and had drowned.

Life went on as was usual after an RAF tragedy, we had all been through many of them during our years of service. Jennie and I continued with preparations for our wedding; with our parents all thousands of miles away it was a DIY effort. I conscripted Tony Bradley to be my best man and Squadron Leader Craven, my Flight Commander, as Master of Ceremonies. Jennie arranged for one of her teacher colleagues, Tony Webb, to give her away. Under Singapore law, we had to go through the civil formalities at the Registry Office in town and effectively we were then married, but after that we had a church wedding in the RAF church, St. Michael and all Angels, at Tengah on the 23rd December.

We set off in the Minivan next day, intending to drive all the way to Bangkok. One thing had us baffled. At every sizeable settlement we saw road signs saying "Utara", but we couldn't find any place with that name on the road map. Eventually the light dawned; "Utara" was Malay for "North". Across the Thai border, we went first to Songkhla, in those days a most attractive small fishing village. There Jennie saw a truly Siamese Siamese cat; she kept a series of them in the U.K. in later years.

While at Songkhla we learnt that the only road from Malaya to Bangkok was impassable, with some of the bridges washed away in the recent heavy rains. We abandoned the idea of driving the rest of the way, left the van at a Missionary establishment in Hatyai and caught the train. Once again I missed seeing most of another of the world's more interesting railway journeys. The train left Hatyai after dark and dawn rose just an hour before arrival at Bangkok. We had dinner in the restaurant car, which was immaculate, with snowy white table linen, solid cutlery and a pewter vase of orchids in the centre of each table and then retired to the sleeping compartment. The locomotive was a wood-burning steamer. Mysterious stops during the night in the middle of the jungle with no sign of life and no trains passing the other way were presumably made at log piles like the ones we saw by daylight next morning.

In Bangkok we did the usual tourist things. Dicing with death in motorised rickshaws. Visiting wats (temples) with their gold-leaf domes. Going in a small boat to the floating market, where the traders sold fish, fruit and vegetables and even hot food from their open sampans. The silk factory, where Jennie stocked up with raw silk cloth in gold and blue. The floating restaurant, where….

Jennie liked curry. All the guidebooks said "Westerners are advised not to try Thai curry, it is too hot." The menu said "Westerners are advised not to order the dishes marked with a *, they are very hot." Jennie asked for one of the * dishes. The waiter said "No madam, it will be too hot for you." She insisted. I tried to dissuade her. No way, her mind was made up. I asked for roast pigeon. Our meals came. Jennie took a forkful, put it in her mouth, gasped, grabbed for the water jug with her face red and her eyes streaming and swallowed a couple of glasses full in about three seconds. When she had recovered, she asked if she could have something else. "You wouldn't listen, you ordered it, so now you'll have to eat that or nothing" I said, somehow managing to keep a straight face.

We lived in a Singapore guesthouse for the first two months of 1966 and then found a flat in Holland Village. Burglary was a common event in Singapore; most houses were protected by metal grilles across windows and doors. Air conditioning was unknown, so it was normal to leave the windows open. We had been warned that the more enterprising thieves equipped themselves with long bamboo poles with a hook or noose on the end and were adept at fishing out anything of value left in sight that was small enough to pass through the grilles. There was no fear of that where we lived. Our landlord, the very wealthy owner of the Thye Hong biscuit company, lived on the forth, top floor of a tower at one end of the building. We tenants were in a row of single story flats joined to the tower. He had run the gauntlet of a kidnap and ransom attempt and was shot in the head while escaping, so he was very security conscious. We had the benefit of an impenetrable 12-foot high fence round the whole compound, with a gatehouse manned by armed guards.

He had even more protection. There were iron grill doors isolating both third and fourth floors of the tower, with more armed guards in between.

Chapter 32
Yacht race, night flypast and parachute descent

Gliding came to Singapore in April 1966, when a T-31 strutted two-seater arrived, sent by the RAFGSA. I did not become a regular attendee at the club; sailing had become the main weekend interest. Seeing Singapore's international airport today it seems scarcely credible that the first day's gliding took place there just thirty-odd years ago. Changi, as it was then, was an active RAF Transport Command base and we soon moved the glider to Sembawang, where there was very little military activity. In July we received a single seat Tutor. We were restricted to flying within the airfield boundary with a maximum height of 2,500 feet. The low performance of both gliders plus these restrictions prevented us from doing much soaring, but I did manage to set a National 2-seater endurance record in September – all of 31 minutes!

By then the Indonesia/Malaya confrontation had simmered down. 64 Squadron was being gradually reduced in numbers of aircraft and personnel and was expecting to disband sometime in the next year. I was transferred to the other Javelin Squadron at Tengah, Number 60. The change made little difference to the social round and the Javelin flying mostly followed the same routine of day and night high and low level practice interceptions.

Jennie and I sailed the Snipe in the annual round the island race that year, a distance of about seventy miles. The start was at midnight, from the western side of the causeway. Normal racing rules were suspended during the hours of darkness; none of the boats taking part had navigation lights so if another boat was not visible it was not possible to give way to it when required. Collisions were inevitable; in normal racing the guilty boat would have had to retire. We fumbled our way down the channel, hearing muffled curses from the unfortunates who had drifted into the bamboo fish traps set at frequent intervals in the shallows each side of the fairway.

When dawn broke we were still within the Johore Strait. The sight ahead and behind us was amazing. Boats of all shapes and sizes and a rainbow of sails covered the water from one bank to the other. At first both large and small vessels were jumbled together, but as the wind increased the larger ones began to pull ahead. By the time we turned the western corner of Singapore Island the fleet stretched ahead as far as we could see. There were not so many boats behind us. The Snipe was smaller and therefore slower than most of the other entrants.

As the sun rose and strengthened I was glad that for once I had prepared us both for a long day. Normally we sailed in shorts or swimsuits with or without a light shirt, but for this race we dressed in hats, slacks, long sleeved shirts and even gloves. It was a little warm that way, but we avoided sunburn. The wind was against us for the long haul along the south coast and past the harbour to Changi and we tacked innumerable times, especially while threading our way between the many ships anchored in Keppel Harbour. Not far short of Changi a comfort stop became a pressing need. Fortunately the beach was almost empty, as was usual in those days.

It was late afternoon by the time we rounded Changi Point and ran with a following wind along the eastern arm of Johore Strait. Darkness fell and so did the wind. It seemed we would never reach the finishing line a short distance before the causeway, but just before midnight we rounded the last corner and saw the lights of the reception committee. We crossed the finish line and made for the bank. Just ahead of us we saw the Royal Navy doing things in style. As another Snipe reached the shore, instead of the crew getting out and de-rigging, a team of sailors picked up the whole kit and caboodle and carried it all, crew included, to its trailer.

Nothing out of the ordinary happened in January 1967, but February was memorable. The Javelin Mk.9's Sapphire engines were fitted with a very simple 'reheat' – also known as 'afterburner' - system. Reheat gives extra thrust by burning fuel in the tailpipe behind the engine. For a reheat system to be fully effective the extra fuel has to be metered and the exhaust nozzle size has to be varied. Nozzle size has to be correct for both the quantity of extra fuel and the aircraft's altitude. The Sapphire's normal fuel control system consisted of a fuel pump, which delivered an excess of fuel and a fuel control unit which, depending on altitude, temperature, airspeed and throttle setting sent the correct quantity of fuel to the engine. The excess fuel was delivered back to the inlet side of the pump. The Javelin's exhaust nozzle had only two positions, normal and fully open. When reheat was selected, the nozzle opened wide and all the excess fuel from the pump was fed into the tailpipe. Unfortunately, low down there was insufficient excess fuel for the wide-open nozzle. The result was that below ten thousand feet or so, with reheat the engines gave less rather than more power and greatly increased the fuel consumption. There was however a quite spectacular tongue of flame behind the engines, especially at night. This gave our Commanding Officer a great idea.

On the 3rd February we were to hold an evening celebration of the Squadron's 50th Anniversary and the Air Officer Commanding Far East Air Force would be attending. It would be dark when he arrived – so a close formation fly-past of four Javelins with eight reheats blazing should make quite a show. Although the power in reheat was fixed, we could formate by using the airbrakes, which were infinitely variable. The formation leader would set his airbrakes slightly open; the other three would use airbrakes instead of throttle to hold position.

Close formation at night, unless there is bright moon or starlight, is not normally a good idea, since judgement of distance by navigation lights alone is difficult. However, the reheat would illuminate the aircraft almost as well as daylight. The problem would be the short endurance. We could not wait until the AOC arrived; the effect would be spoilt. So we needed an advance warning that he was about 20 minutes away, we would then take off and go a few miles to the north where we would be out of earshot from the Squadron area. There we would circle and when he arrived at the camp entrance, we would set off, which should put us overhead moments after he stepped out of his car at the crew room. There would be very little margin for any delay after we took off – for the formation leader. He would have to be in reheat all the time, so that the rest of us could see him. Number two, on his right wing and myself as number three on the left, had our own sneaky idea – we could keep our outboard engines in normal power until the final run in to overhead, the number four in the 'box' behind us would be able to see us clearly. He of course was even better placed; there was no one formating on him, so he could keep both engines in normal power for most of the flight and go into reheat for just the final run in.

It was, by all accounts, a spectacular display. I was exceedingly glad that I wasn't the leader, my tanks were very nearly empty when we landed after just 35 minutes. I hate to think what his fuel state was!

There was another break in the routine at the end of March, when the Squadron flew to Butterworth, on the mainland just across the water from Penang, for gunnery practice on the Phuket range. We expected to be there for three weeks. This covered Jennie's Easter holiday, so on April 9th she set off in the Minivan to join me. She stayed the night in Kuala Lumpur. Next day there was an earthquake; she was delayed for several hours when the road was blocked by a fallen tree. Arriving at Butterworth, she was not best pleased to be told that I would be flying back to Tengah next morning.

Two days before, the pilot of one of our aircraft had experienced an undercarriage failure on his return from the range. One of the main wheels refused to extend. Although landing with no wheels down was a definite no no, two out of three was relatively safe. He made a good job of landing on the nose wheel and one main wheel, but all the Javelins were grounded pending investigations. This revealed a fault in the retraction mechanism and the same fault was found on several more aircraft. It was decided that instead of sending spares and repair teams to Butterworth, we would fly the Javelins back to Tengah, leaving the wheels down all the way. The limiting speed for an extended undercarriage meant flying at an inefficient slow speed; this, added to the extra drag, reduced our range considerably, so we landed to refuel at Kuala Lumpur's civil airport on the way.

Two days after me, a somewhat less than gruntled Jennie arrived back at our Singapore flat. I did make it up to her soon after, when we drove up the west coast of Malaya and spent a week in Penang.

A little later I had the chance to try two new forms of aviation. It started with parascending on the airfield at Tengah, using a surplus emergency parachute and a jeep. Provided there was some wind, the victim could get the parachute to inflate while standing and could then be towed into the air by the jeep. The driver controlled the "flight". If he increased speed the parachute would rise and by slowing down he could gently lower the parascender to the ground. I got the feel of parachuting that way; there was a sensation of buoyancy when the parachute was lifting properly.

A few weeks after that the squadron's aircrew were offered the opportunity to make a static line parachute jump from a Beverley aircraft. It seemed a good idea at the time, but the four days delay between accepting and doing was a bit stressful. The mood graduated from "this will be a great new experience" through "I hope nothing goes wrong" to "I'm going to die tomorrow." The mental agony was slightly alleviated by an incredibly vivid dream the night before the event. I jumped out of the aircraft, realised I hadn't put the parachute on, thought "that's no problem" and went back for it!

We had two hours in the hangar at Changi practising for the jump, with a parachute harness suspended from the ceiling and a set of steps to leap off. We would be going into the sea, so the harness and the technique required had both been modified. To avoid the risk of being entangled in the straps and drowning an extra strap had been added at the rear; this had to be pulled forward under the knees. Then the harness release buckle had to be operated while hanging firmly onto the risers with the other hand. Now one was sitting in something rather like the seat of a child's swing; on touching the water arching the back made a clean exit from the harness certain.

I was the last one of the stick leaving the Beverley. The first thing I noticed was a complete lack of the "leaving one's stomach behind" sensation that occurs when jumping off the top board at the swimming pool. The effect of forward motion imparted by the aircraft initially gives a lift force on the body; the parachute's opening when the static line tightens maintains the lift. As instructed, I looked up to check the canopy. It was slightly disconcerting to see that it was split from rim to apex. I could see that I was overtaking those who had jumped before me, but I felt the same buoyancy I had experienced when parascending, so I didn't operate the second, emergency parachute strapped to my chest.

I was first into the water and hadn't had time to admire the view, so I demanded to be put on the next session two weeks later. The second jump was more normal, if deliberately jumping out of a perfectly serviceable aircraft can ever be described that way.

Chapter 33
End of an era for the Javelin

By June 1967 the Javelin had almost had its day and was being replaced by Lightnings. 60 Squadron was reducing in size in preparation for the arrival of the new aircraft and crews and I was among the first group of pilots and navrads to be posted. As promised when I left 5 Squadron in Germany, I was offered the posting of my choice. This was not such a good deal as it sounds – the choice was limited to a flying instructor course at Central Flying School Little Rissington or a tour as a Fighter Controller at one of the radar stations on the east coast of the U.K. Neither appealed, but CFS was the lesser evil. At least I would still be flying and with my 8-year option of leaving the RAF just 9 months ahead, if CFS proved too much of a pain I could escape.

On the 9th of June I took an RAF photographer in a Javelin to obtain some air-to-air photography of the newly arrived Lightnings. Next day I took part in a Queen's Birthday 19 aircraft close formation fly-past and bid farewell to the Javelin with a total time on type of 1,310 hours.

I had fought a minor battle with the RAF authorities when I was told that Jennie had to leave Singapore with me. This she was not about to do, her contract with BFES had another three months to run. The RAF discovered that pressurising me to make her break her contract was not going to work, so gave in on that, but made me leave Singapore in late June although the CFS course didn't start until the beginning of August. Jennie's parting instructions were "Don't take a married quarter at Bicester and don't buy another Minivan." It wasn't really out of badness, but when she joined me we had somehow been allocated a married quarter at Bicester and I had bought a Minivan. I bought her a second hand Ford Popular as compensation. She found a teaching job not far away at Weston Turville.

Photo 38 - Queen's Birthday fly past over RAF Tengah 10th June 1967

RAF Bicester was an all grass airfield, the home of an RAF Maintenance Unit and of the RAF Gliding and Soaring Association's Centre. No military flying took place there, but gliding was very active, seven days a week. The legendary Warrant Officer Andy Gough ran the Centre and kept a tight rein on glider pilots from Aircraftsmen to Air Marshals. Andy had a marvellous personality; somehow no matter who you were he made you feel that you were a special friend. Sadly he was killed a few years later when he crashed while doing an aerobatics display in a Blanik glider. Investigation found that a spanner had jammed the elevator controls; it seemed probable that it had been lying hidden in the bottom of the fuselage for many years.

With a month's leave before the CFS course, I spent most of the time gliding. My gliding logbook shows 222 launches giving 41 hours 13 minutes airborne for that July, just one hour short of my highest ever monthly total for RAF flying. I had a couple of embarrassments. Most of the launches were in T21's, instructing. On one of these flights I was pre-occupied with the student's erratic speed control and allowed us to get a bit too far downwind of the airfield, over the married quarters. The sports field lay between the airfield and us but goal posts and cricket pitch chains made a landing there without damage unlikely. The only chance was to fly as close to the ground as possible, using ground effect to stretch the glide. We made it – but it was just as well there wasn't a truck travelling along the Bicester-Buckingham road at the time! Since Andy for once didn't seem to have noticed, I grounded myself. A little later he noticed me standing by the control bus. "Why aren't you instructing?" he asked. I told him it was because I had grounded myself and explained why. "You don't ground people here, I do, get back in that T21" he said.

The other embarrassment was an attempted 150 km triangular cross-country in Andy's pride and joy, an Olympia 419. It **was** my first cross-country for three years, but all the same.... I boggled out after 98 km and landed in a large stubble field. Andy sent a Chipmunk to aerotow me out of it. The weather was still soarable, so when we flew into a strong thermal I released and carried on. To no avail. I got 40 km further and then fell to earth at Finmere, another deserted WW2 airfield. A second Chipmunk was sent to retrieve me and this time I was told to stay on tow until we were overhead Bicester!

Chapter 34
Qualified Flying Instructor course

When Jennie arrived from Singapore we moved into a married quarter at Bicester and I began the daily commute to Little Rissington. The aircraft used at CFS were Jet Provosts, a mixture of Mk. 3's and Mk. 4's. I can't remember any difference between the two; both were widely castigated as constant thrust variable noise machines. CFS did indeed prove to be a pain; the object of the instructional staff seemed to be to destroy us so that we could be rebuilt in their own image. I was criticised for almost everything I did; it seemed my operational experience had no value. I didn't dare to mention that I had been instructing in gliders for five years, had taught quite a few people to fly and so far as I knew none of them had killed themselves. I found it difficult to accept the continual emphasis on 'standardisation'. To me, flying had always seemed more an art than a science; I believed there was some room for individuality. I felt that standardisation could mean that if whoever defined the standard got it wrong, then one hundred percent of us would be doing it wrongly. One of my first run-ins with standardisation had to do with take-off technique in the Jet Provost. The 'right' way was to keep back pressure on the stick until the nose wheel lifted off the runway – this required a fairly strong pull. When the nose wheel came up, the pull had to be rapidly changed to a strong push to stop the nose rising too high before take-off speed was reached. It all felt most unnatural. Whenever I was on my own I would just keep the stick roughly central and rotate gently at take-off speed. A year later when I was instructing at Leeming, the standard procedure was changed; the 'right' way became 'just keep the stick roughly central and rotate gently at take-off speed'

It got to the point where I no longer found any enjoyment in RAF flying and felt great relief whenever the weather was too bad or the aircraft was unserviceable. But every weekend, I would be gliding, instructing or aerotowing, at Bicester. A few openings in the civil aviation world started to appear in "Flight" magazine's situations vacant pages and I wrote to British European Airways in response to an advertisement of theirs. In due course a reply arrived inviting me for interview in September. Unfortunately the interview date was one day after the last day I could put in my notice to exercise my eight year option to leave the RAF. I dithered for a week and then decided to go for it. The reaction from the RAF was, I thought, a bit mean. Naturally, I did not expect to remain on the course, I would not have more than two month's service time left for productive instructing when it ended. I spent a few days on administrative duties at Little Rissington while awaiting a decision from Ministry of Defence as to my future and went for the BEA interview. Back at Little Rissington on the Wednesday afternoon I was told that I had to 'march out' of my married quarter at Bicester, clear from Little Rissington and report for duty at Patrington near Hull on Monday morning. Jennie was teaching in the school at Weston Turville and had to serve out her contract until December. The logistics of finding somewhere for her to live and moving our possessions, plus marching out of the quarter and going through the clearance procedure, all in two days was a bit daunting! Added to that, because I would not be available to BEA for six months they had not given me a firm offer of employment in March next year but had just said that they would take me when there was a vacancy thereafter. It had been a most peculiar interview anyway; they'd asked me very few questions and had spent most of the time telling me about BEA's operations, salary and allowance structure! The flying sounded a bit tedious. It didn't take long for me to ask if I could withdraw the six months' notice to leave the RAF and it didn't take long for someone 'up there' to decide that I could be re-instated on the course. No doubt commercial sense came into the decision, my CFS course had already cost a large amount. There was a bit of muttering about my not knowing my own mind!

I didn't exactly cover myself with glory during the rest of the course, but did at least pass out – with the slightly grudging assessment of "Competent to instruct on the Jet Provost". As a group our course didn't cover itself with glory either. One of CFS's traditions involved a top hat. This was awarded to the course member who passed out with the lowest marks; he was required to wear it during the dining out night at the end of the course and to make a speech on behalf of the course members. One of us had the bright idea that the unfortunate hat wearer should conclude his speech with the presentation of a different top hat to the permanent staff. Four feet high and three wide, it was wheeled in on a trolley and placed on the table in front of the Commandant. At the end of our man's peroration, two other members of the course lifted the top hat, to reveal a stripper. All eyes on the top table looked towards the Commandant, waiting for his reaction before they either smiled or scowled. The Commandant sat stony faced. Later in the evening we were advised by the Station Adjutant that it would be a good idea to leave the station very early next morning.

As was usual near the end of a course or a tour of duty on an RAF squadron, we had been asked to nominate three choices of posting in order of preference. By now wise to the ways of the Service, I had made No. 3 Flying Training School Leeming my third choice rather than my first. That was the only FTS where there was an RAF Gliding Club. It was no great surprise when my posting came through to RAF Leeming!

Chapter 35
Pioneering the Yorkshire wave

We moved into number 12 the Coppice in the RAF Leeming married quarters in January 1968. Jennie started work as an assistant teacher at the Wavell County Primary School on the Catterick Army base. I lost no time getting to the gliding club, which flew at Dishforth, just 10 miles south of Leeming alongside the A1 road. During the week, Dishforth was active as a relief landing ground, where the Jet Provosts did much of their circuit training, but at weekends we usually had the field to ourselves. I started gliding there on the 10th January and two weeks later, after all those abortive attempts to find wave at Carlisle, Aosta, Issoire and Innsbruck, at last encountered what I'd so often read about.

It was rough on tow behind the Chipmunk as we climbed towards Ripon, but after we passed below a line of cloud, the turbulence decreased markedly and our rate of climb increased. I released at 2,000 feet just about level with the cloud base. The cloud mass towered like a wall behind me and I turned to fly close alongside it. At first I could barely maintain height in alternating lift and sink, but by making tight s-turns in some of the juicier bits of lift while they lasted I gradually worked up the side of the cloud. Quite suddenly, at 2,500 feet the air went silk-smooth. I could feel the buoyancy as the variometer settled to show a steady 300 feet per minute rate of climb. As I gained height the climb rate increased; passing 5,000 feet the glider was climbing at 600 feet per minute. Upwind I could see the back of the next line of cloud pouring downwards like water over a fall, evaporating as it reached cloud base level and leaving a clear 'slot' stretching left and right as far as I could see. Behind me the cauliflower tops of the cumulus clouds wore smooth caps of lens-shaped alto-stratus and above those, several more of these lenticulars were stacked one on top of the other in the classic pile of plates configuration I had seen so often in the gliding books. At 8,000 feet the rate of climb decreased to almost nothing; it took a long time to reach 10,000 and then the rate of climb increased again. Unfortunately there was no oxygen equipment in the glider and it was getting late. Conscious of the trap that can befall a wave pilot – it can still be broad daylight up high but dark on the ground – I broke off the climb at 11,000 feet, pushed forward into the sinking air and pulled the airbrakes open. Six minutes later I was on the ground.

That was the first of many wave flights, at Dishforth and elsewhere in the U.K. Two months later I went to Portmoak, on the shore of Loch Leven north of Edinburgh. The RAFGSA had organised an expedition there, with half-a-dozen gliders sent from various clubs in England. As I got out of my car one of the GSA pilots, who had just landed in a Dart 17 glider, asked me if I would like to fly it. I was airborne behind the tug within 20 minutes and released from tow at 2,000 feet. After another 20 minutes I was passing 12,000. It seemed that there might be a chance of a Height Diamond, which required a gain of height of 16,400 feet (3,000 metres) but it was not to be, I could get no higher than 16,200 feet.

Three days after that, on the 9th March I made it, but only just. A mile to the east of Portmoak the west face of Bishop Hill provides ridge soaring in a westerly wind. This enables a pilot hoping for a height badge to establish a low point after releasing from tow. I went from 800 feet on the hill to 17,200 in wave very quickly. That was marginally high enough if the altimeter was under-reading. Examination of the barograph trace would decide; that could be done only after landing. I tried desperately to squeeze another few feet of climb, moving from place to place where the clouds indicated the wave might go further up, but couldn't get any higher. The temperature up there was around minus thirty degrees centigrade; the sun through the Perspex canopy kept my upper body warm enough, but my feet were freezing in the shade under the instrument panel. After an hour and a half above 10,000 feet I'd had enough. When I landed I thought my feet were frost-bitten; standing was agony. I was very grateful for the under-floor heating in the Portmoak clubhouse, half an hour walking around in there with my boots off restored feeling to normal. The barograph trace proved that the gain of height was sufficient, so I had Gold C with two diamonds. There was only the diamond distance of 500 kms remaining to do for the full Diamond Certificate.

We RAFGSA pilots, knowing no better, thought this wave flying business was just the job for cross-countries and went roaming off into the mountains wherever the wave took us. The local Portmoak pilots were horrified by our cavalier approach to the lack of good landing fields where we had been. They thought that wave was only suitable for height gains within gliding reach of the airfield.

At work I began on the same "circuits and bumps and stalls laddie and how to get out of a spin" routine that my instructors back at Booker had taken me through. It didn't take long to discover that wave conditions made Leeming a far from ideal place for basic flying training. An aeroplane maintaining a constant altitude is not quite the same as a car on a level road. All aeroplanes have a speed below which more power rather than less is necessary to maintain level flight. Above this speed though, the principle is the same. Press the accelerator halfway, the car's speed increases and settles at a higher speed. Press it to the floorboards, the car accelerates again and eventually stabilises at its maximum speed. The Jet Provost had a more precise power indication than "accelerator halfway" or "accelerator to the floor" in the form of an rpm gauge marked in percentage. Thrust of a jet engine in the higher rpm range is roughly proportional to the rpm. So the "patter" would go on the lines of "O.K. Bloggs, maintain 12,000 feet and set 80% power.... Good.... Notice our speed is increasing.... Now it has settled, what is our airspeed?" Bloggs would say "200 knots, Sir." Then "Right, increase the power to 90%.... Keep the aircraft level at 12,000... wait for the speed to settle... Oh ***** ... Let's try again somewhere else." The airspeed had decreased, instead of increasing, because the aircraft had flown into the descending part of a mountain lee wave and the power was being used to battle against the downdraught rather than to accelerate.

Her Majesty didn't know it, but by providing me with one of her Jet Provosts during the next few years she enabled me to find out a lot about wave that I would never have realised had I not had an engine to take me to interesting-looking bits of the sky. I discovered that wave occurred much more often than had been generally realised. In fact, almost any time there was a wind of 10 knots or more I would find wave somewhere in the local area, maybe just in one or two places or in a limited height range. Although this didn't help the flying instruction, it gave me opportunities to find out where the best spots were in different wind directions. I also saw and remembered many landmarks, which became especially useful when gliding above cloud. A glimpse of some remembered feature through a gap gave the confidence to remain high, instead of descending to find my position. It was only too easy to fall out of wave by getting too low. This would usually mean a field landing and a retrieve.

The acquired knowledge helped a lot on the 20th April. I looked out of the window that morning and saw wave clouds in all directions. When I arrived at Dishforth, Gerry Kemp, the CFI told me our new Ka6E glider had arrived and he thought someone should do a good long cross-country in it. Jokingly I replied "How about Portmoak and back for a diamond distance?" Somewhat to my consternation, he said "right then, you'd better get going – it's all ready, the Daily Inspection has been done." With a 500-kilometre task declared, there was no time to be wasted. I grabbed a barograph, had it sealed and signed by an observer, pulled my camera and map out of the car, photographed the declaration board and settled into the cockpit to do a before take-off check. The tow plane took me to a likely looking spot and I released ahead of a smooth curve of cloud. When I had satisfied myself that the wave was working, I turned north, cruising at 60 knots and climbing gently.

There wasn't a great amount of cloud, just enough lying in lines across the wind to mark where the lift was to be found. When flying cross-country in wave, the technique is to follow a bar cloud leading in roughly the right direction and side-step up or downwind when necessary, either because the adjacent wave bar looks stronger, or to change direction more towards the destination. Visibility was excellent. There was no need to look at the map. I had flown all over this area in the Jet Provost, familiar landmarks came and went and as I climbed above the cloud tops at 7,000 feet, the coast came in sight out to the right.

At around 10,000 feet, the rate of climb started to decrease. It was time to go for speed. When thermal flying, a glider pilot extracts energy from strongly rising air by circling to gain height. In between these climbs he glides in the direction of his next turning point, deviating from side to side towards likely looking clouds or areas of ground where he expects to find another strong 'thermal'. If he encounters weakly rising air, not worth circling in, he slows down and he flies fast through sinking air. This doesn't work so well in wave. Slowing down in faster rising air means that the glider will climb, but in doing so, it will ascend into less rapidly rising air. It is more efficient to stay fairly close to the height of the strongest 'lift' and extract the energy as higher speed. In the extra strong bits, the glider is allowed to climb a little and in the weaker areas, to descend gently. So for the next 30 miles, I undulated along the bars, with the speed varying between 70 and 110 knots and the height between 8,000 and 12,000 feet.

It was a gloriously sunny day up there above the cloud. To the west and ahead the stratocumulus below me was thickening, but still with plenty of gaps. I seemed to be flying above a white sea, with every wave frozen. It was easy to see by the steepness of the upwind curve of the cloud tops where the best lift was to be found. One wave bar led on to another. Near Consett, although I was flying at 80 knots, my rate of climb increased markedly. This was too good to miss. I turned in front of a steep cloud edge below me and slowed right down. The variometer (rate of climb indicator) needle swung upwards, settling at 1000 feet per minute and I was soon passing 13,000 feet. I put on the oxygen mask, but the lift fell away at 14,400 feet. Enough of playing around for height - there was a long way to go. I needed to keep moving, so down with the nose and away northwards again.

Newcastle slid past the right wing tip and way ahead, basking in the near cloudless sky out to sea, lay Holy Island. Dead ahead, some higher, smooth saucer shaped clouds showed where the Cheviot was pushing the air's wave motion higher. As I came overhead Wooler, the variometer indicated another strong lift area and for a few miles I was able to fly at 120 knots while climbing at 3 knots. But things weren't looking so good where I wanted to go. Although the cloud tops were even wavier, the amount of cloud was increasing. I could still see bits of the coast through the gaps, but directly ahead the cloud was almost continuous. A quick turn to look behind showed a more open skyscape, I had a line of retreat if necessary. So I veered towards the coast and a largish gap. This proved to be over Dunbar. I found the lift about a mile out to sea and inland through the hole I could see some good fields for an out landing if one became necessary. It was time to stop and plan what to do next. One definite must was to stay over or at least close to land! I needed to look at the map to see which of the few gaps visible inland was in the right direction.

This was the first problem. In my haste to get away, I had stuffed my neatly folded map into the side pocket of the glider. Now the bit I wanted to look at was inside the folds. There's not a lot of room in even the most spacious glider cockpit to unfold a 4-foot square map sheet. The only answer was "to hell with the expense" and tear off the unneeded bits. With a small heap of confetti piled up on my lap, the map was reduced to a manageable size. "I'm here, it looks like I should try to get close to Edinburgh before crossing the Firth of Forth. So

I need to look for a gap in the clouds about 265 degrees from here. Where's the compass on this aircraft?"

Problem number two. Where **had** they put the compass? "They" hadn't. But I hadn't done a very good pre-flight check of the instruments. All the spaces on the instrument panel had been full, the corresponding dials had checked out as serviceable, but I hadn't gone through a mental list of what should have been present. No compass! A trick learnt in Boy Scout days came to mind. Use my watch. Fortunately digital timepieces were not common at the time and I was wearing an old-fashioned analogue variety. Point the hour hand at the sun and south is halfway between the hour hand and 12 o'clock. Hang on though, we're on summer time. No, the country may be, but my watch is always on GMT. It's now showing 1 o'clock so south is in the 12.30 direction and 265 degrees is in the direction of 3.25 – over there. There are a few holes that way – let's go.

Through the next gap, flat country was visible. The one after that revealed an airfield with tarmac runways and a railway just to the north – it could only be East Fortune. But in all directions except a long way to the south the holes were closing up. There was no indication of bad weather coming in from the west, so perhaps if I waited a while the cloud would start to open up again. If this gap looked like filling in, I'd better pull out the airbrakes and spiral down for a field landing – if I stayed above total cloud cover I couldn't keep track of my position and the sea wasn't far away. The Ka6E was not a flying boat!

So I waited in the lift. The gap started to fill in, I started to spiral down and the gap opened up again. I climbed back up. No gaps opened further west; mine started to close again. Another descent and again it opened up. Same again – and again. Two hours later, it was too late to hope to get to my turning point and back to Dishforth. When the cloud started to break a little more to the south, I called it a day and turned back for home.

The return flight was an anti-climax. The wind, now on the aft quarter, was pushing me along at a great rate and the amount of cloud cover was decreasing. Nearing Catterick, there were few clouds left. I could see Leeming airfield and beyond it Dishforth. Somewhere around there, I completed my 500th hour in gliders. A long final glide, a circuit and 7 hours 8 minutes after take-off, I landed, well before sunset. Perhaps I should have held on longer at East Fortune.

Although I failed the task, it is probable that the flight was the longest out and return solely in wave that had been made in the U.K. at that time, but with the actual turning point not declared before take-off, it set no record. I tried again several times; each time complete cloud cover foiled me. The nearest I got to Portmoak was in April 1971 when I reached Earlsferry on the north side of the Firth of Forth, an out and return distance of 494 kilometres. Nowadays a turning point can be proved by a data-logger connected to a GPS, but in those days it was necessary to take a photograph of the turning point. I was determined to make the first wave-only diamond distance flight in the U.K., but never had the right weather during my remaining time in the Royal Air Force, or during my leave periods from overseas in later years. So in 1990 I gave up on the wave hope and gained the diamond distance gliding badge with a flight of 515 kilometres in thermals.

Chapter 36
Pilot Navigation Training and National Gliding Championships

1968 finished as a good year in terms of flying hours achieved, both instructing on the Jet Provost and gliding. By airline standards the 300 Jet Provost hours were not much, but although the flights averaged around one hour, pre-flight briefing and post-flight debriefing of the students trebled the instructional time. More satisfying to me was the addition of 120 hours gliding. In addition to the time gained at Dishforth, I was given a Ka6E to fly in the Inter-Services competition at Bicester in September. A 6th place put me in the RAF team for the following year's Nationals. As far as my professional career went, I'm not so sure it was a good year. Whether it was because my C.O. thought I was suitable for specialisation or because he thought I was a pretty useless Flying Instructor is something I will never know. Whatever, in December I was sent to RAF Finningley on a Pilot Navigation Instructor's course.

The course ended in February 1969. I was appointed Chief Pilot Navigation Instructor at Leeming, which was not quite as grandiose a position as it might sound. I was Chief of only three PNI's. Between us we taught in Ground School and flew with the students on cross-country navigation exercises; I did most of the final navigation tests. The job involved much less flying and gave me lots of free time. The Chief Ground Instructor was also a glider pilot; between us we set up a plot.

The U.K. out and return distance gliding record was still less than 500 kilometres. Portmoak and return from Dishforth would set a new record. If this could be done by a serving member of the RAF it would be good for morale and Public Relations and would be one in the eye for the Navy, who were doing far too well in the gliding field. There were at least six tug pilots at Leeming who were not RAF aircrew; they had qualified as Private Pilots via gliding. There were also a couple of RAF pilots, of whom the CGI himself was one, who had aerotowed. My duties could easily be covered by one of the other two PNI's. When a suitable wave day was forecast during the week, it should be easy enough to find a wing tip runner and a tug pilot to detach from their duties for an hour or two. They could be sent to Dishforth to launch me before the jets started flying.

The CGI took this proposal to the Station Commander, who was most enthusiastic, so we set it up. Unfortunately it was implemented only three times in the next three years. Although there were many wave days in Yorkshire, they occurred when the forecast showed excessive cloud or rain further north. And as we often complained at the gliding club, the best wave days always came at night! The days when I did set off all came to nothing, on one of them I fell to earth only 50 kilometres away, although another was the Earlsferry 494-kilometre effort.

One of those night "days" gave me some amusement. I was giving a student his final night navigation test in a Jet Provost. His pre-flight planning had been meticulous and exact. The flight went well, his heading corrections to maintain track were good, his estimated times of arrival were within a minute of the actual and he started on his practice diversion perfectly. I'd seen enough to give him a good pass. "Take me back to Leeming" I ordered. At 25,000 feet, approaching the point where he should start the descent I decided to liven up the proceedings. I pulled the throttle back to idle and said, "Your engine has flamed out." He carried out an immaculate relight drill. "Sorry," I told him, "it didn't relight." There was another, emergency relight drill for the Jet Provost. He went through that equally well. We were by then coming down to 10,000 feet. "Tough, it still hasn't relit" I informed him. "Well Sir," he replied, "I can see the runway lights at Leeming down there, but Flying Orders say we must not try to force land at night. I'll make an emergency call, tell Leeming where we are, point the aircraft out over the Pennines and we'll eject." A perfect response. I took over control, congratulated him on his performance and told him that what I was about to do was not in the RAF manual of flying.

It was a beautiful clear moonlit night; there were wave clouds all over the sky. I flew downwind towards one of the bars of cloud. As we approached it, our rate of descent in the glide reduced and reduced again. Just before the cloud

I turned along it, our descent slowed further, stopped and then we began to climb. After twenty minutes or so beating backwards and forwards we had gained 2,000 feet. "There," I said "we could stay up here all night, then when it gets to be daylight, we would be legal to carry out a forced landing."

Photo 39 - Jet Provost T3   Courtesy RuthAS

Never spoil a good story by telling the truth they say. Well, that was the truth, the legend that grew out of it was that I had once landed after being airborne twice as long as the Jet Provost's fuel would last. Not that that would have been impossible. However, there would have been a problem staying airborne in wave with the engine shut down for too long. Even at glide speed, the engine windmilled and drove the oil pump. Jet Provost engine lubrication was by a "dead loss" system; after passing through the bearings, the oil was released into the jet pipe, where when the engine was running it would burn. If the engine ran, or windmilled, for too long the oil would all be used up and the engine would seize.

1969 also saw my first Gliding Nationals competition, held in June at Dunstable. There were two classes. The Open Class was unlimited, which by allowing greater wing span meant higher performance. I flew a Ka6E again, in the Standard Class, limited to 15 metres span. By this time gliding competition tasks had become mostly races, to somewhere, to somewhere and back, or round a triangle. Races were not Le Mans style events, with everyone starting at the same time – that would have been rather dangerous. Pilots could start whenever they liked and would be timed from when they crossed the start line. This went some way to separating the 41 competitors, although every now and then when one pilot started circling in a thermal others within reach would swarm in on him like vultures. This competition was also unusual in that it was scored both handicapped and unhandicapped.

The third day was very peculiar. The task was a 112-kilometre race to Nympsfield, near Stroud. I delayed my start until I thought the conditions would be best and set off when a group of gliders a few miles down track appeared to be climbing well. I arrived beneath them at 2,000 feet; they were way above me by then. I found no lift so pushed on. After that I could never manage a decent climb, I'd get down to five or six hundred feet, find a strong thermal, but at 1500 feet or so would lose it. Cursing myself for my incompetence I'd press on again. This went on until about 30 kilometres short of Nympsfield, when I got the first sensible climb of the day to 3,500 feet. There was a gaggle of other gliders circling ahead of me, so as my thermal died I flew towards them. Then realising I had enough height to reach the goal I flew straight through their thermal and crossed the finish line at high speed. My time proved to be fastest of the day, but on handicap I came second. Sheer luck. The Met forecaster later told me that there had been an easterly wind low down, but it died away rapidly to nothing higher up. All the other pilots had been able to get high and stay high, normally the best thing to do, but they had then been flying in still air, whereas I had a good tailwind helping me along low down.

The next day went quite well also, so at the end of day four I was in second place overall on the unhandicapped list. After that the Gods weren't so kind, I managed to stay well placed on days five and six and was still in with a chance but on the seventh day I landed out not very far away and on the last day made a very slow time round the task. So from second I slipped down to eleventh. Oh, what might have been! The first two pilots, Con Greaves and Andy Gough, both RAF ground tradesmen, obtained places in the British team for the next World Championships, held at Marfa in Texas the following year.

On the domestic front, in September Jennie had been appointed as Head Teacher of the very small primary school at Constable Burton, a few miles up Wensleydale from Leeming. With two years of my 12-year engagement remaining and the assurance that I would not be posted away, we decided it would be a good idea to buy a house. After much searching around the area we settled on a detached two-storey house at Aiskew, Bedale and moved in just before Christmas 1969. I still live there today.

1970 provided me with two exceptional glider flights. The first, on the 18th July was my longest airborne time ever, 9 hours exactly. That was another of the Portmoak and return attempts. Again the weather in the north of the route was not so good; I hung around the Wooler area for two hours. Radio contact with Portmoak finally encouraged me to move on, a gap had appeared in their up till then total cloud cover, but by the time I reached Dunbar the cloud had increased to eight eighths again and it was raining at Portmoak.

The first part of my return was a little harrowing, the wave seemed to collapse and I got low down between cloud masses. I made for the hills at Chillingham, hoping the westerly wind blowing on the ridge there would keep me airborne until the wave reformed. There might have been a problem – I didn't know exactly where the estate with the herd of Highland cattle was and a landing amongst them might have been a bit hairy! Fortunately the wave did reform in the lee of the Cheviot, which got me back up to 10,000 feet. Another bad stretch had me worried, with a low point of 3,500 feet west of Newcastle, but again a newly forming wave saved the day and the rest of the flight was easy.

The eleventh place in the '69 Nationals gave me promotion to the Open Class for 1970. The RAFGSA allocated me an SHK. This, although of wood and fabric construction, was one of the highest performance machines of its time, only a few all glass-fibre sailplanes were rated better. I had not flown an SHK before, so I went to Bicester for some practice in it. Not enough was my excuse; I finished 24th out of 33 in the unhandicapped scores and 29th on handicap. The competition was held at Doncaster in August. I remember little of it except the first and third days. On day one, the cloud base never got above 1,800 feet. I landed out in the Pennines higher than I had been for most of the time getting there. On day three the Doncaster forecast was so bad that we all upped sticks and took our trailers down the M1 in convoy to Husbands Bosworth, near Market Harborough. It was worth it from the competition point of view; we had very good conditions for a 145 km triangle. I got round the task but took far too long to score well.

The second notable flight of the year was in a Slingsby Dart 17 from Dishforth on the 18th October. It was a day with little cloud to mark the forecasted weak wave, not suitable for a long cross-country. Climbing at all was quite difficult, I would slowly gain a few hundred feet, lose the wave, move somewhere else, get a little higher and lose it again. After two and a quarter hours I had managed to pass 9,000 feet and then suddenly I found the express elevator. The rate of climb went to more than 800 feet per minute. It was very foolish of me, but I couldn't resist the temptation to keep climbing despite having no oxygen equipment in the Dart. In no time at all at the altimeter wound up past 20,000 feet. That was enough, I opened the airbrakes and turned down wind into sinking air. Fifteen minutes later I was warming myself inside and out with a coffee in the airfield 'bus.

1970 finished as a boom year for gliding time, with 152 hours. This remained a personal best until my retirement long afterwards. In contrast, my total RAF flying amounted to only 108 hours and if I had not started aerotowing in RAF Chipmunks again it would have been no more than the 82 gained in the Jet Provost.

1971 gliding started well, with several wave flights from March onwards. The big one, 494 km to Earlsferry and return in the Ka6E happened on the 19th April. It was an easy ride going north from Dishforth, with around 6/8 cloud between 3,000 and 8,000 feet, arranged neatly across wind to show where the up going air was and with clear gaps through which the landmarks showed up well. It took only one and a half hours to reach the Tweed, 180 kilometres away, a groundspeed of 120 kph. For a wooden glider that was extremely good going. The good conditions didn't last, just west of Dunbar the wave collapsed for a time and I was scrabbling about low down over the hills surrounded by cloud. After a nerve-racking 20 minutes the wave re-organised and I climbed back to 9,000 feet. There was a small gap in the cloud below, through which I could just see the northern coast of the Firth of Forth, but by the time I reached Earlsferry the stratocumulus layer had become almost continuous, with no breaks to the north or west, just a small gap below me through which Earlsferry itself was visible and very few gaps to the south. I waited around for a while, but the situation didn't improve, so at 15.30 I set off back towards home. By now the cloud tops had risen to 11,000 feet and without oxygen I didn't want to spend too much time above 10,000, so I flew along the cloud valleys below the top of the cloud each side. The lift was stronger there anyway. I saw the ground only four times on the return, at East Fortune, St. Boswell's, Ouston and Barnard Castle. Although I couldn't see the Cheviot, the extra strong and high wave there was well marked by cloud and further south the shape of the cloud tops marked out the North York Moors. I descended through cloud after a timed run on a compass heading from Barnard Castle to where I expected Ripon to be and somewhat to my surprise broke cloud over Ripon!

After my abysmal performance in the 1970 Nationals, the RAFGSA relegated me to the Ka6E and the Standard Class Nationals for 1971. The contest was held from the 29th May to 6th June at RAF Newton, an all grass airfield near Nottingham. Somehow I remember this as one of the most enjoyable competitions of any I flew in. The atmosphere was superb, the organisation brilliant and excellent meals were available in the Airmen's Mess. There were to be only four contest days, but the 9 days at Newton were full of event.

Day one was set as a race to Dishforth. We didn't launch until 15.00; the weather had been a series of heavy showers until then. It became obvious that the only chance of getting anywhere was to make cloud climbs. I was passing 7,000 feet in my first cloud when the glider started to ice up. In a matter of seconds I could not see the wings through the canopy and my air speed, altimeter and rate of climb instruments all stopped working. I managed to find my way out of the cloud, but by the time the ice had melted and things were back to normal I was very low with no chance of another climb so I landed back at Newton. More heavy showers made the prospects of staying airborne remote. I waited for an improvement, but the last launch time of 18.00 was fast approaching. At 17.30 the sky still looked hopeless, so I told my crew to follow me with the trailer immediately and I would at least get a practice field landing. After the launch to 2,000 feet I set off towards the only possible looking bit of sky, at 30 degrees to the way I really wanted to go.

The air was completely dead, not the slightest tremor to give me hope that there might be a thermal to lift me again. I flew on, picking fields suitable for landing ahead of me. At 600 feet, ready to land in the next grass field, the air burbled and the variometer needle twitched. A quick circle and the remorseless descent stopped. Another few turns and 620 feet showed. Slowly, oh so slowly at 50 feet per minute the altimeter wound up as I drifted still further away from track. Then at 1,300 feet it all went dead again. I straightened out heading north and before long was at 600 feet ready to land once more. Another burble renewed hope and an equally slow climb took me this time to cloud base at 2000 feet. The rate of climb in the cloud increased to 100 feet per minute and stayed there until at 3,000 feet it rapidly built up to the maximum the instrument would show, 1,000 feet per minute. This time I straightened up just before 7,000 feet to avoid icing. A few seconds of turbulence, then the air went lifeless again. Flying at the best, slow, speed for distance, concentrating on the turn and slip and compass I carried on, expecting at any moment to fly out of the cloud. More than half-an-hour later, with not a tremor in the air all the way, I was still in the white fog, with the altimeter showing 2,200 feet, worrying about what sort of terrain might be under me. Then the clouds parted and with relief I recognised Finningley airfield. Ahead Eggborough power station offered a small chance of another climb, but unfortunately it was a Saturday, the demand for electricity was low and Eggborough was only ticking over so it wasn't producing any heat to set a thermal going. I made a few kilometres more, which gave me 4th place out of 24. The crew had almost kept up with me so it was a quick retrieve and an early arrival back at Newton.

Sunday was a washout. On Monday conditions looked good and a 206.5 kilometre triangle was set. Until the second turning point, conditions were as good as they looked, but then a sheet of higher cloud cut out the sun's heating and thermals became very weak and far apart. I struggled to stay airborne and at one point was down to 500 feet, but eventually managed a climb to 4000 feet between Peterborough and Grantham. It looked fairly hopeless ahead and I didn't think I would reach Newton, but I couldn't get any higher. From there on it was another dead smooth glide. I made radio contact with my crew, who were still on the airfield. Eventually they spotted me. "He'll make it …no he won't … yes he will … no he won't … yes he will … Oh no!" Thoughts echoed by myself. A marginal final glide can be very nerve-racking, this one was not too much so. The Common Agricultural Policy had not yet converted much of Britain's landscape to monoculture winter cereals, unsafe to land in by the middle of May. There was always a grass or spring cereal field within reach on this day. In the end though, Newton – Isaac, not airfield – won. I would not have cleared the fence before the airfield so I had to pull the airbrakes out and land just yards too short. I left the glider, climbed over the fence and went with my crew, the car and the trailer on the retrieve. It took an hour and a half to find a way into the field! Had we expected it to take so long, we'd have climbed back into the field, de-rigged the glider and passed the pieces across the fence.

Tuesday, day three, was notable for the set task, which was large for those days at 303 kilometres. It proved to be too large for most pilots, including myself – I landed out half way round. On day four, Wednesday, an out and return task of 140 kilometres was set. Unfortunately the wind was rather stronger than expected. The outbound leg, downwind, was easy, but the return leg against the wind was a long slow struggle. No one completed the task. I spent three hours making 40 kilometres from the turning point, which gave me sixth place for the day. It might have been possible to go further, had it not been for a swarm of open class gliders. I found a thermal low down and was climbing well until they joined me. With 10 or so gliders all round, I could no longer keep a tight turn in the thermal core going and my rate of climb decreased. Further climb would mean drifting back with the wind more than the next glide forward would take me, so I left them to it and went on again to look for another thermal. I arrived at the same thermal source around a hundred feet or so higher and found another bubble of lift. Once again I was climbing well until they joined me and again I had to leave when they arrived all round me. After seven or eight climbs, drifting back and glides forward to the same spot, each time being set upon and little higher than I'd started, I'd had enough and tried breaking away to the side of track. Of course, I found no more thermals.

On Thursday and Friday the weather was no good for soaring. On Saturday a race to the gliding site at Nympsfield near Stroud was set. I found one thermal, started and found no more, landing just 12 kilometres away. The field was huge, but something seemed to be going on at one end of it, with a large crowd of people milling around the gate. I landed at the other end and walked across to discover I'd arrived at a sheep dog trial and the entrance fee for a spectator was £1.50, which I was expected to pay! My crew was soon on the scene; we de-rigged and rushed back for a second attempt, which was allowable even from an out landing in those days. I didn't get much further, just 30 kilometres, but nor did anyone else, nobody went far enough to make it a contest day for our class.

I didn't do particularly well overall, finishing 12th out of 24. The contest was unhandicapped, although handicap scores were worked out for interest. By now the higher performance glass fibre ships were more common, so I didn't mind too much being beaten by ten of them. Even more satisfying was being only a few points behind John Williamson who was flying a glass fibre Libelle and being well ahead of him on handicap. John was the winner of several National Competitions.

This was to be my last full year in the RAF. I can't claim that I was overworked, with only 50 hours flying in the Jet Provost. Next year, 1972, January 5th saw my last two Jet Provost flights, a 35-minute joy ride for one of the ground crew and a 30-minute sortie of instrument flying practice for me.

Chapter 37
ATPL, I/R and job search

My service was due to end on the 15th March, but the RAF gave two months resettlement leave for personnel finishing their service during those last months. I used mine to attend ground school at CSE Oxford in January and February in preparation for the Airline Transport Pilot Licence written examinations. Being still in the service entitled me to stay in the Officers' Mess at Bicester so I had a few more weekends of RAFGSA gliding. At the same time I started writing to numerous aircraft operators, seeking employment.

The ATPL examinations were held at the end of March. I passed in all subjects and went back again to CSE for two weeks in April to practice and then take the Instrument Rating flying test. With that passed, there remained one hurdle; the Aircraft Performance ground examination. I took that in May and became the proud possessor of an Airline Transport Pilot Licence complete with Instrument Rating.

Fully licensed and Instrument Rated, the search for employment accelerated. I wrote on spec to many more companies and answered the few advertisements in "Flight International" that did appear. The standard reply to all the letters was "We have no vacancies for pilots at this time, but we will keep your letter on file for future reference." Even in the good times, all aircraft operators try to recruit pilots who already have the Type Ratings for the aircraft they use, or are shortly acquiring. The costs of converting pilots onto new types can be enormous. This wasn't a good time and the only type on my U.K. license was the Chipmunk. There were not many airlines flying those! I should perhaps have gone to one of the organisations offering type conversion training for a fee, but the cost of a conversion onto any of the aircraft in general airline use, such as the Boeing 737, was well beyond the limit of my dwindling gratuity money.

Unemployed and needing to conserve my funds, I had not expected to fly any gliding competitions this year, but in June, Alan White, who owned a Ka-13 two-seater at Sutton Bank asked me if I would fly it with him in the Club Class Nationals at Dunstable. The competition started on the 5th August. As the lowest performance machine in the competition, the Ka-13 was fairly seriously outclassed. We landed out on six of the seven days but we had some good flying and were not over-disappointed with 16th place out of 25.

After six months of unemployment and a couple of days after receiving yet another "Don't call us, we'll call you" response, this one from Fairey Surveys of Maidenhead, I had a letter from the RAF Resettlement Branch saying "Fairey Surveys Limited of Maidenhead require a pilot. For information, contact their Operations Manager at (address and telephone number)." I was somewhat rude when I made the call. "What's wrong with your lot? Two days ago you had no need for pilots in the foreseeable future, now you are recruiting!" "Sorry about that, our girl in the office wasn't in the picture." After a few questions about my past, I was invited to attend for interview. This proved to be more of an information session about the job than an inquisition on my qualifications.

Fairey's main work was mapping photography, although they also carried out magnetometer survey from time to time. The photographs had to overlap in the direction of flight (forward overlap) and sideways onto the adjacent run, the overlaps giving the stereoscopic pairs necessary to enable the terrain height variation to be measured on a stereoscopic plotting machine back at the Company headquarters. Fairey's photographic survey aircraft were flown by a three-man crew, pilot, tracker and camera operator. The tracker's job was rather like that of a war time bomb aimer. Using a periscopic (or on the Dove a 'banana') sight, he guided the pilot along a line marked either on existing maps or on stapled together photographs taken on a previous flight. Just like the bomb aimer, he would be giving a series of "one (degree) left.... one left... steady....one right....." commands. Flying height above ground depended on the scale of photography required and the distance between adjacent flight lines depended on the height. So the tracker controlled side overlap. Meanwhile the camera operator controlled forward overlap and kept the camera in line with the direction the aircraft was moving using an optical system built into the camera.

The Company policy was that any pilot must be a capable tracker. In fact, they frequently operated with two pilots on a crew, taking turns at flying and tracking. My ability to fly an aircraft seemed to be taken for granted. It was evidently of much greater import that I could do a tracker's job. Before being offered employment I was sent on a flight in the Dove to see whether I had any aptitude for this. So I made the acquaintance of the 'banana' sight. This was a Heath Robinson contraption made of straight pieces of wire of about coat hanger thickness, mounted lying fore and aft on a horizontal boom which stuck out through the cockpit wall. A vertical post carried another master wire. The whole assembly could be tilted fore and aft and laterally and swivelled right or left in the horizontal plane. When flying a survey line it was adjusted to the horizontal plane using fore and aft and lateral spirit levels and swivelled until ground features tracked along the wires thus compensating for drift. A sight was fitted on each side of the cockpit, below a Perspex bubble. When tracking a centre line the tracker would set the sight level and then position his head until the master wire lay over the inner lower wire (vertically below the master). He would then give the pilot heading alterations to keep ground features on the line being tracked directly below the two lined up wires. Wires further out indicated the edge of the camera coverage and various amounts of side overlap. Side overlap aimed for was usually 30%.

Back at the Company offices, overlapping pairs of photographs would be set up on special plotting machines. Using the stereo effect, height variation as well as horizontal distances could be measured. The ideal stereo pair would have both photos level fore and aft and sideways, with no skew between the pair, with the correct overlaps and both taken at exactly the same height. Photography that failed any of the criteria might still be useable, but would take longer to set up on the plotting machines, adding to the costs of the final mapping job.

I found tracking to be far more challenging and much more interesting than flying the aircraft. There was a great deal of satisfaction in producing accurate photography with minimum time spent getting lined up for each run and no time wasted by going off line and having to re-fly part of a run. Perfection was impossible; getting as close to it as one could was the aim. Photography that proved unsatisfactory when developed represented a considerable waste of money. There was the cost of flying to the survey area again and the nine inches square film used was expensive in itself. On one of the jobs I went on later, we had over 10,000 nine inch square photo prints piled up in the house where we were living.

Evidently my first efforts showed that I had some aptitude. I was offered employment, subject of course to qualifying on the Dove aircraft. I towed my caravan down to a site near White Waltham and sat the CAA Type Technical ground examination at the beginning of September. While waiting for the result I did the type rating conversion flying training with Jim Storrie and Tom (Jock) Kirkwood, two of Fairey's senior pilots and flew as tracker on several survey jobs. During these few weeks I learnt a little about the end result of photo survey. Fairey's were quite proud of two of the special jobs they had done. One involved a set of aluminium steps, which were to replace the battered concrete stairway up a cliff face to a lighthouse. A few photographs enabled the exact contour of the cliff face to be measured; when the steps, designed and manufactured accordingly were taken to the site they fitted perfectly. The other had to do with the radio telescope at Jodrell Bank. Over the years its performance had deteriorated. Someone came up with the idea that it had become distorted. The dish was turned to face directly upwards, Faireys took a couple of photographs and were able to produce a contour map showing that it needed pushing out a few inches here and pulling in there. Once done, performance was restored.

The Dove was a delightful aircraft to fly and the easiest to put down gently of any I have flown. With its low wing giving a ground cushion effect and the trailing suspension of the main wheels, it could be 'greased on' most times. So much so that on several occasions later one of my camera operators, who had nothing to do on the flight back to base and consequently went to sleep, woke up in panic when I shut down the engines at the parking area and had to be re-assured that we weren't still airborne. But maybe that was because of his dormouse nature. In the Maidenhead office, when we arrived back from an overseas job, people would ask him how long he'd spent in Libya, Yemen or wherever. "Only two weeks" he'd say. "But you left six weeks ago". "Yes, but I spent four weeks sleeping".

There was one problem with the aircraft. Like the Tiger Moth and the Chipmunk, it had De Havilland Gypsy engines, although in this case they were super-charged Gypsy Queens. They were very reliable, but did have a rather high oil consumption. We would arrive at a new airfield, intending to base there for a week or two and on the first encounter with the refuelling crew, would ask, " Have you got plenty of WD 100 oil?" "Oh yes, no problem". "O.K., put two gallons in the left engine and one and a half in the right". Within a few days, with similar quantities needed after each flight, a slightly concerned question would be asked - "Are you staying much longer?"

Photo 40 – DH 104 Dove G-AWFM   Courtesy Geoff Ball/Ringway Publications

Chapter 38
Overseas Survey flying

Ten weeks after starting with Fairey's, on 25 November 1972, I was on my way to Libya with Jock Kirkwood in Dove G-AWFM. The Libyans had plans to build a railway from the coast to the small town of Sabha, about 300 miles to the south, well into the Sahara. In the end, the railway never happened, but I see from an up to date atlas that there is now a road along the approximate route that we photographed.

We flew from White Waltham to Hurn (Bournemouth) for Customs and Immigration clearance. There I had the first of many encounters with Britain's best duty-free airport shop. Run by the airport itself, the prices were really low, unlike the average duty-free where the duty saved is replaced by excessive mark-ups. Unfortunately on this occasion I couldn't take advantage, Libya was very firmly dry (in both senses). After clearing customs we flew on to Jersey and night stopped. A 5½-hour flight next day took us to Ajaccio in Corsica, where the Company's two DC3 aircraft were carrying out a magnetic survey. The gathering of three survey crews plus ground surveyors at the hotel that evening was possibly the largest in the Company's history. Normally the six Fairey aircraft would be scattered singly all over the world.

The following day's plan was for a non-stop flight to Tripoli. Halfway across the Mediterranean a generator warning light came on. This was not a serious problem, the generator on the other engine would supply all the power needed to run the electrics, but we wouldn't want to start a two or three month's survey job with an aircraft not fully serviceable. We reckoned that there would be a much better chance of getting any spare parts needed and of finding maintenance facilities in Malta than in Tripoli. Malta was not far off our route, so we diverted there. By the time our generator problem had been fixed it was too late to go further. I thought that the menu in the hotel we went to looked pretty good, but Jock suggested we went out for dinner – he knew of a part of town where there were lots of pleasant little bar/restaurants. Ever the innocent abroad, I let myself be suckered into an evening over which it would perhaps be best to draw a veil. Suffice it to say that the part of town referred to was officially named 'Straight Street', which is **not** the name by which it has been known to generations of the Royal Navy. It was perhaps fortunate that nearly all the way from the hotel there was a brick wall on our left side. When I abandoned Jock in the early morning hours and returned alone, I was able to find the hotel by feeling my way along the wall, keeping it to my right.

We made a fairly late start next morning and managed not to miss Africa.

During the next three and a bit months I learnt more about the survey pilot's trade. We had to liaise with the Libyan Security authorities and make arrangements for one of their people to fly with us to see that we were not photographing areas outside the survey route. Organising him to be there when we wanted to fly was a little difficult at first, but a bit of diplomacy brought him round. We had to find and rent a suitable place where we could set up our darkroom, in which our ground photographer could develop and print the films. When the films had been processed and before printing, they had to be checked by the Libyans and censored so that no sensitive areas were on the photos. This, in Libya, as elsewhere, was rather farcical. A photograph of several square miles of desert, with a few mud huts, would come back from the censors with one of the otherwise quite unremarkable buildings blacked out. Later on, in the Sudan, I was to see one of our photographs censored with a perfect blackout diagram of an airfield, with three runways and a perimeter track, none of which had been visible from the air because it had not been used for several years and had been covered over by blowing sand!

Although we had maps of the route, there were not enough positive features shown on them for us to track directly. We broke the route up into sections, where the direction or the ground height changed significantly. One run of photography was then flown as best we could along the centre line of each section. When fuel was getting low, we returned to Tripoli. The films were processed and by evening time we would be stapling the prints together to check that they overlapped correctly and were of satisfactory quality. Neither cloud nor cloud shadow was permitted. We could survey only in cloudless conditions, or with complete and even cloud cover above. If the photos were good, on the next flight we would fly runs each side of the original, or if the weather there was not suitable, go further on to new runs. Tracking from photography, even in featureless desert, was relatively easy. Subtle differences in the pattern of sand dunes, rocks strewn on a plain or bushes in the wadi bottoms showed up well.

The weather requirements for photography, even in Libya, limited our operations. In 101 days from our first survey flight to the last, we took photography on 28. Not all of these were full sorties, on around a third cloud developed while we were flying. On another five occasions, we got airborne in hope, but found cloud in the survey area. Met reports on the remaining 68 days gave clearly unsuitable conditions. This gave us opportunities to act the tourist.

On non-survey days in Tripoli, we usually wandered around the city, visited the souk (market), or went to the movies. There were of course no bars, but some of the restaurants still maintained the Italian cooking of colonial days. We occasionally toured further afield. The Roman ruins at Sabratha, on the coast west of Tripoli, were most impressive. At that time it was permitted to walk on the tessellated floors in some of the buildings, I doubt that it is allowed today. Some of the larger floors had however been lifted and replaced on the walls of the museum at the site. One of the busts in the museum caught my eye. I can't remember who exactly was the subject, but the inscription, just fitting on the side of the plinth, read something like JULIUS II IMPERAT$_{OR}$.

The mason had obviously not PLANNED AHE$_{AD}$. One could imagine him chipping away, blissfully unaware until near the end that he was running out of space and then muttering "The hell with it, I'm not going to carve that lot again"

Christmas 1972 away from home and in Libya was not a whole load of fun, although that year, for some reason, foreigners were given a small break from the non-alcoholic rules of the country and were allowed to purchase one bottle of red wine each. We flew a 5½-hour sortie on Christmas day and saved our wine for New Year's Eve. There was no chance at all of a telephone call to the U.K. and at that stage I had still to receive my first letter from Jennie.

Around halfway through our stay, we began to night stop at Sabha after surveying on the way there, continuing with more of the survey on the return to Tripoli the next day. On one of these visits, we spent an interesting evening in the tent of some Bedouin camel traders. One of them spoke a little English; he seemed as fascinated by our nomadic life as we were by theirs. Later on, with the northern part of the photography completed, we moved to Sabha for nine days. The weather was kind to us; we were able to work every day but one. On the day we couldn't, three of us climbed a local jebel (hill) which looked very much like one of the mesas featured in so many Western films. On the flat top, we found many small pieces of fossilised timber. Looking around at the sun baked scenery, it was hard to imagine how trees could ever have grown in the area.

We completed the photography on the 11th of March, but had to remain in Libya while the Ministry of Transport checked that we had covered the required area and that the photography met the contract specifications. I had a new experience, that of having a large sum of money which I had no option but to spend. During our stay we had been paid a local allowance, with no alcohol there had been little to spend it on. It was illegal to take Libyan money out of the country, or to exchange it in Libya. So I had an evening spree in the Souk. I bought a wrist watch and a gold pendant for Jennie, a gold puzzle ring for myself and various pieces of bric-a-brac like a brass tray and coffee set, some leather poufs and reproduction ceramic oil lamps and about thirty minutes later the money was spent.

The return to England took somewhat less time than the outbound trip – just two days, with a night stop in Nice. It was from there that some years previously one of the crews caused a great deal of merriment at the Maidenhead head office. The secretary in charge of distributing incoming telexes received a rather brief message "GAWFM DELAYED NICE WEATHER" and spent a whole morning going from office to office trying to find someone who could explain why the aircraft was delayed when the weather was nice!

We visited Hurn again, for inbound Customs and Immigration clearance. My reception there explains why, from then on, wherever possible, I chose Hurn for arrivals as well as departures on overseas expeditions. To save time, I had a ready-prepared list of all the things I had bought while away and their cost. I copied this onto a declaration form and handed it to the Customs Officer. He conferred with his colleague, they got out their calculators and, muttering one to the other came up with a figure of duty to be paid. I got out my chequebook and started to write. "Hold on a moment" one of them said. "We can do better than that" Further consultations followed. "If we make the wristwatch a gift item and….". The rules were somewhat complex, but the next figure was about two thirds of the original. Once again my pen was poised, but then "Hang on, we've forgotten that…" By now all I wanted to do was to pay up and get on my way home, but they insisted I should wait until they had calculated the most advantageous (for me) way of juggling the allowances and rates of duty. The final amount was about half the first.

Chapter 39

A summer in the U.K. and Eire

After eleven days leave at home in Yorkshire, I was back into the thick of it with survey around Carlisle and Blackpool for a couple of weeks. Then I did get the rest of the leave, almost a month, which my four months in Libya had earned me. With my employment secured, I used what was left of my gratuity to buy a brand-new Pilatus B4 all-metal Standard Class sailplane.

By now it was considered that I could be let loose on my own in charge of aircraft, crew and work to be done, so I spent the rest of 1973 flitting around the U.K. and Ireland chasing suitable weather for the various jobs that came our way. I also became broken in to the uncertain peripatetic life of a survey crew. Except for post-overseas days of leave, we were effectively either flying or on standby seven days a week. We sometimes operated from White Waltham for long periods. If the forecast showed no chance of photography, we would stand down for the day, or what was left of it. I positioned the Pilatus B4 at Wycombe Air Park about ten miles away, so I welcomed days when we couldn't survey because of cumulus cloud – they were ideal for soaring! There were days that were unsuitable for both work and soaring, if I felt really keen I would go to the gliding club and fly the tug aircraft, launching the 2-seat training gliders.

Away from base the airfields we used varied from small, grass, mainly flying club sites like Sywell and Ipswich, to major airports such as Prestwick. Sometimes we would base near a priority job for a few days or weeks and wait for suitable weather. On days when that job was not possible, we might fly off to another target within range and return to our temporary base. If there was no chance of photography we would stand down and do the tourist bit. Other times we moved around following weather slots and did not know from one day to the next exactly where we would be spending the night. There was one occasion when we had completed our work in the Inverness airport area, so we checked out of the Golf View Hotel at Nairn (one of our favourite hostelries) intending to relocate at Glasgow. There was a lot of low cloud about, crossing the high ground below cloud seemed inadvisable, so I opted to climb to around 10,000 feet, hoping to be in the clear on top. We entered cloud soon after take-off and clambered up in the murk all the way to 9,000 feet, which put us just in the clear. Ten minutes or so into the cruise a gap appeared in the cloud below and in the gap was an airfield. There aren't any airfields between Inverness and Glasgow and we certainly couldn't have got to Glasgow 100 miles away in 20 minutes! The wind was so strong that we had gone backwards while climbing and the airfield in view was Inverness itself. We were soon checking into the Golf View again.

Domestic life became very haphazard. The Royal Air Force still had control of White Waltham. I was allowed to leave my caravan in the Fairey area while

I was away, but not to live in it while there. So for those times when I was at home base, I had to move around from one nearby tourist caravan site to another. It seemed that bylaws prohibited more than two weeks on one site. The Company was helpful and let me have weekends off quite often, so I would leave White Waltham when flying was finished or 'scrubbed' on a Friday and drive the 240 miles home, then leave Yorkshire at three in the morning on Monday to be ready for another day's flying. Occasionally during school holidays Jennie would come to White Waltham, or meet me at some other place where we were working.

The 1973 Standard Class Nationals were held at Husbands Bosworth near Market Harborough, starting on the 26th May. I used some of my accrued leave, positioned the caravan there and took the Pilatus in its trailer. Alan White and Jennie crewed for me. I still have vivid memories of the first day, when a 185-km triangle via Peterborough and Henlow was set. The first leg went well, but the second was not much fun. I kept finding bits of lift, but could only stay in them for one or two circles before falling out of them. Progress was painfully slow. I swore at myself for not being able to stay in the lift and my despair was not helped when I kept hearing other pilots reporting positions to their crews from places on the last leg. It was obvious that I had no chance of catching up with them. So I abandoned all ideas of going for speed, just getting round no matter how slowly so as not to lose too many points was the most important thing. Approaching Henlow, I was very low, right over a cricket match, when I found another thermal. The players stopped and watched me as I ground round and round, slowly gaining height. At cloud base, I left the thermal and flew towards the turning point, over which to my dismay a large area of murk had descended. I slid round the turn in dead smooth air and headed towards a patch of sunshine on the last leg, catching another weak thermal low down. A slow climb, another glide, another slow climb and glide and then a final climb put me in gliding range of the finish.

A few miles short of Husbands Bosworth, two other gliders overtook me and I was in a foul mood when I landed. Jennie and Alan arrived with the car to tow me in. "What are you two grinning at?" I snarled. "You're the only one back in your class and only three of the other class got round" they told me! It transpired that all those pilots I had heard calling positions apparently on the last leg had been way off track still on the outbound, second leg. So I won a Nationals day. The other three days didn't go so well and I finished in 4th place overall.

A few days later, back at work, I visited Eire for the first time. We spent a week in Dublin, getting two hours of photography. We stayed at a hotel on O'Connel Street, which according to the newspapers was the scene of a serious riot one evening. Next morning we walked down the street, all we saw was one boarded-up shop doorway. A lesson in not believing all you read in the papers.

The rest of 1973 was occupied with photo survey at sites ranging from home base at White Waltham to Stornoway in the north. We spent four days at

Stornoway, but achieved nothing except sightseeing. I took a circular 'bus trip one day. At one totally deserted point the driver pulled up at the roadside and said "The standing stones are just away down that track, we'll wait here for you for half-an-hour." The other passengers didn't seem at all put out by the delay, the pace of life in the Hebrides was clearly more leisurely than that on the mainland.

Fairey's had a 'bread and butter' contract with the Ordnance Survey, who had a rolling program to update their map coverage of the whole of the U.K. every few years. This meant flying to and fro on parallel lines within large blocks. On one of these we inadvertently found ourselves flying the same line as another of the Company's aircraft, but from the opposite end. With both crews concentrating on staying within a few yards of track and within a few feet of the desired height, we were somewhat close before we saw each other!

My last flight in G-AWFM was on 18 June. Sometime after I left Fairey Surveys the aircraft was retired and used for spares.

Photo 41 - Foxtrot Mike being robbed for spares   Courtesy Clive Glaister

Chapter 40
Further afield

In between the 1973 Dove flying, I did some conversion training on the Beechcraft B80 Queenair, a low wing twin powered by supercharged Lycoming piston engines. In July I passed the technical examinations and the type flying test.

Another Fairey pilot took the aircraft overseas and in early 1974 left it for a major overhaul at Nairobi. Towards the end of February I went with one of our engineers to collect it and take it on to the Sudan, where we had a contract with the Ordnance Survey Overseas Division. We arrived at Nairobi late in the evening and expecting to be there no more than two days I thought, "damn the expense" and just asked the taxi driver to take us to a reasonable hotel. Naturally we wound up at the Norfolk. Next morning I discovered that the aircraft was not ready and wasn't likely to be for a couple of weeks. I might have got away with two nights of high living, but the Company would have had some serious questions if we'd lodged at Nairobi's most expensive hotel for longer. We moved to the Aero Club, where we found rooms at one tenth of the Norfolk rates.

As a free package holiday the next two weeks took some beating. The Aero Club members were most hospitable and took us out for a few memorable evenings. At the Rugby Club we met the Committee members, who were the same people as at the Aero Club, but wearing different hats – the Aero Club secretary was the Rugby Club treasurer and so on. At the weekend we were invited to the Sailing Club on a reservoir near the town, where we were lent a couple of dinghies for a day's racing. We met the Committee members, who were the same people as at the Rugby Club, but wearing different hats. We didn't get to the Golf Club, but no doubt the Committee there were the same people as at the Sailing Club, but wearing different hats. Instead we were taken to an Indian restaurant, where I ate perhaps the best Indian food in perhaps the least chic surroundings of my life. A bare barn of a room with sawdust on the floor, a heavy planked table, no table linen, wooden benches, no cutlery – eat with your fingers – but oh, that curry!

One evening at the Aero Club bar the conversation drifted round to sailplanes. "You'll have to talk to Bim Molyneux" someone told me and gave me his telephone number. I rang through next morning and that was the second weekend taken care of. Bim was the Chief Flying Instructor of a gliding club near Nakuru, sixty miles north of Nairobi and said I was welcome to stay with him for a couple of nights and to do some instructing. I hired a car and set off early on the Friday. Lake Nakuru was reputed to be a great place for wild life, so I went there first. A despondent-looking motorcyclist was at the reservation gate, talking to the warden. It seemed motorcycles weren't allowed in, so I offered him a seat in the car. Serendipity does exist, he proved to be well versed in Kenyan bird and animal life. During the circuit of the lake he pointed out and identified, much that I would otherwise have missed.

I met up with Bim on the Saturday morning and he took me a few miles out of town to the gliding site. The Club was a small organisation, with only three gliders, a T-21 two-seater and two single seaters, a Hutter and a Ka6. The Ka6 was out of action at the time, being overhauled in Bim's garden. Launching was by winch, from a narrow strip through a maize field.

My first day's flying was in the T21, instructing. The first seven flights were routine circuits, up, round and down. The last one became more exciting. The visibility was not brilliant, so I didn't see what was happening until it was nearly too late. We found a weak thermal and climbed to around three thousand feet. Leaving the thermal, we headed back towards the strip and through the murk saw that a large cumulo-nimbus cloud was approaching. Ahead of the storm warm air was being scooped up by the cold air downdraught and outflow from the cloud and we had difficulty descending through the wide spread up-draught. I could see from rising dust and waving trees that the surface wind on the strip would soon become very strong, it would be a race to get safely on the ground in time. In the U.K., or Germany, I'd have flown clear of the storm, tried to stay airborne until it passed and if staying airborne was not possible, landed in a field. Not knowing the area round Nakuru I didn't want to risk an out-landing. It wasn't just a question of finding a smooth flat landable bit of terrain. I had visions of lions and other savage beasts lying in wait for our arrival. But we did make it back to the strip just in time. As we came to a halt the half dozen members present grabbed hold of struts, wing tips and cockpit rim and between us we held the glider down until the wind eased.

Back in Nairobi, the Queenair was nearly ready. My first intended stop on the ferry flight was Addis Ababa, where we planned to stay the night. We left on the 7th of March, but soon after departure Nairobi Air Traffic Control advised us to return, because they had heard that a general strike had commenced at Addis. Back at Nairobi we had a re-think and decided that we should try Juba in the south of the Sudan as a re-fuelling stop. It took another day to get the necessary clearances. It took two hours of flight towards Juba before we could make contact with Sudan Air Traffic Control, only to be told that there was no Avgas (piston aircraft) fuel at Juba. We returned to Nairobi. Next day, the 10th March, it appeared that Addis Ababa was back in business, so we tried again. During the last couple of hours of the flight we heard no other aircraft and on landing the airfield looked strangely deserted. I went to the fuel depot to ask for Avgas. "You will have to wait some time" the supervisor told me, "I have only one driver working" Eventually the fuel bowser arrived. The Ethiopian driver looked absolutely worn out and asked if we had any water on board. "I've just been refuelling a Galaxy (the enormous American military transport) and have made four trips to the depot and back" he told me. We gave him several cans of soft drinks. When he had finished re-fuelling us, I trotted off to the Control Tower to book a met forecast and file a flight plan for the next day. "If you want to get out of Ethiopia within the next month, you had better leave **very** early tomorrow," he said, but would not specify why this should be. I guessed that something more serious than a strike was imminent, but it was too late to leave, the only diversion airports within reach of my Khartoum destination were closed at night.

The French couple owning the hotel we went to apologised profusely for the service we could expect and told us none of their staff had come to work that day. Some of their clients were helping in the kitchen and dining room! For all that, we had a gourmet dinner and some wine on the house. During the night I was woken by the rumbling of tracked vehicles on the road outside. We rose very early and made haste to get airborne as the controller had advised. Three and a half hours later we landed at Khartoum. The Ethiopian troubles continued and in September Haile Selassie was deposed.

Photo 42 - Fairey's Beechcraft Queenairs, author flew Foxtrot Sierra
Courtesy Lyndon Yorke

The Queenair had a periscopic drift sight for tracking, fitted in front of the co-pilot's seat. The co-pilot's control column was removed. The flight crew for survey consisted of pilot, tracker and camera operator. The tracker, camera operator and a ground photographic technician had arrived in Port Sudan later than originally intended, due to my delay in Nairobi. When I flew in from Khartoum on the 12th March they were not happy bunnies. Because of the delay in their arrival our previously booked rooms had been given to a party of scuba divers and the hotel was booked out for months ahead. The only accommodation my crew had been able to find was a flat above some shops and they had spent all their money on the rent and living expenses. The flat was pretty grim. No air conditioning - only one room had so much as a fan for cooling. Although the electricity supply was reliable, water was available only between one and four in the morning. The whole place was alive with cockroaches and the kitchen was indescribably filthy. I was faced with mutiny; the sole solution available was bribery. So I promised that I would find a way to feed them without their having to spend their own lunch and dinner meal allowance, which in the case of the camera operator was almost as much as his pay. I made an arrangement with the hotel that we would take all our meals there (not that there was any other choice!) and that if any rooms became vacant, even for a day or two, one or more of us would move in. At the end of our stay this gave me the opportunity for a little embezzlement, my accounts showed more room nights than we had in fact used and (as was normal) no meals except breakfast paid by the Company. All I had to support my expenditure account for our five weeks accommodation was a till receipt suitably doctored by the hotel, but Head Office asked no questions when I returned to Maidenhead. The total shown for accommodation and breakfast was about half what had been budgeted for when the hotel was originally booked.

The lack of cash was more of a problem. The delay in Nairobi meant I had spent much of the money I had collected there, I needed more, soon. In these days of satellites and mobile telephones it is hard to explain just how difficult communication used to be. My first idea was to try telephoning. There were very few private phones in Port Sudan; a visit to the Post Office was required. There I enquired about making a call to the U.K. "No problem, what number do you want to call?" I gave the clerk the Fairey number in Maidenhead. "When do you want to make the call?" "Well, like now, please." A look of total horror at such presumption came over his face. "Calls are fully booked until Thursday afternoon" he told me (it was then Tuesday morning!).

We had noticed a Cable and Wireless office on our way from the airport so went there in hope of a more rapid connection. "Can I send a cable or telex to England?" I asked. "Yes sir, no problem, would you like to open an account?" Too right I would. So I went through the formalities, filling in forms, giving the Company name, its address in the U.K. and mine in Port Sudan and so on. That completed, the next question was "Did I want to send a cable right away?" "Yes please, I replied." So I filled in the message form. I was somewhat surprised that it was accepted and sent right away, since it ran something on the lines of "We have no money left, send more immediately!"

Our water problem was solved also, after a fashion. Round the corner two blocks away we discovered the Port Sudan British Club. This was a gently decaying relic of Empire, a sprawling, single storey, corrugated iron roofed wooden building. It had an open air sea water swimming pool, a bar, a billiards room, a library and most usefully, a continuous fresh water supply, showers, wash basins and toilets. We met the Secretary and were introduced to the rest of the Committee, by which time we had met virtually the whole club membership. For the rest of our stay the Port Sudan residents were treated to morning and evening parades as we trooped from flat to club and back, clutching towels, sponge bags and changes of clothing.

The area we were to survey consisted of a rectangular block of about 200 by 100 miles. The required scale meant flying at about 20,000 feet, so we were on oxygen all the time. The only available maps of the area dated from 1800s mapping and were printed on linen! They bore very little resemblance to the terrain we could see; in fact by the time we had finished we could identify only three or four features on our photography that corresponded with the maps. One feature we had no hope of finding – it was marked on the map as "Grave of Lieutenant XXX 1845." (I don't remember the name). With no basic mapping to go on, we used the technique of flying one run approximately up the middle of the survey area, processing, printing and stapling together the photography obtained and then flying runs overlapping on each side. We were incredibly lucky with the weather. The first day on the job, 15th March, was partly cloudy and no good for photography, but from then on with only four days of obviously unsuitable weather we finished the work in 29 days. We were able to photograph on 21 days out of the 25 when we did get airborne.

At the airport we were parked next to a Russian AN-2 biplane, powered by a large radial piston engine. Our little Queenair seemed quite pathetic alongside this monster. We attempted "Good mornings" and "Good evenings" whenever we encountered the crew, but stony looks were the only response until well into our stay. Then one morning it was all smiles and greetings. With some difficulty (only one of them spoke a little English and none of us spoke Russian) we ascertained that their KGB watch dog wasn't with them that day, he had fallen victim to the Port Sudan Quickstep, a.k.a. Montezuma's Revenge, Gippy Tummy etc. So we had an exchange visit, showing them inside our machine and then looking inside theirs. Theirs was a strange mixture of ancient and modern, with the latest technology of the time digital radio and navigation kit slotted in between ancient brass cased flight instruments. They were also flying a survey, but in their case it was magnetometer rather than photo.

Next morning it was back to stony faces and no communication, the KGB man had recovered. We did have one further sociable encounter however, when for some reason they were let out on their own one evening and we met them on the terrace bar at the hotel. Somehow, in spite of no common language our ground photographer and one of their crew managed to establish that they had both served as bomb aimers during World War Two. While they were trying to out-do each other's enumeration of the targets they had attacked, the rest of us got stuck into an unstated challenge as to the relative merits of vodka and whisky. Sometime after midnight as we staggered across the maidan singing the Volga boatman song we seemed to agree that there wasn't much in it.

We found the ordinary Sudanese to be very friendly, but were puzzled for a long time when every other new acquaintance asked, "When are you coming back?" Our explanations that we didn't know, maybe never, it depended on whether our Company got another contract in Sudan or not, were met with somewhat blank looks. It finally dawned that they weren't asking when **we** were coming back, they meant "when will you, the British, come back?" Without openly admitting it, they were remembering the law and order that used to prevail and how things used to work in the colonial days. I was to encounter the same sort of reception later on in Nigeria, where the older people remembered how things had been. There, telephone boxes that no longer worked and post boxes that were no longer operative showed that the colonial time hadn't been all bad.

On one of the non-flyable Port Sudan days we took a trip on a small boat out through the harbour and a short way north along the coast. There we snorkelled. It was a spectacular area; an underwater cliff of coral fell vertically through the glass-clear water to beyond the limit of visibility two or three hundred feet down. Thousands of small fish looking like multi-coloured snowflakes swirled around the coral face and larger predators patrolled back and forth. I had seen plenty of coral reefs in Tahiti and Fiji, but have to agree with those who rate the Red Sea as the best.

Near the end of our stay we had another memorable tourist day. We had met some people from Cambridge University, who were carrying out a research programme into the Crown of Thorns starfish. I had seen a few of these in Fiji years earlier. It seemed that in recent years their numbers had exploded in the Pacific. They were predators of coral polyps and had destroyed large areas of the Great Barrier and other reefs. Why this had occurred was uncertain, possibly over fishing of their predators such as the Trochus mollusc (of which the shell was used for making 'pearl' buttons) had something to do with it. Anyway, although the Crown of Thorns was present in the Red Sea, it was not yet abundant enough to cause serious harm. The Cambridge team had a laboratory in town where they kept the starfish and other marine life in seawater aquaria. They also had an outpost on one of the reefs a few miles south of Port Sudan, which was manned all the time. We were invited to spend the day there.

After the hot and dusty drive along an unsealed road it was a joy to board their speedboat for the journey out to the reef. On arrival there, we disembarked onto a scaffold pole and plank construction, roofed with canvas. Over the tent roof a canvas-sailed generator whirled busily. In the shallow clear water, the reef surface below showed a variety of coral formations, with shoals of colourful fish. No fish were allowed to be captured anywhere near the platform. Some of them were individual enough to have been given personal names. They were well trained; after meals the procedure was to drop dishes and plates into the water, a few minutes later these would be spotless, every last scrap of food cleaned off by the fish.

We took lunch with the platform residents and learnt about their research programme. It appeared that the Crown of Thorns tended to hide away during daylight, so the scientists did their census at night. They had a controllable board with elevator and rudder, which they towed underwater behind their motor launch. Insulated communication and power cables attached to the towrope enabled the 'shark bait' of the night, lying on the board, to illuminate the sea floor and report each starfish sighted. They put us to shame when they showed us a superb full colour photo mosaic of 'their' reef. It was as good as anything we could hope to produce with our very expensive survey camera. They had used a radio controlled model seaplane and a 35mm camera.

Back at our Port Sudan flat, we realised what had been perhaps the most enjoyable feature of our day on the reef – no flies!

On the 14th April, with the survey completed, we flew to Khartoum with some of our equipment and returned to Port Sudan to collect the remainder. By the 18th we had ferried everything to Khartoum and obtained our clearance to depart the following morning for our next assignment in Saudi Arabia.

Chapter 41
Deeper into Arabia

Various problems with flight plan, payment of fees and Customs and Immigration clearances delayed our departure from Khartoum, so it was fairly late in the day when we arrived at Jeddah. We parked the aircraft, cleared Customs and Immigration inbound and made our way to a hotel. Next morning we made contact with our agents and were given a briefing on the way things were in Saudi. The most important thing we had to understand was that the IBM business system was in wide use – Insh'Allah, Bukra, Maleesh. Which loosely translates as "God willing, tomorrow, perhaps." In other words, "don't expect to get anything done in a hurry." We soon had an illustration of this when we tried to go back to the aircraft. There was no way to get to the airside of the airport without a pass. "Where do we have to go to get a pass?" "That building over there." "Can we go there now? "Not without a pass." It took the rest of the day, even with the help of our agents, to get round that impasse.

A week later, with all the administrative negotiations completed, we flew south to Khamis Mushayt. Khamis was a Saudi Air Force airfield, with a large presence of British civilian employees of British Aircraft Corporation and some RAF personnel. Our contract was for a large block of photography, about 200 by 50 miles, along the edge of the plateau inland from the Red Sea northwards from the border with North Yemen. Here the Saudis planned re-afforestation.

The airfield and the survey area were just over 10,000 feet above sea level. In the high prevailing air temperature at the required flying height of 12,000 feet above ground the aircraft was close to its operational ceiling. It took a long time to climb to the required 22,000 feet above sea level. Sometimes I was able to put my gliding experience to good use. Thermals, rising to well over 20,000 feet above sea level and often marked by dust devils were very strong. I was able to circle in some of them and use their energy to boost the aircraft's rate of climb.

In a less useful, but great fun way, I would sometimes return low down along the edge of the plateau. The air close to the 8,000 feet from valley floor to ridge top sun facing scarp was warmed by the rock, causing an anabatic wind to blow up the slope. This was strong enough to keep the Queenair flying level at normal cruising speed with the throttles closed. But one had to be **very** close to the ground, lifting the wing over bushes and boulders to stay in the narrow layer of rising air. There was not likely to be anyone around to report this contravention of flying regulations – one is not permitted to fly closer than 500 feet to any person, object or building except while taking off or landing (except for a glider while hill soaring). The Queenair could not be described as a glider! But that ridge, extending for more than 600 miles from Mecca almost to Aden in the Yemen, would be magnificent for record glider flights, if only private flying were allowed in Saudi Arabia.

There was plenty of vegetation down the scarp face, but the country on the plateau top around Khamis was very bleak, a sun-baked tree-less plain of sand and rock, with a few isolated jebels rising another five hundred to one thousand feet. We explored the area on non-flying days, meeting with a troop of baboons on one of the jebels, but seeing very little other wildlife. It was difficult to see how there could be any hope of growing trees in such arid terrain.

By mid-June the weather had broken and cloud formation became too frequent for photography. With about half the contract finished, we left the rest for a return visit in the autumn and flew back to White Waltham via Jeddah, Al Wejh, Cairo, Athens, Brindisi, Nice, Jersey and Bournemouth. I had an embarrassing experience at Cairo, when after landing with a Boeing 707 on finals behind me both my engines cut out just before I reached the turn-off from the runway. I had almost reached the stage of sending the crew out to push the aircraft clear before I managed to re-start one engine and move out of the way.

Back in the U.K. I took two weeks of the leave due to me and 'banked' another two weeks for the Standard Class National Gliding Competition, which was to be held in August at Nympsfield. I went to Kinloss to collect one of our Doves and attempt various survey jobs, but it was not a very good summer for photo survey in the U.K. We had one good week based at East Midlands, but otherwise all my logbook shows is "weather unfit". The main problem was with cumulus cloud forming early most days. Just for once the weather didn't change to a cloudless situation during the competition and we achieved eight contest days out of the ten days there.

In September I reverted to the Queenair for a bit of practice before renewing my Instrument Rating and then on the 1st October it was away overseas again. This time the destination was Baghdad.

At that time it was not necessary to obtain prior permission for a non-commercial flight through France, Italy, Greece, the Lebanon or Syria, so we had no problems with clearances en-route. From White Waltham we made our way to Hurn for customs clearance and continued on to Nice for a night stop. There, at the 'Cave Nicoise' I had my first taste of 'moules mariniere', another item on my wish list for a gastronomic world tour. Next day we were delayed at Brindisi, where the airport authorities would accept nothing except Lira as payment of landing fees. Not having enough, I had to get a taxi to town to find a bank, which of course was closed for lunch. By the time it had opened and I had changed some sterling and got back to the airport, I owed the taxi driver more than I owed the airport. We made Iraklion that evening and next day flew on to Beirut, in those days a cosmopolitan, peaceful place, with interesting architecture and superb restaurants.

Our arrival in Iraq on the 4th October was not so pleasant. Although we had gone there to carry out a survey for the Iraqi Ministry of Railways and had all sorts of documentation giving us clearance into the country, I was arrested on arrival at Baghdad and hauled in front of the Minister of the Interior. I was told that I had broken every aviation law, that I wasn't fit to hold a pilot's licence, that I was lucky that I would only be deported rather than jailed and so on. The Railway Minister appeared on the scene, a tremendous row ensued (of which I understood not one word) and eventually I was allowed to go on my way to town.

The month long stay in Baghdad was quite enjoyable. We had to carry an Iraqi Air Force representative with us to make sure we weren't spying, but he was an affable sort and also reliable, always turning up on time. The hotel was comfortable and its courtyard, with shade trees and fountains, was an oasis from the dust and heat in town. All the Iraqis we met were friendly. The only hassle occurred during one of our non-flying, sight-seeing the town days. We had viewed the sculpture of the forty thieves, walked across one of the Tigris bridges and pottered round one of the bazaars. We left our ground photo technician, who wanted to take some tourist snaps and returned to the hotel. A little later an Iraqi policeman came to see me and told me they were holding our man in jail. I rustled up some help from the Railway Ministry and with the rest of the crew went to bail him out. His 'crime' had been to photograph an old railway locomotive, which stood on a plinth on one of the main streets miles away from the nearest live railway. A strategic target for an enemy perhaps? We eventually got him loose, but his film was confiscated.

Our task was to survey a route for a projected railway from Baghdad to the Syrian border. The base maps we had to work on were at an incredible six inches to the mile scale. To scale, we were flying at 12 inches per minute. This gave the tracker quite a problem! We glued strips of map together and rolled them like toilet rolls on a piece of broom handle. The aircraft was knee deep in unrolled map at the end of each run.

We finished the job on the 22nd October and on the 26th, with our photography accepted by the client, flew on to Jeddah. We were there four days while our agents made the arrangements for us to complete the Khamis Mushayt work. The Souk afforded us many hours of entertainment. We lunched on 'Shwirma' (lamb and onion sliced off a spit) washed down with mixed orange and lemon juice and then roamed the different sections of the market, haggling occasionally for things we didn't really want. The gold area was amazing. Thirty or so small open-fronted rooms, about three metres wide by four deep, were chock full of gold rings, bracelets, necklaces, chains, pendants and other jewellery. No matter how intricate the items were, they were all sold by weight. The most astonishing thing about the set up was what happened when the call to prayer was heard. Each shop must have held well over a million pounds worth of gold, but the only security action taken by the shop-keepers was to draw a cord net across the entrance before leaving for the mosque.

Arriving at Khamis, we booked in to the only hotel in town. During our absence it had changed hands. The new owner was clearly a bit of a rogue. On the first evening the lights went out. They eventually came on again. Next evening they went out again. Then on again. Then off again. It transpired that the 'offs' were because the electricity supply company hadn't been paid and had pulled the main fuse from the supply junction box. The 'ons' were the proprietor putting ever-larger nails in the fuse holder. With various other deficiencies, such as no hot water, a resident population of unsavoury-looking bugs and an evident lack of laundry facilities I was once again facing a mutiny.

A few enquiries led me to a house we could rent, a mud-walled, single story building with three living rooms, a kitchen and a shower/toilet room. It was completely unfurnished, but I managed to persuade the owner to provide a cooker and a refrigerator. We bought rush mats, foam mattresses, sheets, pillows and pillow cases, five wooden chairs, a table, some pots and pans, cutlery and china and then effectively camped in the building, sleeping on the floor. We made storage for our clothes and other possessions using cardboard boxes and scrap planks. There was a small grocery in town, where we could obtain a surprisingly good selection of staples and the market was a gourmet's delight, with a vast variety of root vegetables, greens, squashes and fruit. Each one of us enjoyed cooking, so we took turns at preparing the evening meal. With a glass or two of wine we'd have been on cloud nine. We did try a bottle of illegal 'saddiki' but even diluted with orange juice it was pretty foul.

The flying went very well, with 16 photographable days out of 26, so we did not have too much opportunity for sightseeing. Not that we thought there was much to see, one bit of sun-baked rock looked much like the rest. Then near the end of our stay one of the BAC people asked, "Have you been to Wadi Har yet?" "No, where is it and what's there?" we asked. It proved to be a delightful valley hidden away among a tangle of rocky ridges, with a crystal clear stream no more than 10 feet wide but in places 15 feet or more deep. Lush grass and green bushes filled the valley floor and a herd of very small but sleek cows stood around in the shade. Swimming in the cool water, we felt shoals of minnows trying to eat the hair on our legs. We followed the stream down; eventually it broadened, shallowed and finally disappeared into the pebbles. We made several more picnic visits before the end of our stay.

Garbage collection did not feature as one of the priorities of civic endeavour in Khamis. Roaming herds of goats managed to keep on top of almost everything except plastic. We followed our neighbours' example and jettisoned our rubbish into a vacant lot across the street, until one evening, as Don Yorke our tracker was disposing of another sack full a window flew up in the house next door. A veritable virago of a woman let loose a tirade in Arabic of what had to be invective and Don beat a hasty retreat, stowing the sack in our own back yard. When the time came for us to leave, we thought it would be best to clear all our rubbish out of the house and more in hope than expectation, put it all on the pavement outside. A Yemeni man, with a donkey and cart came knocking at the door, indicating the junk outside. Don rather fancied himself as a trader and with no Arabic except Wahid, Etnain, Tallata etc., (the Arabic numerals) began to haggle. "Four hundred" said the Yemeni. "No way" said

Don, thinking this was a bit much to pay for having it taken away, "Two hundred". The trader looked a bit puzzled, but indicated his agreement – and produced two hundred rials, which he handed over in exchange for the rubbish!

The Khamis photography was completed by the end of November, but we had to remain until the work had been accepted, which kept us there until the 8th December. Back in Jeddah, our agent gave us details of three other small jobs in Saudi Arabia. It was cloudy in the Jeddah area, so on the 10th we set off for Riyadh. We climbed into a layer of altostratus and levelled at our assigned cruising altitude of 11,000 feet. It was perfectly smooth in the cloud and there were no indications of storms anywhere near us, but suddenly there came a flash and a bang – we had been hit by lightning. All our radio and navigation equipment went dead. There was nothing we could do but continue on heading until we flew out of cloud; we could not descend without knowing exactly where we were because of the high ground below us. After a minute or two, our VHF radio came back to life, followed one by one by the different navigation aids, but then the starboard engine coughed and started to wind down. Before I had time to carry out any of the emergency drills, it picked up again. Half a minute later, the port engine did the same. Eventually calm was restored, with everything except the High Frequency radio working normally. When we landed at Riyadh we soon discovered why it had failed – the trailing aerial had been severed. Additionally, the tail navigation and strobe lights had disintegrated and we counted a dozen small, blackened holes in the wings and fuselage.

It took until the 21st to get that lot sorted out. Then it was a working Christmas for us. On the 22nd we photographed around Riyadh and flew back to Jeddah. On the 23rd and 24th we surveyed around the city. On Christmas day there was very little airline traffic, even in Saudi Arabia, so we were able to operate over and around the international airport without too many hold-ups and finish the photography there in one day. With the film in the can we went back to Riyadh for a few days. Next came a job at Al Wejh on the Red Sea coast near the border with Jordan, then Riyadh again and finally a last visit to our agents in Jeddah.

The flight back to the U.K. went fairly smoothly, except for a one-day delay at Iraklion in Crete, where after our night stop we were unable to take off due to too much crosswind. By the time the Queenair's wheels kissed the grass of White Waltham that overseas tour had lasted three and a half months. The month's leave I had earned was most welcome.

Chapter 42
Night landing by headlights

In early 1975 Fairey's decided to add a Britten-Norman Islander to their fleet and I became the conversion guinea pig. After a few non-commercial flights on several different aircraft of the type, I passed the type rating flying test and the ground examinations. Our own aircraft was being modified for survey work at Charleroi in Belgium. For some reason that I never understood it was still officially owned by a Belgian businessman. I was sent to collect it from Charleroi and to base at a small, grass, day only airfield, Amougies, to the south of Brussels, from where I was to fly him on his company's business. I was put up at a pleasant little country hotel near the airfield and sat around for several weeks waiting for a flight, enjoying the food and wine at various local hostelries.

The only excitement was one day watching a hydrogen balloon drift past, hit a power line and burst into flames. The aero club members seemed quite unperturbed by the event. I expected one or two of them might have grabbed a car and gone looking for survivors but no one made a move.

Eventually the 'boss' decided he wanted to go to Shannon, calling in at White Waltham on the way. As there were no Customs facilities at White Waltham, we cleared into the U.K at Gatwick and out at Cardiff. We arrived at Shannon late in the evening and I was asked to be ready to leave for the flight back to Amougies by noon next day. I was ready, but it was late in the afternoon before my passenger arrived. The Islander did not have the range to fly all the way to Amougies, so I elected to refuel at Gatwick. By the time we had completed the re-fuelling and cleared Customs there, it was touch and go whether we could reach Amougies before dark. "We have to go to Amougies," said Monsieur, "I've left my car there." Little use trying to explain that I couldn't stop the sun.

After crossing the Belgian coast it became obvious that we were too late. I asked for and was given clearance to divert to Brussels. Problems over, I thought. We were just about to descend when Air Traffic Control called me to say that Amougies was expecting me and had arranged airfield lighting.

Don't believe everything you read in the papers, they say. Don't believe everything Air Traffic Control tells you either. When I got to Amougies, I found that the 'airfield lighting' was a car each side of the runway at the touchdown end, facing away with their headlights shining on the grass. I gave it a try. Just before the threshold my landing lights lit up the runway beautifully, but as I flared for landing, the lights pointed up in the air and I had nothing ahead to guide me. Amougies was rather narrow, if I veered even slightly I'd be off the edge of the strip. So I opened the throttles and climbed away. After a slightly acrimonious discussion on the radio, I got them to put another car at the far end of the strip, with its taillights towards me to give something to aim at. This worked perfectly; a few years later this method of lighting a runway enabled me to make a night medevac flight from an airstrip in Chad.

The businessman was duly grateful that I had flown him to where he wanted to be, but he didn't ask to fly anywhere else and I was soon back at White Waltham. During a weekend visit home I went to the Yorkshire Gliding Club where I was introduced to Jack Speight, the Chief Pilot of one of our competitors, BKS Surveys. BKS had been an airline operating mostly within the U.K. and Europe, but the airline itself had long before been taken over, leaving only the rump Survey company to carry on the name. Their head office was in Coleraine, Northern Ireland but their aircraft, an Islander and an Aztec, were based at Leeds airport. They were looking for a pilot. Jennie had been promoted and was working as a peripatetic Head Teacher in North Yorkshire. She was expecting soon to obtain a permanent headship in the county and made it plain that she wouldn't want to move elsewhere. I was finding commuting between Yorkshire and White Waltham a bind. When I expressed an interest in the BKS job I was offered it. I accepted and gave Fairey's my notice.

Meanwhile, Fairey's had won a contract for vertical colour photography of the Scottish coastline, from Berwick-on-Tweed on the East Coast, round Cape Wrath and down the west coast to just north of Skye, then from Glasgow to Carlisle and all round the main islands of Shetland and Orkney. As their only pilot experienced on the Islander, with Fairey's other aircraft busy elsewhere, I served out my notice on that job. We moved to Carlisle on the 12th May and flew the first photo sortie on the 15th. A spell of glorious sunny weather began. Even when cumulus cloud formed as the sun heated the ground the coast itself remained clear. We flew and took photography every day until the 21st, with eleven sorties and a total flying time of 38 hours for those 7 days. Then we had to break off to fly to Manchester for the aircraft's 50-hour engineering check. The next week saw us finished with the Carlisle-Glasgow and Berwick-Inverness sections and lodged at the Golf View Nairn hotel again. The following week was a washout. Jennie drove up from Yorkshire and with the crew we took in the local tourist attractions. Then the fine weather returned. Jennie came with us on the Cape Wrath southwards flight and sat in the co-pilot's seat. The Atlantic was calm and to one who was much more familiar with the North Sea, incredibly clear. One of these days I'll go back to the West Coast by road, the memory of that beautiful scenery has never faded.

With the mainland photography completed, on the 10th of June we tackled the Shetlands. It was late in the afternoon by the time we landed at Sumburgh, it seemed a good idea to stay the night. I started telephoning hotels and guest houses from the airport, but those I tried were all full and I soon ran out of change – phone cards didn't exist then. We found a taxi and asked the driver to take us someplace where we could get a meal and a drink. He took us to a hotel a few miles away, one that I hadn't telephoned. I asked if they had any vacant rooms. The landlady said "No, I have four empty rooms right now but they are reserved for a party of Germans who are flying in late tonight" So I ordered a round of beer for my crew, obtained some more change and continued telephoning.

I was on my second pint when it finally became obvious that I would find nowhere for us to sleep on the Shetlands that night. The 'eight hours between bottle and throttle' principle ruled out flying somewhere else. For lack of any better ideas, we had a meal and then returned to the bar, where I switched to 'rusty nails' – that very more-ish mixture of Drambuie and any brand of blended Scotch. Enquiry of the landlady, who was also the bar tender, indicated that closing time was flexible to the extent that the bar would close when we decided we'd had enough. We settled down for an all-night session.

Ten or so rusty nails later, at around one a.m., the landlady clapped her hand to her forehead and exclaimed "Och, This night's the 10th. I thocht it was the 11th. Those Germans aren't coming until **this** evening. You can have those rooms!"

I was up at six the next morning and went for a walk along the beach. After a Shetland breakfast of fruit juice, porridge, poached haddock and eggs, toast and marmalade and half a dozen cups of coffee, by midday I was ready for another spell of survey. There is something special about rusty nails. Drambuie is too sweet; straight Scotch is too harsh. The mixture is perfection – and in my experience doesn't give a hangover. We finished off the Shetland coast and before landing at Kirkwall, photographed all round the Orkneys. Four days later I went to Leeds airport to start work with BKS.

Chapter 43
West Africa baptism

Although I expected to spend as much time away from our Leeds base as I had away from White Waltham, at least I'd be in easy daily commuting distance of home when we were at Leeds. But I found I had drawn the short straw – Jack Speight had retired and since no one else wanted the honour I was appointed as the Chief Pilot. I also found that the company planned for me to go to Lagos, Nigeria, to relieve the pilot who had been out there flying the Aztec for several months. During the next two months we operated the Islander from Leeds to places as far away as Belfast and Prestwick, returning to Leeds each time. On non-survey days I made some training flights on Aztecs at Sherburn in Elmet before taking the day and night type rating flying tests and in the evenings at home I press-ganged Jennie into testing me on the answers to the likely questions expected in the type technical ground examinations. She had just been appointed as Head Teacher of Aiskew, Leeming Bar Church of England Primary School, half-a-mile from our house.

I had the Aztec type rating on my licence by the last week in August and travelled by airline to Lagos on the 28th. While waiting for the connection at Gatwick, I went to see Lemmy Tanner, then living near Redhill, to ask for useful contact names, information and advice on Nigeria. The advice was fairly concise – "Don't go!" Perhaps I should have paid heed. I didn't anticipate it at the time, but I was to spend the next 13 years on duty/home leave rotation between England and Nigeria.

The arrival at Lagos was not too much of a culture shock, but when I took the Aztec to Kano a couple of days later my eyes were opened to a different world. As we walked out of the terminal building to find a taxi, we noticed a man sleeping on the pavement – or so we thought at first. Closer to, the smell of putrefaction made us realise that he was in fact dead and had been for some time. We were to learn that Nigerian medical aid was totally commercial, payment in advance was the rule and if you couldn't pay, then hard luck. Going to the aid of anyone injured or sick meant taking full responsibility for their welfare and accepting liability for the bills.

We spent just over a month in Kano. The weather was not favourable; we flew only eight times and photographed on five. On non-flying days there was always plenty to do. Many day-to-day chores that would have taken a few minutes in the U.K. could take most of a day to complete. All our financial transactions, including paying for fuel had to be in cash – although credit cards had come into use elsewhere, no one in Nigeria would accept them. Going to the bank to cash travellers' cheques was an incredibly slow process, the systems which had been put in place to counter the endemic fraud meant seeing at least four different people before the cash could be handed over. Success in making a telephone call, even to someone in the same town, was an occasion for a champagne celebration. Once I wanted to 'phone Jos from Kano – a distance of 150 miles. After failing a direct connection all morning, I tried calling BKS in Northern Ireland and amazingly got through in a few minutes, passed them the message for relay to Jos and received an answer half an hour later. It seemed the main cause of telephone problems was theft of the copper cables! Another problem was locating a particular address. It might be, say, 121 Abu Damsar Street. Finding the street was relatively easy; maps of the city were available. Finding the building was another matter. Not all the buildings had visible numbers, but starting at one end one might see number three on the left and number six on the right. Then seven on the left, and twelve on the right. Great. But some way further on, one would see number 160 on the left and 43 on the right. Then totally out of sequence number four on the left. We learnt that buildings were numbered in the order they had been built. Some of the streets were a mile or more long; if the office you were looking for didn't have its number displayed, what then? It wasn't much use trying to telephone for guidance. Unless you had half a day to spare!

After leaving Kano, we spent two and a half months wandering around Nigeria, basing for varying periods near to contract areas at Kaduna, Enugu, Jos, Ibadan and Lagos. It was quite usual to set off on a flight expecting to return to our temporary base, but on finding the weather not suitable for photography at the first target, to go somewhere else, land at the nearest airfield when the fuel was getting low and end up staying the night. We had to be careful doing this – Avgas (piston aircraft fuel) was a continual problem. Most airfields almost always had turbine fuel but Avgas supply was very uncertain, we often had to break off our survey before we got out of reach of a place we knew had fuel for us. Accommodation was another difficulty. Being unable to book ahead (because we didn't know where the weather would be suitable) we would arrive at a new place after a day's work and then hunt around for a hotel with available rooms, working down the scale and often ending up in some fairly insalubrious hostelry. We usually managed to find somewhere to stay in the end, but a couple of times, finding nowhere in one town, we went back to the aircraft and flew to another. One time the substitute town really let us down. We found rooms at the Bus Terminus Hotel in Jos, but got very little sleep. A loud disco kept us awake until 2 a.m. and then a flock of turkeys gobbled noisily until the goats started bleating at 4. At 5 the bus station started up with its piped music and loud announcements of bus departures and arrivals and that put paid to any hope of further sleep.

Later on Jos proved to be the most enjoyable place we operated from in Nigeria, when we stayed in a bungalow owned by Makerie Smelters, a tin-mining company that had some vague association with BKS. The town was situated on top of a 4,000 feet high plateau, which made for a much cooler climate – cool enough to grow peas, potatoes and even strawberries. There too we could buy fresh milk and cream to go with the strawberries. UHT was unknown then, elsewhere in the country the only milk available was either tinned or powdered. The plateau top was fairly bare of trees, with occasional granite tors surrounded by large grassy areas. This was a cattle-rearing and staging area; sand-coloured tracks across the plateau marked drover's trails which began in neighbouring Chad and led eventually to Lagos 350 miles to the south-west. In those days the airfield was all grass except for a single dirt runway; it had the feel of a typical flying club airfield like Sywell or Sherburn-in-Elmet, with an old-fashioned rectangular control tower and a couple of small corrugated iron hangars. Later on, some distance away, a new airport was built with a tarmac runway capable of taking Jumbo jets.

A flight to Lagos to collect one of our Company Directors and take him back to Jos became quite exciting. I had emphasised to him that with no runway or airfield lighting at Jos we would need to leave in good time to arrive at Jos before dark, but of course he turned up later than arranged. I told him that we were probably too late to reach Jos, it depended on the en-route wind, but if we didn't get there in time we would divert to Kano where there was lighting. The wind was against us and shortly before reaching Jos the sun set. I then heard from another aircraft that Kano had a total electrical power failure. From previous experience I knew this could last for hours; there was no other airfield with night facilities within reach. In the standard tropical fashion it grew dark very rapidly and there was no moon. I continued towards Jos and was relieved to see the lights of the Makerie Smelting Company's compound, which I knew was just to the side of the runway approach centreline. Ahead was the black hole of the airfield, with just a few scattered lights from buildings around the perimeter. Then, in the dim starlight I picked out a faint difference in texture between the laterite runway and the surrounding grass. I reckoned if we were going to crash we might as well get it over with and with no real visual cues as to when to flare for landing did a flying boat low speed steady rate of descent type approach until we hit the ground. It worked.

Our aircraft's Aerial Work maintenance schedule required checks by an engineer licensed on type every 50 hours of flying. Unlike Faireys, BKS did not employ engineers. In the U.K. this was no great problem, we were never too far from Leeds, where the Yorkshire Light Aircraft Company did our maintenance. When overseas however, places where we could have checks carried out could be a long way from where we were operating. The survey pilot's motto was "fly and find out' – if there was a chance of the weather being suitable for photography, go try it. This was all very well when maintenance checks were easy to accomplish. In Nigeria the only maintenance facility available to us was at Lagos, a seven-hour round trip from Kano. With the dire state of the Nigerian telephone system it was almost impossible to let the maintenance company know when I was coming. I could only turn up out of the blue and hope they were not too busy, but a maintenance visit always meant three days minimum away from site and sometimes a week. It was always a fine judgement whether or not to risk wasting flying hours on a sortie when the chance of success was uncertain. Nigeria was in a very unfavourable part of the world for survey weather. A fair part of the country had been photographed during or soon after World War Two, but some areas were still not covered despite many attempts since then. Some of the maps even had blank areas with "Cloud" printed in them!

We did our best, but when we were due to be relieved by another crew in mid-December we still had not photographed some of our jobs. It was not really our fault with one of these. We were asked to survey a coal mine not far from Enugu and were given the latitude and longitude of the site, with a hand drawn sketch map of the immediate area. Each time we were passing nearby en-route to or from another target we'd have a try at finding it without success. We were of course looking for colliery winding wheels and spoil heaps, but what really worked against us was that the client had given us the longitude figures as the latitude and the latitude figures as the longitude. The error was not obvious because in that part of the world the two positions were close together. We did stumble across the place on a later Nigeria visit, when we discovered it was a very small open cast quarry, only 100 metres or so across.

Chapter 44
An eventful ferry flight

At home in January 1976, after a Christmas leave ski-ing with Jennie in Austria it was back to the Islander around the U.K. In 1976 there were many more coal-fired power stations operating than today. Every six months or so they needed to assess their stock. It was far quicker and cheaper to do this by aerial survey than by physically measuring the coal heaps, so the National Electricity Board contracted BKS and other Survey companies to carry this out, giving each company a group of targets. We would set off on a grand tour. Even from our flying height of 1000 feet the target area could be covered by a single stereo pair, so cloud or cloud shadow was not such a problem as in normal survey. If a cloud or cloud shadow partly covered a target we could orbit until the cloud moved away. When we had used most of our fuel, run out of daylight, or run into unsuitable weather we would land at the nearest airport and stay the night. Battersea power station (now Tate Modern) was then in full operation. I can distinctly remember passing directly over Buckingham Palace on the line-up run to the tall chimneys on the bank of the Thames. Meanwhile airliners were not far above us on their approach to Heathrow and a helicopter was on its way to the Battersea heliport.

A four-month overseas session that year with BKS was notable for the number of incidents which, though similar to ones I had already experienced, did not usually occur quite so close together. The Company won several more contracts for surveys in Nigeria and bought a Piper Navajo to add to the Islander and Aztec. I took the type rating technical examinations and on 31st March went to Stapleford Tawney in Essex for the flying tests on the type. By mid-April all was ready, I had the type on my licence and the aircraft had been modified at Fairoaks with a camera hatch, a tracking periscope and all the associated electrics. We left Leeds on the 24th April, dropped in at Fairoaks for some last bits of paperwork and flew on to Hurn near Bournemouth, for customs clearance. We loaded up with duty-free and that evening reached Perpignan in the south of France. A recommendation from Air Traffic

Photo 43 - Piper Navajo G-BBEI   Courtesy Malcolm Clarke

Control led us to a splendid family restaurant. With the meal, the owner suggested his own vineyard's wine. This was so more-ish (not to mention cheap) that we bought a couple of cases each.

Next morning, when we tried to leave for Algiers, our VHF radio was not transmitting, although we could hear Air Traffic Control. A local radio engineer spent the rest of the day working on the installation. This was not an easy task, he had to lie on the cockpit floor and reach up behind the instrument panel to get at the connections, but by evening the radio seemed to be working properly. The following day we set off once more, but as soon as we were airborne we again lost transmission.

There was nothing for it but to return to Fairoaks to have the people who had modified the aircraft rectify the problem. Flying back without radio was not however a simple matter. It was necessary, for legal reasons, to stay clear of cloud and out of various airspace areas within which radio was mandatory. This required many changes of direction to go round, climbs to go above, or descents to go below these no-go zones. In some places there were gaps of only a mile or two between adjacent areas. Contrary to the general belief, visual navigation by map and compass is no simple matter and staying within even five miles of track is sometimes the best one can manage. It is far easier to fly from radio beacon to beacon along airways, letting Air Traffic Control sort out all the problems of airspace and 'Notices to Airmen' (which detail temporary restrictions on where one can fly), but to do this requires two way voice radio communication.

There was one small trick to help the situation. The Navajo was fitted with a transponder. This, when it received a radar transmission from a ground station, responded by 'squawking' back with a code dialled up by the pilot. I had set the appropriate code to indicate "I can hear you but cannot transmit". No one in France took any notice of this as far as I could tell, but passing near Jersey the Air Traffic Controller, presumably having received my flight plan passed on from Perpignan called "Aircraft squawking XXXX (a four digit number), are you Golf Bravo Bravo Echo India? If affirmative, squawk XXXY, if negative squawk XXXZ." I squawked XXXY and then by a series of yes or no questions, the controller ascertained that I had enough fuel and wanted to go on to Fairoaks. He then gave me headings and altitudes to fly, cleared me through a bit of controlled airspace and eventually handed me over to the controller at Fairoaks.

The problem came after landing. Fairoaks was a "Customs on Request" airfield. With radio, I'd have been able to give advance notice so that the Customs Officer would be there to meet us. When the Controller discovered that we had not flown from Jersey, but from France, he was a bit concerned and made us wait in his office until he could get a Customs Officer to come over from Heathrow. When he arrived, he wanted to charge us duty on the duty-free we'd taken from Bournemouth and on the wine we'd bought in Perpignan. Expecting to leave for overseas again in a day or two, we weren't very happy with that. Eventually we devised a system. We put all the booze in a couple of our aluminium camera boxes, he put a lead seal on them and he agreed that to save a Customs visit on our next departure the ATC controller would check that the seal was unbroken.

After two days at Fairoaks with the radio being worked on, fixed, checked and checked again, we made another start on 28th April. This time we routed via Hurn to Bordeaux, night stopped and then next day flew on to Palma, Majorca. Here we had to wait a day for our clearance to enter Algeria. On the 30th the intention was to start early and, depending on how long it took to refuel and clear through Algiers, press on as far as possible before dark.

The first setback occurred when I contacted Algiers Air Traffic Control. The controller asked me to report reaching the Control Zone boundary, which I did. He then told me to turn onto a heading of 020 degrees. This was back the way we had come. I thought perhaps he had an aircraft on departure and needed to delay my arrival, but after several minutes with no other transmissions on the frequency I queried the reason for this heading instruction. "It's your heading to the airfield," said the controller. A session of "Oh no it's not", "Oh yes it is" followed, until I managed to convince him that since I was over water and not sand the airfield could not be to the north east of me. After we landed the controller apologised, explaining that he had been using a CRDF (cathode ray direction finder) to find my bearing. This was a new piece of equipment to them and he wasn't used to it, so had read the bearing to the aircraft as the direction to steer (180 degrees out).

I found the refuellers and left my crew to supervise, while I went to check the weather, file a flight plan for the next leg and pay my landing fees. The landing fees became the next problem. On departure from the U.K. the Company had provided me with Traveller's Cheques, a substantial quantity of sterling and dollar notes and what other foreign currency had been handed in by crews who had returned from countries I would be visiting. The landing fees clerk would accept nothing but Algerian dinars. I didn't have any. He was adamant; I could easily change sterling or dollars at the bank just outside the terminal building, that's what I must do.

To get to the bank I had to go through Immigration and Customs. No problem at Immigration, they would keep my passport while I went to the bank. No problem at Customs. At the bank I changed just enough Sterling for the dinars I needed. Back at Customs, "How much Algerian money do you have?" the Customs Officer asked. I told him. He replied "You can't take that amount out of the country." "But I'm not taking it out of the country, it's to pay my landing fees." "Doesn't matter what it's for, you can't take that amount past here". Impasse. I went back outside to where I'd noticed a hole in the fence, snuck back in and went to pay the fees. Out again through the same hole and back to Customs, now no problem. Then Immigration to recover my passport. By then, refuelling had been completed, so we were on our way. Except that when I tried to call ATC, once again the radio had quit. We spent another day trying to get it fixed locally without success, then turned tail and fled back to Fairoaks. This time we paid the customs duty and took our liquor home.

My memory fails me regarding the next ten days. I see from my logbook that I flew the Navajo from Fairoaks to Leeds on the 5th May, I guess this was for maintenance at Yorkshire Light Aircraft, our usual maintenance organisation. On the 7th I set out for Oxford (I don't know why, perhaps to collect some spares to take with us) but had to return to Leeds with an undercarriage problem. I made it to Oxford and on to Fairoaks on the 10th for more work on the avionics installation and did a couple of test flights on the 15th.

We left Fairoaks on 17th May and wended our way via Hurn again towards Kano, this time deciding to fly round the West African coast because it was easier to get clearance to enter or overfly the countries en route. We stopped at Madrid for the first night and sampled Spanish cooking in a working man's restaurant. On the 18th we made an early start and landed at Casablanca to refuel. Just before landing, I was quite thrilled to have the opportunity to relay a radio message from Concorde, somewhere out over the Atlantic on flight trials. Then we went on to Las Palmas and night stopped. On the 19th we continued with a $5^1/_2$-hour leg to Dakar, memorable for the frog's legs I ate in a down town restaurant. Next day we made two legs, the first from Dakar to Bamako. That day I learnt yet another way to be caught out in the aviation world. Before departure from England I had carefully listed all the topographical air maps I would need for the route to Nigeria, including adjacent ones to allow for possible diversions. I had taken those we already had in the Leeds office and purchased those we didn't have. Approaching Bamako the weather began to deteriorate and a diversion became a possibility. The alternate airfield had no radio navigation aids and would have to be found by map reading. I unfolded the roughly one metre square map to the bit where the alternate should have been and discovered that someone had cut that section out of it. I guess that same someone had been operating in that area on a previous occasion and had wanted a more conveniently sized map, but he might have had the sense to scrap the bit he didn't want! Fortunately the weather didn't get too bad and we were able to land from an instrument approach at Bamako.

I particularly remember the excellent French bread sandwiches we bought from the airport restaurant, which we ate on the next leg to Niamey in Niger. There things went a bit pear-shaped. A soldier marched me off to the police station, prodding me in the back with a .303 rifle. Although I showed my copy of the telex from the Niger Civil Aviation Department giving me landing clearance I was interrogated for an hour. I was accused of landing without permission plus various other crimes. Once I had made it obvious that I wasn't going to hand over cash to get out of the situation, but was prepared to wait until they gave up trying, they let me go. The quality of the hotel and meal in Niamey made up for the unpleasantness.

We arrived in Kano, Nigeria on the 21st, cleared aircraft and equipment through Customs and made contact with the client. We flew our first photographic survey on 23rd and for the rest of May, the whole of June and the first week of July chased the weather around the country. During a week at Enugu, we had an interesting event on return to the airport after a flight. Selecting the wheels down produced only the nose and left wheel green lights. When I went round again I was given a strong telling off by the Air Traffic Controller. "You were cleared to land, why didn't you land? When I clear you to land, you **must** land. Land immediately." Some argument then took place before I convinced him that it wasn't a good idea to land until I was sure all the wheels were down and locked. Alternatively, if I couldn't get all the wheels down it **would** be a good idea to fly around until there was very little fuel left in the tanks, that way, if the landing went wrong, there'd be less to burn. Meanwhile I was going through the emergency procedures. The first was to check that the problem was not simply a bulb failure, but the working bulb from the left wheel indicator did not illuminate when transferred to the right side. The controller, by now understanding the problem, said that he could see that the wheel was actually down. "Not good enough" I replied, "It may be down but is it locked down? I'll fly low past the control tower and swing the aircraft, please watch to see if the wheel moves." After the low pass, he told me the wheel was not moving. Fair enough, but I would really prefer to see three green lights. Raising the undercarriage and lowering it again still gave only the two greens. Two tricks left – one was to pull up sharply as the undercarriage was selected down, the 'g' force applied by this manoeuvre would help to force the wheels over centre to the locked position. The last option would be to bounce the aircraft hard onto the runway on the good wheel. Fortunately the first of these did the trick.

Obi, our regular taxi driver when we were in Enugu on this and previous occasions had been waiting for us and had seen our fly-past. He said that when I swung the aircraft from side to side the right wheel had been swinging up and down. I had more faith in his observation than in the controller's. Obi had a fair amount of flying experience, he often came along on our survey trips, although he did tend to fall asleep soon after take-off and would wake up only when we landed. On these occasions he was of course right there when we needed him to take us back to the hotel. Somehow he also always managed to be there ready for us on the days he didn't fly, despite our uncertain arrival times.

We didn't have much luck with our accommodation at Enugu. One of our directors, a noted tightwad, had booked rooms for us at the Destiny Airport Hotel, presumably because it was a) very cheap and b) within walking distance of the airport, which would save taxi fares – or maybe he just liked the name! We checked in and I went to my room for an urgent appointment with the toilet. When I'd done, I found that there was neither flush water for the toilet nor water from the washbasin tap. A visit to reception produced the information that this was normal, the only water available was from a tap in the yard, where there was a bucket in which I could wash my hands. When I did so, I felt something in the bucket and pulled out several beer glasses belonging to the hotel bar. We went looking for somewhere else. The only decent hotel in Enugu was full, but they offered us their 'annexe' rooms. These turned out to be what had been intended as changing/shower rooms next to the swimming pool. There was just enough space to fit in a single bed, with a foot-wide gap alongside giving access to the shower and toilet. We took them – with the option to take rooms in the main hotel any time they were available, even for a single night. Needless to say, that didn't happen more than twice. At least we didn't have far to go for a swim.

Towards the end of June word came from BKS that we were to do as much as we could to finish the jobs in Nigeria, but we had to be in Swaziland by the middle of July. I immediately telexed Coleraine to say that I would need more funds for the transit, but foolishly let the Company persuade me that with my Diner's Card for hotels, food and transport and a Shell carnet for aircraft fuel, there would be no problem. We left Kano on the 13th July, for Yaounde in Cameroon. There was a bit of drama not long after crossing the border. Large thunderstorms lay across our track and we were unable to stay out of cloud. Turbulence in thunderstorms can be bad enough to damage or destroy aircraft. The most severe conditions are believed to occur at around one third of the height of the cloud, so sometimes it is possible to stay low to avoid the worst. This we could not do because of the mountains across our track, the highest, Mt Cameroon reached over 12,000 feet. Jet aircraft can fly well above the severe turbulence level, our Navajo couldn't go that high and with no pressurisation or oxygen, nor could we anyway. So we were stuck with penetrating the weather at the worst level. Nowadays most aircraft, even small ones, are fitted with weather radar, which enables the worst conditions to be avoided even when flying blind, but we didn't have this. With a lot of twisting and turning towards clearer bits of sky we managed to find a way through, but we took a fair bit of shaking about.

Not until after landing did we discover that there was no avgas available at Yaounde. It was by then too late in the day to fly to Douala on the coast where we were assured there would be some fuel. Although Douala was equipped with the lighting needed for night landings, there was nowhere else with night facilities as an alternate within range of the limited fuel remaining.

After Nigeria, Yaounde turned out to be a little bit of heaven. We asked the taxi driver to take us to a good hotel, the one he chose for us had bungalows scattered around among coconut trees in a manicured garden. It reminded me of 'Les Tropiques' in Tahiti, though without the lagoon. Perhaps this was mainly due to my once again having to communicate in French while in a tropical setting. We checked in and then walked to the centre of town. Where two wide boulevards crossed we found a tropical version of Montparnasse. Old colonial two or three story buildings had shops, cafes and restaurants on the ground floor, with balconied dwelling apartments above. There were tables, chairs and umbrellas on the pavements outside the cafes and buskers providing western and African music. We drank French wine and sampled a mixture of French and Cameroon cooking. Most impressive of all, after three months of erratic electricity and water supply in Nigeria, the lights stayed on all evening and the taps at the hotel gave hot or cold water as required whenever required.

Next morning we flew to Douala for fuel. Strangely, this was one of only two occasions in my flying career when I was asked to show my pilot's licence, other than when flying with an examiner. Fortunately all the required certificates and signatures were in place and valid and we were able to carry on to Kinshasa on the Congo river in Zaire, the only small problem being that I had to pay cash for fuel, the oil company at Douala would not accept my carnet. The same applied at Kinshasha and again next day passing through Kananga to Lubumbashi. When once again I couldn't use my fuel carnet, the cash situation became serious. Between the four of us, we raised enough of our personal money to partly fill the fuel tanks with enough avgas to get us to Blantyre in Malawi. My Diner's card sorted the rather splendid hotel we night stopped in and paid for our meals and a few beers. We put our faith in being able to get fuel on the carnet at Blantyre and fly on to Matsapa in Swaziland, where our client would provide us with an advance of cash against the work we would be doing.

So on 16th June we departed from Lubumbashi and headed on towards Blantyre. Approaching the Malawi border, I called Blantyre Control on the high frequency radio. I passed my flight details and got the response "You do not have permission to enter Malawi". I pulled the relevant bits of paper out of my flight bag and having found the one I needed, replied "Yes I do, telex reference XXX of YY June". Back came "You do not have permission, if you land in Malawi you will be arrested". With the Niamey experience still freshly in mind, my thoughts ran on the lines of "Not again, is there any way out of this?" At that moment Salisbury (now Harare) radio came on the air. "Salisbury weather at 1100 hours 3 Octas at 4,000 feet, visibility 30 miles, wind 180 degrees 10 knots." This seemed like an open invitation, so I asked if they (Salisbury) would accept my entry into and landing in Rhodesia (as it was then). "No problem, you're welcome."

There was a minor difficulty. We had enough fuel to reach the first airfield in Rhodesia with some to spare and, if nothing went wrong, to get to Salisbury with not quite empty tanks. From our position at the time going direct to Salisbury meant crossing over a tongue of Mozambique. We had clearance to overfly Mozambique from Blantyre to Swaziland, but not from where we were and not until the next day. We had nowhere near enough fuel to fly round the enclave or to fly in circles while we negotiated with Mozambique Control but I reckoned we could slip across with no one the wiser, the chances of being intercepted by a Mozambique fighter were about zero!

We didn't need a map to know when we crossed the border into Rhodesia. We had been flying over bush country for the last few hours and then the scenery changed abruptly to well-kept farmland. Green crop fields and cattle pastures stretched ahead as far as we could see. The first airfield appeared off to the side, I re-calculated the fuel remaining and found we could easily make the next one. A whole string of airfields followed and eventually Salisbury itself was assured, although we landed with only 15 minutes worth of fuel remaining. I went happily off to the fuel depot and then discovered that I had jumped from the frying pan into the fire. I hadn't thought about the full implications of the sanctions then in force against the Ian Smith Government. My fuel carnet was no use and by now between us we had barely enough to pay for a taxi into town.

We went to one of the better hotels where I asked if they accepted the Diner's card. I didn't say it was one issued in the U.K. "No problem" was the answer. So for the next three days we lived on tick at the hotel while I tried to get hold of some cash. I telephoned BKS but because of sanctions there was no way they could transfer money through the banking system, or by any other method. They would see if the client in Swaziland could do anything, but as the weekend was coming up it would be a few days before any results. It began to look like we would either have to find some work locally or sell the aeroplane! Trying to let Jennie at home in Yorkshire know what was going on led to some amusement. I made a reverse charge call. When the operator told her "I have a reverse charge call for you from Salisbury, will you accept the charges?" Jennie, thinking of Salisbury in Wiltshire, promptly said "No, I don't know anyone in Salisbury" and hung up. Next time I got the operator to specify Salisbury Rhodesia.

On the Saturday, with time on our hands, I suggested to the crew that we should walk out to the nearby Salisbury gliding club. We were invited to a party that evening and were given a lift to the house where it was being held. There I found the solution to our problems. I met a girl who was hoping to visit Europe on holiday, but she did not see how she could manage on the small amount of money that Rhodesian currency laws allowed her to take out of the country. I gave her a U.K. cheque in exchange for enough Rhodesian money to cover our hotel, fuel and other expenses and on Monday we were on our way.

We survey aviators frequently complained that we worked only in the less pleasant parts of the world. Swaziland was an exception for us. The scenery was magnificent, the climate mild, the food excellent and the ambience altogether different to the run of African and Middle East states we had previously visited. Unfortunately for me, I enjoyed only seven days there. Three days after arriving at Matsapa, I had to take the aircraft to Johannesburg for maintenance and four days after my return my relief arrived. I flew back to England with no problems – sitting in the back of a South African Airways 707!

Photo 44 - Dove G-AWFM was rescued and restored in South Africa

Courtesy Pawel Bondaryk

Chapter 45
Saved by the cameraman

After the four month Fairoaks to Swaziland epic I did expect to have at least four months in the U.K. before going away again, but it was not to be. There was time to fly in a gliding competition at Dunstable in August, but in mid-September a problem arose in Sana'a, North Yemen. The Company had taken on a new pilot and he had flown the aircraft there from Leeds. One of our trackers, who had been an unlicensed aircraft engineer, went with him. On the way, the undercarriage had started to extend every now and then, without being selected down. The tracker said they should have the fault rectified, but the pilot said there was no need, he could raise the undercarriage back up using the hydraulic hand pump. On the first flight in the Yemen, the fault recurred several times, until eventually the wheels could not be raised this way. More seriously, they could not be lowered either, because all the hydraulic fluid had leaked away! The pilot then used the emergency undercarriage lowering system, a pressurised carbon dioxide bottle which, when activated by a switch, discharged into the hydraulic lines and blew the undercarriage down. Unfortunately it also ruptured the seals on the port undercarriage hydraulic jack. I was sent out with spare parts and the task of dismissing the pilot.

I found a bizarre situation on arrival. The crew were staying in a house rented by the client, most of whose own staff were not due to arrive for several weeks. The arrangement was that the client's house staff would do the housework and laundry at no charge to us, but we would pay for meals (at a very reasonable rate) out of our meal allowances. Our hero was having none of that – he had a suitcase full of Vesta ready-cooked meals and such and would look after himself. This might have been acceptable, had he not been helping himself to the fridge contents when no one was watching. Not only that, but our camera operator had met the crew of a cargo 707. They made regular flights into Sana'a and had promised to bring in a couple of cases of beer for us every week, at cost. The pilot collected the first consignment, but instead of taking it to the house, went to an expats' club down town and sold it to them! Even without the dreadful airmanship he'd displayed, there was no way the crew would have worked with him.

When I said I was sending him back to the U.K., he went to the British Embassy and told them I was operating illegally, because I was flying outside the aircraft's weight, altitude and temperature limitations. Sana'a, at over 10,000 feet above sea level, was indeed so high and so hot that the 'WAT' limitations would be exceeded, but they applied only to Public Transport operations, not to Aerial Work or private flying. The Embassy accepted my explanation, ignored him and he left.

We now had a big problem. There were no maintenance facilities in the Yemen. We couldn't fly the aircraft safely with the undercarriage down. Our

Aztec had difficulty maintaining height on one engine even with the undercarriage up; an engine failure with the undercarriage non-retractable would inevitably lead to a crash. So I couldn't take it to the nearest place (which was Dubai) where we could have it repaired. I could carry out the repair myself, provided I then flew without passengers to the nearest place where the repair could be checked and 'signed off' by a licensed engineer. But Dubai was about 15 hours flying time away. The only sensible option was to have an engineer flown out from the U.K. While awaiting his arrival, we started to make preparations.

We needed to put the aircraft on jacks. I had made the acquaintance of a friendly Yemen Air Force pilot who was flying Mig 15s based at Sana'a. The Mig was a Russian designed single jet fighter, contemporary with and very similar to the American F86 Sabre. The two types had met in combat during the Korean War. Having flown the F86, I had been trying to scrounge a flight with him in the Mig17 two-seater version of the Mig 15 to see how the rival fighters compared, but the presence of Russian military advisors made this impossible. He was however very willing to help with our problem and showed us some aircraft jacks we could borrow. East is east and west is west … They were no use. The jacking points on the Aztec are protruding cones that fit into a corresponding hollow on the jacks. The Mig had the hollows in the aircraft wings and the cones on the jacks.

Lateral thinking was required. I remembered what someone in Singapore had told me about seeing a Chinaman changing a truck wheel without using a jack, by digging a hole in the road. We pushed the Aztec off the hard standing onto a patch of sand, built pyramids of concrete blocks up to the jacking points and then excavated around the wheels. When the engineer had arrived and fitted the new parts, we carried out retraction tests. Once we were satisfied that the undercarriage went up and down properly, we filled the holes as far as the wheels, then with four of us lifting a wing tip, the engineer was able to pull out the top concrete block on that side. Round to the other wing for the same treatment and finally, when we had dug sloping ramps from each wheel up to ground level, I started the engines and taxied out of the sand onto the hard standing.

Once we had flown an air test, we began what became the most successful month's surveying of my career. We flew on 20 out of 27 days and took photography on 19. The main job covered the route of a proposed new road from Sana'a south along the edge of the plateau for a few miles, then down the escarpment and across to the Red Sea coast. In this area the scarp was less distinct that further north, with many razor-backed ridges running out into the coastal plain. Our photography required flight at 5,000 feet above the ground, much of our flying was well below the 8,000 feet ridge tops around us which required close attention so as not to bump into the spectacular scenery. On our way to or from the survey area we were able to have a look around. The 45 degree or steeper sides of the ridges were intricately terraced, with high dry-stone walls. Few of the terraces were more than thirty yards long or two wide. Here and there villages of one or two storied houses straddled the ridge crests, which were so narrow that the path through a village was literally through it, passing under or in and out of the houses. At each end of the villages open water cisterns quarried out of the rock could be seen. Presumably these could be filled only by rainwater, most water having to be hand-carried from the streams many thousands of feet below. The valleys seemed narrow enough for the inhabitants of one village to be able to converse with the villagers on the opposite ridge without raising their voices; a visit would have taken hours.

For us, living at 10,000 feet took some getting used to, even with the luxury of water on tap. The control tower was about eighty feet high and the office where one had to go to file flight plans was almost at the top. There was no lift. It felt like a day's work just climbing the spiral staircase each morning. We stayed at a hotel that had been a palace in years gone by. When we first checked in, unannounced, we were given rooms on the ground floor, but as time went by we were moved further and further upwards, as visitors with reservations from earlier on arrived. By the time we had been relocated to the top floor, the effort of walking down the stairs for dinner and up afterwards became too much to bear. What it must have been like for those Yemeni women fetching water is hard to imagine. We took the easy way out and shopped on our way back from the airfield, carrying the makings up to one of our rooms and dining en suite. Our favourite dinner became local cheese and local grapes; both of these came in great variety.

The door of my top floor room slanted sideways. Inside, the two foot thick walls were whitewashed. Black, rough-hewn wood beams held up the plastered ceiling. A small multi-paned window was deeply recessed into one wall and sheepskin rugs partly covered the planked floor. Had the muezzin's calls from the surrounding mosques been replaced by the bleating of sheep, I would have thought myself to be in a Devonshire farm cottage.

Sana'a city was a fascinating place. A maze of streets and alleys, many wide enough only for pedestrians or donkeys was surrounded by a high mud brick wall. Inside the wall most of the buildings, anything up to five stories high, were ornately decorated with horizontal bands of geometric figures. Many had heavy, studded wooden doors. Yemeni men, all with daggers at their belts and some carrying rifles, strolled the streets. Others, their cheeks bulging grotesquely sat in corners chewing 'kat', a mildly narcotic leaf.

Central Government had very loose control over the out-lying settlements; many of these had virtually their own armies. A highly casual attitude to weapons prevailed. Any celebration was excuse enough for loosing off not fireworks, but shotguns, rifles, antique field guns and on one occasion we heard of, a surface to air missile. The Yemeni approach to other hazards was equally casual. I vividly remember taking our car to the filling station. The attendant, lighted cigarette in one hand and petrol nozzle in the other watched us in bewilderment as we hastily retired round the corner.

We had not finished all the Yemen work by the end of October, but with unfavourable weather expected during the early winter left the Aztec behind for another crew to collect and take to Nigeria. We returned to the U.K. by airline. The Navajo left Swaziland in December for Nairobi and a maintenance check. At the beginning of January 1977 I went there to collect it and fly it to Sana'a. BKS had transferred money to a Kenyan Bank to pay for the maintenance work and I was to collect the balance in the form of traveller's cheques as funds for the ferry flight. There was one small snag with this apparently sensible idea. The balance to collect was a little over £4,000. The highest denomination traveller's cheque available was the equivalent of around £10. By the time I had finished signing four hundred cheques any resemblance between my normal signature and the last one was purely imaginary.

The political situation in Ethiopia was by then calm, so we flew via Addis Ababa and Djibouti to Sana'a. BKS had secured more contracts in the North Yemen, so they had rented two houses, one for an Area Manager sent out from Coleraine and the other for the crew. This was a more satisfactory arrangement, we could set up the photo-lab in our own house instead of, as on the previous visit, some distance from where we lived and there was much more room for our equipment and photo-mosaicing work. Unfortunately I was not to achieve much this time. After three days with short partially successful flights, the weather turned and we stayed on the ground for a week. We tried again on the 21st, 22nd and 23rd of January. On the 23rd I had another drama.

I had been suffering occasional and not too serious backache since my RAF Germany days, without thinking too much of it. At Leeming, the RAF doctor had given me heat treatment and once a few years later when it had persisted longer than usual I had tried an osteopath. This time it was serious. We had been flying for an hour when my back 'locked up' with excruciating pain. On previous occasions I had found that standing up eased the ache, so I engaged the Navajo's autopilot and got out of my seat. A minute or two later the pain stopped, but as soon as I tried to sit down again the agony resumed. I stood for longer. No good, I still couldn't sit down. Had there been no other option, maybe I might have managed to get the aircraft back on the ground myself, but luckily Philip Byrne, our camera operator, had recently gained his private pilot's licence. He had flown only fixed undercarriage, single engined Cessnas, but he took over the pilot's seat and with myself standing behind him telling him what to do, took us back for a perfect landing at Sana'a.

I left for the U.K. by airline next day. Sitting down for the take-off was agony again. As soon as the seat belt signs went out, I was on my feet and stood all the way to Heathrow. The next flight to Leeds was even more painful, the weather was rough and I had to stay strapped in. Then we were diverted to Manchester. On the coach to Leeds I stood again, but by then the combination of exhaustion and painkillers caused me to fall down twice. I was not amused when one of the other passengers complained to the stewardess that I was clearly drunk!

Three days later I was in traction at the Friarage hospital in Northallerton.

Chapter 46

Stretched on the rack

I quite enjoyed my hospital stay. BKS were continuing to pay me, so I had no immediate financial worries. The pain had gone, I was waited on hand and foot (literally!) and without the pressures of work I was able to relax, catch up with reading, talk to visiting friends and, with headphones, listen to the radio. I narrowly escaped being committed to the psychiatric ward one day. It must be just a little unusual for someone being stretched as if on the rack to burst into loud, uncontrollable laughter. It was all Kenneth Williams' fault, his contribution to that day's "Just a Minute" BBC radio problem was particularly zany.

There was one small irritant. I was visited once by a Civil Aviation Operations Inspector. It seemed that the pilot I'd sent back from Sana'a had made a complaint against me. The Inspector took a statement from me and soon after I heard that CAA were treating the complaint as unjustified.

The traction lasted six weeks. That wasn't the end, a further six weeks in a neck to groin plaster cast that made me feel like a tortoise followed. Eventually that too was over and I was flying again by the 2nd of May.

I had a few days on the Islander in Eire during which I experienced an example of Irish well intended but slightly screwed up helpfulness. The Met officer at Shannon had told us that the next day would be fine and cloudless. At the hotel I thought it would be a good idea to organise early calls for my crew and myself. No problem. "Which rooms?" asked the receptionist. "5, 6 and 8" I told him. "What time sorr?" "Seven o'clock" I replied. We had a splendid meal and a few Murphy's in the bar before retiring. I was well away, sleeping like a baby, when the telephone blasted off next morning. "Good morning", I mumbled. "Good morning to you, sorr and to be sure, in thirty minutes toime it'll be seven o'clock" came the reply.

In mid-May 1977 I travelled by airline to Kano, Nigeria where the Aztec was waiting for a new crew. We had work all round the country, from the Niger border north of Kano to Sokoto in the northwest, Lagos in the south and Maiduguri near Lake Chad in the northeast. We had a fairly productive two months, especially around Maiduguri, with occasional breaks when one or other of us succumbed to local varieties of the 'Kano Quickstep'. We found that wherever we went, once we had suffered, we could then re-visit that particular town with no further problems.

We could continue to operate when either the tracker or the camera operator was sick; the tracker had some camera experience. I could manage the tracking, by engaging the autopilot, moving over to the right hand seat, peering down the drift sight and reaching across to twiddle the autopilot heading knob to stay on track. This would have been a bit hazardous in the U.K., but in Nigeria there were very few aircraft flying around at our level.

In Kano we had received a telex from BKS, with information they wanted passing on to our team of ground surveyors, who they thought were currently "somewhere not too far south of Maiduguri". The next time that we were there we hired a taxi and set off to look for them. English is the "Lingua Franca" of Nigeria, so we didn't need an interpreter. At the edge of town the tar seal ended and we made our way along a backcountry bush road. It had been dry for some time and the surface had been ground into a talcum powder-like dust. Every now and again where the dust was too deep we had to divert off the track and wend our way through scattered acacia trees and other low bushes. We came to a small village and asked if anyone had seen four Englishmen with poles and tape measures. "They were here three weeks ago and then went that way" we learnt. Further on we came to another village, where the school was in session. Benches were set out in the shade of a large mango tree. A blackboard was nailed to the trunk and the small pupils were all clutching slates. Their eyes widened in surprise – we were the **second** lot of "ayibos' they had seen that year, they told us. They said the others had passed through two weeks before and then they went 'that way'. So it went on for a few more villages, with a few false turns and some backtracking, until some 60 miles from Maiduguri we were told "They have tents along that path a bit." No one was home when we arrived at their camp. We decided we had best wait for them, our chances of finding them were slim and without a compass we could easily have become lost in the bush. An hour later they came in. There was only one possible way to greet them - "Doctor Livingstone and party, we presume".

At the end of July we were relieved by another crew. I had somehow found out that Schreiner Airways might be recruiting for their Nigerian operation (Aero Contractors of Nigeria or ACN), which offered a regular schedule of work and leave. I telephoned them and was asked to go to their Scheveningen base in the Netherlands. "It will be for a couple of days; bring your wife with you and she can have a holiday while you are over here, we'll pay your fares and hotel" they said. This seemed very encouraging. The interviews went well, including a session with their psychiatrist. I had the impression that his job was to make sure I **was** insane, which anyone intending to work in Nigeria had to be! A check flight in a Navajo at Rotterdam also seemed satisfactory. I was told all the details of ACN's pay scales, local allowances, leave cycle, travel arrangements, accommodation and so on and I was offered employment, subject to a medical examination. There it all fell down. When I mentioned my past back problem, the doctor asked if I'd had an operation to sort it out and when I told him that I had not, I'd spent six weeks in traction, that was it. He considered there was too much chance of a recurrence. But at least Jennie and I had a free return trip and we spent a few extra days touring.

Chapter 47
Eire and the Gulf States

A few days after the Schreiner interview I was flying a Blanik two-seat glider in the 1997 Northern Regional Gliding Competition at Sutton Bank. People often asked me why I flew gliders on holiday when flying was my livelihood. The explanation that I flew powered aircraft because that was the only way I could earn enough to glide generally left them nonplussed! Sailboat fanatics will understand how much more satisfying it is to go from one place to another using only the forces of nature than it is to use an engine.

That autumn, using the Islander, we worked from Inverness, Cork, Shannon, White Waltham, Southend, Shoreham, Glasgow, Belfast, Blackpool, Newcastle, Bristol and Teesside – and even from our Leeds home base a few times! At Cork, we had another of those delightful Irish "don't tell them anything they won't like hearing" experiences. The people at the first hotel we tried were most helpful. "We are closed for the season" said the manager, "But never mind, we can give you rooms for the night" We checked in and he told us he'd send someone down to the bar if we wanted a drink. We did. The Murphy's were sliding down nicely and a cigarette would have completed the bliss. I had none left. "Do you have any Benson and Hedges?" I asked the barmaid. "I'll go and look", she replied. "Sorry, we're all out of Benson and Hedges, to be sure" she said when she returned from the store behind the bar. "Rothmans would do" I replied. Away she went again and "No, to be sure, we're all out of Rothmans" was the answer. I lowered my expectations through any tipped cigarettes, then several specified brands of untipped, finally saying "Well, any sort of cigarettes" Do I need to say what the final answer was?

At the beginning of November the Navajo was in Abu Dhabi and the crew were due for relief. I went there to complete our Gulf States work and then set out towards Sana'a. We needed to stage through Dahran and Jeddah for fuel, so we left before dawn hoping to reach Sana'a that day. En-route from Dahran to Jeddah, the weather at Jeddah went below limits, so we diverted into Riyadh. Next day we tried again. We were fairly close to Jeddah and past the point of no return to Riyadh when once again the Jeddah weather deteriorated. An aircraft on the ground told us it was in fact raining mud! Somehow a dust storm had started and then a rainstorm had spilt into the dust. My planned alternate was Medina to the north, but another problem had arisen. We were flying just below a continuous layer of cloud and the air temperature was slightly below zero degrees Celsius. There were mountains between us and Medina, to go there meant climbing into the cloud to get above the high ground. In cloud with a temperature below zero we would have been in serious danger of icing. We had no anti-icing equipment fitted and if we did ice up, would have been forced down blind into the high ground. So I told Air Traffic Control that I would divert to Taif, to the south. "You can't divert there, it is a military airfield, you must go to Medina" came the reply. I tried to explain the problem. "You can't go to Taif unless you have an emergency". I decided I did have an emergency and went there anyway.

I was a little apprehensive on arrival, especially when the Taif Controller told us to stay in the aircraft until an escort arrived. A Landrover duly appeared with a couple of armed soldiers and took us to the airfield Commandant's office. Expecting the worst, we found the experience something of an anti-climax. The Commandant asked why I had diverted there and I explained the dilemma. He then told us that we would be taken to "the hotel" - he didn't say which - we were not to go outside of the hotel and we would be picked up next morning. Did I want to file my onward flight plan now, or in the morning? From this I gathered we were not about to be arrested as spies.

The end result was that I feared I'd be in more trouble with BKS than with the Saudi authorities. The hotel turned out to be the Mecca Hilton. As was to be expected at the hotel chosen for the United States President Jimmy Carter when he visited Saudi Arabia it was horrendously expensive; our one night stay cost around ten times as much as had any previous hotel. I had though saved a little on the ferry fuel costs. By going to Taif we had cut the corner from the normal route and were able to fly direct to Sana'a.

A week later, on the 20th December, we left the Navajo at Sana'a and flew back to the U.K by airline. That had been a very short overseas trip, just five weeks, but the uncertain life of a survey pilot was starting to pall. The date of return from overseas jobs was never foreseeable. It was usual for a crew to stay with a contract until it had been completed, although if there was still a lot to do after three or four months they would be relieved. When back in the U.K. the situation was even more uncertain. Suitable weather was infrequent and short lasting. To avoid missing what opportunities there were, meant being ready to go anywhere at short notice, seven days a week. Home and social life was totally disrupted; even a planned shopping expedition with one's wife might have to be cancelled. I was given a hard time by management on one occasion when we missed an opportunity to survey because I allowed my camera operator to keep a dental appointment for which he had waited two weeks. Of great significance to me, gliding competitions were usually over-subscribed; one had to enter well in advance and I could not be certain I would be able to take leave or even be in the U.K. for any of them.

Early March 1978 found me back in Nigeria with the Aztec. On a previous visit I had gone to Bristow Helicopters in Lagos seeking assistance with maintenance and had found them very helpful. We had a fuel pump problem in Kano on the 19th and I flew to Lagos by Nigeria Airways to see if Bristows had a spare I could purchase. They hadn't, but while I was there I learnt a bit about them. Although they were as their full name suggests a helicopter company and had bases all over the world, they had a fixed wing operation in Lagos, flying Islanders on contract to Shell. There was a possibility that the piston-engined Islanders might be replaced by Twin Otter turboprops by the end of the year.

Of more interest to me, their personnel were on a strict work/home leave rotation and knew a long way ahead when they would be at home. They were on a twelve-week/four week schedule, but were expecting an improvement to eight weeks/four weeks. Furthermore, their British personnel were all non-resident for U.K. tax purposes. As long as they spent no more than 90 days a year in the U.K. they were exempt from U.K. income tax.

We had exceptionally good survey weather this time and had finished the work by the 24th. I returned home again by airline. There I wrote to Bristow Helicopters head office at Redhill in Surrey, expressing an interest in joining their Lagos operation, but only if the eight-weeks/four-weeks rotation and Twin Otter plans came good. The answer was that neither was yet certain, but they would let me know if it happened. A month later I was away again, joining the Navajo which had moved to Abu Dhabi from where I had left it at Sana'a. We finished a small job in next-door Dubai before returning to Sana'a via Jeddah and had another very productive two weeks there. Feeling slightly dizzy, we retraced our steps back to Dubai and on 31st May flew to the Oman.

Although Swaziland was the most pleasant country we had worked in, Oman came a close second. Muscat, the capital city, was clean, with reliable water and electricity. There were good restaurants in the hotels, which were not dry as in Saudi Arabia and well-stocked shops, including one excellent bookshop. One of the hotels even had draught Worthington E in the bar.

We had a day sightseeing by road when we had to take a message to our ground surveyors who were staying at an oil company base on the edge of the Empty Quarter. The scenery was quite spectacular. A bare, jagged mountain range stretched along the coast, sloping down to the west into the desert sands. Between the hills, water from clear streams was diverted into irrigation channels, watering bright green plots of fruit and vegetables. We stopped and walked up one of the streams. It was full of small fish and there was much bird life. Driving further along a good tar-sealed road we came to the Oil Company's establishment. Set in a rocky plain with almost no vegetation, we found modern housing with lawns and colourful gardens, green sports fields, tennis courts, a riding stable and a virtual English pub, with wood beams and leaded windows. But to us the best thing of all in Oman was the Shell Oil Company's beach, a crescent of white sand between rocky headlands just north of Muscat. We went there on non-flyable days to windsurf and snorkel. Although not up to Red Sea standards, there was some coral and a great variety of fish.

Our job in Oman was photographic survey for a projected pipeline from the oil fields in the south of the country to Muscat. We were able to cover most of the route with out-and-return flights from Seeb airport at the Muscat end, but eventually, to reach the far end, had to make arrangements via the client to land for fuel at an oil company strip way down to the south. We were by then well past the hills and into the featureless, flat, stony desert. Without the non-directional radio beacon at the strip we would never have found the place. The only indication of the two 'runways' was two parallel sets of oil drums; the runway surface was otherwise indistinguishable from the surrounding terrain. There was no sign of life when we arrived overhead and no apparent habitation as far as we could see in any direction. We just had to hope that the message of our intended arrival had reached whoever it was that would be bringing the fuel. If it hadn't we'd have been fairly poorly placed, with too little fuel to get back to Seeb. We landed, taxied to the runway intersection, shut down and scanned all round the horizon. Twenty minutes passed and we were beginning to worry and then a plume of dust appeared in the distance. It drew nearer and finally revealed a Land Rover, which drew up alongside the aircraft. "A truck is coming with your fuel" the driver told us. With the tanks re-filled, we finished the last part of the route to its southern extremity at Ghaba and had enough fuel left to fly direct back to Seeb.

We had completed the work by the 29th June. After a week waiting for the client to check and accept the photography, we set out to return to the U.K, stopping at Dubai for two days for a maintenance check. The route home involved several rather short legs. This was all to do with the difficulties of arranging 'diplomatic' clearances through some countries from an overseas location at short notice; sometimes over-flying without landing was not permitted. It took four days to reach Fairoaks, with stops at Kuwait, Amman (Jordan), Damascus (Syria), Larnaka (Cyprus), Athens, Bastia (Corsica), Nantes (France) and Bournemouth. A real Cook's tour, but unfortunately with no time for sightseeing.

The peripatetic life in the survey game was becoming even less appealing, so on my return I advised BKS that I was looking for a change of employment and gave them my notice, which took me to the end of my due leave. August and September were spent writing to various aircraft operators. The pilot market was opening up; I had quite a number of interviews and offers, but for reasons connected with Jennie's career (more successful than mine up to that date) and her desire not to leave the U.K. I took none of them up.

There was a bit of an Indian summer that year. I was kept busy freelancing for BKS with the Islander in October. We had a very successful eleven-day session based at Shannon and then on the 22nd we flew from Leeds to Aberdeen. I was more than a little frustrated to be flying an Islander rather than a glider; there was superb mountain lee wave all the way. Somewhere around Wooler I succumbed to temptation, did a practise engine shut-down and then with the other motor at idle followed the wave cloud for thirty minutes without losing height. The problem came when I tried to re-start. It was well below freezing at our height and the engine had got very cold. When I finally managed to get it going I decided that I wouldn't try that trick again.

There was some compensation for missing a good gliding day. I always carried my fly fishing kit when flying around the U.K. The weather was unsuitable for survey on the day after our arrival, so I bought a day ticket for salmon fishing on a stretch of the River Don and caught one fish of around ten pounds weight. At the hotel I asked if they would keep it in their deep freeze until we left. Checking out two days later with the survey completed, my salmon was handed back to me – already gutted and packed in a long raffia-tied parcel complete with carrying handle! That's what I call service. I was car-less at this time, usually travelling from home to Leeds airport and back by motorbike. Whenever we flew, we would take spare clothes, washing kit and such on the aircraft in case we overnighted somewhere. After an away trip I would have to travel home by 'bus to take my suitcase home for replenishment. On this occasion I had the suitcase, two thigh waders and a salmon to carry. There was only one way to manage. I got some funny looks from the other passengers when they saw me clutching a wader with a large fish tail sticking out of the top.

Early in November 1978 a letter arrived from Bristow Helicopters. They **had** gone to an eight-week/four-week leave rotation in Nigeria and the Twin Otters were definite – one had been bought and would be in February. An interview was arranged and I travelled to Redhill by train. On the way there my back, which had been quiescent for almost two years began to ache. I got through the interviews, but by the time I went for their medical it was clear that this was more than a minor problem and I had to cry off. By the time I got home I was in a very bad way. The only way of easing the agony was to lie on my left side on the floor. One of Jennie's Head Teacher colleagues had suffered a similar problem a year or two earlier and had told her about the surgeon who had sorted him out, a Mr Myles Gibson. I don't know how it came about but Jennie took charge and got me an immediate appointment with him. It seemed that there was some risk involved with a laminectomy but I couldn't face another session of traction; that would probably be no more than another temporary cure. By paying for the operation myself I was able to go straight into the Leeds General Hospital and onto the operating table the following day.

The next couple of weeks were, speaking colloquially, a pain, but not in the least physically painful, apart from a sore throat from the anaesthetic tube. Mr Myles Gibson was clearly a genius! I learnt some time after that he had been one of the pioneers in microsurgery and with an engineer friend had developed the necessary surgical implements. Within twelve hours of coming round I was feeling fine. The nurses kept trying to give me painkillers and wouldn't believe I had no pain to kill. They almost had to tie me down to stop me getting out of bed. After four or five days I was allowed to get up and walk once round the room with a nurse each side holding me steady, with difficulty I persuaded them to let me walk around on my own and they had to move fast to keep up with me. From then on I pleaded each day to be allowed to go home, I could see those hospital fees mounting and my savings weren't unlimited. Finally they let me out.

Chapter 48
New Year in Nigeria

Six weeks after the Bristow interview I was able to tell them I was fit again. I was asked to go back to Redhill so I drove there with Jennie on the 28th December. Next morning their Chief Fixed Wing Training Captain, David Collinson and I travelled to Manchester by airline where he had arranged to hire an Islander so that he could give me a flight check for employment. The Islander was not ready when we expected, so we did not get airborne until shortly before sunset and it was pitch dark well before we landed. Flying at night was not something survey pilots did much of. I had not flown at night for seven months and my total night time for the previous seven years amounted to only 20 hours. Given that I also hadn't flown at all for two months, the gods could have been kinder. That was the roughest flying weather I had ever encountered in the U.K. The wind on the ground was not over strong, but as soon as we were airborne we were into vicious turbulence. We flew a short cross-country to check my flying accuracy (holding a steady airspeed, height and heading) and navigation (including estimated time flying of arrival at checkpoints). The turbulent conditions proved to be due to a very rapid increase of wind speed with height, which I discovered when an estimated 10 minutes for a fifteen mile leg (allowing for a 40 knot headwind) became an actual 18 minutes (headwind of 80 knots). Meanwhile merely keeping the aircraft the right way up was enough of a problem; accuracy went for the proverbial ball of chalk. As far as I was concerned merely getting the Islander back on the ground in one piece would be a bonus. Evidently that was enough for David as well; two days later, New Year's Eve 1978, I was employed by Bristows and on a British Caledonian flight to Lagos.

I was greeted with relief by the pilots already there; someone who should have returned from leave had 'done a runner', a not uncommon occurrence in the ex-pat community in Nigeria. Some years later the ultimate example of this nature happened, when a newly arrived recruit took one look at Lagos, turned round and caught the next flight back without leaving the airport terminal building! My arrival meant that the pilot who should have been relieved could now go on leave.

Naturally, on New Year's Eve things were happening. I was taken along to the Country Club in time to see the New Year in. Just before midnight we were sitting on the veranda drinking 'Star' beer when we heard the skirl o' the pipes. Out of the darkness across the open grass area an advancing line of disembodied white spats and sporrans came into view. Not until they approached within a few yards of the clubhouse lights were the dark faces, hands, kilts and jackets of the Nigerian Police Pipe band visible. Next day we drove out to Badagry. After paying our way through a traffic barrier, a bit of private enterprise by the local youth, we crossed the lagoon in a Nigerian canoe and spent the day on a magnificent sandy palm fringed beach. I returned to Badagry with my windsurfer many times.

That was the start of a twelve-year session with Bristow Helicopters in Nigeria. It took a week to obtain a Nigerian licence, a few days for Islander line check and base check and on the 15th of January I made my first scheduled flight as Captain. Shell Head Office was in Lagos; they had large residential and office compounds at Warri and Port Harcourt to the east. From these Bristows flew helicopters to and from the oil rigs in the Niger delta and out at sea. So our usual route on the Shell contract was Lagos-Warri-Port Harcourt-Warri-Lagos; I flew it several hundred times in the following years. The legs were short; about 80 minutes between Lagos and Warri and 40 between Warri and Port Harcourt. Many of our passengers were ex-pats returning from or going out on leave; we would be most unpopular with the latter if we didn't make the schedule. Airline flights out of Lagos were usually full; missing their flight could mean days, even weeks, waiting for a seat.

Photo 45 - On the lagoon at Badagry

The Islander was not ideal for the job. It had only eight passenger seats, although it was allowable to fly single crew and carry a passenger up front instead of a co-pilot. We needed four of the Islanders, sometimes flying two round trips a day with each one. More significantly, our Islanders had no weather radar. In the dry season this was no problem. The 'harmattan' wind brought very stable air down from the Sahara. Mornings would usually start foggy, the fog would lift into low stratocumulus and this would burn off to leave thick haze up to six thousand feet or so. The haze could be a problem, often enough there would be no airfield in the country with more than one kilometre visibility, but the visibility would not worsen rapidly so one could be confidant of being able to land at a destination airfield or an en-route alternate. From about April through to November it was a different story. Thunderstorms were frequent, often widespread and although a reasonable overall probability of their frequency could be forecast, exactly where or when they would occur was completely unpredictable. En-route, without weather radar, the prime aim was to stay out of cloud, so as to see where the larger build-ups were and avoid them. This would involve much twisting and turning, climbing and descending through gaps, sometimes going down to 500 feet or less and often enough doing an about turn to retreat and look for another way through.

That was problem enough; finding out about bad weather at destination early enough to divert elsewhere, or obtaining the weather at the alternate was a bigger problem still, due to the lack of ground-to-ground communication in Nigeria. In Europe, when requested by a pilot, any airfield would have, or be able to obtain quickly, up to date information about the weather at any other airfield; there were landline connections between them. Alternatively one could tune in to a radio frequency on which a continuous broadcast was made giving up-to-date weather at a selection of airfields. In Nigeria the only connection between airfields was by high frequency radio, which was completely overloaded by many different stations and aircraft, all trying to use the same frequencies at the same time. When the weather at the intended destination was below limitations, it was legally required that one should depart for the alternate when the fuel remaining was down to that required to fly to the alternate and to arrive there with enough to hold for another 45 minutes. Setting off for the alternate without knowing what the weather **there** was doing was something of an act of faith. When flying at low level, one would have to be very close to the new destination before being able to talk to its Air Traffic Control.

The lack of ground to ground communication caused other severe problems. The standard practice everywhere in the world is to file a flight plan by completing a written form at the departure airfield. In most places the details are then passed by landline (or these days by satellite) to all the other Air Traffic Control units along the intended route. As the aircraft continues along its flight, it is controlled by each Unit in turn acting on the flight plan details received and directing the pilots to follow an appropriate route and height to avoid conflict with other aircraft within that Control Sector. At some time while they are within the sector, up-to-date information on their progress is sent to the next Control Unit which is asked if it can accept the traffic. Rarely, due to overloading, it may be unable to do so and the aircraft will either be put into a holding pattern or re-routed. When the aircraft is approaching the end of a Control sector, it is 'handed over' to the next sector; the pilots are instructed to 'contact xxxxx Control on frequency yyyy'. The new sector already knows of the traffic. This didn't happen in Nigeria. The first any new Control agency knew of an aircraft entering its sector was when it was close enough to make radio contact. It was then necessary for that aircraft to file an airborne flight plan, that is, transmit its point of departure, destination, last check point, time and altitude there, estimated time for next check point, number of souls on board and remaining endurance. A long-winded procedure, which at most airfields did not matter because there were not too many aircraft in their area. Lagos was different; nearly all the inbounds would be landing, so the airport was busy. It also had a very large terminal controlled airspace area around it and aircraft had to obtain clearance by radio to enter this. For us, flying low down, there was a very short distance between coming into radio range and reaching the edge of the area. Getting a word in to obtain a clearance was sometimes extremely difficult.

Occasionally things would become more difficult still. When the President was travelling by air, the airport would be closed without prior notice for an indefinite period. It was a nail-biting exercise for inbound aircraft – hold while hoping the airport would soon re-open or divert? Just to make the decision more difficult, the only near-by airport had no fuel most of the time! Not so bad for us in the Islanders, a few drums of Avgas could be sent by road reasonably quickly.

Another trauma would occur when the Nigerian Electrical Power Authority (known as No Electrical Power Again) electricity supply failed, a frequent happening, and then the airport's standby generator also failed. On one of these fortunately rare occasions the Duty Air Traffic Controller, who was extremely capable, commandeered a DC-10 aircraft that had started its engines and operated both Approach and Tower control from its cockpit!

We sometimes carried Shell employees' families on non-business trips. On one of these Air Traffic Control, knowing what the normal passenger number for an Islander was, queried my 'one eight souls on board' airborne flight plan report. It was correct – pilot plus nine adults and eight babes in arms.

The en-route scenery between Lagos and Port Harcourt was unspectacular; no hills, just a level plain with a few remaining small patches of rain forest and much secondary jungle with semi-cleared areas where millet, maize, yams and other vegetables were grown. The Niger Delta region around Warri was a tangle of distributaries, ox-bows and cut-offs amongst extensive mangrove swamps, with more extensive rain forest on the higher ground. In the Delta itself, long dead-straight lines of lower vegetation running in various directions still showed clearly where seismic exploration had been carried out years previously. Here and there man-made canals connected oilrig platforms to the natural waterways, enabling transport of non-urgent or heavy equipment by boat at much lower cost than by helicopter.

The Twin Otters, both of which were on line by early May, introduced a little more variety into our schedules. I had converted onto the type in March and in April flew one of the newly started rest and recreation flights that Shell had laid on for their employees and families. We took them from Lagos, Warri or Port Harcourt on Saturdays to Jos on the Central Plateau, returned empty and collected them on Mondays. The scenery was more interesting on these routes; there were hilly areas and many rivers including the Niger itself. We sometimes passed by the red cliffs on the Niger River bank at Idah and the Niger/Benue confluence at Lokoja, two of the major landmarks of the early African exploration days. It was strange to realise that the distance from the confluence downstream to the sea, 300 miles, was the same as that from the river's source in Guinea to the Atlantic coast. In between the river flowed eastwards and then south for 2,200 miles.

The new aircraft were not much faster than the Islanders, but had the advantage of carrying twice as many passengers and, with turboprop jet engines, used Jet A1 fuel which was much more readily available in Nigeria than Avgas. They were also a little more comfortable, in that there was standing headroom in the cabin. It might have been this factor that influenced the Shell Managing Director to travel around the country much more than in the past. I had some interesting flights with him to out of the way locations, small airstrips in the bush, which probably saw no more than half a dozen aircraft a year. When we switched off the engines after landing on a seemingly remote and deserted runway it was quite astonishing how quickly a horde of children would appear from the undergrowth. Persuading them to stay clear when we wanted to start up again was a problem.

In those early days of my time with Bristow, we lived in a number of houses scattered around the GRA (Government Residential Area), a relic of Colonial days. Approximately half a mile square, with the houses, mostly bungalows, set in large flower and tree-filled gardens, the GRA was a far cry from the surrounding shanty districts. It was however rather run-down from its pre-independence days. In addition to the unreliability of NEPA, the water supply was also uncertain, especially when the authorities decided to dig some new drainage ditches with a JCB and simply ploughed through all the individual branch pipes from the mains into the houses. Little road maintenance took place and potholes abounded. I encountered a most unexpected hazard once when driving on the GRA. It was the rainy season; large puddles abounded, often stretching right across the carriageway. I had driven through several a few inches deep with no problem when I came to one at a road junction. Fortunately I had slowed down to take a corner when the front wheels dropped into a two-foot deep trench hidden under the muddy water and I came to an abrupt halt! But this was a minor event compared with the many that occurred on the dual carriageway we joined on our way to the airport. Rumoured to figure in the Guinness Book of Records as the most dangerous stretch of road in the world, the Ikorodu Highway was either a go-slow or a no holds barred stock car track. The central reservation was used as an either way extra lane, with cars, trucks and buses dodging from one side of it to the other and then often enough driving the wrong way down the opposite carriageway. At night, the smaller amount of traffic made much higher speeds possible and it was a brave (or foolhardy) man who ventured on it. One morning we passed a flatbed truck which had broken down on the left-hand (fast – they drive on the right) lane of the east bound carriageway. It was carrying several long steel girders which overhung about twenty feet behind and a Volkswagen Kombi van was impaled on these. Two days later the Kombi had gone, but the truck, with its overhanging load, was still there. The following morning, a Peugeot 404 taxi had replaced the Kombi! In the go-slow mode, I once watched a single Nigerian pushing a broken-down Kombi in the outside lane. He frequently had to stop to avoid running into the back of the traffic ahead of him!

We were a multi-national bunch of people in the house where I lived; the other occupants included an Australian, a Filipino, a Frenchman, a German, a Kenyan and an Icelander. During the years I was to spend with Bristow many other nationalities came and went from the Nigerian operation, including Swedish, American, Malaysian, Indian, Singalese, Portuguese and Irish.

It didn't take me long to discover that the rigid 8 weeks on site 4 weeks leave cycle was not that rigid. Shell kept a beady eye on us to see that we maintained the contracted number of people on site, so no one could go on leave until their replacement arrived. People's plans were frequently disrupted when someone went sick while on leave, or simply quit and didn't come back. Even if the leave cycle had been held to, one's dates at home would rotate from year to year. I wanted to be on leave every year for the National Gliding Contest and for one at least of Jennie's school holidays. I made an offer that I would be flexible, would stay on, come back early, stay on leave or go early at short notice, so long as the 2:1 ratio was held overall and I could have two periods of two weeks each, selected well in advance by myself, when I would be untouchably on leave. This would reduce the disruption for everyone else. The proposal was agreed and it worked well for a good few years. Then we had a new Chief Pilot, who expected the flexibility without the two certainties.

The flexible arrangement did enable me to fly in the 1979 15 metre National Gliding Championships at Husbands Bosworth. The Gliding fraternity is a rich source of stories about the retrieves from landings in fields that cross-country flying without an engine inevitably leads to, amusing in retrospect if not at the time. I had one such during this competition. I landed in a field near Chipping Norton and walked into the town to find a telephone. A hotel in the main street looked like a good spot for a meal later on and there was a wide expanse of tarmac between it and the road that I thought would be useful for a car with a 30-foot long trailer attached. Back at the field I waited for Jennie. She arrived with the trailer. We de-rigged the glider into the trailer and then Jennie drove the car and trailer back into town. I saw the hotel and told Jennie to turn right onto the tarmac. As we straightened up we heard a loud scraping noise and the car came to an immovable halt. On investigation we found the rear end of the trailer had grounded and the trailer was suspended between tow hitch and rear end with the wheels six inches in the air. There was no way we could lift it off the tow hitch. We went into the hotel's bar thinking we might have to get a room for the night – and encountered the town's fire brigade on a night out! Hearing our problem, they went away to fetch their engine and soon had us sorted out. Beers all round seemed the least I could offer.

Undeterred by the experience, Jennie crewed for me in almost all the competitions I flew in after that one.

Photo 46 - Jennie crewing at Sutton Bank

Chapter 49
Conned into training

Because of my experience as an RAF instructor, in early 1979 David Collinson had asked if I would take on the duty of Training Captain in Nigeria. I wasn't very keen, but on being assured that all a Training Captain did was check the other pilots' proficiency at six month intervals I let myself be persuaded. Had I known what the job would eventually entail I would certainly have turned it down. Bristow had other fixed wing operations and most people had the chance to move from one to the other, but with my Training Captain position I ended up trapped in Nigeria.

I took the Bristow Training Captain course at Redhill in August after the Husbands Bosworth gliding competition. Back in Nigeria I began to carry out the required base (handling and emergencies) and line (route) checks. Very soon an embarrassing situation arose. Bristows, back in England, hired another pilot for the Lagos operation. He arrived and turned out to be my bete noire from Sana'a. I was worried that if I did his check flights it would be difficult not to let my previous experiences with him affect my judgement. I might easily pass him when I should not, over allowing for bias against, or fail him when I should not, because of bias against. So I passed the job to the Chief Pilot who promptly did fail him. The Company then insisted that I flew with him – and the result was again a fail. He left.

The next training commitment arose. "We need someone to convert new pilots onto the Twin Otter, would you be prepared to become a Type Rating Examiner?" asked the Company. I agreed and waited for the arrangements to be made for me to fly with a Type Rating candidate while being observed by a Civil Aviation Flying Unit Examiner.

While I was waiting, two other major events took place. A brand new Twin Otter had been ordered for the Bristow operation at Miri, in Borneo and it was due to be ready at the end of November 1979. David asked if I would do the ferry flight from Canada to Gatwick with him and then take the aircraft on to Miri with someone else as co-pilot. This sounded like fun, but the ferry interlude would interfere with rostering for the Nigeria operation, I would have to be there over Christmas and Jennie's school holidays. Bristows had a company HS125 twinjet which made frequent flights from Gatwick to Nigeria, but I was really only joking when I said "Yes, if Bristows will fly Jennie out to Lagos over Christmas". To my great surprise, this was immediately agreed to with "We'll send her the visa forms and she can send them back to us with her passport and we'll organise the visa"

So there David and I were in Toronto on 29th November about to carry out an acceptance test flight on our shiny new toy. "There's no anti-icing gear on it" I said. "Of course not" David replied, "you don't get icing in Borneo!" "This ferry could be **very** interesting", I thought. The test flight was satisfactory, so we went to complete our flight plan ready for departure next morning.

The Twin Otter's normal fuel system consisted of two tanks at the bottom of the fuselage with associated pumps and pipelines feeding the engines. This gave around four hours of cruise at about 150 knots, 600 miles range, depending on altitude. As with all jet powered aircraft, even turboprops, 'the higher the further', but with no pressurisation the maximum normal flying height was relatively low so the full potential of high level economy could not be utilised. For the ferry, extra fuel was needed. Fifteen inter-connected 45-gallon oil drums were strapped onto a palette fixed to the cabin floor. Manually operated taps at the front and rear could be opened allowing fuel to flow by gravity from the drums into the forward and aft normal tanks. The procedure was to use the fuel in the main tanks until the gauges showed about a quarter full, then open the taps. When the main tanks were nearly full the taps had to be turned off otherwise the main tanks would overflow through the vent pipes and fuel would be lost overboard. This ferry system increased the cruise time to around thirteen hours.

For ferry purposes, without passengers, the maximum allowable take-off weight was 15,000 pounds, compared with the normal 12,500 allowed for passenger carrying operations. When passenger carrying commercially, a twin-engined aircraft must be able to climb away when an engine fails during take-off. At 15,000 pounds there was no way the Twin Otter would climb on one engine. So it became like a single engined aircraft, where an engine failure means a glide landing (or crash) – except that there were twice as many engines to go wrong! The extra fuel, plus the weight of the ferry tank system, aircraft spares, tools, survival kit and our own baggage put us close to the higher limit. For this reason we had to take off from a runway which pointed at open country.

In the morning we kitted up with heavy rubber immersion suits, gloves and woolly hats and took off for Goose Bay in Labrador. With the heavy fuel load, we used an awful lot of the runway and climbed very slowly once airborne. It was a fine, clear, but rather short day up there near the Arctic Circle and we landed just before dark. We thought we would be away early next morning for Reykjavik in Iceland, but during the night it began to snow and next morning conditions were impossible. During the next two days we tramped at frequent internals through deepening snow to the Met office and back, wearing our immersion suits whenever we poked our noses out of the hotel.

At the weather office on the evening of 2nd December the met man said there should be a weather window next day if we started early. So we took off before dawn, into a clear sky, with the stars shining brilliantly in the arctic night. With the full fuel load, we climbed slowly out across the Atlantic. About four hours later we saw cloud starting to form below us. Gradually the tops of this cloud rose towards our cruise height. Another hour and we were just clear of the tops. With no anti-icing equipment, we had to stay out of cloud.

Although severe icing was unlikely, even a small amount could increase the aircraft's drag, requiring more power and therefore greater fuel consumption. We didn't have that much fuel to spare. There was no way we could descend below icing level, the temperature at sea level was below freezing. And we were too far on our way to turn back, we'd had a strong tailwind, turning back would mean an equally strong headwind. So we had to climb higher. The problem was we had only one small portable oxygen bottle between us.

It is generally reckoned that for anyone who lives at or near sea level, 10,000 feet is as high as is desirable for continuous flight without oxygen, although 12,000 for half an hour maximum is acceptable. We were now approaching the limit, but the cloud was getting higher all the time. We passed through 10,000 feet, climbing further, but in less than 30 minutes reached 12,000. The cloud tops were still rising. We had no option but to continue climbing. From then on we took turns to have a few drags at the oxygen bottle, doing our best to keep an eye on how the one without the bottle was coping. Eventually, approaching Iceland, we were at 19,000 feet and just above the cloud tops. Then Air Traffic Control at Reykjavik told us it had started to snow! Although our alternate at the other end of Iceland was still clear the situation was looking rather unhappy. But fortune smiled, a few minutes later the cloud broke below us, we could see lights on the Iceland coast and ATC said the snow at the airport had stopped. We made a very rapid descent, landed and put the aircraft to bed (pitot, static, engine intake and exhaust covers, propeller ties, control locks and chocks) and went off to find a hotel. We had been airborne for eight hours.

The weather next morning was too bad for us to continue on to Gatwick, so we had a wander round the town and did a little shopping for Christmas presents. I was fascinated by the open-air geothermal swimming pool near the centre of town. Despite the time of year, it was fully occupied. Steam rose from the surface, but all the swimmers were wearing hats!

On the 5th the weather had cleared, so we brushed the snow off the aircraft and continued the flight to Gatwick, routing overhead Stornoway and Glasgow and then along the airways to the London Terminal Area. It was clear along the Scottish coast and we had a magnificent view of Skye.

The ferry flight to Borneo was planned to start on the 13th December. I was sent to continue my interrupted leave with the assurance that my co-pilot, very experienced but not yet Twin Otter rated, would prepare all the maps and charts, do all the flight planning, get the required diplomatic clearances and so on. All I had to do was turn up on time for the departure. I took this with a grain of salt and went back to Redhill two days in advance. I found that he was an optimist and although he had obtained all the maps for the planned route and the airport charts for the planned re-fuelling stops, he had none for any diversions from route or stops. I rushed around and found the necessary items. As it happened, on the very first leg, while flying across Italy we were informed that our planned destination, Rhodes, was closed for maintenance and we had to stop short at Brindisi after 7 hours 35 minutes in the air. Next day we went on to Damascus, a 7 hour 40 minutes flight and the day after that we reached Dubai in 6 hours 50 minutes. We had some messages and equipment for the Bristow Dubai helicopter operation, so on the 16th we had a late departure and a short flight of 3 hours 50 minutes to Karachi. Next day there was some problem with clearances across India; instead of making one long flight across to Calcutta we had to land at Ahmadabad for clearance into the country. That took several hours, but we were able to get away in time to fly on to Calcutta the same day, arriving after dark with a total flight time for the day of 7 hours 45 minutes.

There was another problem when I went to file my flight plan next morning. I was required to certify that my aircraft's High Frequency radio could transmit and receive on certain frequencies. Up to this point I had not needed to use the HF set. When I checked (which of course I should have done before leaving the U.K.) I found that the set was crystallised for Oil Company and Bristow's own radio communications only. Just in case the Indian aviation authorities came to check the aircraft, I hastily wrote a card showing the (fictitious) frequencies we carried and taped it on the instrument panel next to the radio. No one turned up to verify the truth of my statement, but on the next leg I almost wished that they had and that they had stopped me from going further until the required frequencies **were** installed. We had to overfly Burma; there was an ADIZ (Air Defence Identification Zone) on their west coast. All aircraft are required to make radio contact before entering an ADIZ; an unidentified aircraft is likely to be intercepted and forced to land – or worse, shot down. With the correct HF frequency I could have established radio contact well in advance, but at our low level, we were still out of VHF radio range at the ADIZ boundary. Expecting any moment to be intercepted by a Burmese fighter, I kept going. Fortunately I hadn't gone far when I made contact with Air Traffic Control. They didn't seem at all concerned by our sudden arrival in their airspace and cleared us on across Burma into Thailand. We landed at Bangkok after a flight of 5 hours 15 minutes.

Next day, the 19th, I had some documents to be delivered by hand. The recipient was 'not on seat' until late in the afternoon, so we had another night in Bangkok. On the 20th an early start and a 4 hour 50 minute flight got us to Kuala Lumpur, where my co-pilot left to obtain a Malaysian validation of his licence and I continued on my own for another 4 hour 50 minutes to Kuching in Sarawak, Borneo. Night fell before I needed to top up with fuel from the ferry tanks; it felt a bit eerie going to the rear of the cabin to turn on the tap in the dark while 'George' the auto-pilot looked after flying the aircraft.

In the dark I couldn't see much of Kuching, but it had clearly changed a lot since my Javelin time there. As I remembered the town from 1965 it had been a backwater, with only one hotel of any standing and that was an old colonial style two-storey building. The taxi driver took me to a modern multi-storey tower block hotel, which was very comfortable but could have been anywhere in the world. There was none of the adventurous feeling of being on the edge of unexplored territory that I remembered from my RAF time in Kuching, when we lived in palm thatch and bamboo 'bashas' on the edge of unbroken rain forest. I saw no more of the town next morning, when I made a pre-dawn departure. I arrived at Miri, in Sabah, ten minutes after sunrise.

That was the end of the ferry flight. If you've time to spare, go by air they say. From Toronto to Gatwick, three legs, six days and 20 hours 55 minutes flying time. Gatwick to Miri, ten legs, nine days, 50 hours 35 minutes flying time. I wasn't quite finished though, two of the Bristow pilots at Miri needed base checks on the Twin Otter and the aircraft itself had to go to Kota Kinabalu to be put on the Malaysian register. I did one of the checks on the way to and the other on arrival at KK. Kota Kinabalu is such a mouthful that the locals all abbreviate it – in syllables they'd have done almost as well by keeping its old name of Jesselton.

I had to wait a few days before an airline flight back to the U.K. was available and flew on to Lagos without going home.

Chapter 50
Jennie arrives in Nigeria in time for coup

Jennie arrived at Lagos on the Company HS125 on the 28th December. Somewhat jet-lagged, she flew with me in the Twin Otter to Warri, where we night-stopped. Next day she sat in the co-pilot's seat on the Jos weekend R&R flight, with return via Kaduna to Lagos. She visited Lagos another six times in the next six years. On one of these visits she was not very impressed when there was a military coup on New Year's Eve during her stay. As usual on these occasions the airport was closed and movement around the city hazardous. It was a relatively mild coup, with only a little shooting. The rest of us relaxed and kept our heads down in our residential compound, entertaining ourselves with a barbecue by the swimming pool, sunbathing, squash and the bar. Our only complaint was that we had no flying scheduled on New Year's Day anyway, that day of the coup was a waste. But Jennie was very conscientious in her Head Teacher' job and was agitated that she might not be able to get back to school for the start of term. In fact, the coup was over very quickly and her planned flight back to the U.K. was one of the first to get away when the airport re-opened a couple of days later.

The second major event was the acquisition in February 1980 of a Mitsubishi MU2 Solitaire aircraft for use as Shell VIP transport. At the time it was the fastest twin turbo-prop in existence; it also had an extremely short landing capability (although it wasn't so hot on take-off!). Designed by the Japanese for Japanese, it was fairly diminutive. Although I could fit in reasonably easily, some of my longer-legged colleagues had to adopt a praying mantis-like attitude with their knees around their ears to get into the pilot's seat. It was pressurised and we normally cruised it at around 30,000 feet.

The Chief Pilot and I went to Houston, Texas, for the Flight Safety conversion training course and then flew the aircraft to Redhill via Cleveland Ohio, Goose Bay in Labrador, Narsarssuaq on the West Coast of Greenland, Reykjavik in Iceland and Gatwick. We had brilliant, cloudless weather into Narsarssuaq and could see the whole of the approach up the narrow, twisting fjord into the airfield. During the Second World War it was known as Bluie West One and was used as a staging post for military transatlantic flights. One of Ernest K Gann's novels narrates a hair-raising event when an American bomber arrived there in bad weather, short of fuel and with no way of turning back out of the fjord.

Four days after our arrival at Redhill we left on an uneventful flight, ferrying the aircraft to Lagos, via Malaga, Las Palmas, Dakar and Abidjan. In Nigeria it took two weeks to complete the formalities of Certificate of Airworthiness issue and crew licensing for a new type on the Nigerian register and for Registration as 5N-ALP. Since no one in the Nigerian Civil Aviation Department had any experience of the type, we were asked to set the ground type technical examination ourselves; it was then assumed that, having set it, we knew the answers, so we automatically passed! On March 1st, we carried out the aircraft's Nigerian Certificate of Airworthiness air test and on the 3rd did some trial short landing tests at Ibadan. I left Lagos on the 7th for the U.K. Type Rating Examiner check flight on a Twin Otter at Glasgow. Interestingly I passed my test because I (correctly) failed the candidate! I returned to Lagos on the 10th, had my brand new U.K. Twin Otter TRE rating validated for Nigeria and extended to MU2 and Islander and was appointed as Bristow's Chief Training Captain, Fixed Wing Operations, Nigeria. With three different aircraft types (later four) and around twenty pilots, all requiring six-monthly type proficiency ("Base") checks and annual route checks on each type they flew, plus conversion training onto new (for them) types, I soon became very busy and began to wish I'd said "No" to the Training Captain job.

In April 1981 we moved into a new residential compound, purpose-built for Bristow ex-pats at Isolo, a mile south of the airport's new international terminal. It was surrounded by a security wall, with a guard house at the gate. One block of flats, for those of bachelor status, included a kitchen, dining room, sitting

Photo 47 - Pond in Bristow Residential Compound Isolo

area and bar. Another block was for married accompanied personnel and there was a row of quarters for the Nigerian houseboys. There was also a smallish swimming pool and a squash court, with a patio area, barbecue and open-air bar. Between the buildings there was room for lawns and gardens. The builders had made two concrete tanks sunk into the ground outside, so they could have a water reserve when the town supply ran dry, as it frequently did. I converted these into fishponds and soon had Amazonian Angelfish and Zebra Danios breeding in them, amongst local water lilies and bull-rushes

At one time or another I flew check flights with every pilot and co-pilot on the operation. The co-pilots were all Nigerian and for the first ten years I was there, the Captains were all expatriates. Shell's requirements made it impossible for our co-pilots to be promoted within the Company. The normal promotion route for co-pilots is via the accumulation of command under supervision time (i.e. with a qualified Captain acting as co-pilot but still in command), but Shell demanded 1,000 hours actual command time for Captains on their contract. We had no other operation where the co-pilots could fly on their Nigerian licences, so we had nowhere we could send them when they had sufficient command under supervision time (and of course had shown the ability) to fly as Captain. This was somewhat demoralising; those with sufficient get up and go did just that. The Twin Otter was legal for single crew operation so I was able to give those I could trust a little confidence boost. On empty sectors I would tell them to wake me up after we had landed and then I would retire to the back of the passenger cabin before they started the engines. I remember one empty sector flight from Bauchi to Jos, when I left it all to Enid Otun. We landed to refuel and for once the re-fuelling chief was right there when we stopped by the underground tank. I opened the passenger door from inside and walked down the steps. The re-fueller looked at me and then up at the cockpit where Enid was completing the paperwork. "That's a very small boy to be flying such a big aeroplane," he said. When I told him it was in fact a very small girl but she had been flying for many years and had lots of solo time he wouldn't believe me.

The airstrip at Warri, in the Niger Delta, had one short and narrow tarmac runway with no taxiways and very little clearance each side between trees, buildings, hangars and radio masts. The main road leading east from the town crossed the runway threshold at the northern end. Aircraft lining up for take-off to the South turned round on the road. Pole barriers were lowered to stop road traffic when an aircraft was approaching to land or taxying for take-off. I took a photograph of the Bristow Twin Otter on the road some years later and sent it to "Flight" magazine, who put it in the Roger Bacon column and paid me an unsolicited £25.

Photo 48 - Lining up on the road at Warri

The Mu2, because of its small size, appeared to onlookers to make its landing approach at a much higher speed than the Twin Otter, although in fact it was a few knots slower. At Warri the proximity of the trees and buildings on the approach exaggerated the MU2's apparent speed even more and it soon became known as the 'Rice Rocket'. There was no difficulty whatsoever in stopping it in the available runway length; taking off was a little more problematical. We had been flying in and out of Warri for more than a year when it was realised that the performance figures we were using were the "raw" data. We had been used to the U.K. system, where the graphs from which we calculated minimum runway length and maximum take-off weight included the safety factors; the American graphs gave actual distances and weights and the safety factors had then to be applied. That began the demise of the MU2 on the Shell operation; we had to severely restrict the load we could carry out of Warri. I also found out the hard way that the aircraft didn't like water on the runway when we ran through a puddle after landing and an engine flamed out. No great problem after landing, but from then on I wouldn't take off if there were puddles on the runway, an engine flame-out at a critical stage of take-off would have been disastrous. Eventually Shell decided they didn't want the aircraft any more. With no other use for it, in 1986 Bristows sold it.

Chapter 51
A very relaxed client

In December 1981 we obtained another contract. We were asked to operate a Beechcraft Super Kingair 200, registered in Nigeria as 5N-ALW, for the Ashland Oil Company. This was something a bit less toy-sized, with standing room in the cabin for a small passenger. Low winged and with a retractable undercarriage, it was powered by two Pratt and Whitney PT6 turboprop engines, a different version to those on the Twin Otter, but equally reliable. The only thing I felt slightly uncomfortable about was its extremely rigid wing. In turbulence there was no 'give' to absorb the shocks. It was a little slower than the Mu2, but also pressurised and we operated it at similar heights.

Photo 49 - 5N-ALW ceased flying on the Ashland contract in December 1966 and was thereafter operated in the U.K. by Bristow Helicopters registered as G-BFOL.
Courtesy Charlie Stewart

Ashland's routes were mainly between Lagos, Port Harcourt, Eket and Calabar near the Cameroun border. If we really went for it we could do the Eket – Calabar leg in less than eight minutes.

Flying for Ashland was much more relaxed than flying for Shell, because whenever things went wrong with planned flying schedules, they tended to think it was their fault rather than ours. It wasn't always! On one occasion the plan had been changed so often that I ended up losing the plot. As we taxied clear of the runway after landing at Eket, one of the passengers said, "This doesn't look like Calabar!" "Oh, were we supposed to be going there? Never mind, sit tight and I'll get you there in about ten minutes", I replied. There was no subsequent flak from Ashland. Had it been a Shell flight I'd have been lucky not to be taken off their contract.

One event that certainly was Ashland's fault occurred when we were asked to fly from Lagos to Calabar at 6.00 a.m. to take some of their people to a very urgent meeting. This was not simple to arrange; there was a bit of tension in the country and all departures had to be attended by one of the military. They tended not to want to get up that early. However, all went well, the passengers for once arrived on time for the planned departure and the soldier was there. We had no Air Traffic delay and were soon up to our cruising level. We had HF radio on the aircraft; when I made the usual call to the Ashland Lagos office they said, "There's been a change, you have to land at Port Harcourt on the way to Calabar. Another passenger will be arriving there on Nigeria Airways at 7.30 and he has to be at the meeting too." I told my passengers of this on the P.A. system and we landed at Port Harcourt at 7.10. We went to the Ashland terminal hut to wait. Ashland's Port Harcourt representative gave us coffee and then went off to the main terminal.

Time went by. My passengers were looking at their watches and muttering to each other. 7.40., 7.50., 8.00 – still no sign of our man. At 8.15 the representative returned alone. "Nigerian Airways was late, but anyway, Mr xxxx wasn't on it" he told us. "What? But **I** am Mr. xxxx!" said one of the people I'd brought from Lagos.

Ashland were also very concerned that we should be fed at some time during the day. Schedules were usually arranged so that we would be at Calabar at lunch time. On one occasion we had a flight from Port Harcourt to Enugu, northwards from our usual routes. The Port Harcourt despatcher went with us to deliver some money. When he returned from his business down town, he told us we were to go to Calabar. We arrived there, were met by a driver and went off to the Ashland staff house in town. After the usual very good lunch, the despatcher said it was time to return to Port Harcourt. "Where are our passengers?" I asked. "There aren't any," he told me. "So why did we come here instead of going from Enugu to Port Harcourt direct? We will have flown an extra 100 miles for nothing," I enquired. "Well, you had to have your lunch," he replied!

Another interesting Kingair flight saw us en-route past Jos towards Bauchi. The cloud base was rather low and we were flying along a valley penetrating the Jos plateau. The Jos Air Traffic Controller wanted to know our altitude and could not accept what we told him, because it was lower than he was. He next told us to contact Bauchi. They were not listed in our flight guides as having radio so I asked for the frequency. When I called the Bauchi controller he was annoyed that I had left it so late to tell him we were arriving. However, we landed and the controller said "Come to Control to file your flight plan." We looked around, but could see nothing like a Control Tower. So I told him "I will taxi round in a circle, when I am pointing at you, please tell me to stop."

He said "Stop!" The co-pilot and I fell about laughing. About 200 yards in front of us we saw a table, two chairs and a large black umbrella arranged in the shade of an acacia bush, with a radio aerial poking through the tree's branches.

I did many of the training flights and much of the line flying with the five Nigerian co-pilots who qualified on the aircraft while it was with us. After leaving Bristows one of them quit flying for a business life, another went to a European airline and was last heard of flying the BAe 146 four-jet. Enid Otun joined Pan-African, a Lagos-based operator of small twin-engined turboprops and jets and rose to become Chief Pilot. Dayo Awobokun went one better, becoming Chief Pilot and then Aviation Manager of Mobil Nigeria.

The star performer, Reece Oni, TRE IRE etc. became Chief Pilot of Aero Contractors of Nigeria, with a fleet of five De Havilland Dash 8 turboprops, plus an HS125 Jet and one Twin Otter and 38 pilots to command.

Two of Bristow's Islanders had gone in early 1979 and a third by early 1980. The last remaining, with one of the married accompanied pilots, was based at Port Harcourt and hung on there until late in 1982. The pilot was on a five month/one month rotation; his absences on leave were covered by one of us from Lagos. I had two spells of two weeks as relief pilot living in his bungalow on the Shell compound; it made a pleasant change from the Lagos routine. Even the chance to cook for oneself was refreshing. One of nature's more extravagant displays was an occasional feature. At certain times of the year, just after sunset, the sky would be full of millions of large fruit bats, all flying southwards towards the coast. Luckily I never encountered them during our few night flights in the area. Nor did I hear of any aircraft bat strikes. Maybe their flight path was clear of the airport, or perhaps their sonic system enabled them to take evasive action.

For a short time, we had all four aircraft types in use and I was doing line or training flights on them all. I never flew all four in one day, but I did manage three on one occasion. Nowadays this would be illegal and I would have been pleased had it been then. On many occasions I found myself reaching for a switch or control on one type in the position where it would have been on another. Such is the force of habit and routine.

Chapter 52
Line Squalls

A pilot obtains his first U.K. Instrument Rating by passing a flying test carried out by a U.K. Civil Aviation Flying Unit (CAFU) examiner. Thereafter his renewals can be done by a CAFU approved examiner from his own or any other aircraft operating company. A prospective Company examiner obtains his approval by attending a course run by CAFU and after the course, carrying out a renewal test on a random candidate while being observed by a CAFU examiner. In January 1983 Bristows sent me to Stansted where the course was run at that time. It involved two weeks of morning HS125 simulator flying and afternoon lectures and discussions.

The system in the simulator was for the CAFU pilot to act as an Instrument Rating Renewal candidate, with one course member acting as both examiner and co-pilot. Another course pilot sat in the jump seat to observe and (during the debrief) to comment on how both the 'candidate' and the 'examiner' had performed. The CAFU pilots were adapt at doing things which constituted definite fail errors but were often very hard for the trainee examiner or the observer to spot. They were equally adept at treading a fine line between fail and pass. They caught me out as 'examiner' when we were simulating an Instrument Landing System approach in bad weather, ready to go around if we hadn't seen the runway by our minimum descent altitude (MDA) 300 feet above the ground. There was no way we would see the runway in the simulator, it had no visuals, so the test was to see that the candidate did start the go-around at the correct height and that the procedures were followed accurately and smoothly. I knew there was something wrong, but couldn't put my finger on it. At the MDA, just as I was expecting the 'candidate' to open the throttles, there was a thump, rumble, rumble.... We had landed. The CAFU examiner and his side kick acting as Air Traffic Controller at the simulator console fell about laughing, they had worked a bit of jiggery pokery with the altimeter setting figures the 'Controller' had given. I should have picked this up as we crossed one of the markers on the approach, by comparing the altimeter indication with the altitude shown on the approach chart, but another thing the CAFU guys were adapt at was distracting the 'examiner' at a crucial moment by asking him to do something that the co-pilot is required to do when requested by the Captain.

Crest-fallen, I was ready to be sent home, but "Don't worry, we catch 80 percent of those we try that on and it wouldn't happen for real because you would see the ground," they said. When doing a real test, the candidate's view is screened so that he can't see outside, but of course the examiner must be able to look out, for other aircraft as well as the ground.

The console operator had his own special talent acting as an Air Traffic Controller. If the flight was simulated into Cardiff, he had a perfect Welsh accent, going into Liverpool it would be pure Scouse and his Geordie came straight from the Scotswood Road.

I got through the rest of the course, then carried out the observed Instrument Rating Renewal flight on a real candidate and returned to Lagos with the appropriate certificate, which was then validated on my Nigerian Licence. One difference between the Instrument Rating Examiner's endorsement and the Type Rating Examiner's was that the latter was valid only on specified aircraft types whereas an IRE could carry out IRR's on any aircraft type. I did a few on exotic (to me) types, such as the Cessna 425 twin piston and the HS125 and Citation twinjets.

The new qualification let me in for another two unexpected interludes. At that time there were problems with Nigerian Initial Instrument Ratings. There was no equivalent to the U.K. CAFU examiner flight test arrangement for Initial Ratings or for approval of Company examiners. Nigerian pilots obtained foreign licences and gained their Initial Instrument Ratings on those licences. Their Nigerian licences were then validated with the Rating. Renewals were carried out by examiners holding Nigerian validated, overseas issued, IRE endorsements.

There was a Government run Flying Training School at Zaria in the north of the country. In July 1983 half a dozen Police Air Wing Cadets had completed the course there and needed Initial Instrument Ratings. I don't know quite how it was legalised but Derek Jordan, another Bristow pilot with an IRE endorsement and myself were asked to carry out the flying tests for their Ratings. For a couple of days we flew to Ibadan in their Aztec in the morning, flew rating tests with them there and returned to Lagos in the evening. Between us, in some cases after partial passes and re-tests, we ended passing most of them, but the experiment was not repeated.

A year later I did some flying for the Nigerian Civil Aviation Flying Unit. They had obtained a Beechcraft Super Kingair fitted with the equipment needed to flight test the country's ground navigational aids and some of their pilots needed training on the aircraft. I made a dozen flights with them, but we didn't get much training done through being hampered by various Government Ministers who demanded to be flown here and there. I finally told them I wasn't interested in being a taxi driver any longer. But I did get to see some new places, like Yola in the hilly country on the eastern border with Cameroun. This flying was to have a repercussion twelve years later, when I met one of those CAFU pilots in somewhat different circumstances.

Line squalls were not uncommon during the rainy season in West Africa. A few of them would be many hundreds of miles long and most were too long to escape by flying round the end of the line. Compared with the teddy bear variety I'd experienced in England and Germany, these were sabre tooth tigers. We had weather radar in the MU2, the Kingair and both our Twin Otters. This was not a totally effective device for avoiding the severe turbulence found in storms and squalls. The radar echoes showed only where heavy rain was falling; this was normally, but not always, associated with the areas of roughest air. Also it could only show the next bit of heavy rain ahead. A nearer storm cast a shadow in which more bad weather could be lurking and this would only show up on emerging from the first storm. So the radar was helpful, but not infallible. Of numerous line squall incidents, I vividly remember two.

On one occasion I was taking the Shell Managing Director and his family from Lagos to Kaduna in the MU2. There was a line of widely separated echoes across the screen. We were in the descent, passing 20,000 feet when we transited between two of these, well clear of both. It was not a pleasant experience; it became so dark that we had to turn the cockpit lighting fully up. Lightning was flashing away all round us, it was almost impossible to see through the rain beating on the windscreen and the aircraft was lurching all over the sky, at times it seemed bodily sideways, rocking from side to side and bouncing up and down so much that I half expected the wings to come off. A few minutes later we were clear, the air smoothed out and we continued down to land. The aircraft was needed back in Lagos right away, but I was, and still am, a devout coward. There was no way I would return through that lot now I knew what lurked there. We took off as soon as we had refuelled, but I went at right angles to track some one hundred miles parallel with the squall line until it came to an end. We heard later that a Boeing 737, which had penetrated that same squall, was actually damaged, some rivets had pulled out and there were wrinkles in the wing.

Another time I was returning from Jos to Lagos in a Twin Otter. It had just become dark when a serious line squall started to show on the weather radar. One of the problems in Africa in general was the dearth of airports that stayed open after dark. Nigeria was no exception. Behind me Jos had closed down. Kano was a 24-hour airport, but way out of reach of my remaining fuel. If there had been anywhere open and in reach on my side of the squall I'd have turned back. My alternate was Cotonou, like Lagos on the other side of the squall. In daylight I'd have used the same old technique as in the Islander, descending in visual conditions before the squall and flying low below it. At night and unable to see the ground I had to stay well above the high ground across track. That was just the wrong height to be penetrating thunderstorms, but the Twin Otter was unpressurised so there was no way of climbing above the weather. I made the usual passenger announcement about expecting turbulence and fastening seat belts in as casual a voice as I could manage, turned the cockpit lighting fully up, disengaged the autopilot and manoeuvred to line up with a gap between two of the slightly weaker returns on the weather radar screen.

As we entered the squall, all hell broke out. One moment we were climbing at two thousand feet per minute and the next we were slammed down at the same sort of rate. Loose items like maps and en-route flight guides literally hit the roof. Even with my earphones on, I could hear the passengers screaming behind me. My co-pilot, wanting something to hang on to, took a death hold on the control column and I had to hit him to make him let go. There was nothing to do but let the aircraft ride the gusts, try to hold a level attitude with minimum control movements and wait. It didn't last too long; about ten minutes, but I died several deaths before we broke out into a clear starry night on the Lagos side of the storms.

There was a flip side. Sometimes line squalls were helpful. Ahead of and close to them smooth rising air was the norm. It was usually easy to find this area; a vertical wall of cloud would have a higher shelf extending outwards a mile or so and the most strongly rising air would be found in the angle between wall and shelf. A few times I found a squall almost lined up with my desired track and was able to throttle right back yet still maintain height and speed for fifty miles or more. Several times I used squalls to save fuel and get to my destination when otherwise I would have had to go to an alternate. On our Lagos - Warri - Port Harcourt route, there was no fuel available at Warri. With full fuel from Lagos, we had enough to land at Warri and then depart with the legal requirement of fuel to destination (Port Harcourt), plus fuel for missed approach, flight to alternate (back to Warri) and 45 minutes holding. There was very little to spare, ten minutes extra holding at the most. So we could not hold off at Warri for long if the weather was bad. This time Warri was below landing limits with heavy rain, low cloud and bad visibility brought in by a line squall. I was able to soar the squall with the throttles at idle, reducing the normal hold fuel consumption from 350 pounds per hour to 100. This enabled holding for over thirty minutes, by which time the squall had passed through Warri and the weather had cleared.

Chapter 53
Gone are the honeymoon days

My early years with Bristows were very enjoyable, but after Alan Bristow, the Company's founder bowed out, things changed. In particular the bean counters began to gain control.

At first, when we lived in various houses around the GRA, we were taken to and from the airport by car as and when required. When we first moved to the new Residential Compound at Isolo, which was on the opposite side of the airport from our hangar in the domestic flights area, we had an on the hour every hour minibus service to take us to and from work and to and from the compound for lunch. The bean counters decided this was too expensive and reduced it to a run to the airport, timed for the morning scheduled departures, one back to Isolo around noon, with the inbound pilot and the engineers (the latter for their lunch), another to the airport after lunch with the engineers and the pilot for the afternoon schedule and a final return around 5.00 p.m. when the engineers had put the afternoon arrival to bed. The afternoon pilot had to wait until the engineers were finished. For the line pilots, this was no problem; the transport waited for them if they were delayed en route. Many of my training flights were at unscheduled times. Even on line check flights, which were carried out on a normal passenger scheduled flight, I had to spend half an hour or more on a debriefing after we landed. By the time I had finished at the hangar the transport would have left. I was often refused out of schedule transport, no matter how much I protested and I would have to wait three or four hours for the next.

The Company paid for our travel to and from Lagos and had arrangements with some airlines for discounted (ID50) fares. Depending on which airline happened to be the current international discounter those of us who lived in the U.K. flew via Heathrow, Gatwick, Amsterdam, or Frankfurt and then to or from our nominated airport. That had to be one to which a discount fare was also available. We paid our own way from there to home.

I had been travelling via Teesside with British Midland to wherever the current transfer point was with my fares paid, when out of the blue I was told my fares would be paid only for Lagos to London or London to Lagos. This was because British Midland would no longer give the discount on the Teesside-London leg. Bristows would not pay a train fare; it was against Company policy. So for a while I paid my own way between Yorkshire and London. I did manage to beat them after a while when we had a choice of London or Amsterdam en route. The fares from London to Lagos and Amsterdam to Lagos were the same. I was able to get to Amsterdam from Teesside with an airline that would give the discount but not to London. The discounted fare to Amsterdam was more than the full fare to London, but the rules said they had to pay my fare that way!

Our contracts specified that our travel would be during our leave time. Later on when discounted flights were unavailable for one reason or another the Company started to buy standby tickets for our leave travel, or sent us on roundabout routes where they could get cheaper fares. This often meant an extra day or more of leave used in travel home. When one of our pilots complained to our Area Manager about this situation, he was told "If you don't like it, go and work for someone else – Twin Otter pilots are ten a penny." The pilot gave him a penny and said "There you are then, go and find yourself ten because I won't be coming back." And he didn't.

Another personal aggravation was that because of my position as Training Captain, I had to spend quite a lot of time on Company business, including some flying, during my U.K. leaves. The vagaries of weather and aircraft availability could mean several days away from home and so days of leave lost. Company Policy (again) was to recompense for this on a two days leave for five days worked basis. Our eight week four week rotation gave us two days leave for four days worked. The disruption to already limited home life, holidays with Jennie and gliding was bad enough; being short changed this way didn't make me a great fan of Management.

An encounter that was to have considerable significance a few years later occurred around this time. I landed at Port Harcourt and parked next to one of Aero Contractors of Nigeria's aircraft. The pilot, a tall thin man of Middle Eastern appearance came up to me and asked, "Are you Sam St. Pierre?" When I admitted to this, he told me his name was Nabil Haqui and said he had been one of my students at Leeming. He had gone on to fly helicopters in the RAF and had spent a few years with Bristow's before joining ACN.

By late 1985, with the last Islander gone and the MU2 no longer operating, we were down to the two Twin Otters and the Kingair. The Ashland contract lasted until October 1986. After that, Ashland did want the option of ad-hoc chartering and an attempt was made by the Lagos management to put together a consortium of oil company charterers, but management back in the U.K. were interested only in single-user long term contracts. The Kingair sat around Lagos until June 1987 with no more than a few training flights, its Certificate of Airworthiness Test flight and one flight to Kaduna and return on a Shell charter. It was then flown back to the U.K. and put onto the British Register as G-BFOL, to join Bristow's fixed wing operation at Gatwick. My last flight in it was from Carlisle to Teesside on the 16th March 1989, when I renewed my Instrument Rating during my home leave. I sat in it for the last time two days before the end of that leave. My U.K. Instrument Rating Examiner and Type Rating Examiner endorsements were due for renewal. The Company had arranged for a Civil Aviation Flying Unit examiner to observe me carrying out an Instrument Rating renewal on another of our pilots, at Gatwick, to renew **my** examiner qualification. I had already spent a couple of days there waiting for the aircraft and CAFU examiner to be available. Unfortunately, when we started up, one of the navaids that was necessary for part of the renewal was unserviceable. The examiner could not wait around until it was fixed and he was not available again until the day I was due to be returning to Lagos by airline. Bristows were sending another Captain from Lagos to Redhill for some training, when I suggested they kept him at Lagos for a couple of days so I could renew my qualifications, I was told I could do that during my next leave. That was the last straw. Before going on my next leave I told the Area Manager that I was resigning my position as Chief Training Captain and would no longer carry out any training duties after my return. Somewhat to my surprise, I wasn't told not to bother to come back but was kept on as a line pilot. I did in the end renew my Instrument Rating Examiner qualification while on a later leave in the U.K., but not through Bristows. I was approached by the Chief Pilot of a small charter operator based at Teesside and after a flight renewing the Instrument Rating of one of their pilots while being observed by a CAFU examiner I became their IRE for a couple of years – until they went out of business.

Chapter 54
First retirement and Aero Contractors

At the beginning of November 1990 I was two months short of the Bristow Helicopters normal retirement age of 58. I was completely disenchanted with Bristow's by then, so made no attempt to have my employment extended. I took two weeks leave and went to Nairobi, then on to the Seychelles to see what jobs were available. Nairobi looked promising, there were several opportunities with smaller Kenyan companies, but the pay was rather low. I had a slightly embarrassing experience at the Nairobi (Wilson) Airport. I saw someone approaching from the other direction dressed in a khaki shirt and slacks with the four rings of a Captain, thought "Gosh, he looks very like Nabil Haqui" and greeted him with "You **must** be Nabil Haqui's brother or cousin or something." "No I'm not, I **am** Nabil, Sam" he replied. I'd seen him many times in Nigeria, but in the Aero Contractor's (and almost every other Company's) black trouser white shirt uniform. Out of context, I hadn't believed what my eyes had told me.

The Seychelles proved to be a dead loss work-wise, they had more than enough pilots of their own and didn't need ex-pats. The Twin Otter operation, flying from Mahe to some of the outlying islands, sounded idyllic and I'd have leapt at it if I'd been offered the chance. At least I had a few days holiday in a place that was reminiscent of my South Pacific days. Mahe, though much smaller, was a 'high' island like Tahiti, with a mountainous interior, fringing lagoons and coral reefs.

Back in Lagos on November 13th, I continued on the Lagos-Warri-Port Harcourt routine until 6th December for a three-week total of 59 hours flight time. I was due out on final leave on the 7th. A few days before my last Bristow flight I walked the three hundred yards from Bristow's to Aero Contractors, saw Nabil and asked if Aero could use me for a couple of months on their Twin Otters. I wanted to stay out of the U.K. until April for tax reasons, but I didn't really want to stay in Nigeria longer than that. A change of scene or retirement was more to my liking.

I was welcomed with open arms, they would have liked me to start right away, but I would have to go to their parent Company, Schreiner Airways in Leiden, the Netherlands, for the Company hiring procedures. Would I go there right away and come back immediately? I said I could call in at Leiden on the way home, but I really should spend Christmas with Jennie in Yorkshire. We agreed that I would return shortly before the New Year. There was another small problem; they said that Schreiner would not take me on a temporary arrangement, I would have to take a two-year contract, but they, Aero Contractors, would see to it that if I wanted to leave they would fix that.

The Schreiner interview was a bit of a formality. The Company still had a file on me from 1977 when I had passed their flying test and had been certified by their tame shrink psychologically suited (i.e. insane) to fly in Nigeria. With my back problem having been sorted out by the operation, the Company Doctor no longer had reason to reject me either, so it was just a matter of filling in the appropriate bits of paper and signing the contract. One thing that the Personnel Manager made a point of telling me was that my fares **would** be paid to and from whatever U.K. airport I selected. I suspect he had heard of the Bristow trick! My employment start date was the 1st January 1991, which meant I would be paid by both Bristow and Schreiner until my Bristow terminal and accumulated leave ran out. With continued income assured I took Jennie to San Francisco for Christmas, her first visit to the USA.

Schreiner's pay scales were very formalised, with set increments for type of licence (Commercial or Airline Transport), pilot grade (co-pilot, Captain, Senior Captain), seniority in the grade, total flying hours, aircraft types on one's licence flown by the Company and additional responsibilities such as Chief Pilot, Training Captain and so on. They were generous to me, giving me seniority for pay purposes. With my Bristow pension kicking in I started on about the same income as I had in Bristow's. Schreiner's pay was however denoted in Guilders. Over the next few months I watched with delight the increasing strength of the Guilder versus the Pound Sterling, which eventually gave me an effective pay rise of around 25%.

The flying with Aero was mostly on the same along-the-coast routes as Bristow, with the exception of the 'Escravos Shuttle". Escravos was an important base for Chevron Oil, with a tank farm, machine shops and a depot for all the bits and pieces needed for oil exploration and production. Situated on the coast south of Warri, at the mouth of one of the Niger's distributaries, it had a long tarmac runway for fixed wing aircraft.

A number of helicopters were also based there, flying workers and material to and from the oilrigs offshore. Many of the workers commuted to and from Warri in the Aero Twin Otters and expats flew to and from Lagos for their home leave journeys. So we would fly from Lagos to Escravos in the morning, then shuttle to and from Warri as many times as needed, finally returning to Lagos in the evening. We would keep the starboard engine running during the shuttle turn rounds except when we needed to refuel at Warri. Escravos to Warri took a little over 15 minutes, so the shuttling part of the day could be somewhat frantic, with the ground time filled with loading, weight and balance calculations and various other bits of paper work. I only got as far as four Escravos-Warri shuttles in one day, but other pilots had done more.

Not long after starting with Aero, on a return flight with the week-enders from Jos, I had another brush with a line squall. Once again I had no option but to fly through it. I warned the passengers that "there may be a little turbulence for a few minutes". I was soon fully occupied with finding a way through the rough bits. We got through into the calm air and I looked round to see how they were – and they were all wearing their life-jackets! Maybe they thought they would act as parachutes if the wings fell off.

I was familiar with such Nigerian-English expressions as "Put the light on off", "Put the brake on on" and "The Manager is not on seat" but one I heard while with Aero caused me some amusement. One of the co-pilots arrived in a terrible mess, with his uniform torn and blood all over his face and hands. "What on earth happened to you?" "Oh, I had a disappointment on the way here" (He'd crashed his car).

Like Bristow's, Aero's leave rotation for ex-pats was supposed to be 8 weeks on, four weeks leave. My first tour was extended when in mid-February I ferried one of the Twin Otters to Maastricht in Holland. I had of course flown across the Sahara many times as a passenger in a high-flying airliner; taking a small aircraft across at low level was more humbling. I felt very insignificant in the immensity of the Sahara. For hours on end, there would be no sign of human existence among the sand and rocks below us. We night stopped halfway across at Tamanrasset, a name as evocative perhaps as Timbuctou. From Tam we flew on via Palma to Marseilles, but there we had a problem. Our transponder, a mandatory piece of equipment for flying in controlled airspace in France failed shortly after take-off and we were ordered to return to Marseilles by Air Traffic Control. The weather was too bad for us to fly outside controlled airspace under visual flight rules and was forecast to stay that way. I found a radio maintenance engineer who could repair the transponder, but it took three days.

Maastricht airfield was vastly different from when I had last seen it in the Minimoa nearly thirty years before. Then it had been an ex WW2 aerodrome, with crumbling runways, used by no more than a few flying club light aircraft and some gliders. Now it was a busy airport and a large maintenance base for big jets from all over the world. That wasn't the only difference I found from my memories of the area. Schreiner's had a car that needed delivering to Amsterdam. My flight from there back to Lagos by airline was not until three days later, so I was told I could use the car for touring around if I would deliver it for them. It seemed a good idea to drive down to Heerlen, cross into Germany, visit some of the old haunts from my RAF Germany days, then drive from Geilenkirchen to Laarbruch as I had done so many times to visit Jennie. I saw practically nothing that I recognised. I couldn't find the splendid little pub in Ubach-Palenberg where we so frequently went for steaks and beer after gliding on Saturdays. The sandy track we used to use as a short cut had vanished under acres of tarmac and where the pub had been among the houses of a farming village there was now a business centre with multi-storey office blocks.

On arrival back in Lagos, I was asked if I would extend that first tour until the middle of March. I had spent nearly all my allowable days in the U.K. for that tax year; three more would put me over the 90-day limit so extending suited me very well. Jennie would be on holiday for Easter and I could get a very cheap flight from Lagos to Los Angeles with Varig via Rio de Janeiro, so

I asked her to meet me in LA. Also, having found the Aero ambience far better than Bristow's, I decided that I could bear a bit more time in Nigeria, so made no move to leave the Company.

The Varig schedule gave a day and a night each way in Rio. This was my first and only visit to South America, until then my only unvisited continent unless one counts passing through the Panama Canal. I took the compulsory tourist ride in the cable car to the top of the Sugar Loaf and the compulsory walk along Copacabana Beach. I had had dire warnings from my ACN colleagues about Rio. One of them claimed to have had his pocket picked three times in ten minutes; the third pickpocket gave him back all that was by then left to steal – his comb! As ever, when I strolled around the back streets of Rio, ambled through the Botanical Gardens, caught a bus and generally ignored all the warnings about being mugged or molested, I saw nothing to cause alarm and encountered no trouble. Perhaps I just look too much of a tramp to be worth robbing!

During the next duty tour from 8th April to 19th May I told Nabil that I very much enjoyed working for Aero, but would like to spend more time at home. I asked if I could be a part-timer and indicated that I would accept a considerably lower pro-rata salary. "We may have something coming up that would suit you, but it's all hush-hush at the moment. See me again when you get back from your next leave" he said. When I returned, it transpired that Aero had won a contract to operate two Twin Otters in Chad, for Esso. The ex-pat crews would do two weeks in Lagos and 4 weeks in Chad, then have 4 weeks leave, but the salary would be the same as for the Lagos 8 and 4 rotation. I could be part of this if I wanted. I did!

After the leave I returned to Lagos for the expected two weeks and then on July 8th took one of the Twin Otters via Kano to N'Djamena, the capital of Chad. Next day we flew on to Sarh, 270 miles to the southeast and officially took over the contract from the Canadian Company that had until then been operating it. For various settling-in reasons this first stay went over the expected four weeks to six, but I hardly noticed the fact, the Chad experience was like a very well paid holiday. In the contract, Esso provided us with living accommodation in their headquarters compound and since there were no catering facilities there, paid us a meal allowance, in U.S. dollars, sufficient for three meals a day in the restaurants in town. In addition, Aero Contractors paid us an extra so-called 'hard living' allowance while we were in Chad. Altogether we were coining it; our Nigerian co-pilots were especially pleased, their allowances added up to more than their basic pay.

In the French colonial days N'Djamena had been known as Fort Lamy; the radio beacon at the airport was still Morse coded FL, Foxtrot Lima. Sarh had been Fort Archambeau; again the beacon there coded Foxtrot Alpha. There was still a sort of Beau Geste atmosphere about the place. Outside of a circus visit, it would be a little unusual to see camels being ridden down the main street of any other capital city, but it was unremarkable in N'Djamena. The presence of many French Legionnaires added to the ambience. There had been frequent civil wars at intervals since independence from France in 1960 and even at the time of our arrival two years after the last coup rebels were still operating, with occasional incursions right into the city. Most of the buildings in town were heavily pockmarked with bullet and shell holes. Esso were fairly paranoid about security, we were forbidden to go outside the city, even to some areas within it, without an armed escort. In fact the main reason for our presence was to provide the means for emergency evacuation from the country should it be required. We also provided medevac facilities from the oil exploration and drilling bases and carried personnel and materials to and fro. With one of the aircraft on permanent standby and four crews on site, the flying load was very light.

I spent most of that first tour at the Sarh oil drilling camp. Life was fairly restricted there; it was almost like being in a prisoner of war camp. The compound was around 250 metres square and surrounded by a high chain-link fence; other than going to the airfield we were not permitted outside the gates unless escorted. One corner, about a quarter of the site, was given over to office and living accommodation, all in the form of portakabins. The remaining area was practically filled by racks of drill pipe, cranes, a mobile drilling rig, vehicles and tractors of all shapes and sizes and even a large steel boat. The sleeping accommodation portakabins contained two double tier bunks each, leaving room for nothing more than an upright steel locker per man, one very small table and one chair. The only real entertainment facilities were a book library and a video library. There was also room for a jogging track round the

Photo 50 - Sarh oil exploration camp accommodation

inside of the wire. The oilies were busy with work every day, but for us, flying just a few hours every other day or so, time hung heavily. But the food was first class.

It would have been rather difficult to find our way to some of the airstrips we flew into had it not been for the then fairly new Global Positioning System equipment, with which Esso insisted our aircraft must be equipped. The terrain in most of our usual operating area was flat Sahel, dry laterite soil sprinkled with bushes, mostly acacia, with very few outstanding features. The few roads were almost all unsealed and apart from the main Chari river and a couple of its tributaries near the Central African Republic to the south there were no other water courses except for a brief spell during heavy rain, when the normally dried-up wadis were liable to flash floods. The only aviation navigation aids on the ground were the VOR Beacon, Non-Directional Beacon and Instrument Landing System installation at N'Djamena, a VOR Beacon at Moundou 220 miles to the south and a Non-Directional Beacon at Sarh. However, unlike the navigation aids in Nigeria, they were reliable and worked 99% of the time.

With the operation in place and our competency established, some re-negotiations of the contract took place. Esso had not envisaged 'their' crews being used outside of Chad and insisted that they wanted us to work a four-week duty/four-week leave rotation. We changed to this in the summer. One consequence was that Jennie found herself making more frequent visits to the USA. The limit of 90 days maximum per year in the U.K. to maintain my status as non-resident for tax purposes was even more difficult to satisfy. One day too many and I'd be liable for tax on the whole year's income. So I had the choice between paying tax or paying for three months holiday elsewhere in the world. Since my income put me well into the top tax bracket of around 40%, economically there was no choice. When Jennie's school holidays coincided with my leave we went to California, either meeting there or travelling from London together. My gain was the British economy's loss; the foreign exchange I was earning went to the USA instead of the U.K. I often wondered how many billions of pounds from Britain's ex-pat workers were lost this way.

Photo 51 - A glider pilot's Eden

Another change was a move out of the Esso compound into a house of our own. This also gave us the opportunity to arrange our own catering. We were told by all and sundry that we would have great difficulty finding a cook;

this proved to be only too correct. Our first cook was a total disaster; described by one of our members as an unemployed camel driver, he knew little more than stew. Later we were lucky to acquire a cook who had worked for one of the American oil exploration companies and from then on we ate very well.

As a result of the bombing of an Air France aircraft flying from Chad to Europe a few years earlier, Esso had decided for security reasons to fly their own and their contractor's personnel in and out of Chad in a chartered Boeing 737. With the change to four weeks on and four off, we ex-pats no longer needed to go to Lagos and we started to travel in style on the 737 rather than in the cattle class of normal scheduled flights. The 737 was never more than one third full, so on the late evening flights out of Chad we could stretch out on three seats and sleep all the way to the refuelling stop at Palma.

In November 1991 I was asked to take over as Pilot-in-Charge of the operation, back to back with another Captain on the 4-week rotation. Although we were now providing an extra Twin Otter, the task was not onerous. It took no more than a morning to hand over/take over the finances and other details. The amount of flying had gone down even more, there was plenty of time to deal with the small amount of administration involved. Rostering was the major difficulty, with so little flying to do it was difficult to share it out fairly. I was achieving an average of 20 hours per tour, as much as or more than the others were. At one stage I threatened to institute a new system. When Esso called for a flight, everyone should line up at the gate to our compound, I would fire a starting pistol and the first two pilots to reach the aircraft on foot would have the privilege of flying it. Subject to my veto, because I might want to fly it myself.

What extra work there was for me proved to be a bonus; there was not a great deal else to occupy my time. Generally it was too warm outside during the day to take part in strenuous activities. I had played squash regularly in Lagos, but there were no courts in N'Djamena. I couldn't get the hang of tennis, but with practise regained some of my schoolboy table tennis skill. When the wind wasn't too strong we played outside by the Esso swimming pool. I spent many hours there, reading, sunbathing and leaping into the pool to cool down at intervals. It was a peaceful spot until one afternoon when someone loosed off a rifle shot; I heard the bullet pass by very close. Another time the main Esso building was hit by a shell.

There were some very large 'Kapitan' fish in the Chari River, we bought them occasionally from a trader who visited the house with fish, meat and poultry. The largest kapitan we bought was about 25 kilos but they grew very much bigger. I tried fishing myself with little success, although my colleagues believed that I had actually caught the one they found me with when they returned to collect me on the riverbank one day. Some passing netsmen had saved my reputation as a fisherman; I didn't confess the truth.

When we flew over Lake Chad the first time, it was not what I expected. Instead of a vast tract of open water, I saw narrow ribbons of sand with small areas of water and a lot of reed beds in between. It seemed that my time in Chad coincided with a low rainfall period. A few years earlier, one of the oil exploration conveys taking a short cut across an arm of the lake had been trapped by a rise in the water level. The vehicles were abandoned and had been completely submerged for some months.

Photo 52 The tide has gone out

Rig Rig, to the east of Lake Chad, was a typical oil company strip. It was located where previous surveys had indicated that drilling might be worthwhile and was several miles from the nearest settlement. Cleared among the scattered acacias of the Sahel terrain, the surface was unsealed laterite. It had been used intensively while drilling took place, but once oil had been found the well was capped and the strip was visited no more than three or four times a year to check that nothing was amiss. I flew there for my first time on one of these inspection trips in January 1992. Arriving overhead, I was a little puzzled by what looked like just one side of a vehicle wheel track meandering along the full length of the strip. In places there was a similar mark alongside, but the two weren't parallel. As I was descending to investigate these markings, in case they were deep ruts and a hazard for our landing, the explanation hove into sight. A donkey appeared at the end of the runway and ambled slowly along one of the tracks. So I circled around waiting for it to move away. Which it did, at the touchdown end of the strip – just as two more appeared at the far end! Enough was enough, I buzzed them and they galloped away.

We touched down, taxied to the end of the strip and turned onto the stony ground at the side. I switched off the engines. The silence was eerie. Our oil company men climbed down and prepared to go off to the well head. Then we heard a vehicle engine and a half-truck arrived in a cloud of dust. Five or six men, wearing a motley variety of camouflaged combat gear, all armed and bandoleered stared at us. The situation was a little tense. There were still many rebel groups roaming around Chad and we could not be sure whether this was one of them. Then their leader got out of the cab and one of our passengers recognised him as an old acquaintance from previous visits. We all relaxed. The Chadians escorted our oilmen away to the well and we waited in the shade of the aircraft's wing. As usual, I had a paperback with me. If I had a pound for every book I've read while waiting for passengers….

I was well settled in to the Chad operation by this time. Jennie was in the middle of a school term during my February leave, but I had to stay out of the U.K. for those same tax reasons. I went to the USA on my own, during which, without telling her, I treated myself to a tandem free-fall parachute jump at Hemet, near Los Angeles as an early 60th birthday present. After that, Death Valley was a must-do. In February the temperature there was in the low seventies, giving perfect shirtsleeve weather. I walked for miles. Then I moved on to Phoenix Arizona and spent a couple of days gliding at Maricopa. The airfield was about 1,500 feet above sea level, I climbed in a thermal to cumulus cloud base at 12,000 and then found wave, which took me on to nearly 15,000. The controlled airspace of Phoenix International was a circle with a bite out of it, which allowed gliders to soar the mountain range lying close to the west of the airport. It was quite an experience looking down at the jumbos landing and taking off almost below me.

In March, a few days after my return to Chad from leave and before I had even started flying Jennie telephoned me with bad news. She had been diagnosed with an ovarian tumour and was to have a hysterectomy. Aero Contractors came up trumps again and let me depart from Chad immediately, giving me as much unpaid leave as I needed to look after her. The tumour proved to be a non-malignant cyst and three months later she was back at school. I went to Lagos in mid-June for a couple of days, to have a proficiency check before going back to Chad on the crew change Twin Otter flight. To my considerable pleasure, the check pilot was Reece Oni, the Bristow Kingair co-pilot of earlier times. After having been on the receiving end of the checks I used to give him, it must have been very satisfying for him to check me.

During my months away from Chad Esso had scaled down their operation and reduced their flying requirement. One of the three Twin Otters and two of the crews had returned to Nigeria, but even then our remaining pilots were averaging little more than seven days flying and twenty hours per four-week tour. I calculated that with my tax-free salary and allowances plus full board and lodging while on site, my take-home pay per hour of flying was probably more than a British Airways 747 Captain's! My own flying hours increased at a snail's pace, but during a flight from N'Djamena to Sarh in December I passed the 10,000 hours pilot-in-command figure and 12,400 hours including co-pilot and student time. Considering that during all but a tiny fraction of my previous

40 years I'd made a living by professional flying, those were not very impressive figures!

Life seemed settled and serene, with Jennie's operation successfully accomplished and myself in a well-paid, not too strenuous position, but as ever fate has the habit of creeping up behind with a sock full of wet sand and belting one on the back of the head. The Nigerian Civil Aviation authorities brought in a maximum age of 60 for Public Transport pilots and for me it seemed the game was over. My impending second retirement was announced at the Company Christmas party.

As was typical of ACN's regard for their employees, the Company arranged for me to spend the two weeks before my January 9th 1993 60th birthday in Lagos, so that I could renew my U.K. Instrument Rating, which would be essential if I did go looking for flying employment elsewhere. I did the renewal on a non-revenue flight with the Chief Pilot on the 7th January and on the 8th made what I thought might be my last commercial flight, Lagos to Warri and back.

As it happened, by casting its bread upon the waters the Company was rewarded almost immediately. While clearing up my affairs and packing for my final departure I heard that they had a problem with their contract in Guinea, on the West African coast. They provided a full time pilot and an engineer when required for a Twin Otter owned by CBG (Compagnie Bauxite de Guinee). This was therefore classed as a private operation, not Public Transport. The pilot was on a five months on site, one month leave rotation and was due for leave, but Schreiner/ACN had no pilot available for his relief. I suggested that, since it was not a Public Transport operation and the aircraft was on a Guinean, not Nigerian registration, I might be legal to fly it on my U.K. licence and another month of employment would not come amiss. This was agreed and I went home for a week on leave before travelling to CBG's head office in Brussels to get a Guinea visa. A few days later I arrived at Conakry, the Guinean capital and boarded the Twin Otter as a passenger for the short flight to Kamsar, the bauxite port.

Chapter 55
Guinea holidays

Guinea had been a Communist state, closed to all but a few foreign workers from 1958 until 1984 when the military took over. It had then remained under military control until the presidential elections of 1993. It was a very poor country. There was very little public electricity supply even in Conakry – individual generators were the rule. At Kamsar, the Company provided electricity for its own offices, port facilities and housing and also a small amount of street lighting, but in the villages, when darkness came, the only illumination seemed to be from wood fires. Between Kamsar and Conakry just the first 50 km of road, to Boke, was sealed when I first went there; the rest was dust in the dry season and almost impassable mud during the rains.

After showing me round the routes between the usual destinations of Kawass (Kamsar airstrip), Sangaredi (the open-cast bauxite mine) and Conakry the regular pilot left me in the care of Sory Diallo the Guinean co-pilot and went on leave. I was given a suite in the Resident Bachelors' Quarters, a complex of living accommodation, mess room and bar. I could step directly out through the French windows of my suite to the swimming pool and did so a lot during my time at Kamsar – the flying schedule was very light. Flight time from Kawass to Conakry and return was only 1 hour 15 minutes; the Kawass - Conakry – Sangaredi – Kawass or reverse triangle took 30 minutes longer. Often one or the other of those was all we did, usually we were finished by lunchtime and we didn't fly every day. After lunch, armed with a book from the Company library, I would seek the shade of one of the pool side umbrellas, stretch out on a lounger and read through the afternoon, with frequent dips into the pool to cool off. Most afternoons I'd be on my own there, everyone else was working.

Some amusement was provided by the local crows, which sat in wait on a nearby tall water tower. Every now and then a flock of vultures, sometimes with pelicans and gulls, would drift past while soaring in a thermal. This would spark off a massed 'scramble' by the crows, which would climb above the other birds and then swoop down like Spitfires on a Luftwaffe bomber squadron. The crows were highly manoeuvrable and would often perform flick rolls and other aerobatics. I once saw a crow perform a full-blooded two-turn spin and recovery. After their rout of the vultures they would fly back to the water tower and perch there chattering away nineteen to the dozen. I could imagine the conversation … "There I was, diving at never exceed speed with this big black vulture right in my sights, when a b****y pelican flew in front of me and…"

On February 19th I made what should have been my final Guinea and third final retirement flight, a Kawass-Sangaredi-Conakry-Kawass triangle. We landed at Kawass in the early afternoon. As we taxied towards the terminal hut,

I saw flags flying, a large crowd and a band. Puzzled, I asked Sory if we had a VIP on board. He didn't know of any such. As we disembarked, I was greeted with a glass of wine, a burst of music and the information that the show had been arranged by the engineer to mark my retirement. Unfortunately what he didn't know was that before leaving Kawass that morning I had had a message from Schreiner Airways saying that CBG had asked for the permanent pilot to be removed from Guinea and asking if I would be prepared to stay there until they found a replacement! Which I had agreed to do. With a bit of luck I might be able to stay within the 90 days in U.K. limit until the end of the tax year on April 5th.

The permanent position involved a five month on one month off rotation. Schreiner knew there was no way I would have taken it. Jennie was firmly established in her school and ten months a year away from home was not an option for me. The permanent position was advertised. An applicant was offered the job and was expected to arrive early in March, but he decided that the education possibilities for his children in Guinea were not acceptable. A further advertisement brought another applicant, this time a bachelor. He was able to come in the first week of April, but for only three months on his first visit. So my one month of extra employment became three months, saving me a lot of tax and I was also offered the opportunity to become the permanent relief pilot. This was on the same terms as my Nigerian employment; one week's paid leave for every two weeks on site. Three months' pay for two months away from home each year suited me very well; I wanted to spend more time at home with Jennie. She could use a bit of househusband help.

Life was very relaxed during the next couple of years. I did the one month leave relief five times and visited Lagos twice for Instrument Rating renewal flights. I was free for most of Jennie's school holidays; we went to California again several times and once to Seattle and the Warburton and Glacier National Parks. In Guinea CBG supplied me with a 4 wheel drive vehicle, primarily for going to and from the airstrip, but also freely available for personal use. The countryside near Kamsar was flat, with rice fields cleared among the low trees and with mangrove swamps along the coast and creeks. Further inland there were low hills, mostly bush covered, but with some natural grass clearings. For many miles to the south and east the surface was rocky, with a peculiar pattern of long straight crevasses, mostly water filled, in a rectangular grid pattern. Some of these were so straight, with such smooth vertical walls and of such regular width (around 25 feet) that they looked man-made. When fishing in one of them I tried plumbing the bottom, but reached the limit of my line at 80 feet or so.

The usual preconception of those who have never been there is that in Africa there are all sorts of wild things whose sole aim is to leap out of the bush and kill you. It really isn't like that. In Nigeria, the most common snake I saw was the flat snake. Totally harmless – squashed on the road. I saw perhaps as many as ten live snakes in all my time there, of which only one was even slightly dangerous. In all my tramps through the Guinean bush, I saw none. There were lots of birds, but I saw very little other wild life apart from lizards, monkeys, a few gazelles, some squirrels and of course a myriad of insects. Small lizards abounded, but there were also some large iguanas. When one of them appeared on the apron at Conakry there was great excitement among the airport workers, who abandoned their work to pursue it all around the tarmac. Eventually it was caught and killed for its meat.

We often had monkey trouble at Sangaredi. Many of them lived in the surrounding bush and from time to time when we arrived overhead they would be on the runway. We would have to fly a low pass down the airstrip to drive them away.

On one occasion we had a somewhat different monkey incident. At Sangaredi, where there were no refuelling facilities, we normally kept the starboard engine running while disembarking and embarking the passengers. There was a small hut to the side of the runway where the passengers could shelter from sun or rain. About 40 yards of concrete path led from it to our parking spot. I would position the aircraft with the passenger door (on the left side of the Twin Otter) at the end of the path and the co-pilot would go back down the cabin to open the door and supervise the passenger and cargo handling. I was sitting there while he did this one day, idly gazing around, when one of the European mine employees came out of the hut, leading a small child, dressed only in a nappy, by the hand. "Good heavens," I thought. "I've seen plenty of dark-skinned children in West Africa, but that one is about the blackest I've ever seen". As they drew closer, clearly intending to board the aircraft, I saw that the 'child' was not only very black, but also very hairy! Sori, my co-pilot, seemed quite accustomed to such events. I looked back into the cabin as he strapped the young chimpanzee into a window seat and its owner sat down next to it. I looked back again several times on the way to Conakry; the animal seemed quite blasé about flying, gazing out of the window and looking as bored as the rest of the passengers.

Another occasional and rather more prestigious passenger, was the President's wife. Now and again we would receive a message that she wanted to travel with us to or from Conakry, so we would delay our departure. Her arrival was a very low-key affair; a Landrover would turn up on the apron with no more than a couple of soldiers as escort. She would climb on board the Twin Otter, make her way to the front of the cabin, look into the cockpit, give me a big smile and a "Bonjour Capitaine," and then sit down, get out her knitting and click away with the needles all through the flight. At the other end it was "Merci Capitaine", another big smile, another Landrover with two other soldiers and off she went. She would usually have a selection of fruit and vegetables and some plants with her. I once caught my Guinean co-pilot helping himself to some of her grapes when we were loading the baggage. I was horrified, but he shrugged it off with the explanation that she was a friend of his and wouldn't mind!

With the Twin as it was affectionately known being a private Company aircraft there was no commercial pressure on the operation. Some of the passengers were travelling on duty, or to or from leave, but many were on non-business travel, visiting relatives or friends. I never worked out why we always seemed to carry sacks of rice and cartons of soft drinks to Conakry and carried different sacks of the same sort of rice and different cartons of the same variety of soft drinks back again. What I did find very difficult was persuading the CBG Dispatchers that there was a limit as to how many passengers and how much cargo and baggage we could safely carry. I would watch over them as they weighed the load and filled in the manifest, when all was done and everything was in the baggage compartments I'd be starting the engines and then notice the baggage door unlocked light come on. Looking round, I'd see them trying to put another three sacks of rice in the rear baggage hold.

Eventually CBG decided they would provide their own pilot and in July 1995 the contract with Schreiner was not renewed. Life for me became even more relaxed, I was quite happy to hang up my headphones and finally retire from power flying. But once again it didn't happen. After nine months of idleness, in early April 1996 I telephoned Nabil Haqui in Lagos, just to say hello. After catching up on each other's news, he told me that the Nigerians had raised the age limit for commercial flying back to 65 and said he had been thinking of calling me to see if I would be interested in going back to work for Aero Contractors. Three weeks later I was back in Lagos, on an 8-weeks/4-weeks rotation to start with.

Chapter 56
A Cameroun break

ACN had changed some of their procedures while I had been away and had put much emphasis on their supervision and training. It took rather longer to get on line this time than before. After seven hours refresher training, followed by a Proficiency Check and an Instrument Rating renewal, I spent two weeks and 25 hours flying as co-pilot, covering all the routes and airfields that the ACN Twin Otters normally used, before being let loose as Captain. Another change was that whenever possible they would roster two Captains together, one experienced and the other newly promoted, flying leg and leg about during the day. I did as much flying as co-pilot as I did as Captain during the next three weeks.

Much of my flying on this first tour was, to my amusement, for Shell. Bristows had been having problems with their aircraft and had to turn to chartering us to keep their operation going. Many of their passengers greeted me with big smiles and "Oh Captain, we are happy you are back" Unfortunately it was on an intended Shell flight that I was thrown off the aircraft in Lagos by one of the Nigerian Civil Aviation Flight Operations Inspectors.

The Nigerian Civil Aviation Administration was at the time in a state of disarray, the bureaucrats couldn't keep up with the red tape and paperwork they had themselves brought into being. Pilots had to have medical examinations at regular intervals, every six months for older pilots. The medical examiner produced a report that showed whether or not the pilot was fit to fly. Instead of this report being sent to the authority and a medical certificate page that pilots could insert into their own licences being sent back, or the medical examiner himself completing a medical certificate page, the authorities required that our medical reports had to be sent with the licence and the whole licence renewed. It was taking several weeks to get the licence back; legally one had to carry a valid licence with one when flying. Clearly no aircraft operator could afford to have pilots sitting around waiting for their licences; we carried on flying with photocopies of the licence and the medical report. This had caused a problem when a Nigerian crew had been grounded somewhere overseas because the authorities there would not accept a photocopy licence. So rather than speed up the administration, the Nigerian authorities instituted a purge on pilots who did not have current licences with them.

I had completed the load sheet and other paperwork at the Bristow hangar where our aircraft was parked and was in the cockpit carrying out the pre-flight checks when the Operations Inspector arrived. He showed me his identity card; the name rang a bell. "Show me your licence" he demanded. I told him it was at his office for renewal and proffered him the photocopies. "These are no good" he said, "and anyway, how old are you?" I told him I was 64. "That is too old, you cannot fly in Nigeria, get out of this aircraft" he shouted. A wise pilot does not argue with an Operations Inspector. As I picked up my headphones and flight bag and turned to leave the aircraft, I remembered where I'd met him before. Just to show I bore no ill will I thought I might lighten the tension with a polite remark. "Do you remember flying with me when I did some training of you guys in your Kingair?" I enquired. Mistake. He went ballistic, said he'd done all his training in the USA and had never seen me before. I thought I'd better not press the point by showing him his name in my logbook!

I wasn't too bothered that I might soon be unemployed again, but I felt a bit guilty at the thought that I might have let ACN down in some way. Back at our hangar I told Nabil what had happened. After some discussion between him and the Chief Pilot I was assured the problem would be sorted out, but it could take a while so I might as well go on leave early, they'd let me know when to come back.

A month later, in mid-July, I was back in Lagos and flying the south coast routes again. I had another embarrassing West African experience when a severe and long-lasting thunderstorm kept Lagos unlandable and caused me to divert to Cotonou, in the next door country of Benin. There was very little friendship between Nigeria and Benin; I was not allowed to let the passengers disembark. Dealing with the gendarmerie, customs, immigration and airport authorities took a long time; with no air conditioning it soon became uncomfortably hot in the passenger cabin and after an hour or so the need for toilet facilities became pressing. Eventually the passengers were allowed to leave the aircraft, but they had to stay close by it out on the apron. The grass got well watered. Meanwhile I was coping with another major difficulty. I had to pay for fuel and landing fees. By sheer chance, as a result of a recent holiday in the States, I had a stock of US dollar travellers' cheques with me, but the fuel company and the airport wanted payment in local, Benin, currency. It was long past normal banking hours and I was expecting to have to wait until next morning. I was wandering around inside the terminal building, dreading the moment when I'd have to go back and face my passengers when the P.A. announced an impending International flight arrival – and the Bureau de Change shutters flew up. Phew!

In mid-August I returned to Chad, again as pilot-in-charge on the 4-week/4 week back-to-back basis with another Captain. I found that there had been significant changes during my absence. An Administration Manager had been appointed, which made my job even easier. We had moved into a different house, nearer to the city centre, just round the corner from "Number One", one of N'Djamena's Boites de Nuit. Esso no longer chartered the 737 from and to Europe; our ex-pats reverted to cattle class on Air France. On crew change days, a Twin Otter arrived from Lagos with the Nigerian pilots and the occasional ex-pat that had needed to visit Lagos for medical or check flights. However, the majority of check flights could now be done in Chad. Our flying had become more varied, with more sites to visit in Chad and with oil exploration expanding into Niger.

Esso had had work done on an old airstrip at N'Guigmi in Niger, just across the border to the west of Lake Chad. The scrub that had grown up over the years had been cleared. The dirt runway had been lengthened and marked out with tyres. I made the first landing there on August 15th. The airstrip was difficult to see from above, not helped by the fact that the aeronautical charts showed it to the west of N'Guigmi town, when it was in fact to the east. We had been given the same latitude and longitude co-ordinates as were shown on the chart. This would not have mattered had the arranged radio communication worked, but the man with the ground radio was still on his way, almost bogged down in the talcum-powder like dust of the track from the north where the exploration site was located. I climbed to nearly 10,000 feet to increase our radio range and was about to return to N'Djamena with minimum fuel before we established contact and found out where the field really was. A few weeks later a ground radio beacon was installed, enabling operations down to low visibility.

Considerable reserves of oil had by now been discovered in Chad, but there was as yet no production. One problem was that the country, being completely land-locked, had no port from which to export the crude oil. Negotiations had been taking place with the Cameroun Government with the view to construction of a pipeline from the Kome field in the south of Chad into Cameroun, passing close to the Cameroun administrative capital, Yaounde and on to the Atlantic coast at Kribi. On the 18th August I took a delegation of Chadian politicians to a meeting at Yaounde. We stopped to refuel and clear Customs and Immigration at Garoua. This had an incredibly long runway; it was apparently built as an emergency landing strip for the space shuttle.

I had been looking forward to seeing Yaounde again, but the pleasant little Paris in the jungle of 25 years earlier had become a sprawling industrialised city. Maybe if we'd had more time to look around I'd have found some trace of the old town, but we left next afternoon to fly back to N'Djamena.

By the time of my next duty tour, in October, the Niger oil exploration team had pushed further north, setting up depots and temporary camps at suitable locations as they went. Apart from the obvious need to be near a geologically promising area for oil, one of the criteria for suitability was that an airstrip could be constructed or an abandoned one restored at the campsite without excessive earth moving work. This was primarily for medevac capability, but also for the supply of food and materials. One such location was in a shallow, flat-bottomed valley about 75 miles north of N'Guigmi at Bedouaram. An airstrip had existed there in the past, but over the years it had completely disappeared under a blanket of soft sand blown from the surrounding dunes. All strips, or additions to existing ones, had to be approved by the Niger authorities, but the bureaucracy involved was far less in the case of an existing strip, no matter how derelict. So the exploration team cleared the old strip.

Unfortunately it lay north to south across the prevailing wind. The first attempt at landing there was beaten by very poor visibility in blowing sand and the second by a howling crosswind that was way above limits. We took the supplies back to N'Djamena, expecting to have another attempt the next day. That didn't happen; back at base we found that another Cameroun flight was scheduled.

This was arranged to enable a visual inspection of the proposed pipeline route, mainly for an ecological assessment of the likely impact on wildlife, farming and existing settlements. The flight planning took me back to my photographic survey days, but now I had the advantage of GPS. I was able to put all the turn points into a route stored in the Garmin 100 GPS unit. This enabled very accurate tracking, which would have been very useful for mapping, but was wasted on this flight. The ecologists and engineers wanted to see the route out of the windows, not to be directly above it. At some of the more significant features I had to circle back and then fly along the other side of the line so that those sitting on the other side of the aircraft had a chance to see where the pipeline would go.

On the first day we flew to Garoua for customs clearance and then followed the pipeline route to near N'Gaoundere, where we landed for more fuel and lunch. From there on, first southwards and then bending south-west, we passed over ever more verdant terrain as we left the dry wooded savannah behind and flew over a carpet of tropical rain forest. Occasionally we glimpsed water between the trees, but only the very largest rivers showed for more than a few yards. With such dense vegetation, unsurprisingly we saw no animals, although we disturbed many flocks of brightly coloured birds. There was little sign of human activity; even the occasional roads were mostly hidden beneath the tree canopy.

We night stopped at Yaounde again and set off early next morning for the run down to the coast. The scenery became even more extravagant, with steep-sided mountains hung with tall trees and threaded with waterfalls. After one last high ridge, the palm-fringed Atlantic coast at Kribi, with a shining sandy beach came into view. The area of the proposed terminal looked idyllic as a peaceful weekend picnic spot. We circled a few times; I couldn't help thinking of Ghana's Tema Harbour and the hauntingly evocative song:

> *"Sing a song of Tema Harbour,*
> *Climb a coconut tree,*
> *Catch a fish and light a fire,*
> *Drink some wine with me."*

It seems an oil terminal and a refinery were built at Tema, presumably after the lyric was written. I expect Kribi has gone, or will go the same way.

We were back at Yaounde for lunch and hoped for another night stop there, but our passengers decided they had be in Douala that evening to make sure they wouldn't miss their airline flight next morning. We left Yaounde just after sunset. It was a bit touch and go whether we would get through the dramatic thunder storms that sprang up on the way, but after an hour in the middle of a spectacular fireworks show of cloud to cloud and cloud to ground lightning we intercepted the Instrument Landing System glide slope and landed at Douala without difficulty. A visit to a splendid restaurant with almost the longest menu I'd ever seen followed. I chose the Osso Buco; it was another item for my gastronomic world tour of place and time. After that there was no alternative but a visit to one of Douala's nightclubs. With no passengers, there was no rush for our departure back to N'Djamena the next day and we made a night of it.

Back at the N'Djamena operation another crew had succeeded in landing at Bedouaram and the exploration team had reconnoitred further north still, well into the Sahara. They had found another disused strip near Karam and wanted to know if it was useable. I flew to Bedouaram as passenger in our Twin Otter and next day was taken to the Karam airstrip in a four-wheel drive vehicle. With GPS on board, there was no problem knowing which direction the strip was from us, but finding a route to it was more difficult. We wove our way between sand dunes and rock outcrops, occasionally back-tracking when we ran into soft or excessively rocky ground. There was very little vegetation, just a few scattered low bushes in the dried up wadis and a sprinkling of straw-coloured sun-baked grass, but we saw several groups of up to twenty gazelles. With boundless space all around for flight from our intrusion, it was almost beyond belief that one of the animals should choose to dash across so close in front of us that we grazed it with the front bumper. But we were not far south of the Tree of Tenere...

When I first went to Nigeria, I bought a map, about a metre square, of the whole of Africa. I was intrigued to see marked in the north east of Niger "L'Arbre du Tenere". A tree marked on a map of the whole continent? I discovered that it was indeed just an acacia tree, not a village or oasis. It seemed that it was the only tree within several hundred kilometres and was known to be at least 300 years old. In 1973, with limitless space all around to avoid it, a Libyan truck driver managed to knock it over!

The Karam strip was marked out by large earth-moving vehicle tyres at each corner, with another lead-in line of tyres stretching half a kilometre from the western end. Surprisingly, these had not been covered over by blowing sand during the years since the strip had last been used, or more likely they had, but our arrival coincided with the cyclical pattern of covering and uncovering common in the desert. The surface was in good firm condition and although it was not over long the ground beyond the eastern end was flat, smooth and hard enough for our Twin Otters; lengthening the runway would need no levelling or other preparation, just some more tyres to mark it out. The surrounding terrain was almost featureless, a bare sandy plain with a low ridge to the south.

I returned to N'Djamena from Bedouaram as a passenger again and a few days later set out to make the first Karam landing. By now Esso had provided N'Guigmi with a terminal building (wooden poles, guy ropes and thatched roof) complete with a large pedestal scale for weighing freight and baggage. They had installed a ground VHF radio and a non-directional navigational beacon and had trucked in a large stock of Avtur jet fuel in 45-gallon drums. The runway, although still unsealed, had been further lengthened and would have been almost long enough for a Boeing 737; it was more than adequate for us. A Niger customs and immigration official had been positioned there from Niamey and we could truly re-title the strip as N'Guigmi International Airport. We left N'Djamena, flew across Lake Chad and landed at N'Guigmi to re-fuel. I don't remember why it was that we had to land at Bedouaram before going on to Karam, but we did have to and couldn't, again because of a howling crosswind. So with nowhere at N'Guigmi to night stop we returned to N'Djamena.

Photo 53 - N'Guigmi International Terminal Building

Early next morning we tried once more. We landed at Bedouaram with some difficulty – crosswind again – but the wind rapidly increased and we were soon in the middle of a full-scale sandstorm. The strip consisted basically of compacted soft sand, there was nothing firm to anchor the aircraft to, so we did our best, tying some very large JCB tyres to the wing picketing points and retired to the oil camp around mid-day. Driving there was interesting, with visibility reduced to a few yards. All the rest of the day the wind was howling round the Portakabin accommodation, the resident oilies told us that sandstorms there sometimes lasted for a week! We watched several videos, had a superb meal and retired to bed. I woke up in the middle of the night; it was eerily still. Outside the visibility was fantastic and the sky was blazing with stars.

Esso's security rules forbade night travel; to beat the wind's expected arrival we left the camp at sunrise. At the airstrip we were alarmed to see the Twin Otter tipped over with the left wing, normally around twelve feet above the ground, at head height. Panic subsided when we found that there was no damage, the wind had been from one side and by rocking the aircraft had caused the left wheel to work its way deep into the soft sand. It took considerable digging out! However, we were on our way before the wind started. Karam proved difficult to see from the air; we were almost overhead by GPS before I spotted the line of tyres. We landed, shut down for a cigarette and then returned via N'Guigmi to N'Djamena

I visited Karam only once more, during December in my next tour. Two of Esso's people arrived at N'Djamena one evening from Europe and we were to take them to N'Guigmi early next morning, where a helicopter was to meet them for a flight on to Karam. During our pre-flight checks I found that our GPS had failed. This was no great problem, there were good landmarks on the way to N'Guigmi so I decided to go. Unfortunately, when we reached N'Guigmi we found that the helicopter had failed and we were asked to take the passengers on to Karam ourselves. I explained my predicament to the passengers. There would be no ground features to navigate by, so without the GPS I could only try to find Karam by flying on heading and time. If the wind from N'Guigmi onwards was different to what we'd had on the way (and even if it wasn't!) we could easily miss Karam. "Oh, I have a GPS that I bought in Amsterdam, but I don't know how to use it yet" one of them told me. "Did you get batteries with it?" I asked. Our luck was in; he had bought batteries to fit. I read through the instructions for putting in waypoints and operating the 'GoTo' function, entered the latitude and longitude of Karam, started the unit on its initialising procedure and set off with it resting on the instrument coaming as near to the windscreen as it would go. Every now and again I had a look to see if it was working but for the first thirty minutes or so it gave no indications of use to me. Probably the metal cockpit roof had been screening the satellite radio signals on which it depended, because to my great relief it finally began to give occasional ranges and bearings and with this information there was no problem finding Karam. The passengers were not returning with us, but I wasn't worried about finding N'Guigmi, I couldn't miss Lake Chad even from a long way off track and that would enable me to locate landmarks leading to the strip.

There was a Schreiner helicopter at Karam when we landed. Luckily I had my camera with me and the light was just right with the sun in the best direction for this unique situation. Schreiner later used the resulting photograph for their calendar. The orange Schreiner marking on the two aircraft complemented by the sandy background and the absence of bushes, rocks or other features captured the feeling of a back of beyond desert location with great effect.

Photo 54 - Desert Meeting

That tour was the slackest ever, I flew on only four days out of the 28 on site for a total of 11 hours and 35 minutes.

1997 began well enough, with a February tour flying around Chad and for variety, a trip to Lagos at the end of the tour for my medical. Other ex-pats could have medical examinations in their own country while on leave to medically validate their Nigerian licence, but the Nigerian authorities insisted that, because of my age, I could have my medicals done only in Nigeria and then by only one doctor. He had been the Chief Medical Officer in the Nigerian Air Force, had been on Aviation Medicine Courses at RAE Farnborough and had set up his own clinic. The equipment he had installed was very impressive, with among other things an ultrasound scanner. I was also impressed by the examination, which was about the most thorough I had ever had. There was only one snag – his clinic was in Kaduna, about 380 miles from Lagos. Travelling there by road was impractical and by air, uncertain, with most internal flights full. I had a few unplanned nights in Kaduna's Durbar Hotel when no return seat was available. The Durbar's night fighters were particularly active and difficult to evade.

I was now just coasting gently along, with five more tours and four more leaves scheduled before my final and definite retirement date just nine months away. The pay was good and although I was now paying U.K. tax at the higher rate I was able to use a personal pension plan with carry back and carry forward facilities to reduce the tax bill enormously. There was enough flying in Chad to avoid boredom, but plenty of free time for other pursuits. Life in N'Djamena was quite enjoyable; there were some excellent restaurants, bars and discos and my ACN team got on well together. With the generous leave there was plenty of free time for flying my sailplane – often involving time consuming waiting around for suitable weather and sometimes even more time consuming retrieves from fields with the de-rigging and rigging that was involved.

Photo 55- Rigging the DG200 at Sutton Bank

At home, Jennie seemed to be fully recovered from her hysterectomy. She was well established at her school and had decided not to look for further promotion involving a move. She would be due to retire two years after me; I had hopes of persuading her to take early retirement. Meanwhile, I was on leave for half the time and while on leave was able to take some of the load off her, in the school as an unpaid secretarial assistant and in the house as chief cook and odd-jobber. I was a little concerned that after months of waiting, she had been given an appointment for an operation on the knee she had damaged while skiing a few years previously. The date fixed would be during my July tour; I was contemplating asking ACN if they could juggle my dates, or if it wouldn't be a problem replacing me, let me retire early, so that I could be at home while she was recuperating.

Chapter 57
The Aouk dispute

As it happened, fate's sockful of wet sand got me in the back of the neck again and in the process took care of my domestic concern. It all began to fall apart when I returned to Chad from leave on the evening of Friday 16th May. My opposite number, Rick Garbinski, told me that the Esso Chad Managing Director (a Frenchman) wanted to fly on the next Friday to Aouk, a disused airstrip on the Central African Republic border, for a hunting trip. The MD had been there a few weeks earlier and had arranged for the strip to be cleared. Because of the remoteness and lack of roads ground access would be very difficult in the time available. So he (Rick) had agreed not to follow the normal procedure of an inspection visit of a newly constructed or cleared strip by ground transport before flying there. We (meaning I) would fly there without passengers and if it appeared safe to do so would land and check whether anything else needed doing before we took passengers there. Rick gave me information on the length of the strip and told me about the hunting lodge, surrounded by trees just off the eastern end. The length sounded fine, the trees might mean landing towards and taking off away from them.

First thing Monday morning I went to see the MD to find out a little more about what had been done and to make arrangements for the flight to be incorporated in the existing schedule. He told me he had had the runway widened to 20 metres. Perhaps that should have sowed a seed of doubt in my mind, but I thought, "that's wider than many of the runways I've landed on" and did not query what he said. It was agreed that I would take the aircraft on its planned Tuesday N'Djamena-Moundou-Kome-Sarh flight and night stop at Sarh. On Wednesday I would check out Aouk, then return to Sarh and make the afternoon flight back to N'Djamena.

I was looking forward to the possibility of seeing wild life at such a remote place; our usual landing strips were in fairly densely populated areas where the larger animals had all been killed off. We took the Esso Security chief with us as supernumerary crew to communicate with the hunting lodge staff. When we arrived overhead Aouk, I was disappointed to see that in addition to the trees at the eastern end there were forty foot high trees close to the edges of the grass runway at the western threshold end one side and halfway down on the other. One of those halfway down was so close that its canopy actually overhung the runway. In addition, there were low bushes close to the runway edges all along. I made an approach down to just above treetop height, from there I judged that there might be about a foot clearance each side of the Twin Otter's 65-foot wingspan. It was most definitely not possible to land there safely. The **runway** was indeed twenty metres or so wide, but an aircraft needs a clear area at least one wing span wide each side of the actual runway. Especially twin-engined aircraft; the possibility of an engine failing on take-off and the aircraft swinging has to be allowed for. Even the best pilots will take a few seconds to straighten out the flight path in this event. We circled the strip and I had my co-pilot (another Captain) draw a sketch of what we could see, then returned to Sarh, re-fuelled and continued to N'Djamena. About 45 minutes after our departure, our other Twin Otter took off from Kome, about 60 miles west of Sarh, on a Kome-N'Djamena schedule.

Our flight back became interesting when with about 80 miles to run our weather radar started to show a line of storm cells to the north of the airport. As we got closer, it became apparent that this was a very active line squall and that it was moving towards N'Djamena. We had enough fuel to return to Kome or Sarh, where there was fuel available, but if the squall arrived at N'Djamena before us we could not wait around for long waiting for the weather to clear. There were several other useable airstrips not so far away where we could land, but they were all unmanned and with no fuel. Diverting to those would mean bringing fuel to us, a process which could take days by land, or involve a night in the bush for our passengers while we organised the other aircraft to fly fuel in.

As we drew closer, we could see the thundercloud tops reaching high above and the dark mass of lower nimbostratus stretching across our track, with continuous flickering of lightning illuminating the clouds from within. It looked a bit touch and go whether we or the squall would arrive first, but eventually it became clear that we were winning. We landed in calm conditions, with the squall around fifteen miles to the north and getting closer.

Now I was concerned about the other aircraft. Our staff house was very close to the airport; at the house we had our office and communication centre with HF radio and telephones. It also had a flat roof, from which I would be able to see how the storm was developing. I asked the Esso Security chief to tell the MD that Aouk was not useable and went to the staff house. For the next twenty-five minutes I was running up to the see the storm's progress and running back down to the radio to keep the other pilot informed. While I was busy with this, our office assistant came to tell me that the MD wanted to see me in his office, which was half a mile away. I asked him to explain the situation and to say I would be there as soon as our aircraft was either safely on the ground at N'Djamena or had turned round to go back to Kome. A few minutes later the assistant returned with the same message and I repeated mine. A third message, "he says you are to go there immediately" coincided with the arrival of the squall at the airport. I told the Captain of the inbound aircraft of this and he decided to divert back to Kome.

At the Esso headquarters I found representatives of the company whose people in the field were supposed to have done the Aouk airfield clearance, the Esso Security Chief and the MD. I wanted to apologise for the delay in my arrival, but I wasn't given the chance. "Esso has done everything Aero asked for, why do **you** want more?" he demanded furiously. "I am fed up with Aero" he continued. His question was similar to the "When did you stop beating your wife?" conundrum, with its implicit statement of unverifiable and possibly untrue fact. I'm not good at quick answers; various responses went through my mind. "No they haven't" was clearly out; perhaps they hadn't, but it could be that Rick had not asked for enough. I had no way to find out if this had been the case; Rick was on leave in the USA. "How do you know Esso have done everything Aero asked for?" "What did Aero ask for?" "Who told you what Aero needed?" "I don't believe I want more than Aero asked for." None of these seemed likely to calm the situation. I couldn't say, "I want more than Aero asked for because the strip was too narrow"; that would in effect be saying that Aero **had** given the wrong information on what was required. I floundered; the best I could think of was "Well, if Aero did expect me to land at a strip like that, I would resign and look for a job with another company." Which was an attempt to show that if the whole thing **was** Aero's fault, I was as fed up with Aero as he was, while diplomatically indicating that he might be wrong and that what had been asked for hadn't in fact been done.

From then on the situation went rapidly downhill. He ranted some more about how he was fed up with Aero. My co-pilot produced the sketch he had made and I showed it to the MD. He seemed to calm down for a short time, then said, "Which trees do you want me to cut down?" When I started to answer, he screamed "I don't want details". From then on, each time I tried to speak, he cut me short, finally telling me to get out of his office. As I left, he was telling all and sundry "I want to see his boss." He meant our Admin Manager. I didn't bother to tell him that the Admin Manager was not my boss; he was in charge of administration, I was in charge of operations, we were both subordinates of the ACN Lagos MD.

The Esso MD's behaviour had been so abominable that I felt like fighting back, but Aero had treated me so well that I didn't want to jeopardise their contract with Esso, or their chances of another Esso contract that was in the wind. There was also my concern for Jennie and my own feelings that I'd had a pretty good run. I didn't need the extra six months of work before I reached the maximum age for commercial flying with passengers and I would rather be in England full-time for the coming summer than miss half of it by being in Chad. Telephone calls to Nigeria were almost impossible so I sent a message via SITA[8] to Nabil Haqui explaining what had happened. I said that after the manner in which I had been treated there was no way that I would have anything more to do with the Esso MD. I didn't want to return to two and one terms in Nigeria. I thought it would be best for all concerned if I resigned and I was doing so.

Back at the ACN compound I got our Admin Manager to take the Esso MD a diagram of what we needed for the airstrip to be useable. The word came back that what we needed would be done. Also that the MD wanted me

---

[8] SITA was a communications system something like telex organised by aircraft operating companies.

removed from the operation because "St. Pierre couldn't tell him what needed to be done" and "St. Pierre has a history of problems with Esso" The first was in a sense true, I couldn't – because he shouted me down each time I tried to speak! The second could only have been a reference to a couple of occasions when I had refused to do things which were dangerous and illegal under aviation law, both long before this particular MD's arrival and which had been resolved in my favour. I sent another SITA to Nabil detailing these, but said I still wasn't going to stay in Chad.

On Thursday afternoon we were told the work was finished. Another pilot went to check this but the trees overhanging and close to the runway were still there. On Friday one Twin Otter left N'Djamena for Sarh and Aouk with the MD and his party on board. Meanwhile the other Twin Otter flew to Aouk for another check; the trees were still there. The MD insisted on continuing the flight; the two aircraft passed each other halfway. By the time the MD's aircraft arrived at Aouk the worst tree had at last been cut down. The pilot landed on his own initiative. His written report when he returned to N'Djamena included "After landing I instructed Mr. ***** (the Esso MD) what needed to be done to bring the strip up to aviation standards." Which made me wonder why the pilot landed there in the first place! I can only assume he did so because he felt under pressure and didn't want to get the same treatment as me. I learnt that a certain amount of hasty clearing took place before he took off again and that before the Monday flight to collect the MD returned to Aouk, still more clearance was done, apparently even the MD's wife spent much time wielding a machete.

During the rest of my four week stint I left what little flying there was to the other pilots, attended to the small amount of administration remaining to me, packed up my belongings and said my farewells. The ACN Deputy Operations Manager came with the crew change Twin Otter on the last Friday of my tour; he tried to persuade me to continue flying for ACN in Lagos, but I told him that I needed to be at home anyway to look after Jennie. He asked if I wanted him to discuss the events with the Esso MD, but I said that it would be better to forget about it; even with an apology from Esso I wouldn't stay. I flew out of Chad on an Air France Airbus late in the evening of Saturday 13th June 1997.

I never flew a powered aircraft again.

It was a disappointing way for a 47 year long career in professional flying to end, but perhaps it was better to finish unexpectedly rather than to continue until my 65th birthday, like a condemned man with an execution date set and no possibility of a reprieve. I didn't bother to keep my licence valid for private flying and I don't have any desire to fly powered aircraft again. Unless someone offers me the chance to fly solo in a Spitfire of course!

Postscript/Epilogue

I finished my professional flying career with the relatively low total of 13,150 hours, of which 4,650 had been on the Twin Otter. Roughly 300 hours per year actually doing what I was paid to do had given me a good living, I could not complain that I'd been over-worked.

Jennie had her knee operation at the end of July 1997, but a few weeks later she was diagnosed with breast cancer and in September she went into hospital for a mastectomy. Despite my urging her to take early retirement, she insisted on going back to work. I took her to New York during the autumn half term in October and then in November she started a six-week radiotherapy session. We went to New Zealand for her Christmas holidays and I took her to some of the places I had last seen in the 1950s. In Auckland, I discovered that the Solent flying boat ZK-AMO was now in the Museum of Transport and Technology. MOTAT was near the Zoo; we went to the Zoo first to see a kiwi, which it was unlikely we would see in the wild. Then we rode the tram to MOTAT and found the hangar where the flying boat was housed safely under cover.

The normal impression on seeing places or things unvisited since one's youth is how everything has shrunk. When I passed through Devizes after a thirty-year absence, I was astonished at how low the Roundway Downs had become. Even the trees we used to climb seemed quite small. But the Solent amazed me – I could hardly believe it really was the one I'd flown, it seemed so enormous. Of course, I'd seen it mostly when it was afloat. In the water, five and a half feet depth of the hull were out of sight below the surface. In the museum, with the beaching wheels fitted, the normal water line was around six feet above the floor.

From Auckland we drove to the Bay of Islands, where the small town of Russell was much as I remembered. Then we headed south to the Chateau Tongariro area. The glow worm cave at Waitomo didn't seem quite so impressive as it was in memory and Rotorua shocked me. The small Maori village I remembered had grown to a large industrialised city and the lakeshore, which had been mostly bush or farmland, was now largely built up.

We flew from Auckland to Christchurch and toured around South Island. I tried to find Bill Kofoed's farm and in fact a few years later discovered we had driven right past it without me recognising the place. At Queenstown the surrounding scenery, the Remarkables, the Crown range, Lake Wakatipu and the mountains to the west were as I remembered, but the town had grown much larger than the small lakeside settlement it had been. The Earnslaw was still there, chugging its way round the lake and the jetty near the town centre still sheltered shoals of monster trout. We stopped at the old bridge in the Kawarau gorge; Jennie wouldn't let me watch a bungy jump, let alone try one.

When we arrived back home in Yorkshire in January 1998, Jennie returned to her Headship. At intervals she went for further consultations and tests and from what she told me all seemed to be going well. She had some more tests just before we went to New Zealand again at the end of December; it was a short holiday and we rushed back from Christchurch to Auckland in three days so that she would be back in time for the new term at school. She had an appointment with the consultant two days after term began. He told her that the pre-Christmas tests had shown she needed to have the lymph glands on her right side removed, the cancer was still active, she needed more radiotherapy and she should stop working. She still wouldn't ask for early retirement but took sick leave instead.

After the operation and the radiotherapy, we had a few months of retired life together. We had taken up bird watching and visited distant sites like Spurn Point and Blacktoft Sands at least once a week and our local Nosterfield and Marfield Reserves almost every day. Jennie appeared to be doing well; I didn't believe she would not be cured. We planned and booked a month's holiday before Christmas and another month after New Year. Before Christmas we would visit two of the places, Aitutaki and Suva, that I had been to in my Solent days, then we would continue to Australia to see the Blue Mountains, the nature reserve at Dunk Island and the Barrier Reef. After New Year we'd have a really leisurely tour around New Zealand.

It was not to be. Until the middle of June she seemed normal, but the end came very rapidly. She was admitted to hospital on June 30th and died there early in the morning of the 9th July.

I was in a state of desolation for a while, but life goes on. I drove myself into making the trip to Australia that December, but Aitutaki, Suva, Dunk Island and the Barrier Reef without Jennie would have been miserable. Instead I took a hire car up to the gliding site at Lake Keepit in the north of New South Wales and flew a few hours there. Then to another gliding site, Tocumwal on the New South Wales/Victoria border. I've been back there three more times, pushing my best distance in one flight up to 860 kilometres.

On the way to Australia on one occasion I had a whole day in Singapore. I hired a car and driver and went looking for the places I remembered but there was almost nothing left, the whole island had been rebuilt and rebuilt again in the 36 years since we lived there. The only thing I did recognise was St. Michael and All Angels church where we were married. I couldn't get onto the air base, now occupied by the Singapore Air Force, but I found a place where the church, almost hidden by tall trees, was just visible through the fence. The trees were recently planted saplings in a well-kept lawn in 1966.

Another time I revisited New Zealand, with a week in the Cook Islands on the way. The Boeing airliner landed at Rarotonga; then I flew in a smaller Bandeirante to Aitutaki and once again experienced the breath-taking view of a coral atoll from the air. I had never been to the main island before, so not knowing what it had been like in the past there was none of the "its all been spoilt" feeling that Singapore had given me. I went on a tourist boat tour around Aitutaki lagoon, run by the son of one of the TEAL girls of the 1950s. There was barely a trace left of the scaffold pole and sawn-off oil drum seaplane runway markers in the lagoon, just one or two single rusted spars. I was dropped off at Akaiami motu for a few hours. The coral jetty was half crumbled away and of the three huts only the concrete floors remained. But the well was still there and it still held drinkable water.

Back in Rarotonga, a scuba dive fulfilled another of my ambitions and in New Zealand I made the bungy jump from the Karawau Bridge. Tandem para- and hang-glider flights from the Crown Range continued the theme – my friends accuse me of having a death wish – but I believe "try anything once" is a good approach to staying active. The main problem now is that with gliding, trout fishing, bird watching, the garden and (minimal) housework, there's little spare time left for anything else. I'd rather like to go back to my old job in Chad – for a rest.

John Whittier wrote "For all sad words of tongue or pen – the saddest are these: 'it might have been'" implying that good things were missed. But that doesn't allow for the fact that life might have been less pleasant, less interesting, whatever; a slight alteration of his words gives the more positive "For all glad words of tongue or pen – the gladdest are these: 'it might have been worse.'" Looking back on my life, there were many forks in the road. If I had the chance to go back to any point and take the other direction, which point would I choose? Should I have gone to University before National Service? If I had, I might never have flown except as a passenger. Should I have taken the BOAC offer? But then I wouldn't have had the flying boat and South Pacific experience. Perhaps I should have taken the DC6 conversion with TEAL? Then I wouldn't have had those years in Germany and Singapore and met and married Jennie. There were good times and bad times, but the more I look back, the more convinced I am that I went the best way. Except perhaps that day last year when I went fishing and caught nothing on what turned out to be the gliding day of the century.